A GOOD GERMAN

also by Giles MacDonogh
A Palate in Revolution:
Grimod de La Reynière and the Almanach des Gourmands

A GOOD GERMAN

Adam von Trott zu Solz

Giles MacDonogh

THE OVERLOOK PRESS
Woodstock, New York

First published in 1992 by
The Overlook Press
Lewis Hollow Road
Woodstock, New York 12498

Library of Congress Cataloging-in-Publication Data

MacDonogh, Giles, 1955-
    A good German : Adam von Trott zu Solz/Giles MacDonogh
    p. cm.
Originally published: London; New York: Quartet Books, 1989.
Includes bibliographical references and index
    1. Trott zu Solz, Adam von, 1909-1944.   2. Anti-Nazi
movement—Germany—biography.   I. Title.

DD247.T766M33   1992
943.086'092—dc20
[B]

91-37266
CIP

ISBN 0-87951-449-3

In memoriam
HWP
1959–1987

'Cut is the branch that might have grown full straight,
And burned is Apollo's laurel bough . . .'

Contents

Preface

This book was conceived at the hospitable table of Douglas and Lucy Blyth in Suffolk. During lunch it was mentioned that there was a need to produce a clear and unequivocal book on Adam von Trott's short life which would clear up some of the misunderstandings which have circulated in this country and the United States since the war. My conviction was, and is, that the importance of Trott's life lies in his role in the German Resistance and the part he played in the abortive plot of 20 July 1944. With this in mind I have skirted over those things which I feel are of doubtful importance in the light of his later destiny. The reader will not find here, for example, a detailed discussion of the dissertation which Trott wrote on Hegel at the age of twenty-one, and which so fascinated Christopher Sykes in his 1969 biography. The thesis has been reprinted and I advise those interested to look at it themselves. I have sought to place Trott in the context of his time and within the framework of the movement for which he gave his life.

Any attempt to write this book would have been impossible without the help of Trott's widow and the Hon. David Astor. Frau Dr Med Clarita von Trott zu Solz not only opened up her archive for me, but treated me with consummate kindness during my visits to Berlin. David Astor introduced me to Clarita, answered my naïve questions and lent me books when I had trouble finding them in London. He and his wife Bridget also entertained me in their home and gave me unstinting help. Thanks are also due to Peter and Christabel Bielenberg, who had me to stay in their house in Ireland, and Mr and Mrs David Hopkinson, who gave their time to see me and to give me information. I am grateful also to Trott's younger daughter, Professor Dr Clarita Müller-Plantenberg and her family, who not only put me up for a night in Berlin but also filled me in on certain questions of recent Resistance historiography. I am also indebted to Simon Acland, Sir Harold Acton, Sir Isaiah Berlin, Douglas and Lucy Blyth, Dr Penny Bullock of Balliol College, Oxford, Tim Clarke, C.E. Collins, Patric Dickinson, Nicolas Elliott, Dr Robin Fletcher of Rhodes House, Oxford, Peter Hamilton, Professor Peter Hoffman, Philip Mansel, Marielle Ruskauf, Dr Eric M. de Saventhem, Dennis Sewell, Katharine and Charles Sheppard, Ingrid, Countess Spinelli, Sir Peter Tennant and Simon Wallis. In Washington John Aycoth and Brian Harte made strenuous efforts on my behalf, trying to locate papers in public archives. Clarita von Trott, David Astor and Susanne McDadd also kindly read the proofs and provided me with constructive criticism.

I must also express my gratitude to the staffs of the British Library, the Goethe Institute and the Imperial War Museum in London, Balliol College Library, Rhodes House, the Bodleian Library in Oxford and University Library in Cambridge, the Embassy of the Federal Republic of Germany in London and the Bundesarchiv in Koblenz.

Finally, I must acknowledge the contribution of my friend Roderick Blyth who took great care in reading both the manuscript and the proofs, despite his busy practice at the Bar. I owe him even more than even *he* knows.

Giles MacDonogh
London 1989

Introduction

On 26 August 1944, Adam von Trott zu Solz was hanged in the Plötzensee Prison in Berlin. His execution came as the inevitable result of his long-standing involvement in the plot to kill Hitler which had ended in dramatic failure little over a month before.

The Nazi authorities did not announce his death to the press until 10 September when it was reported in *Völkische Beobachter*. Two days later, with customary flair, the *Daily Telegraph* in London reported the hanging of Trott's father, the former Prussian Minister of Education (who had died in his bed in 1938). Others in Britain, however, were less vague as to Trott's identity. On 18 September, Lord Elton, chairman of the Rhodes trustees, wrote to the Warden of Rhodes House in Oxford:

> I heard indirectly that he had thrown in his lot with the Nazis and I was told that he had privately expressed the hope of bringing them to a more liberal policy... Much later rumours came to my ears that he was probably involved in some mysterious negotiations and there was a hint that he had been in touch with our FO reps in Ankara and Stockholm. Of course, everybody was very discreet about it and I could not make any exact enquiries. It now seems certain that he was engaged in the plot to overthrow the Nazi regime as early as 1942, and that he was very active in it. As this was known over here, it seems incredible that it was not also known to the Gestapo. Anyhow, I'm afraid they got him in the end, and he has died at the same time as Goerdeler and the others.* I take it we are to record him as a casualty of war and I propose to include him in the casualty list in the Annual Statement. He was a charming man of distinguished family, and his latter history seems to make it certain that he was on the right side, though at one time it seemed a little dubious.[1]

Dr, later Sir, Carleton Allen, the Warden of Rhodes House, reacted cautiously. He had had mixed views about Trott ever since the latter's time at Balliol when Trott had been involved in left-wing politics.[2] On 19 September he wrote both to the Master of Balliol, A.D. Lindsay (later Lord Lindsay of Birker), and to Heinz Koeppler† of the

---

* *Goerdeler was not, in fact, executed until February 1945.*
† *Heinz, later Sir Heinz, Koeppler, founder of Wilton Park – 'best described as a training centre for the indoctrination of foreigners' (Jo Grimond, Memoirs,*

Intelligence Department of the Foreign Office in London,[3] echoing Elton's opinion that 'we ought to record him as an honourable casualty of war'. On 27 September, Koeppler replied: 'We have a good deal of rather vague information concerning his anti-Nazi activities. I agree there is a great temptation to say *de mortuis nil nisi bonum* in this case, but I rather feel at present the evidence is still too conflicting to allow any definite estimate (*sic*) of the motives of his actions . . .' Koeppler suggested that Allen wait till the conclusion of hostilities before making Trott an honourable casualty of war. In the meantime he wrote, 'I should like you to meet Mr Wheeler-Bennett, the historian, who is working in this department.'[4]

Koeppler's advice was enough for Allen. On 4 October he wrote back: 'Dear Koeppler, many thanks. I agree that discretion is wise at present. Thank you for your suggestion. I should certainly like to meet Mr Wheeler-Bennett.'[5] In the meantime, through Trott's old friend Isobel Henderson,* Allen had received a translation of an article from the Swedish newspaper *Dagens Nyheter* dated 12 September.[6] The article was unsigned, but the author was the future West German chancellor, Willy Brandt. Brandt's piece was in the form of an interview with an unnamed political personality who had been in contact with Trott in the course of his final trip to Stockholm in June. The hanging of the seven conspirators mentioned in the *Völkische Beobachter* article had 'effectively destroyed the central opposition group in Germany'. The group's liaison man was Trott 'who arrived in Sweden in order to establish contact between the considerable group of internal opposition and the Allies. Such contacts were also made elsewhere, but Trott's action is nevertheless one of the most important.' On Trott's politics Brandt was quite clear: 'He was never a National Socialist. Before Hitler's rise to power he stood somewhere between the Democratic and Social Democratic parties, but he succeeded in maintaining himself in the Foreign Office owing to his particularly good connections and generally acknowledged efficiency.'

On 15 September, Brandt's *Dagens Nyheter* article was used as the basis of a British account published in the magazine *The Week*.[7] Nonetheless the presence among the dead of the well-known Nazi Berlin Police Chief and former SA leader Count Helldorf continued to give rise to considerable suspicion as did the ease with which Trott was able to travel to neutral countries. In Oxford, Wheeler-Bennett and his friends at the Foreign Office had effectively prevented any moves to have Trott's death recorded as an 'honourable casualty of

---

1979). For Koeppler's denazification work in England, see Terence Prittle, My Germans, 1933–1983.

* *Widow of the historian Charles Henderson who had been a member of Trott's circle when he was an undergraduate.*

2

war' but correspondence continued to fly between the colleges. The Master of Balliol wrote to Allen, the Warden of Rhodes House, on 11 October to inform him that he had been aware of Trott's Resistance activities all along: 'I had myself known a certain amount about it, because I got a message from von Trott in the summer of 1942, which I answered to the best of my judgement.'[8] Isobel Henderson had also received a letter from Lindsay: 'Roger Hinks saw him in Stockholm and believed in him. But he was a bad conspirator. The Master of Balliol writes to me that Adam sent him a message in 1942, mentioning the *coup d'etat* and asking about terms – which seems to me almost incredibly indiscreet.'[9]

Caution and distrust have continued to mark British and to some degree American attitudes to Trott long after other leading figures of the German Resistance have achieved recognition and respect in this country.[10] Similarly, evaluations of his life in English have tended to trivialize the man, denying his stature within the Resistance movement, or judging him in a misleading context, either as lover or as some sort of muddle-witted German who dulled his mind with too profound a reading of Hegel's philosophy.[11] The attitude stems from his Oxford contemporaries who never forgave him for wishing to return to such an uncongenial Germany in 1933. It can equally be attributed to the Foreign Office in London, where, as Richard Lamb discovered, resentment against Trott was so great that even forty years after his death surviving officials could not be induced to alter the jaundiced views expressed in internal memos written at the time.[12]

A memorandum circulated by the Hon. Con O'Neill (who had been a Balliol contemporary of Trott's) in October 1944 gives a glimpse of those bitter attitudes. The paper was written in response to one by John Wheeler-Bennett, who had poured scorn on Trott's overtures to the Allies a year before. 'I don't sympathize with what seems to be really the main burden of complaint against him in Mr Wheeler-Bennett's paper in C5218 of 1943,' O'Neill wrote, 'namely that he did not quite succeed in being an Englishman. That he was a German was perhaps his misfortune, but not his fault; and at least it was to his credit that he at last made up his mind to act in what he took to be Germany's interests – we can hardly complain if he did not consider England's, though possibly the two coincided for a moment at this point – and lost his life in doing so.[13]

Whatever Wheeler-Bennett's motives were, he continued to obscure an earlier collaboration with Trott for the rest of his life. He was bitten late with the Vansittartist bug,* and perhaps for this very

---

* *Sir Robert, later Baron, Vansittart (1881–1957), Germanophobe Permanent Under Secretary at the Foreign Office and, from 1938, Special Diplomatic Adviser to the government.*

reason, had more trouble shaking it off after the war. For Wheeler-Bennett and a great many other people Trott's problem was that he was a *German* patriot. His background and education had instilled in him a deep love of the German ideal and a determination to serve the state in whatever capacity. This love was at the bottom of his attraction to Hegel, who in so many ways defined the concept of 'Prussianism' which Trott espoused. Although Trott's career was blighted by Hitler's *Machtergreifung* or seizure of power in 1933, he none the less returned to Germany. He could not conceive of a life which did not represent his country's interests.

The same patriotic sense of duty made him return to Germany in 1938 and again in 1940. Even after the dramatic failure of the 20 July plot, he refused to countenance leaving his country, explaining to his friends at the time that he not only wished to protect his family from Goebbels' dreadful *Sippenhaft* (the concept, apparently derived from old German law, of punishing the relatives for a man's crimes), but that he also felt it incumbent upon him to stay and share in the fate of the others.

Richard Crossman, despite his doubtful behaviour towards Trott during the war, was one of the first to point out how Trott's patriotism had undermined the sympathy the British might otherwise have had for him. In a review of Christopher Sykes' biography of Trott, *Troubled Loyalty* (1969), he wrote, 'It was the untroubled loyalty of von Trott to the German idea which troubles Christopher Sykes – along with most other Englishmen.' In the same article Crossman wrote, 'Adam was that very rare thing, a "good German" who did not hate his "bad" countrymen.'[14]

The Germans themselves have never been in two minds about Trott. Even before the end of the war, he was being venerated on the same platform as the Weimar Socialist leader Rudolf Breitscheid and the pre-1933 Communist leader Ernst Thälmann,[15] both of whom had been slaughtered in concentration camps. At the end of the war, the veteran German Socialist Friedrich Stampfer contributed his assessment of Trott to an *emigré* New York paper, the *Neue Volkszeitung* : 'Everything about Trott must have filled this new tyranny with fury: the aristocrat versus the vulgarian, the Christian versus the heathen, the respecter of religious liberty versus the suppressor of freedom of belief, the German versus the despoiler of Germany, the Socialist versus the betrayer who abused and violated the name of Socialism.'[16]

'. . . I owe more to Oxford than I can say,' Trott told Christabel Bielenberg in the spring of 1944, 'but it's a strange thing. When I decided to come back to Germany in 1933, I would have thought I did exactly what most of my Oxford friends would have done if they were faced with a Hitler in their own country. Yet the very fact that I *did* come back aroused, I think, nothing but distrust – damaging distrust. I sometimes wonder how many friends I have there now – I mean real friends.'[17] The answer was, sadly, very few. The news of Trott's death in September 1944 provoked precious little reaction from his former circle among the younger fellows of All Souls, except to inspire A.L. Rowse to pen a brace of singularly tasteless poems.[18] Maurice Bowra, whom Trott had once referred to as 'very nearly a real friend,'[19] celebrated the news with the line, 'That's one Nazi who was hanged.'[20]

Oxford not only served him ill among the dons who remained on their foundations during the war, it also contributed nothing to his reception at the Foreign Office where the ranks of the service had been temporarily swollen by an influx of hundreds of academics into hastily conceived departments connected with the war. One of these was the Foreign Office Research Unit on Germany, which was actually based in Trott's old Oxford college under the headship of Professor Tom Marshall.*

Communication was a considerable problem with Trott. Although he had spoken English as a child to his nurse and his half-American mother, his style was often convoluted and cloudy. His writing is difficult to follow and many of his friends yielded to the temptation to be lazy in the reading of his letters. His correspondence with Shiela Grant Duff has recently been published,[21] revealing the frequent misunderstandings which arose from his style. To add to the confusion, his desire to thwart the Nazi censors led to his adopting a code which not only defeated them, but also the majority of his friends.[22]

Increasingly from January 1933, it must have taken strength of mind not to fall in with the Vansittartist view of Germany. The worst fears of intelligent observers were confirmed from 1935 when Hitler began to unveil his *Stufenplan* or step by step policy for German aggrandizement. Confirmation of his policy could be found in *Mein Kampf* – though the first unabridged English edition was not published until 1939 – where Hitler had made it abundantly clear that he would not stop at remedying the grievances resulting from the Versailles settlement, but would go further in a quest for *Lebensraum* in the east. This balmy pursuit of Eastern European domination probably impressed few other than his most hardened followers, but for patriotic Germans there was a considerable temptation to accept a leader who promised a solution to border problems in the east, where

---

* *Among Trott's Balliol contemporaries were the future ambassadors, Paul, Lord Gore Booth of Maltby, the Hon. Sir Con O'Neil, Sir Charles Hepburn Johnston, Sir Duncan Wilson (who worked in the German section of the Political Intelligence Department during the war), Richard Heppel and Brian MacDermot. (see Balliol College Register, Oxford 1983).*

the new Polish state had absorbed a number of previously accepted German homelands. Consciously, Hitler succeeded in blurring the two ambitions, national and colonial, leading Western observers – like Miss Grant Duff – to believe that National Socialists and Germans were calling for the same thing.

The issues surrounding the Polish Corridor, Sudetenland (where Czech policy in the early twenties had exacerbated the problems between the Austro-Germans and the Czech minority) and the independence of Austria (a largely pointless state after Versailles) were keenly felt by all Germans. Many German liberals like Adam von Trott were also aware that if Hitler succeeded in changing the post-Versailles map, he would gain such kudos that it would be years before there was a chance to unseat him. In Trott's view the Germans had legitimate grievances, and he became over-sensitive when foreigners gave too glib an interpretation to questions of internal German policy. When, in 1934, he wrote an ill-conceived letter to the *Manchester Guardian* on the subject of the persecution of Hessian Jews, his friend Isaiah Berlin said to Shiela Grant Duff: 'What really distresses me is that by his action he should have shifted himself into a terrible region which I see in terms of sheer black and white . . . That he was a patriotic person before everything else was patent always.' Shiela Grant Duff adds, in case we had forgotten, that patriotism was a dirty word, 'Isaiah's remark was not meant as a compliment.' In summing up the incident, she explained, 'Adam regarded criticism of his country as one regards criticism of one's family.'[23]

Later, once the war had begun, many people recalled how free Trott had been with his criticism of Britain. According to one story, on 29 June 1933 he had caused offence to a large number of people by wolf-whistling the Prince of Wales, who had come to Oxford on an official visit. Incidents of this sort are common among students and do not, as a rule, influence people's judgement of a man in later life. It was a misfortune for Trott that he found himself on the wrong side after the outbreak of war, and that stories of this sort were naturally brought out of mothballs.

It was also held against him that he should have chosen to work for the Nazi administration, at first informally and later as a member of the German Foreign Office. Trott, however, whose knowledge of life in a totalitarian regime was somewhat greater than most people's in Britain and the United States, felt that the only way to fight the evil was from the inside. His decision to apply for Party membership, which alone gave him the freedom from suspicion to enable him to travel to neutral countries during the war, was one of the most difficult he ever had to make. While he was in America, and not yet a Party member, he asked the anti-Nazi journalist Paul Scheffer: 'Am I doing more to destroy the Nazis by staying in my job than I am assisting them by keeping the machine running?' As Scheffer commented after the war,

'This was Adam's basic dilemma, and it was on this point that we came to agree in New York. Adam and his friends were in a strange situation. In order to be effective at all they had to co-operate with the enemy.'[24] Had Trott not done so, he would probably have survived the war, an obscure legal official in Hessen. Ultimately, Trott's participation in the conspiracy *necessitated* his joining the Nazi party.

One way in which he co-operated with the Nazi enemy was through a not very convincing attempt to bring down the British Empire, while his old friends across the divide tried to keep it afloat in its moment of crisis. Trott's propaganda campaign for Subhas Bose against the 1942 Cripps Mission led to a singular division in Trott's loyalties. He was torn between a genuine desire to see India independent and his friendship with Stafford Cripps, founded on mutually held commitments to greater social justice in Germany and Britain.

How much Trott's dangerous double game contributed to his failure to reach an understanding with the Allies remains a question mark hanging over his life. Sadly, in a regime such as the Third Reich, there was no alternative to duplicity. Trott's familiarity with the leading personalities in the Allied camp proved his biggest stumbling block when it came to achieving recognition in Britain and America, both during the war and afterwards. That the problem vexed Adam von Trott is an understatement. As his widow remembers, he was woken by a dream some time in the course of 1942. In the dream he had formed part of a squad storming a Japanese fortress. When they entered the building, Trott found it to be occupied not by Japanese soldiers, but by the Master of Balliol, the Warden of New College and the Warden of All Souls College, Oxford. In his dream Trott broke into a lively argument with the three heads of houses, but unfortunately woke in the middle. He tried vainly to fall asleep again so that he might continue his conversations. His inability to do so distressed him greatly.[25]

1
Family Traditions

Adam von Trott's intense patriotism stemmed from a lineage impressive by any standards. He was born into the *hessische Uradelstand*, the old nobility of Hessen, who could date their profession of arms back to before 1400. In its insistence on the year 1400, the Hessian court resembled the French before the Revolution, where the *noblesse d'Epée* were also required to prove their coats of arms were issued before the fifteenth century before they could present themselves at court.[1]

The first Trott to bear arms, and therefore the first noble, was Hermann, who became steward to a Hessian prince in 1253. Hermann's descendants continued to serve Hessian princes and electors until the state ceased to exist when it was swallowed up by Prussia after the Seven Weeks War of 1866. The Trott seat was the castle at Solz, a small town on the edge of the Trottenwald forest, whence they derived the name.

The first Trott of note, and the first Adam, was born in 1504. Unable to find a suitable career in his native land, he emigrated to Brandenburg, entering the service of the Elector Joachim II as counsellor and later field marshal to his armies. Although his own line died out in the course of the eighteenth century, he was much venerated by nineteenth- and twentieth-century Trotts, his portrait hanging on the walls of Solz and at nearby Imshausen,[2] where a branch of the family was established by Rudolf Ludwig von Trott zu Solz (1738–1814).

The Trotts formed part of the hereditary knighthood or *Ritterschaft* which made up the vast bulk of the Hessian nobility. They were untitled. 'Virtually all Hessian noblemen were equal in rank. They were simply nobles with the prefix "von".'[3] Despite their profession of equality, many lusted after the title of 'Freiherr' or baron which was more common in other parts of the Holy Roman Empire, but the court was not inclined to allow a substantial number of knights to adopt this style. Despite the court's injunctions, many Hessian nobles continued to call themselves Freiherren in correspondence and when travelling or resident abroad.* In the manner of nobles in minor German states,

---

* *After 1871 the Kaiser appears to have granted them the right to use the title of Freiherr, but only outside Germany.*

eighteenth- and nineteenth-century Trotts served in the army and civil service of Hesse-Kassel or Kurhessen as it was called (Electoral Hessen).

In the nineteenth century the Trott family had a virtual monopoly on the directorship of the Stift Kaufungen, a charitable foundation whose directors were 'leaders of the knighthood'. Stift Kaufungen had been given to the Hessian nobility at the Reformation to compensate them for the disappearence of the convents where nobles had hitherto lodged their unmarried daughters. The income from the foundation was used to pay the dowries of the daughters of poor or deceased nobles.

For minor German nobles the alternatives were simple: one joined the army or the civil service, or one administered an estate. Although the Trotts were in many ways a fairly typical *Beamtenfamilie* (i.e. civil-service family), during the nineteenth century they none the less produced three men of significant local importance: Adam von Trott's great-grandfather, August von Trott zu Solz (1783–1840); Friedrich von Trott zu Solz (1794–1855); and Otto von Trott zu Solz (1810–76). Curiously, perhaps, for the patriot that he was, Adam von Trott had a particular affection for the first of these, who had taken a single-minded stand in favour of the Bonaparte monarch during the time of the short-lived Kingdom of Wesphalia. After the Treaty of Tilsit in 1807, Napoleon included Kurhessen in the German kingdom which he carved out for his brother Jerome. Jerome had sought to give his court an aura of legitimacy by enlisting as many local nobles as possible to work with him, offering the incentives of good pay, rapid advancement and post-French-revolutionary thinking – a considerable breath of fresh air in the stultifying atmosphere of the German petty principalities of the time.

August found the chance to show his conviction in 1808 when he helped King Jerome to suppress the Dörnberg conspiracy which had brought together a group of reactionary Hessian nobles in a plot against Bonaparte under the leadership of Colonel Freiherr Wilhelm von Dörnberg. August's loyalty to Jerome earned him a prefecture in the new Kingdom. Despite an amnesty declared in 1815 in favour of those who had collaborated with the Kingdom of Westphalia, the Elector ordered Trott's arrest the following year. He was eventually allowed to leave Hessen and ended his days as the Foreign Minister of Würtemberg.

After the restoration of the Hessian royal family, a feud broke out between the king and the nobility over the former's contemptuous treatment of noble privileges, which led to a curious alliance between the right-wing nobles and the liberal party. Adam von Trott's great-uncle, Friedrich von Trott zu Solz, was a conservative who later joined forces with the Hessian liberals in their opposition to thg policies of the Elector. The nobility had been incensed by the Elector's

9

ennoblement of the children from his mistress's first marriage. Elector Friedrich-Wilhelm's high-handed treatment of his nobility drove them into the arms of the bourgeoisie.

Despite the alliance with the left, the essentially reactionary Trott was not tempted by the liberal ideas which had floated into Hessen from France after the revolution of 1830. His efficiency had earned him the rank of Geheimer Rat, or privy councillor in the Ministry of Justice. In 1831 he was elected to the presidency of the Hessian assembly and early the following year his popularity made him Minister of Justice. Later in 1832, Trott was made Foreign Minister of Hessen, a post which he occupied for the next five years. He was again President of the Assembly in the years 1847–8 when his stand in the face of growing revolutionary agitation was praised by the liberal press.

The last Trott to achieve prominence before the eclipse of the Hessian state was Otto von Trott. In 1847, while his cousin controlled the assembly in Kassel, Otto von Trott convoked a meeting where a list of grievances against the Elector was drawn up by the nobles present. Otto von Trott was a conservative opponent of the monarch who had no time for the liberals of 1848. He sought to form an alliance with the democrats in order to prevent the former's pro-Prussian policies. Opposition to the Elector had reached such a height by September 1850 that he was forced to appeal to the Emperor of Austria for assistance in putting down the revolt. The snub to the King of Prussia, who would normally have been called upon to control the situation, brought the two German powers of Austria and Prussia to the brink of war. The Prussians backed down at Olmütz, thus disappointing the liberals who saw unity with Prussia as an essential condition for achieving their policies.

In the wake of the Prussian humiliation, Otto von Trott became the leading spokesman of the conservative nobility and a convinced anti-Prussian. When war broke out between Austria and Prussia in 1866, the left and right wings were united in their opposition to Prussia. Trott found himself in alliance with Adam Trabert, the leader of the Democratic Party in the Assembly, and said:

It has been jokingly suggested that the far right and the far left are united here. I have always found this far left to be honourable, one always knows where one stands with them, and in this case I see Herr Trabert as a true Hessian and true German and believe that under no circumstances does he want to be made into a Prussian, a feeling which I naturally share with him . . . Frederick the Great has often been called the gravedigger of German Unity, but I find that Bismarck is its real gravedigger. You think the Prussian government may change, that a different one may come to power, but the whole policy of Prussia is that of the Emperor Napoleon, it is that which leads to caesarism. If Prussia succeeds in accomplishing what it has set out to do, do not be so naïve as to think this is being done for the benefit of liberalism. You will soon see what kind of politics you will have under Bismarck's regime.

10

The alliance of left and right was sufficient to defeat the liberal motion in favour of joining the war on the Prussian side, but it was soon clear that they had backed the wrong horse. On 3 July, Moltke's Prussian army routed the Austrians at Königsgrätz. On 8 October, Hesse-Kassel was amalgamated into the Prussian state.[4]

It was from the cadet – Imshausen–branch of the family that Adam von Trott came. His grandfather, Werner von Trott (1819–58), served in the Hessian diplomatic corps as Legationsrat or counsellor in Würtemburg. When he died at the age of thirty-nine, Adam von Trott's father, August von Trott, was only three. For August von Trott, there was no longer a Hesse-Kassel to serve. By the time he was ten years old the centre of power had shifted from Kassel to Berlin with the elimination of Kurhessen.

August von Trott was born in the Herrenhaus or manor at Imshausen in December 1855. After his schooling, he proceeded to the University of Göttingen in nearby Hanover. Göttingen had enjoyed a considerable reputation for liberalism after its foundation in the first half of the eighteenth century, a cachet derived from the fact that Hanover's electors were kings of England until 1837. In that year the thrones divided as a result of Hanover's adherence to Salic law – which required the rulers to be male. The results were soon felt in Göttingen, where the new elector promptly removed a number of liberal teachers, including the brothers Grimm. August von Trott chose Göttingen rather than the traditional Hessian centres of learning at Marburg and Rinteln. Göttingen had a more cosmopolitan and aristocratic reputation and, unlike the Hessian universities, attracted students from all over Germany. Like most other young men destined for the civil service, August von Trott studied law and public administration before becoming a Landrat or provincial administrator in Hesse-Nassau – as Hesse-Kassel, as a Prussian province, was now called.

From Kassel, Trott moved to Berlin and the Ministry of the Interior, where he was appointed Vortragender Rat (literally 'lecturing counsellor'). In Berlin he came into contact with the future German chancellor Theobald von Bethmann-Hollweg, with whom he was associated until the fall of the latter's ministry in 1917. In 1899 both Trott and Bethmann-Hollweg were despatched to different ends of Prussia as Regierungspräsidenten or chiefs of local administration. In Trott's case he was sent to Koblenz at the confluence of the rivers Rhine and Mosel. The following year he was shifted to Kassel, the old capital of Kurhessen.

In 1905 Bethmann-Hollweg was made Minister of the Interior for Prussia and Trott was summoned to Potsdam to become Oberpräsident (head of the civil administration) for the province of Brandenburg.

The post had been previously held by Bethmann-Hollweg, and the latter was not slow to show Trott a patronage which was to be consistently demonstrated in the course of what became a meteoric rise.

In 1909 Bethmann-Hollweg became Minister-President of Prussia and Chancellor of the German Reich. His appointment had been occasioned by the fall of Prince von Bülow. It was an unprecedented step to appoint a civil servant to such a political post. In the same month August von Trott became Prussian Kultusminister.

Trott remained essentially a civil-servant in his mentality, and his new post did not require him to adopt any of the underhand practices of political life. As Kultusminister he was responsible for both religion and education. In the latter capacity he was in charge of the Prussian universities, the Royal Academy of Sciences, the Royal Academy of Art, the Berlin scientific institutions, the National Gallery, the Observatory, the Charité Hospital and other similar bodies. In 1911, with the theologian Adolf von Harnack, Trott played a seminal role in the foundation of the Kaiser Wilhelm Society for the Advancement of Science. Throughout the eight years of his tenure of office, Trott enjoyed a reputation as a diligent and efficient administrator 'who embodied in his person the fully majesty of the state'.[5] When Bethmann-Hollweg's career foundered on the issue of electoral reform in the summer of 1917, Trott felt it incumbent upon him to resign from office. Clearly he had to take the rough with the smooth as Bethmann-Hollweg's man.

As he was still a member of the Prussian civil service he was able to slide down into a new administrative appointment as Oberpräsident of Hesse-Nassau based in Kassel. He also sat for the province on the Reichsrat or Imperial Council. Proximity to Imshausen meant that they were able to reoccupy the family house in 1919. The following year, at the age of sixty-four, August von Trott retired from the civil service assuming the role of elder statesman to his by now numerous children.[6]

August von Trott had married late. Late marriages had been something of a rule for members of the Hessian nobility whose sons had chosen to wait until they occupied a well-enough paid job in the administration before taking a wife. August von Trott, however, does appear to have been extremely cautious as he was already quite an important figure as the Regierungspräsident of the large city of Kassel when he married Eleonore von Schweinitz on 28 February 1901. He was then forty-five years old and she was twenty-six. The average age at which men in his peer-group married was thirty-two and a half; for women it was twenty-four.

His bride was the daughter of Lothar von Schweinitz from a noble Silesian family. Schweinitz (1822–1901), 'a notably sober-minded soldier diplomat',[7] was on his mother's side a direct descendant of

Field Marshal Adam von Trott. Having begun his career in the Foot Guards, he was sent in 1854 to Frankfurt-am-Main with a contingent of federal troops. There he got to know Otto von Bismarck, at that time the Prussian ambassador to the Imperial Diet. The meeting was not, perhaps, as fortunate as that of August von Trott and Bethmann-Hollweg. Schweinitz was to suffer at the hands of the temperamental future Chancellor, even though Bismarck clearly appreciated Schweinitz' abilities and marked him down for future use.

Following his appointment in Frankfurt, in 1857 Schweinitz became adjutant to the future emperor, Prince Frederick-William of Prussia. In 1861 he was gazetted military attaché in Vienna thus commencing a long and important diplomatic career. Schweinitz served in the Prusso-Danish war of 1864 on the staff of Frederick-William (by now crown prince) and was named the following year as head of the Prussian military mission to St Petersburg. He served in the Seven Weeks War of 1866 between Prussia and Austria, interrupting his service in Russia, and was appointed major-general soon after. Despite his good relations with Czar Alexander II, in 1869 he was removed from St Petersburg and dispatched to Vienna as the envoy of the North German Confederation, those states which had fallen into the Prussian orbit after the war in 1866. After the conclusion of the French war in 1871, Schweinitz was raised in rank to Imperial Ambassador to Vienna with the rank of a Prussian lieutenant-general. Later he was promoted to the rank of general of infantry.

In 1875, as problems began to mount in the Balkans, Alexander II asked that Schweinitz be returned to St Petersburg, where from the beginning of the next year he was closely involved in the negotiations leading up to the Congress of Berlin (1878), the Dreikaiserbund 'and other notable milestones of late nineteenth century international relations'.[8] Schweinitz' close relationship with the Czar was a frequent impediment when it came to his collaboration with Bismarck who was not happy with the ambassador's insistence on probity in diplomacy. At least once the Chancellor threatened to dismiss his ambassador to St Petersburg. Finally, in 1892, two years after the fall of his difficult patron, the 'long-suffering'[9] but very distinguished ex-ambassador retired to Kassel.

If August von Trott married notably late, Lothar von Schweinitz had married notably later. The future ambassador was nearly fifty. His twenty-three-year-old bride was Anna Jay, the daughter of John Jay, the American minister in Vienna. Jay was the grandson of George Washington's first chief justice of the United States and therefore a member of a class with a natural claim to represent the aristocracy of the new nation. Despite the wide difference in age between Schweinitz and his bride, ten children were born. August von Trott's bride-to-be, Eleonore, was born in Vienna in February 1875. When she came to marry and have children of her own, she could add to the long and distinguished history of her husband's family a no-less prestigious background which united a Silesian-Prussian military and diplomatic world with the strong puritanical tradition of the American founding fathers. The strange mixture was to be noticeable in August and Eleonore's son Adam.

In the first nineteen years of marriage, Eleonore von Trott gave birth to eight children, the last one in February 1920 when she was very nearly forty-five. Friedrich Adam was the second son, born on 9 August 1909, soon after his father's appointment as Kultusminister, and baptized with the name of Trott's most distinguished ancestor. Up until that time the name had fallen into disuse within the family. For his family and friends he was always 'Adam' and never Friedrich. The only time he was ever called Friedrich was on the occasion of his marriage to Clarita Tiefenbacher in 1940. 'Adam' was thought to be too 'Semitic' for the sensibilities of a Nazi registrar.[10]

A few days after his birth, the child was placed in the competent hands of an English nanny, Louisa Barrett. As the minister's wife, Eleonore von Trott was too busy with official engagements to devote very much time to her brood and it appears that Louisa Barrett was a model nurse for the five years that Trott was in her care. As an enemy alien Louisa Barrett was obliged to return to her country at the outbreak of war in August 1914. Trott reproached her with only one thing – her poor pronunciation of German when she read him his nightly fairy tale.

Trott's earliest memory, as he told A.L. Rowse, was of 'the daily drill on the great dusty barrack square before our official residence in Potsdam'.*[11] His first school was the French lycée which he attended from the age of six. The war years were marked by chronic shortages caused by the Allied blockade. When his father took up his post as Oberpräsident in Kassel, Trott went to school there, starting his first year at the gymnasium in 1919.† With the family's installation at Imshausen and August von Trott's retirement, Trott was removed from the gymnasium and sent to cram with a pastor in Solz. The boy was happy with this arrangement as it left him time to explore the Trottenwald with his cousin Bobbi (Friedrich) von Trott zu Solz, who was exactly his age, hunting for small game. Bobbi became a lifelong

---

* *Frau von Trott insists that the family lived on the top floor of the Ministry of Culture in the Wilhelmstrasse in Berlin. Perhaps the drilling took place in the nearby Unter den Linden?*

† *The gymnasium resembles rather more the French lycée than the old-fashioned English grammar school. It covers the period from the age of ten to university entrance. Like the lycée and the grammar school it was intended for brighter pupils who were likely to take on higher education.*

friend and far more than just a cousin; when his eldest son was born in 1939, he was christened Bodo Adam.

This happy period was cut short a year later at Easter 1921 when Trott was sent back to the gymnasium in Kassel, boarding with a pastor in the city, who had previously had charge of his eccentric elder brother Werner (1902–66). The pastor was further required to give the boy extra tuition to speed up his path through the school. Trott, then aged twelve, found himself at odds with the clergyman and his attitude to prayer. In May he wrote to his mother: 'I can't understand Herr Pfarrer's brand of Christianity, all this so called "quivering and quaking". We should be courageous, not endlessly praying and praying (it sounds to me like crawling), but rather doing good through our actions.'[12] It was an early indication of Trott's attitude to religion – rather more humanist than dogmatic.

Poor health, which troubled Trott throughout his life, must have been a considerable bane to him during his years at school, especially as it meant not taking part in outdoor games with the other boys. It is not impossible that this incessant badgering by ill-health was brought on by the very rapid change in the family's material circumstances – suddenly reduced from the level of ministers at court to that of pen-pushers in a provincial city. There is some evidence that the young Trott was teased about his father's change of status by his schoolfellows and therefore avoided contact with other boys of his age in Kassel. Added to this his mother was in poor health herself and rather remote. His relations with his father were even more distant and formal. Trott never lost sight of his desire to please the latter – all the more so, perhaps, because of the oddity of his elder brother Werner whose scrapes caused his parents to despair.

One distraction which Trott did appreciate, and which brought him into contact with the outside world he loved so much, was the Nibe-lungenbund. The Nibelungenbund was a branch of the Wandervogel movement which had captivated German youth in the years since the turn of the century. Seen in the light of Baden-Powell's boy-scout movement, its contemporary in Britain and the Empire, it loses the sinister importance which some people might choose to attribute to it were they to accuse it of being a forerunner to National Socialism's Hitler Youth. The Nibelungenbund was the conception of Lothar Freiherr von Biedermann but its 'real leader' was Gustav 'Gösta' Ecke. Ecke, the son of a professor of theology, had completed his university studies with distinction and served as an officer in the army throughout the war. In 1923 he emigrated to China.

Adam Trott's major involvement with the Wandervogel movement came to an end in Easter 1922 when he was transferred from the Kassel gymnasium to a boarding school at Hannoversch-Münden. The Alumnat des Klosters Loccum was a comparatively minor German private school situated about twelve miles north-east of Kassel on the road to Göttingen. Trott, who rarely reproached his parents on the question of his upbringing or anything else was later to regret the fact that he was not sent to a better school like Rossleben, where his friends Peter Yorck, Kessel and Nostitz went, and where he might have found companionship with boys who were his intellectual equals, or indeed decent teachers.[13] As it was, his teachers had an unfortunate tendency to pry into his reading and even to intercept his post. Trott, who could be discreet to the point of obscurity, responded by asking his parents to place their letters in sealed envelopes and to cease sending postcards.

Still, Trott's experience of boarding school was not universally negative. The Alumnat was to instil a deep love of German literature, especially of Goethe and Schiller, as well introducing him to a number of foreign writers including Ibsen. In a touching letter to his wife written in November 1943, Trott summed up the years spent at Hannoversch-Münden in a romantic, somewhat melancholic vein:

> Yesterday, while I was rescuing objects from the ruins of the Kurfürstenstrasse [i.e. the Foreign Office Information Department], on one of the walls I lit upon a delightful, antiquated picture of Hannoversch-Münden. It was in the style of Merian,* only bigger and more naïve. For a curious moment it brought back to me the memory of those lovely, slightly cloudy, slightly menancing, yet at the same time uncomplicated youthful years in this town set among unending woods and river valleys. One day I shall show it to you. In a way I loved my existence there and was from time to time very happy.[14]

---

* *Matthaeus Merian (1593–1687), the founder of a dynasty of painters in the city of Basle. He was noted for his landscapes and aquatints.*

2
Student Years in Germany and Oxford

In the spring of 1927, Adam von Trott took the state *Reifeprüfung* examination and was marked *gut* in this *Abitur* or matriculation certificate. As a result he could now pursue any course of study he pleased in one of the German universities of the day. Even at school in a small provincial town, Trott must have been aware of the turbulent events which had taken place in Germany since the Weimar Republic had come into being eight years before. From his family's point of view there was little reason to love the new constitution; after all, August von Trott, like his father-in-law Lothar von Schweinitz, had owed his entire advancement to the Bismarckian Reich and the 'Prussification' of Germany from 1864 onwards.

In 1927, however, the worst years of Weimar Germany seemed to be far behind. The Germans' record of achievement since 1924 had distanced the country from events like the Kapp Putsch of 1920, when the flimsy regime was all but toppled by a right-wing civil servant at the head of a Freikorps, or acts of political murder like those which eliminated Matthias Erzberger in 1921 and Walter Rathenau in 1922. The terrible inflation which rocked the nation in 1922 and 1923 probably had little effect on the Trotts as their money was in land, and chiefly in their extensive forests which surrounded the estate at Imshausen,[1] but the French invasion of the Ruhr in 1923 had caused a serious blow to German pride which must have been felt even in young Trott's cloistered world.

In the autumn of that same year, Gustav Stresemann had come to power as the saviour of the young republic. Communist uprisings in Saxony and Thuringia were put down by the army under General von Seeckt, who also saw off the attempted *coup* of Adolf Hitler and his supporters in Munich. The young nation appeared to be on the road to recovery. When President Ebert died in 1925 he was replaced by the veteran Hindenberg who, as a monarchist war hero, could be safely seen to unite the German right behind him, and therefore bring those disaffected groups within the pale of the republic for the first time. The following year Stresemann as Foreign Minister took Germany into the League of Nations.

The political and economic insecurity which had plagued Germany prior to Stresemann was reflected in the Reichstag where there were

17

already thirty-two National Socialist members in 1924. By 1928, as a result of Stresemann's policies, the number had dwindled to twelve. Stresemann died after a stroke the following year, but even had he lived it is hard to see how he could have averted the effects of the world economic crisis which swept through Europe after the Wall Street Crash. As Golo Mann writes,

> The first republic came to grief over the economic crisis of 1930 and it is impossible to say with certainty that it would have come to grief otherwise. One cannot say that the normality of the years 1924 to 1929 was an illusion and had no genuine chance of lasting. One can only say that the equilibrium of those years was always threatened from within and that the sources of danger are more apparent in retrospect than they could be at the time. A man may survive a serious illness, but when it comes to the last crisis his previous medical history will count; the weakened organism cannot support what a stronger one might have supported.[2]

In May 1927, Adam von Trott matriculated at the University of Munich. His subject was predictably law and public administration, allowing him to style himself *student juris* on the visiting cards which he had printed.[3] By taking up the study of law, Trott was declaring his intention to follow in the tradition of a *Beamtenfamilie* and serve the state when the time came to do so. In Munich he was rapidly drawn into the standard pursuits of aristocratic German undergraduates, learning to fence and to ride as well as going for cycling expeditions up the River Isar which bisects the city.

In the course of the semester he also witnessed a Nazi meeting in the capital of the movement, recording that the spectators that day were 'uneducated and useless'. Trott seems to have been impressed by the sheer energy of the Führer himself, writing that 'he's quite a chap'.[4] But for all that, the event does not seem to have made a deep impression on him. Trott's time in Munich was troubled by illness which had him bedridden through much of the short semester. During that time he read voraciously: Dostoyevsky, Gogol and his favourite German poet, Hölderlin. In June he left for Vienna and Budapest, thinking it neccessary to apologize to his mother for not visiting the German embassy in the former where her father had been ambassador and she herself had been born. In July he was lured back to Hessen by the prospect of shooting in the forests.

Trott did not return to Munich after the summer. German universities differ from most others in the freedom they accord students to come and go at will. With a completed semester one was and is able to travel on to a new faculty, often lured by the reputation of a teacher in a particular subject. Trott spent a total of eight semesters at three different German universities as well as one more 'in residence' while he prepared his doctoral dissertation. Instead of returning to Munich, Trott went on to Göttingen.

One of the advantages of Göttingen for a Trott zu Solz was the chance to join the select corps of the Göttinger Sachsen. Trott's father was a member of this, and an interested *Alte Herr* – or old member. The German student corps were in origin dedicated to friendship and mutual assistance. In the nineteenth and twentieth centuries, however, they developed into the equivalent of the better university and college clubs in a British or American university – free from political or religious significance and rather dominated by the upper classes.[5]

The hallmark of corps membership was the *Mensur* or student duel. The name derived from the measurement of the boundaries of the duelling ground. The purpose was to exhibit self-control and strength of character in the face of armed combat. One who had fought a duel and who exhibited the scars on his face to prove it was deemed *satisfaktionsfähig* or 'able to give satisfaction'. Duels of this sort were still common under the Weimar Republic despite their being banned by law. The social exclusivity of the corps meant that they were, for the time being at least, little sullied by Nazi membership, though in the late 1920s the Nazis formed their own NSDStB, or National Sozialist Deutsches Studentenbund, in an attempt to produce a rival organization.

During his first semester at Göttingen, Trott was an enthusiastic *Fuchs* (literally 'fox' or novice member) of the Sachsen, his social life revolving around his fellows in the corps. In their society he made excursions to the Universities of Halle and Bonn and engaged in drinking bouts which are not unusual in any university.

Through the Sachsen, Trott met two men who were to remain his friends till the end of his life, Götz von Selle – who married the sister of a friend from Hannoversch-Münden days, Hans von Bodenhausen – and Ernst-Friedemann Freiherr von Münchhausen.[6] After the war Münchhausen recalled the striking appearance of his friend in that first Göttingen semester of 1927: 'Under the high forehead and heavy eyebrows were dark blue eyes with an expression which at the same time brought forth the clear depth of understanding and showed the compelling force of feeling . . . Whoever met him once felt that he was one of those gifted persons that one only seldom meets.'[7]

In the summer semester of 1928, Trott proved himself amply *satisfaktionsfähig* in a duel against a boastful opponent, standing unharmed while he cut his rival three times, twice drawing blood. His activities at the time were by no means all so violent, but they betray none the less an interest in the less serious side of university life despite his studies under professors Julius Binder and Herbert Kraus (the latter taught international law and diplomacy – subjects already dear to Trott's heart). So, for example, on Thursday 10 May, in company with other members of the Göttinger Sachsen, Trott had spent an hour, from eight to nine, small-bore rifle-shooting before going on to an hour's fencing lesson. Sporting activities were interrupted for an hour for a class but resumed with a ride between eleven and twelve. Another class intervened before lunch which was followed by an hour's fencing theory. In the evening he went to the theatre.

That summer Trott attended a meeting in Geneva that was to have enormous subsequent significance for him and was to ring the knell for the more frivolous side of his student life. Through her American mother, Eleonore von Trott had inherited a strong puritanical strain which she expressed in her membership of numerous religious bodies. In the summer of 1927, while her son was travelling in eastern Europe, she had attended a conference for Christian youth leaders at Dassel in Hanover. In the course of the meeting she met the Reverend Tracey Strong, Dr W.A. Visser't Hooft and Robert Abernathy, three church leaders then based in Geneva. Through Strong, Frau von Trott arranged for her second son to spend part of his vacation in Geneva, thus satisfying to some extent Trott's yearning for further foreign travel.

When Trott arrived on 3 September Geneva was still feeling the effects of the Pact of Locarno. Three years before a non-aggression treaty had been signed between Germany, France and Belgium, which had been guaranteed by Italy and Britain, giving the cue for a new peaceful Europe of international co-operation. It had been followed up by the Kellog-Briand Pact in which sixty-eight countries, including Germany, had agreed to renounce war as a means of foreign policy.

A week later Trott attended a talk given by George Bernard Shaw which impressed him to the degree that he considered writing an article about him. Also in Geneva he met Geoffrey (later Sir Geoffrey) Wilson, then an Oxford undergraduate, and the Reverend Charles Freer Andrews, a friend of Tagore and Gandhi who introduced Indian culture to Trott for the first time. Andrews made a deep impression on Trott who soon became an enthusiastic supporter of the call for Indian independence.

An important contact was Dr Willem-Adolf Visser't Hooft whom he encountered on 20 September. Visser't Hooft later wrote that he had been 'strongly attracted to this very intelligent student'.[8] Trott seemed already aware of the dangerous and tragic situation in which German youth found itself. In his personal life, Visser't Hooft found Trott to possess the 'timidity of a young man desperately searching for a foundation for his existence'. After what he described as 'an overdose of spiritual good' received from his pious mother, Trott had discovered that he could no longer read the Bible. The novels of Dostoyevsky now provided him with the faith that the Bible could not.

In political terms Trott admitted to being a Socialist – though of an English sort, as he saw the need to maintain historical continuity, respecting tradition yet crusading against inhumanity and injustice.

Trott returned to Germany via a cousin in Zürich. He was much impressed by the lake, the sight of which touched his deep-rooted romantic strain, as did the prospect of 'the whole horizon with zig-zagged, snow-covered mountains, bathed in the red glow of the sinking sun'.[9] While in Geneva, at the house of Tracey Strong, Trott had met Conrad Hoffmann of the World Student Christian Association who arranged through his friend Canon Tatlow in Britain for him to attend a Student Christian Movement Conference in Liverpool in the New Year. The conference was planned to run from 2 to 8 January. For the time being, Christianity in Geneva, Liverpool and Oxford was a means to discover new horizons and to travel beyond the narrow confines of his traditional German background.

The following semester at Göttingen, Trott fell ill with a kidney complaint and had to spend much of his time in bed and convalescing in Imshausen. It was at this time Trott decided that following the Liverpool conference he should like to spend the next term at Oxford. Canon Tatlow's secretary Margaret Wrong was put to work to arrange something and came up with the offer of a term at Mansfield College. At that time Mansfield was not strictly a part of the university but a Congregational college where students read for the Bachelor of Divinity degree. Trott, however, was to be allowed to follow politics and philosophy courses which were in line with his Göttingen studies. Distant from the centre of university life that Mansfield was, it was to provide an introduction to Oxford, one that was to bring much pride and bitterness in the rest of his short life.

The theme of the Liverpool conference, 'The Purpose of God in the Life of the World', was a fairly hefty one for a man on the verge of losing his faith. Trott seems nonetheless to have taken the heavy religious content in his stride and he set about using the session in order to make further contacts and friends who would be useful both now and later on. Throughout his life Trott had an extraordinary knack of being able to pick up people who would be useful to him and keep them in cold storage until such time as their use became clear. There was certainly a trace of opportunism about his character, though not one which appears to have troubled his friends.[10] In a letter to Diana Hubback written from Oxford in the autumn of 1932, Trott revealed how little point he saw in male friendships, considering men only as 'contacts'. Trott wrote 'my ultimate wish and ambition [is] to be of the greatest possible political service to my country' and this was the thing on which 'my friendships with men are more or less directly dependent'.[11]

For a while during the conference Trott's plan to spend a term at Oxford began to look doubtful.[12] However, the project was rescued by Margaret Wrong who was able to introduce Trott to the principal of Mansfield College, The Reverend W.B. Selbie. Selbie was an authority on German Protestant theology, the author of a book on Schleiermacher and a friend of the same Adolf von Harnack who had founded the Kaiser Wilhelm Institute with the help of August von Trott as Kultusminister. Naturally he read and spoke German fluently and this may well have helped him to come to an understanding with Trott junior.

Apart from Selbie, Trott made several other useful contacts during his week in Liverpool. One of these was Professor W.G. Adams, the Warden of All Souls, the college where, as an undergraduate, Trott was to find a very large part of his society. Another was G.J. Scholten, a Dutch student with whom Trott discovered a certain affinity. Later Scholten provided a valuable link with the war-time Dutch Resistance. He also met Hans Gaides, a working-class German student who gave him an *entrée* into a world vastly removed from that of his student corps at Göttingen.

After a short break Trott went up to Oxford on the 20 January. At Mansfield it would have been hard for Trott to enter fully into the swing of the university and much of his time must have been isolated in the extreme. He had one or two means of escape. He had arranged for a couple of political science tutorials a week, which took him out of the chilly world of the nonconformist church, and he had also begun to assemble a few Oxford friends. One of these was Geoffrey Wilson, whom he had got to know in Geneva and with whom he explored the colleges in the afternoons. Another was the Indian student Humayun Kabir who later that year came to stay with the Trott family at Imshausen.*[13] Kabir was later to become Minister of Culture in New Delhi. Trott was already a convinced Hegelian while Kabir was a devotee of the philosopher Kant. This led to the occasional intellectual fight in the course of their afternoon walks.[14]

The third of his younger Oxford friends from the Mansfield days was A.L. Rowse. Rowse, who later went on to enjoy a distinguished career as an historian and literary critic, was at that time a left-wing junior Fellow of All Souls, six years Trott's senior. Two years before his meeting with the young German, Rowse had decided to fill an obvious gap in his knowledge by learning German. An interest in Rilke, 'possibly the greatest poet of our century', Hölderlin and others, including the socialist writer Otto Braun[15] who had died young on the Western Front, excited him to take up the study. Braun, whose

---

* *Trott was absent at the time but Kabir was impressed by his parents, describing the father as a 'venerable man' and the 'moving spirit' of the family. Eleonore Trott, he thought 'one of the most distinguished persons I have ever met'.*

stepmother later became Trott's friend, Rowse called 'a kind of Rupert Brooke but not a poet'. At the end of 1926 he moved to Germany for a while in pursuit of his aim. After spending a while in the industrial Rhineland town of Hagen in the house of a Lutheran pastor, Rowse went on to Munich and Vienna, gathering along the route a profound hatred for the Germans and their ways of thinking.

'Adam was first brought over from Mansfield College – where he was outside real university life – by General Swinton, the inventor of tanks, who knew people in the German Army,' Rowse writes in his volume of autobiography entitled *A Cornishman Abroad*. In the course of the term he came to tea with Rowse twice, and later, at the end of term, Rowse entertained him to dinner in hall. Not surprisingly Trott 'fell for All Souls', then as now a unique institution populated entirely by graduate fellows, many of whom were distinguished academics, diplomats and politicians. The older fellows gathered around the erect figure of the young German in the buttery before dinner, asking him about his grandfather, Ambassador Schweinitz. Rowse, however, wanted to talk about Werfel and Thomas Mann and Trott seemed more enthusiastic about modern literature than Schweinitz' relations with the Iron Chancellor. At the end of the evening Rowse escorted Trott down Beaumont Street, as the latter wished to say goodbye to a friend who had rooms there. Rowse was stunned by the casualness of the handshake with which Trott bid him goodnight. He returned to his rooms in All Souls to survey the scene left after the German's visit.

My top row of German books knocked a little askew where he had picked out Rilke's *Stundenbuch* to read while I dressed for dinner. The cigarettes open on the chimney-piece, the blue ashtray by his chair; the cushion which had fallen back while he talked with such earnestness; the reading lamp on the chair where I placed it to read a sonnet of Shakespeare's by . . . [16]

It was, Rowse confided to his diary,

the strangest evening I ever spent, just in talking quite ordinarily, one each side of the fireplace. I had thought of him as a youth, charming and sensitive, intelligent, radiant with his beauty and inevitable happiness. But no: he was anything but this last, and to an extraordinary degree. He has based his whole outlook in life upon his acute and even morbid sensibility, upon his own feelings and the intuition of others, personal relations have become the stuff of his mental universe – which seems incredible to me. It made me go back a long way in my own emotional history to achieve a state which was in sympathy and in tune with his. His feeling of defeatism for one so young was difficult to comprehend, it took constant intellectual effort to follow him. I made it, for tonight I fell in love with him. I felt here is the one I have always hoped to find; someone beautiful in all ways, mind and body, and who could go along with me the way I want to go. No woman or man I had ever come across was this that I longed for. [17]

What Rowse chose to see as an 'ideal love-affair, platonic in the philosophic sense', was almost certainly never construed as one by Trott. Rowse himself admits that Trott was 'fundamentally hetero-sexual' and although he was prepared to be drawn into a form of 'romantic friendship' with the older man he certainly shied away from physical contact with Rowse. Later, after Trott had come into residence at Balliol, he wrote to his mother in terms which reveal his own feelings on this score, feelings which Rowse clearly resented. 'Rowse I see only very seldom, as he is currently teaching in London – when we meet we get on extremely well, if with one or two difficulties (which above all spring from the earlier misunderstanding)'.[18]

From the beginning the friendship was fraught with difficulties. Rowse was, by his own admission, an 'oversensitive Celt',*[19] immensely conscious of his obscure Cornish background in the public-school world of Oxford. 'Adam once and again asked me to stay, I never would. At Oxford, with All Souls behind me, I remained top dog.'[20] At Mansfield Trott had been far removed from the romance of Oxford; his initiation into the rarified preserve of All Souls revealed another Oxford to him, one which he 'fell for' and which, for the time being, was represented by Rowse.[21] Trott had been sufficiently impressed by Oxford to wish to spend three years in one of the traditional colleges and to follow the degree course. That evening in All Souls he asked Rowse his advice. Rowse suggested that Trott should attach himself to one of the German newspapers, perhaps as a 'stringer' in London. Trott told Rowse that he had made an unsuccessful bid to interest the London correspondent of the *Frankfurter Zeitung*. Rowse's next idea was the diplomatic service, but that would have involved putting off the return to England to such time as he had qualified in Germany. Finally, in Rowse's account of the conversation, he suggested that Trott apply for a Rhodes Scholarship,† backed with his recommendation. Here Rowse clearly had some prior knowledge that there was soon to be a decision to restore the German scholarships which had been suspended in 1914.

Trott had gone down after his dinner at All Souls and Rowse was anxious to receive a letter from him. He did not have long to wait and there ensued a correspondence which endured for a number of years. It must soon have dawned on Rowse, however, that his 'young man out of Dostoyevsky' was not quite the godsend he took him to be. For a start there was Trott's growing interest in the philosophy of Hegel, something bound to cause no little friction, more indeed than it had caused with his friend Kabir. 'I *detested* Hegelianism, and the

---

* *'50% of A.L. [Rowse] 's well-known behaviour is unsureness and 50% a closely connected scorn; there's another Celt!' (Trott to Diana Hubback, 26 January 1934.)*

24

perpetual, fruitless self-analysis, and the analysis of everything it led Adam into – until it seemed there was no solid ground for existence whatever.'[22] The other problem which raised its head was Trott's already well-formed interest in girls. There had been a relationship at Göttingen and Trott had told Rowse about a German girl he was seeing at Oxford. From Berlin, Trott wrote to his friend about a new romance. Trott it seemed was not interested in anything more than a physical relationship with the lady in question and, thinking that he might make a gesture to his first 'male' friendship, he wrote to Rowse for his advice. 'I resolved to tell you about this [i.e. the affair]; if you believe that in order to preserve our friendship I should drop the girl – who loves me – I will do it.' 'What an extraordinary thing to say!'[23] wrote Rowse some fifty years later, while he dismissed his rival as 'some ordinary little German girl'. He was clearly shaken by the revelation and from that moment onwards his expectations from his young German friend must have diminished sharply.[24]

The fits of melancholy which Rowse had observed continued to plague Trott until he met Miriam Dyer-Bennet in Göttingen and fell in love for the first time. He went back to Germany still tormented by unhappiness. In an essay he wrote at the time, comparing the existences of German and English students, Trott gave vent to his emotions: 'I feel that just at this moment the best who are most truly involved in this conflict are silent about it . . . silence and suffering seem to me the greatest destiny and privilege of the thinking man, and the deeper the question, the greater the answer may be.'[25] The essay, was published in the YMCA journal, *The World's Youth*.[26] Much of the paper is high-flown adolescent stuff, but occasionally there are intimations of the mature Trott, especially in this passage which Trott was to return to in his now lost memorandum, '*Deutschland zwischen Ost und West*'. 'The position of Germany is now peculiar and her problems very complicated. She is midway between a communist East and a highly individualistic West that has succeeded in adjusting itself to the conditions of the modern mechanical age.'

Trott did not return to Göttingen, where his third semester was drawing to a close, but after stopping for a few days to see his new friend Scholten in Holland, went to his parents at Imshausen. The following term he chose to spend in the more 'cosmopolitan setting' of Berlin. In May he formally ex-matriculated from Göttingen and entered the law faculty in the capital. In Berlin he had family like his Schweinitz cousins. Trott's first lodgings were near the Kurfürsten-damm in the bustling 'West End' of the city. After a while he found the noise began to erode his concentration and distract him from his work. While he looked for a quieter billet he briefly moved in with his well-connected uncle Eberhard von Schweinitz who lived in the admirably roomy accommodation of the old royal *Schloss* in the very heart of Berlin. The *Schloss* had been empty since the fall of the monarchy in 1919, but Uncle Eberhard was there in the capacity of trustee. In the course of his visit to Berlin in 1931, Trott took Rowse to inspect his old quarters.

His uncle had a flat in the *Schloss*, the immense imperial palace of the Kaiser; he was a von Schweinitz whose father had been Bismarck's ambassador to Russia. In the evenings Adam and I used to roam around the palace. I well recall the Kaiser's study; the telephone cords looking as if they had been just cut, the big desk made of timbers from Nelson's *Victory*, the books, half German and half English, half Lutheran theology, half contemporary history and biography. I still recall among them Churchill's biography of his father Lord Randolph and Bishop Boyd-Carpenter on prayer. Behind the doors everywhere, I was surprised to see, were stacked pictures of the *Allerhöchste* in peacock attitudes, eagles in his helmet, flunkies bowing before him — just stacked in the corner and waiting for his return.[27]*

From the *Schloss*, Trott moved to a room in the Pariserstrasse of which his new friend, Albrecht von Kessel, has left us a description: 'cheap and gloomy digs, on the sole wobbly table of which were arranged in a truly artisitc still life, Marx's *Das Kapital*, Hölderlin's poems, a hairbrush, and a slice of bread and butter'.[28] On the walls Trott had hung the two portraits which accompanied him throughout his life – one of his grandmother, Anna Jay, and the other of the early nineteenth-century Prussian statesman, the Freiherr vom Stein.

Kessel, the son of a former Landtag deputy and a career diplomat, was part of a circle of people he met at this time, possibly through Hugh, later Monsignor, Montgomery, then a third secretary at the British Embassy in Berlin. Others were Gottfried 'Gogo' von Nostitz and fellow Göttinger Sachsen, Josias von Rantzau. With Montgomery Trott had a fierce argument on whether or not the *Mensur* (see above, p. 19) was justifiable. Trott defended the tradition vigorously, citing British barbaric customs, like fox-hunting, in his defence.

When he was not attending embassy parties Trott was mixing with a wholly different social milieu in his desire to develop a relationship with working-class and socialist groups. Hans Gaides, his friend from the Liverpool conference proved useful in this. Through him Trott was brought into contact with the Sozialistischer Arbeitskreis, or socialist working group, writing to his no doubt bemused father that he believed himself 'finally to be on the right track'. Trott was surprised himself that he was so easily absorbed into working-class socialist circles, even more so as a former corps student. Through the Arbeitskreis, Trott made a further contact of importance in the person

---

* *The* schloss *was dynamited by the Russians in the 1960s, only one bay of the façade being preserved.*

of the Regierungsrat (government counsellor) Dr Hans Muhle from the Prussian Ministry of Trade. Trott also attended meetings of the Sozialistischer Studentenbund – or socialist students' union.[29]

Although Trott was able to see the positive side of Socialism and was deeply attracted to some of its tenets he was never taken with Marxism. 'I am constantly impressed by the underestimation in Socialist (especially Marxist) circles of the values which form personality and create friendly co-operation.' In his time in Berlin, Trott was increasingly influenced by the writings of Gustav Landauer, the libertarian socialist murdered in Munich during the revolution of 1919, who with his anarchist leanings had been strongly opposed to Marxism. Trott himself found the rigid formula and social divisiveness of Marxism inadequate in the face of political reality.[30]

Trott decided to remain in Berlin for the rest of the academic year. He was involved in his work in Berlin and the city had the virtue of being far removed from his hearty corps-brothers in the Göttinger Sachsen. Trott's drift to the left would have been hard to explain in what was an essentially conservative body.

By the late spring of 1930, when Adam Trott was once again settled in Göttingen, he had begun to worry about his ability to do justice to the state Referendar exams in law that he would have to take at the end of the academic year. Looking around for someone to pace him in his work, he asked his cousin Adalbert von Unruh to 'fill in some of his gaps'. Unruh later became Professor of Aeronautical Law at the University of Frankfurt before being killed in the war on the Russian front. The work with Unruh did not come off, but it was the latter who suggested Trott go back to his earlier teacher, Professor Kraus, for supervision of his doctoral dissertation. It was in Kraus's seminar that he began to study Hegel's *Philosophy of Law*, a book which was to have a profound affect on his thinking for a number of years.[31] Hegel's thought clarified the model of Prussian/Socialist synthesis which was forming in his mind.

Another result of his working under Kraus was his meeting with Alexander Werth. Trott met Werth, who was to work closely with him throughout his time in the Foreign Office, in Professor Kraus's office. They introduced themselves to one another then together went off for a long walk along the Professorenweg. The fruit of their discussion that afternoon was the decision to work together for the coming exams, a practice relatively common at Göttingen at the time.[32]

That term at Göttingen Trott met another person who was to play a big role in his life – Miriam Dyer-Bennett. She was an American woman of forty, with five young children, who had taken the unusual decision to come to Germany to finish her doctorate. Trott very quickly fell in love with Mrs Dyer-Bennett and by midsummer he had moved into the same *pension* as her, from there shifting to a villa in the autumn. Clearly Mrs Dyer-Bennet was in many ways a mother figure to the twenty-year-old Trott,[33] giving him a new confidence and curing the bouts of melancholy which had troubled his adolescence, but his love for her was still undiminished in his first year at Oxford and with occasional hiccups their friendship remained close, although sometimes stormy, until Trott's last visit to America at the beginning of the Second World War.

Trott had been discreetly distancing himself from his corps brothers at Göttingen which allowed him to experiment with a more varied social existence. Miriam Dyer-Bennet had socialist leanings and through her Trott met Franz Golfing, a Viennese Jew who became Trott's best friend at the time. Through Golfing, Trott was introduced to Socialist groups in Göttingen and later made contact with Socialists in Vienna.[34] Golfing introduced him to Klaus Ziegler, who was then the head of the Socialist Students' Union in Göttingen which Trott was anxious to join. Ziegler, on the other hand was cool, seeing Trott's membership of the student corps as being incompatible with participating in his organization.

Trott achieved his majority in August 1930 and thus became eligible to vote. Elections came up in September of that year and Trott, demonstrating how much he had moved to the left in the past year, cast his vote for the Socialists of the SPD (Sozialdemokratische Partei Deutschlands). Trott's decision to abandon class interests in favour of a radical social solution distressed his father, who envisaged his running into difficulties with his friends in the university. Trott, however, at a time of considerable uncertainty in Germany with the Weimar Republic tottering on the brink of collapse as a result of the economic crisis which followed the Wall Street Crash, had made up his mind. Unemployment in Germany had risen to over six million. Lacking support in the Reichstag, Chancellor Brüning had been reduced to governing by decree. The elections of September 1930 were a call to give him a clear mandate to govern.

The results were ominous. Though the Socialists remained the major party in the Reichstag, there had been substantial gains by both the Communists and the Nazis. The latter had made something of a comeback in German politics after the wane of Weimar's prosperous middle years under Stresemann. The Nazi gains were even more worrying than those of the Communists in that their total seats had risen from twelve to 107, making them the second biggest party in the assembly. Trott believed that in voting for the Socialists he was opting for German reconstruction. His conservative father remained distinctly doubtful, but chose to respect his son's decision none the less.

Much of Trott's time was being taken up with his study of Hegel – a philosopher then much in vogue among German students as a result of the increasing polarization of the German political scene. Another theme of Trott's was his avowed desire to reach a synthesis of Socialism and 'Prussianism', by which he meant 'readiness to render service, openness towards social questions and the primacy of the community before the individual'. Trott's source for his idea of Prussianism was probably Oswald Spengler's book *Preussentum und Sozialismus*. The synthesis of unstinting dedication to the state and socialistic ideas was clearly an attempt to reconcile the mental conflicts which beset Trott at the time in the wide divergence between his family tradition and his own radicalism. In concocting this philosophy Trott saw an alliance of the aristocracy and the proletariat as a feasible notion, combining against the selfish interests of the middle classes.

Trott took his Referendar exams in the winter of 1930. The examinations were held in the city of Celle, to the north-east of Hanover. The written papers were in November and the orals a month later just before Christmas. After the *viva voce* he was judged *voll befriedigend* [35] — or fully satisfactory — and achieved the status of Referendar, or probationary counsel. In the normal course of events he would have gone on to complete the second part of his exams, the *Assessorprüfung*, which would have enabled him to practise at the bar and was taken after three years' service in the courts. Trott elected instead to submit a doctoral dissertation and therefore returned to Göttingen and Professor Kraus.* The subject that Trott chose for his doctorate was 'Hegel's Philosophy of Law and its Relationship to International Law'. As he was no longer formally obliged to be a member of the university, Trott ex-matriculated but remained in residence in order to accomplish the task. He worked throughout the winter, spring and summer, reading voraciously on the subject as well as attending the classes of a Professor Binder on political theory. Trott thought Binder an extreme Nationalist who used Hegel to justify his hero-worshipping of the state as the supreme embodiment of reason. Trott was not wholly at ease in Binder's classes. The first part of his thesis was ready by 6 July, two weeks later he went before the examiners for his *viva voce*.

On 18 July 1931, Trott saw Professor Kraus and his board. His doctoral thesis was accepted and marked *summa cum laude*, the highest distinction possible. Now all that stood between him and the title of Dr Jur. was to have the thesis bound and submitted to the university. He intended to provide a second part to the thesis, one

---

* *The pre-war German doctorate should not be confused with the British or American D.Phil. or Ph.D. which are submitted several years after the end of undergraduate studies and must constitute a 'contribution to original knowledge.' The German dissertation could be offered any time after the completion of the first state examination and resembled an MA dissertation. The equivalent of the British Ph.D. was the Habilitationsschrift.*

which implied a fundamental critique of Hegel. Even at the outbreak of war he had not wholly shelved the project. He was not yet twenty-two, yet he had shown himself to be a master of an immensely complicated subject. 'His ambitious work on Hegel's political philosophy was a remarkable (and almost unbelievable) achievement for one of his age and experience,'[36] but despite its subject, Trott was by no means as enamoured of Hegel as Oxford contemporaries suggest. In a notebook of the period Trott wrote of the need to find a philosophy which, in contrast to Hegel's 'beautiful description of the past', would actually lead to a *future* based on the triumph of human personality.[37]

There had been a further incentive for Trott to complete his doctoral dissertation as quickly as he could, one which went back to the conversation in Rowse's rooms at the end of Hilary term of 1929 – i.e. the chance of Trott winning a Rhodes bursary. Rowse was clearly aware that moves were underway to revive the awards which had been suspended at the outset of the First World War and officially abolished by private Act of Parliament in 1916. In October 1929, Lord Lothian, the chairman of the Rhodes Trustees flew out to Berlin to vet the selection committee. From the beginning he feared for the scholarships' political independence, a fear that was justified when the Nazis came to power and tried their best to use them for political ends.[38]

The Rhodes Scholarships had been created by the terms of Cecil Rhodes' will of 1899–1902, which envisaged the use of Oxford, a university which Rhodes himself had attended at a comparatively advanced age, as a 'modern Athens' for the white, Anglo-Saxon peoples. This involved not only scholars from the colonies and dominions, but also from the United States and Germany, the latter being seen as racial cousins.[38] Between 1903 and 1913, fifty-five Germans availed themselves of the awards, fifteen of which were granted annually. Among those who had been to Oxford on the scheme was Trott's uncle, Eberhard von Schweinitz, who had gone up to Balliol with the first bunch in 1903 after a term at the University of Lausanne. Another was Albrecht von Bernstorff who was later linked to Trott through his unrelenting opposition to Hitler and who died, one of the last victims of the blind revenge of the SS, shot in the back of the head on a tract of waste land by Moabit Prison at a time when the Russians had already occupied the greater part of the city.*

The man who had been responsible for the selection of the earlier German scholars was Dr Friedrich Schmidt, later Schmidt-Ott.

---

* *Although in general those chosen by the Rhodes Committee were not to be found among the Nazi ranks, there was a notable exception in Lutz Graf von Schwerin-Krosigk, Finance Minister from 1932 to 1945 and Foreign Minister in Dönitz's short-lived government. He had studied at Oriel College, Oxford before the First World War.*

Schmidt-Ott was an official in the Ministry of Education who became Kultusminister in 1917 after August von Trott's resignation from the post. In 1929, while he was studying in Berlin, Trott had been to see Schmidt-Ott, probably with a view to asking his advice in the event of the scholarships being revived. When the scholarships were restored in the course of the year, Schmidt-Ott by dint of past experience was put at the head of the selection committee. The revival, however, was not on the old generous basis, the number of Germans eligible being reduced to two. The first of these, Fritz Schumacher and William Koelle, went up to Oxford in 1930. The former, the author of *Small is Beautiful,* went to New College where the following year he was to become a close friend of Trott.

Trott was alerted to the scholarship deadlines for 1931 by his Uncle Eberhard. As the closing date fell on 25 November 1930 he was obliged to send in his application in the middle of his Referendar exams. Of the six referees required, three were drawn from Trott's Göttingen teachers, while the others were made up of Eberhard von Schweinitz, Dr Selbie of Mansfield and A.L. Rowse. The latter took the credit for the success of Trott's suit, though in the long term it is unlikely that the German committee would have been as impressed by a young Oxford don as they were by the distinction of the other referees.[39] Trott probably appeared before the committee in Berlin in the January of 1931, receiving notice of his acceptance on the 9th. He was asked to submit a list of preferences among the colleges. Trott selected Balliol 'not only because it was my uncle's college but because from all I know it would meet my tendencies most', by which he meant that Balliol had a reputation for being politically progressive.

As Trott's father could not be guaranteed to approve of his son's shelving of legal qualification in Germany for the sake of studying in England, Trott was anxious to have senior status at Oxford which would allow him to take the degree course in two as opposed to three years. The university required the doctorate for the granting of senior status and Trott was keen to get the dissertation out of the way before going up in October 1931. The doctorate was finished by July and in the intervening time before going up to Oxford Trott decided to start his career as a Referendar in the German courts.

The Referendarship meant an attachment to a series of courts and positions whereby the potential advocate of the German bar was able to learn from experience the ways of every branch of the German legal system. Trott's first posting was to the court at Nentershausen, only six kilometres from the family home at Imshausen, and it may be that the former minister had a hand in ensuring that his son was not given too arduous a task in his brief first role as a *Gerichtsreferendar* or court assistant.[41] While he was working in the court he was able to find the time to expand his thesis into a one-volume work to be published in a series edited by his supervisor, Professor Kraus.

Trott was aware that as a German Rhodes Scholar he would be an ambassador for his country, a task which made him nervous at a time when Brüning's coalition contained no representatives of the Socialist Party. Before he went to England the Rhodes Committee required him to attend a four-day orientation course in Berlin in order to deck him out for this irksome mission. The idea of going to Berlin, however, was more attractive to him, as it allowed him the opportunity to visit some of the friends he had made in his year at the university; both those in the diplomatic circle as well his Socialist friends. It was Hans Muhle who introduced him to a new circle in Berlin, that of the *Neue Blätter für den Sozialismus*, a Socialist ginger group whose writings were edited and published by the Protte Verlag in Potsdam. Acquaintance with this group meant that Trott was able to get his friend Rowse's book *Politics and the Younger Generation* translated and published in German.[40]

The editorial board of the *Neue Blätter für den Sozialismus* contained a number of names that were later to carry considerable weight on the left wing of the German resistance to Hitler: Paul Tillich, the theologian, who later emigrated to the United States; Carlo Mierendorff, the Social Democrat deputy, whose death in an Allied raid in 1943 was to deprive the German Resistance of one of its best heads;[41] Theodor Haubach, who was to die on a Nazi gibbet only a few months after Adam von Trott; and Adolf Reichwein, one of the most sensitive of all the Socialist conspirators who were executed for their part in the July Plot. Trott and Reichwein were later to meet often at the gatherings of the Kreisau Circle during the war and it is tempting to think that some empathy existed between them based on a similar interest in and wide experience of the world.

Following a tragic period in his life in which his little son was accidentally drowned and his first marriage broke up under the strain, Reichwein took a year's leave for research in the late autumn of 1926. Here he was helped by the Minister of Culture, Becker, who took a fatherly interest in him. He went round the world, in a way one would hardly have expected from someone travelling on a scholarship, in order to study the economics of the world's raw materials and much else. He drove at his leisure in an old Ford across North America, had an accident in the Rocky Mountains, wrote, drew and went to the fur-trappers and lumberjacks of Alaska. He served as a sailor, helping out as navigation officer, went to Japan and China, and then back to California. He crossed Mexico on a horse and in a boat. The *bueno* he brought back; he always subsequently spoke with the invincible *joie de vivre* of a scholar of a peculiar kind – one who had taken his doctorate in nature's school, and who said of himself that he loved life in all its forms because only this love brought knowledge.[42]

3
Rhodes Scholar at Oxford

Trott became a member of Balliol College Oxford in the Michaelmas Term of 1931. Arriving in England at the beginning of October, he spent a few days in the house of a schoolfriend of his mother's before taking the bus up. As the vehicle crossed the bridge over the Cherwell into Oxford proper, Trott was 'almost overcome with emotion' at the sight of Magdelen Tower.[1] His own college lacked the immediate aesthetic appeal of Magdelen's medieval quad and deer park. It was a gloomy collection of chiefly nineteenth-century buildings squat among the traffic at the junction of Broad Street and Magdelen Street. Balliol's attractions were cerebral rather than physical; even in the 1930s it could stake a claim to being the intellectual power-house of the university.

This intellectual ascendancy of the college was as recent as its buildings. Founded in the mid thirteenth century, it had, apart from a brief flowering in the fifteenth, never before then been one of the university's more prestigious institutions. At the beginning of the nineteenth century it abandoned a scholastically unsound tie with a provincial grammar school and began to offer its places to the cream of the reformed public schools. As the century progressed the Balliol Scholarship became the badge of excellence among Oxford men, and all the more so after the accession of Benjamin Jowett as Master in 1870. From late Victorian times, 'Balliol men' began to occupy a vastly disproportionate number of key positions in the British Empire, and the incentive for schools to send their brightest candidates to sit the Balliol examination became all the greater. The college also began to attract brilliant students from abroad. The peak of the college's ascendancy arrived with Asquith's Cabinet of 1908, when half the portfolios were assigned to members of the Prime Minister's college, including the Foreign Secretary, Sir Edward Grey, and the Lord Chancellor, Lord Loreburn. A little over ten years later the Versailles Peace Conference created the republics of Eastern Europe out of the vacuum created by the departure of three ruling dynasties, imposing crippling terms on a defeated Germany. Some sixty-five per cent of the British delegates who performed this feat were from Balliol, something which made the young diplomat Harold Nicolson immensely proud.[2]

At about the time that Adam von Trott himself came into residence, the college received a visit from his extraordinary brother Werner. Clearly the idea of his brother attending a foreign university called for some drastic action on his part and he made the trip in order to see that the 'loathed and despised' English had accommodated Trott in a befitting style. The rooms in question were to the west of the vast college hall built by the architect Waterhouse who was also responsible for the modern half of the cramped front quadrangle. Werner Trott approved the first-floor rooms and thereupon returned to Germany.*³ In the 1960s the college pulled down these nineteenth-century staircases, replacing them with wholly incongruous new buildings in the then fashionable brutalist style.

Trott had elected to read for the Honour School of Politics, Philosophy and Economics, known as 'PPE' or 'modern greats', the latter to distinguish it from 'greats' or Literae Humaniores – the study of classical languages, history and philosophy. PPE was a new school, created only a few years before Trott's admission. Theoretically it provided for those undergraduates who, coming from state schools, had insufficient knowledge of Latin and Greek to read for 'greats'. Trott's tutor was Humphrey Sumner, the future Warden of All Souls, who referred to Trott obsequiously as 'Baron'.⁴ Apart from Sumner, Trott was tutored by the Master, A.D., later Lord, Lindsay, and John Fulton, later the first vice-chancellor of the University of Sussex.

Oxford in the early thirties was not the giddy, party-giving university it had been ten years before when, as a reaction to wartime austerity, it had been led by a colourful 'aesthetic' element. By 1931 the pendulum had swung back as a result of the depression and students were moving in great numbers to the left and adopting attitudes of heightened social-awareness which were more congenial to the serious-minded Trott. Going up to Balliol at the same time were a number of men later to distinguish themselves in one or another branch of endeavour.†

---

* 'This journey abroad was one of only two (the other being to Italy) voluntarily made by Werner in the course of his life. He heartily disliked both.' (Sykes, Troubled Loyalty.)

† Among these were: the Hon. David Astor, the second son of Lord Astor and his wife Nancy (Britain's first woman MP), who was editor of the Observer for twenty years; Peter Calvocoressi, the historian, publisher, writer and don; Christopher Hill, later Master of Balliol; Donald, later Sir Donald, MacDougall, ultimately Chief Economic Adviser to the Treasury; the American architect Joseph Irwin Miller; the Hon. Sir Con O'Neill; and Faiz Hasan Tyabji and Jai Kumar Atal, later Indian ambassadors to Japan and Italy.

During his two years in the college, Trott also came into contact with some of the undergraduates who came up before or after him: the American political scientist Samual Beer; the writer Somerset de Chair; Arthur Gore, later the

Having achieved senior status in the university by virtue of his doctorate, Trott could proceed directly to the more interesting work for his final examinations. In the meantime he had to catch up with the first-year work by reading biographies and works on English history. Some of these he sent to his mother to translate into German so that his father might annotate them and return them to him in Oxford; a rather novel way of dealing with a heavy academic workload. It was not until his second year at Balliol that he was able to return to his beloved philosophy, and then to the much less congenial Kant. Some consolation however, was to be found in the Hegel-based systems of Croce and Gentile.[5] In his passion for Hegel, Trott would have received some sympathy from the Master, Lindsay, who had given a lecture on 'Hegel, the German idealist' at London University the previous year.[6]

Apart from academic work, in his first year in college, Trott was tempted by other university pursuits, rowing an hour a day, doing a little boxing and playing squash. In the evenings he attended rather serious club meetings, being a member of the philosophic Jowett Society, and later its first German president, the legal Bryce Club, the Labour Club and the German Club, of which Fritz Schumacher was president as he was of the '*Weltbürgerliche Tendenzen*' (cosmopolitan tendencies) in which Trott also participated.[7] He was also a member of the Oxford Union where he made a brace of speeches on 'neutral subjects'. The only record of either of these is a facetious comment in one of the university papers to the effect that the only thing which was memorable about it was the length of the speaker's name.

Almost as soon as Trott arrived at Oxford, he went out of his way to befriend all the more interesting dons and undergraduates, many of them through his membership of the Labour Club. Trott was, without a doubt, introduced to the club by Geoffrey Wilson – his friend from the Geneva conference – who had been president the previous year. The institution was not always as high-minded as the name would suggest and had termly dances at which Socialist sympathizers got together for a shindig. Patricia Spence, who later married Bertrand Russell, remembers meeting Trott at the club. Someone had asked her to make a speech and, petrified at the prospect, she had hidden under the table. One of the members had just pulled her out in a dishevelled state when she encountered Trott. Together they went to a café and

journalist Lord Arran; the future leader of the Liberal Party, Jo Grimond (later Lord Grimond); the biochemist Alexander Ogston; the art historian John, later Sir John, Pope-Hennessy: the distinguished medieval historian Richard, later Sir Richard, Southern; the music critic Philip Hope-Wallace; the sometime Indian Home Secretary Venkata Viswanathan; and the author and glass engraver, Laurence Whistler.

drank vodka, 'to show how Socialist we were'. After the drink they proceeded to dance and ended the evening 'walking about the dark streets, talking'.[8]

Also at the Labour Club, Trott made the aquaintance of Patrick Gordon-Walker and Richard Crossman, both of whom were to be in the Cabinet of Harold Wilson's first administration. Gordon-Walker and Crossman were also linked by their wartime experience when they worked together on the German-language service of the BBC. Another Labour Club friend was the Communist sympathizer and later Party member Jack Dunman, who was part of the group who formed a rival association with a number of other Balliol men called the October Club. The October Club was specifically designed for the veneration of the Russian Revolution. After the war Jack Dunman told Christabel Bielenberg that without Trott's patient explanations he would never have understood *Das Kapital.*[9]

In the summer of 1932 Dunman was in a punt with Diana Hubback and others when they saw the tall figure of Adam Trott propelling himself towards them. 'Here comes the enemy!' came the cry from the first punt, 'We shall meet in opposite trenches.' Dunman did not agree. 'No, he will be fighting at the barricades on our side.'[10] The following day, Diana Hubback received a note from Trott saying that he had regretted not being in her boat.[11] Diana Hubback was another Labour Club friend with whom Trott was to form 'an attachment which was to plague and sustain them for a number of years.'[12]

They had met at the end of their first, Michaelmas, term at the university at the club's end-of-term dance. Diana Hubback was 'dancing with an unskilful partner . . . I bumped into a very tall figure who was dancing with Shiela . . . Recovering myself, I saw Shiela's partner smiling at me, rubbing his hurt arm while I was rubbing my head. It struck me that he was an exceptionally beautiful man.'[13]

Adam held his 6 foot 4 inches magnificently and made many gentle gestures with his long hands which were most expressive. He had an immensely high, narrow forehead. His hair was a crisp light brown but he had started going bald in front in his early twenties which gave even greater height to his forehead. His large grey-green eyes* were deeply set, drooping slightly, with heavy eyelids, thick lashes and darker eyebrows. He had strikingly high cheekbones with slight hollows beneath them and a fair skin. His nose was long and slightly curved above a large mouth with full lips. On his lower lip he had a scar, a relic of his duelling days. His habitual expression was one of great candour and serenity. His English accent was excellent. He was completely familiar with the language, which he had spoken as a child with an English nurse and spoke at home with his half-American mother. He had a most beautifully modulated and expressive way of speech.[14]

---

* *Dark blue or violet are the colours normally given by his friends for Trott's eyes.*

Trott's dancing partner that evening was Shiela Grant Duff, a schoolfriend of Diana Hubback's who had come up to Oxford with her.[15] From the spring of 1932 till the outbreak of war, Diana Hubback, Shiela Grant Duff and Miriam Dyer-Bennet were, at one time or another, to provide the emotional support Trott required in order to guide him through his increasingly tormented existence. For the time being, however, Trott was still very much in love with the American woman he had lived with in Göttingen. Diana Hubback, remembering (in 1968) her efforts to get to know Trott better, found herself thwarted by a barrier of high-minded German seriousness: 'I met him again at the German Club, and as we stood on the steps outside Rhodes House admiring the starry skies, he asked me if I had read the works of Jean-Paul.* As I had not even heard of him this did not further our relationship.'[16] On another occasion she saw him running across the Garden Quad at Balliol when she was on her way to a tutorial with John Fulton and noticed that 'he moved with startling grace and speed, though he was no athlete.'[17] Their relationship finally took off that Trinity term of 1932, after an evening when they had been trapped in the University Parks by the closing of the gates. Trott sent her a letter in which he said, 'One should never forget that one is just as much a part of nature as the summer all around us.' The letter ends with a transcription of Hölderlin's poem 'An eine Rose' beginning *Ewig trägt im Mutterschosse.*†[18]

Another person who has left a description of Trott in his first year at Oxford is Charles Collins, a fellow PPE student from the East End of London:

---

* *Jean-Paul Richter, 1763–1825, known as 'Jean-Paul'; a writer much admired by the composer Robert Schumann.*

† *'Eternity is carried in the womb'.*[19]

  Ewig trägt im Mutterschosse
  Süsse Königin der Flur,
  Dich und mich die stille, grosse
  Allbelebende Natur;

  Röschen! unser Schmuck veraltet,
  Sturm' entblättert dich und mich,
  Doch der ew'ge Keim entfaltet
  Bald zu neuer Blüthe sich!

  Roderick Blyth has offered the following translation:
  All time resides
  In your Insides
  Sweet Queen of scented meadows
  You and I
  Encompassed by
  Nature's still enormity;

The impression he made on meeting one was immediate; it was produced by his very tall figure, striking features and a sense of power in his manner. But one came to like him for more important things than these; for his quick sympathy and understanding, his good humour, his great kindliness, his intelligence and his complete integrity of purpose. He was always good company. No one to my knowledge ever found any serious flaws in his sense of humour; he would equally readily joke at other people's expense and take a joke at his own ... It would have been easy for anyone with so much natural dignity of appearance, as well as his other claims to distinction, to be conceited or pompous, but he never was. I always was impressed by the ease with which he got on with all classes of people, both in Germany and in England; and he had the same ease of manner with children, who at once took to him.[20]

A demonstration of his sense of humour is also given by Charles Collins: 'On one occasion at a concert, when I had been trying to explain to him the exact meaning of the English expression "old fogey", a party of elderly gentlemen passing down the hall caused Adam to ask in the solemn, serious voice which was sometimes his, *much* too loud, "Are they old fogies?" '[21]

Although Trott had been absorbed into a typically Oxonian existence – rowing, punting, attending club meetings and parties – he had neither lost sight of events in his native land nor lost his essential Germanness. Many of his English friends, then and after his death, failed to see the importance of Trott's country in his make-up, deciding that as a friend he had achieved the status of being 'an honorary Englishman'.[22] It was partially for this reason that they so much resented, and misinterpreted, his desire to return to Germany in the summer of 1933 and to work against the regime. One of Trott's friends who did not fall into this misconception was Charles Collins. 'He was deeply German, and no foreign influence, not even an English influence, ever overlaid this fundamental characteristic. When we walked in the Quad of his Oxford college in the moonlight, it was German poetry which came into his mind. This devotion to his own country was obvious; he had no need to express it.'[23]

This overriding Germanness often made him exasperated at the frivolity of England and the English language. In a letter to Diana Hubback sent during the long vacation of 1932, he wrote, 'This is a

---

Rosebud scorning
Tired adorning
Come the Storm to strip us bare
Not withholding
But unfolding
Burst and bursts with blooms again.

German letter and it ought to be written in German and not in your social and, as it seems to me, sometimes somewhat gossipy tongue.'[24] Trott was aware of the German notion of a *Sonderweg* (special way), even when it came to his love affair. Diana Hubback recounts a story of an exchange of views on Hammersmith Broadway in London: 'Maybe I am in love with you, if you mean by that what an Englishman means. But I am not in love with you in the higher German sense.'[25]

Trott was especially aware of the problems posed by political developments in Germany. Soon after coming up, he had spoken out against the Nazis at a meeting of the German Club, which they were making a bid to infiltrate. Admission of his forthright attack on the movement had led to an exchange of letters with his mother, who patriotically took the view that Nazism was a 'national movement' and as such, not something to talk about outside Germany. In making his point about politics Trott wavered between a tight-lipped ambiguity and a form of reckless frankness which occasionally led him to make wild statements for the sake of hearing the reaction. To those who knew him, however, there was no doubt about his conviction, and his desire to see a socially united Germany take its place in a European framework; as Richard Crossman put it, 'This was Adam's vision when I first met him as a student, it was still his vision when he was hanged on an iron hook by Adolf Hitler's orders for his role in the July plot of 1944.'[26]

The results of the elections to the Landtag (provincial assembly) of Trott's native province of Hesse-Nassau, when the Nazi seats increased from one to twenty-seven, alerted him to the possibility of Nazi power. After the results had been declared Trott confided in his friend Pat O'Gorman at Ruskin College that 'upon his return to Germany he hoped to become part of a new movement, constructed from the ground up rather than being fashioned from the ruins of the old, which would oppose the extremism represented by National Socialism.' In this context, Mr O'Gorman answered the question, frequently asked, concerning when Trott made a deliberate decision to fight against National Socialism. 'For him, the war against Hitler began in 1931.'[27]

In his determination to fight the Nazis, Trott made two key contacts in Albrecht von Bernstorff and Hans-Bernd von Haeften. Bernstorff, the grandson of Bismarck's ambassador to London and the nephew of Joachim-Heinrich von Bernstorff, ambassador to Washington at the time of the outbreak of the First World War, was himself a Rhodes Scholar and diplomat who had been one of the prime movers in the restoration of the scholarships in 1929. Just when Trott first made the acquaintance of Bernstorff, an uncompromising anti-Nazi who was removed from the Foreign Office after Hitler's coming to power, is not clear. In February 1932, however, Trott made a journey to Cambridge in order to attend a meeting where Bernstorff was to be present, and from that moment onwards Trott's contact with him remained close.

Trott's links with Hans-Bernd von Haeften were to be of even greater significance later on, when the two of them worked together in the German Foreign Office during the war. They were eventually to face trial together in 1944. They met at a conference in Oxford in January 1933 where Trott was employed as an interpreter. At this time Haeften, who had spent an academic year at Trinity College Cambridge, was working as secretary to the Streseman Foundation. The conference was attended by Otto Gessler the former Reich's Defence Minister. Gessler was to work closely with ex-Chancellor Wirth in trying to negotiate with the Allies from Switzerland during the early days of the war. In Oxford Gessler formed a bond with the Master of Balliol, A.D. Lindsay.

In philosophic terms, Trott was still trying to align Socialism with 'Prussianism', a concept which had him branded as a 'red' by Schmidt-Ott when he visited Oxford to see the German Rhodes Scholars in Trinity term 1932. Trott's idea of Prussianism bore no resemblance to that generally accepted in England. British minds were still haunted with the notion that the Prussians had been behind the carnage of the First World War. By extension, the 'Junkers' or East Elbean nobility were viewed as a warlike caste, hell-bent on European domination. The view that the Prussians, and not the Germans, initiated the conflict was still current in the 1930s and few appreciated the true nature of Prussia and the concept of total dedication to state service which was the idea enshrined in Hegel's philosophy. There was little appreciation in England that the Prussian concept had been *harnessed* by the Kaiser in his war of aggrandizement. In his attempts to synthesize positive elements from both the right and the left of German politics, Trott was able even to see some positive sides to National Socialism, or at least understand something of its appeal. 'Although Hitler's movement is largely carried out by immature and desperate enthusiasts, it gives voice to justified grievances which makes a large number of sober and sensible people join them.'(*sic*) He wrote to Tracey Strong on 5 April 1932: 'The reparations issue has got hold of the people's mentality primarily and they believe that Germany's cause is not represented rightly by the present government, I have full confidence in Brüning and am supporting his line.'[28] Brüning, however, was dismissed in May and the President, Hindenburg, instead of appointing the Oberbürgermeister of Leipzig, Carl Goerdeler, to the Chancellor's office, made the fatal mistake of choosing Franz von Papen.

That summer Trott wrote to Diana Hubback from Germany,

Germany is in a bad way politically. The present government however, is, I believe, shrewd enough not to let things pass into turmoil. You, anyway, will always be safe in your journeys. Hitler has repeatedly proved that he is a fool and the large organizations formed against him, though the foreign press doesn't make much of them, are in full existence.* I have re-established contact with my political friends and shall be much happier about that in the future.[29]

At the end of the Trinity term, Trott had gone down to stay with Diana Hubback in Treyarnon Bay, Cornwall. The gathering was billed as a reading party, though Diana Hopkinson later admitted that 'little reading was done . . .' 'Adam climbed the castellated rocks and crawled across a narrow natural arch connecting two islands with a drop of forty feet below him. A photograph shows him like a prehistoric man exploring his domain.'[30] At Trethias Cottage, Trott met the philosopher Bertrand Russell, though their meeting was perhaps a disappointment. Trott, who could be shy from time to time, found himself too much in awe of the great man to let himself go in Russell's company.[31] They did nevertheless, have a talk and thirty years later, Russell remembered, 'I liked him and admired him. The only thing I remember at all vividly about him is a walk to a very stormy Cornish coast during which he expressed his admiration for Hegel as to which I disagreed.'[32] From Treyarnon Bay, Trott went to stay at Penmount with the historian Charles Henderson, and then to A.L. Rowse, who also lived nearby.[33]

Trott returned to Germany in July to lodge with Miriam Dyer-Bennet and her children on the Island of Sylt in the North Sea.[34] From there he proceeded to Berlin to attend a Socialist conference. To some extent the seriousness of the occasion and the crisis brewing in Germany were sufficient to put the more frivolous aspects of Oxford in perspective and to bring him back to reality. Writing to Diana Hubback from Berlin-Charlottenburg, Trott confessed to being 'very reluctant to go back to Oxford'.[35] Oxford, however, returned to him, in the shape of Charles Collins and another Balliol friend who pitched up that summer. At one moment they found themselves outside Hitler's Berlin headquarters in the Kaiserhof Hotel.

> . . . We were at a loose end and, having nothing better to do, 'Hitler must have a dull life, let us,' we decided, 'drop in on him' . . . It was courteously conveyed to us on the Führer's behalf that he was unfortunately too busy to see us at that time, but we were cordially entertained, and had we been able to stay in Berlin long enough a meeting would very likely have been arranged; it would have been Trott's first encounter with the man whom later he sought to kill.[36]

Collins and his friend were also introduced to Berlin friends like Gaides, Gross and Muhle.

---

* *When Hitler did achieve power it came as a considerable shock to Trott. In a letter of 30 January 1933, Douglas Jay wrote to Shiela Grant Duff, 'Von Trott told me on Saturday that Hitler was definitely finished.' (Shiela Grant Duff,* The Parting of the Ways.*)*

Muhle was at that time drawing up contingency plans to be used in the event of Hitler achieving power. Through Muhle, Trott met Curt Bley, a former Socialist student leader from Heidelberg University, who was to be active in the resistance to Hitler, through the Roter Stosstrupp organization, in the early years of the Nazi regime. From Berlin, Trott went on to attend a Trade Union Conference at Bernau where he met Helmut Conrad, a working-class student from Halle who, like Bley, was to remain a devoted friend until the end.

Even if Trott still dismissed Hitler as a fool, he was sufficiently alarmed by the situation in Germany to doubt the sagacity of returning to Oxford. In September 1932 he wrote to Diana Hubback,

> I am still a little uneasy about this having to go back to Oxford, not because it frightens me in any sense but because it now seems like a boy-world where I shall have to contract my movements in an artificial and undesirable way. And yet there is much in it that I deeply admire, but sometimes it seems to me as if that part of it must be dead and what remains is only the tomb and some ceremonial memories.[37]

Diana Hubback, on the other hand, had decided to send herself down from the university, though during Trott's final year she was a frequent visitor, arriving from London virtually every weekend to see him. In the meantime they communicated by a stream of letters.[38]

Although Trott was less close to Rowse than he had been during his Mansfield term, many of Trott's best friends were to be found in All Souls. One of these was the philosopher Isaiah Berlin, or 'Shaya' as he was to his friends. In 1984, Berlin recalled their meeting:

> We met at lunch . . . , at the end of which he suggested that we might go for a walk that afternoon. We became friends almost at once. He had exceptional charm, great distinction of mind and manner, was extremely handsome, had both wit and humour, and was, at all times, a most delightful companion. I was completely captivated. He had a far wider view of history and culture than most of my Oxford friends: his conversation was interspersed with references to Schiller, Hegel, Kleist, Goethe – not names often mentioned in those days by students of the school of PPE, and he aroused in me an interest in those thinkers which has stayed with me ever since. Oddly enough he did not, as far as I can remember, talk to me about contemporary politics, either then or, with one or two exceptions, later, as he evidently did to others of his friends. In 1931–33 he seemed to me gay, carefree and invariably exhilarating. Even with Hitler's rise to power, he did not speak to me about it. If I brought up the subject, he tended to wander into fascinating, somewhat general, historical disquisitions.[39]

Berlin was often baffled by Trott's very convoluted manner of speaking, which may have led some people to underrate his very considerable intelligence, especially about his favourite subject of

Hegel. Berlin recalls that Trott used to say, 'I fall back on Hegel here, like an acrobat falling into a net.' Isaiah Berlin once told Jo Grimond after a four-hour walk with Trott that he had not understood a word the latter had been on about.[40] Hegel was very much in his mind that term, for on 18 November 1932 he received a copy of his expanded thesis, issued as part of Professor Kraus' series on international law. Trott was not happy with the printing, referring to the book as looking 'like a miserable little scientific pamphlet'.[41] His mind was on Germany when he wrote to Diana Hubback two days later about the life he would have on leaving Oxford, 'a life in which even you, my Diana, may seem to have been a beautiful but somewhat unarrestable interlude . . .' He was reconciling himself to the need to complete his law exams before he could enter state service and be of use to his country. 'It does seem dreary to think of law cases and codes and horrid officials and hours wasted instead of spending them getting ready for the real difficulties which will face one in politics outside and after the law . . . I begin to understand that my chances depend to almost one hundred per cent on the development of external circumstances in Germany.'[42]

During the Michaelmas term 1932 he became closer to Richard Crossman. Another new friend whom Trott found difficult – he seems to have had problems getting him to leave his rooms in the evening – was Thomas Balogh (later a fellow of Balliol and economic advisor to the Wilson Government).[43] Trott went down to London in December. He had a full programme of dances, given among others by a Lady Trotter whose name he found comic. Trott was a keen dancer, an enthusiasm which he shared with Diana Hubback, going to *thé dansants* and the Palais de Danse in the Tottenham Court Road. At a similar occasion at the Royal Thames Yacht Club, Diana Hubback fainted in the middle of the Blue Danube Waltz, to be seriously upbraided by Trott when she came round with, 'What a damn fool you are! Just when we were dancing better than ever before.'[44]

From London, Trott went to Brussels where Bernstorff had fixed him up with an introduction to the German minister Graf Lerchenfeld. In theory Brussels would give Trott the opportunity to revise the economics for his 'schools' while at the same time mugging up his French – a language for which he had only a small aptitude. He was joined in Brussels by Miriam Dyer-Bennet . In the German embassy in Brussels Trott had the opportunity to meet Herbert Mumm von Schwarzenstein, a diplomat member of the family which had, until 1914, owned the champagne firm in Reims. Mumm was obliged to leave the Foreign Office after Hitler's *Machtergreifung*. Arrested for plotting to kill the tyrant, he was murdered by the SS in the same batch as Graf Bernstorff.

The time spent in Brussels did not, it seems, do much to alter the heavy weather Trott was making of economic theory. He jokingly went so far as to write to Diana Hubback, 'Can't you read Keynes for me and give me an idea of what it is all about? . . . My Teuton mind is simply too clumsy.'[45] He returned to Oxford, at the beginning of January 1933. On the 30th of that month Adolf Hitler was asked to form a government in Germany. Charles Collins remembers Trott's reaction to the tragic news as he sat in the junior common room of the College.

> He knew at once that a terrible disaster had befallen his country; that the prospects for his own future had undergone a fundamental change; it was a future in which a bitter struggle would be needed to achieve even the smallest result; that many of his friends and acquaintances were at once in personal danger. A number of things he was sure of immediately: that overt resistance to the regime would be useless for a long time to come; that nevertheless he must oppose it by all means in his power; that a common ground must be found for as many opponents of the regime as possible, and that he himself would try to find that ground in a struggle for the 'liberal' rights; that although it would certainly be at the cost of handicap for his own career, he would not join the Nazi Party unless it should ever become his clear duty to do so in furtherance of his anti-Nazi activity.[46]

Two weeks later he wrote to his father,

> I have to say that the news, though meagre, of the German situation, worries me greatly – continual dismissal of political officials, often arbitrarily and suddenly, encouragement of provocative demonstrations, and above all the arming of the SA [Sturmabteilung] as election police! Are we really at the beginning of German fascism, of the domination of the state by this party which excludes large parts of the population, not only with regard to their beliefs, but also as regards social class, and will have to suppress them brutally in order to hold on to power. I feel very downcast when I think of the injustice which must happen day by day to the most serious and responsible civic attitudes, and such injustice by people who – as far as the Nazis are concerned – owe their present strength only to abnormal conditions. As far as I myself am concerned, all this makes me very depressed because it is clear to me that I too shall be condemned for a long time to a passive role. As much as I believe I agree with you about almost all questions of responsible political leadership, we have a very different opinion, I believe, with regard to the positive rights of the individual and the masses. One can discuss responsible political leadership only if these rights are held sacred, and for that neither Hitler nor Papen offers the slightest guarantee. To neglect these rights will cause a very severe reaction and there will be a need for creative forces to direct justified impulses in such a way which makes for lasting order. *For that* I shall prepare myself – and in the meantime, not enter into any alliance whatsoever with this authoritarian nationalism. To determine how best I can serve this goal, whether as a judge, civil servant, university professor or author – we shall have to wait till my return and, I regret to say, even till after the end of my training. Serving the rights of the individual – of 'man' as the advocates of natural law say – in connection and conflict with all the external orders and obstacles is far more important to me than service to the state (which is transformed into tyranny).[47]

It was now far more difficult to represent the decent side of his country, a country which had given support to Hitler, and this was frustrating for Trott. In the college he snapped at Samuel Beer, when the latter tried to make a joke of Nazism. He avoided many of his old friends, seeking comfort from the music of Haydn and Beethoven. One person to whom he moved closer was David Astor. Astor had met Trott on his very first day in the college, when they reported together to the porter's lodge to pick up their keys. He had some sympathy for Germany, partially inherited from his family, and partially from having spent a term at Heidelberg before coming up to Oxford. Astor remembers Trott's feelings that February at Balliol.

> Trott's first reaction, as I recall, was gloom, tempered by challenge. I remember a walk in the country when I told him that if he defied the Nazis they wouldn't answer him with arguments. I tripped him up and pushed him to the ground to suggest what they would do . . .
>
> He also spoke of the hatred that the rest of the world felt for Germany during the Great War and feared that Hitler would inevitably bring it back. He yearned to retain some sense of common humanity between nations and hoped that Germans could be seen as part of the normal world, not as a uniquely criminal people.[48]

According to Astor, Trott drew the greatest comfort from the reaction of the Berlin workers. Berlin had always been less smitten with the Nazi bug than many other parts of Germany. From Goronwy Rees in Berlin he received the report that there had been a thousand-strong joint meeting between the Nazis and the Communists. Hitler, he told Diana Hubback, had received an ultimatum from his followers; 'This may mean the beginning of a revolution in Germany.'

> My chief worry [he continued] is that the Social Democrats will not take the right stand – if manoeuvred into a position of defending the present order it will have lost what may have been the last chance of integrating the radical workers and forming the spearhead of a rational application of Socialism . . . Germany is a beautiful and creative country and, perhaps, even my generation will be rewarded for a time of great effort and pain preceding the attainment of the right political order.[49]

Through his son John Cripps,[50] another Balliol contemporary, Trott had been introduced to Sir Stafford Cripps, the Socialist MP. On 27 February, at the end of a month which had brought Trott's destiny into stark perspective, Cripps invited Trott to dine with him in the House of Commons. The evening was clearly a success as only a few days later Trott was invited again, this time to the Cripps home in Montague Square. The situation in Germany had brought Trott round to the idea of emigration, carrying on at Oxford by attempting to get a fellowship at one of the colleges. Trott was still very taken with All Souls, where

A.L. Rowse had been encouraging him to take up a project to produce the equivalent of Burckhardt's *Civilization of the Renaissance in Italy* for Northern Europe. Trott rejected the idea – something which Rowse later put down to the malign influence of Hegel.

At the end of Hilary term 1933, Trott flew straight out to Berlin. His brother Werner had become a Communist, and was in danger under the new Nazi regime. He found lodgings on the Holsteiner Ufer, on the banks of the River Spree. The 'room looks out to the Spree . . . on the other side there is a red-brick factory building, and frequently heavy and slow boats pass by'.[51] To baffle the Nazi censor, his writing became more and more obscure and convoluted, ranging from a simple code – Jack's friends (i.e. Dunman: Communists) or Dick's friends (i.e. Crossman: Socialists), children (Nazis), etc., – to clumsy attempts to find a periphrasis which would not be recognized by a third party, such as 'abnormal delegates' for Nazis.[52] As Diana Hubback recorded later, 'It had an unfortunate effect . . . in that it made his English, sometimes already obscure and difficult to understand, yet more clouded in meaning.'[53]

During the Lenten term the Reichstag building had been set alight by the Dutch former Communist Marius van der Lubbe. Whether this act was performed with Nazi connivance or not, the Nazis were not at a loss to know how to benefit from the removal of the Democratic platform of the Weimar Republic.[54] On 23 March they passed the Enabling Act and fell mercilessly upon their enemies. To this end the SA, who had been roped in to act as auxiliary police, designated a number of 'wild' concentration camps where their victims were imprisoned, beaten up, tortured and murdered during the next few months. Among these victims were a large percentage of the country's elected representatives* as well as Communists, Socialists, church-men, conservatives who had made clear their revulsion for Hitler and his gang, Jews, homosexuals and anyone against whom the SA had a personal vendetta. The wild concentration camps gave way in their turn to more permanent institutions run by the SS.[55] In the years leading up to the outbreak of war roughly a million German political prisoners were to do stretches of varying length in these institutions.[56]

One of the first groups to come forward and resist the new regime was Curt Bley's Roter Stosstrupp (Red Raiding Party). The organization produced an underground newspaper of the same name, which brought together the remnants of a variety of youth groups (Socialist, workers', Catholic) and two Jewish groups (the Kameraden and the Deutsch-Jüdisch Jugendverbund). The leaders of the Roter Stosstrupp,

---

* *According to the incomplete figures of Günther Weisenborn (who himself spent the war in a KZ), eighty-nine Reichstag members were killed, seventy-seven emigrated and ninety-nine suffered periods of imprisonment. For the federal Landtags and figures are forty-six, twenty-five and sixty-nine respectively.*

Bley, Carl Zinn and Rudolf Küstermeier, were all to the left of centre but the paper represented a broad anti-fascist line. Originally published in batches of 1,000 every ten days, its success was so marked that it went over to weekly production and with duplication arrived at a print run of more than 20,000.

The Roter Stosstrupp came to grief in November 1933 when it was flushed out by the Political Police (the forerunner to Rudolf Diels' Gestapo). In October twenty-five copies of the paper were seized by the police when they were delivered to the house of a Communist they were watching. A few weeks later in November a larger haul of 250 copies was opened at the post office. The press was located by tracing the postmark on the packet. Rudolf Küstermeier was sentenced to ten years' imprisonment and was not actually released until the British liberated Bergen-Belsen at the end of the War.[57]

Trott's friend Curt Bley escaped detection at this time, though the incident must have served to warn Trott of the danger of becoming too closely involved with the dissident groups. For the time being it was enough to be in Berlin and in a position to be able to transmit news to friends in Britain. To Shiela Grant Duff, for instance, he wrote of the unsocial habits of the Germans and their inability to run their public affairs properly – a problem which resulted in the reigning political alliance of Nazis and National Conservatives. This was, Trott wrote, 'like wanting to play marionettes and real theatre on the same stage . . .'[58]

Trott returned to England in April, and travelled down to Cornwall to spend a short spell with Diana Hubback at Trethias Cottage. He was still nervous of his Oxford friends and how they would see him and Germany after the suspension of the constitution in Germany. At the beginning of the month he had written that he feared 'the development of things here [i.e. in Germany] – painful enough in itself – will estrange my new friends in your country . . . there are only a very, very few that I . . . can be sure of'. One that he was not certain of was the historian E.L. (later Sir Llewelyn) Woodward at All Souls, with his 'utterly blind and sweeping generalities' (sic).[59]

When he was back in residence for his final term at Oxford, the philosopher R.G. Collingwood gave a party for him. People crowded around Trott to ask him about the state of Germany. Trott seemed in despair. Isaiah Berlin heard him tell someone, 'My country is very sick,'[60] which for Trott was unusually indiscreet. Lionel Gelber* was informed that Trott was considering joining the German army, as he believed that the General Staff was now the only institution capable of resisting Hitler. While mooting projects such as these he was also casting about for advice from his seniors. On 16 June he applied for an

* Lionel Gelber, born 1907, sometime assistant to the Prime Minister of Canada and writer on international affairs.

extension of his Rhodes Scholarship. This was accepted by the trustees in view of what Trott called his 'rather uncertain future' and elicited a kind letter from A.D. Lindsay. He even wrote to the veteran Socialist politician George Lansbury and received a boobyish letter in reply.[61]

Though he was distinctly wary of the growing number of German *emigrés* in Britain, who had taken flight at the first wave of Hitler's persecutions, Trott had not yet ruled out emigration for himself. However, to Victor Gollancz, with whom he stayed in the latter's Berkshire home, he explained that he had decided to return to Germany to fight Nazism from within. To Professor Brock of Cambridge he said, 'I don't know which is the more difficult at the moment for a good German, whether to remain in Germany or to stay abroad. In the one it will be sour, in the other bitter.'[62] His plans to remain in Britain hinged on the idea that he might be able to win a fellowship at one of the colleges, preferably at All Souls. Candidates for this élite prize fellowship would normally have obtained first-class honours in 'schools' or their BA examination. Trott was therefore anxious to do as well as possible in the June exams.

Trott had grown tired too of Oxford undergraduates, writing to Diana Hubback, he lamented 'the worst is that I cannot get through to my friends [in Germany]. I have no friends here. Oxford is half over, it is really finished now.'[63] In May he went to stay with Stafford Cripps in his house near Lechlade in Gloucestershire. 'In him,' he wrote, 'I find a person most helpful and encouraging to talk to, together with Gollancz, to whom I spoke before leaving London.'[64]

After schools, Trott, David Astor and Jo Grimond decided to travel north to one of the Astor houses on the Isle of Jura. As Jo Grimond recounts in his memoirs, in a slightly satirical vein,

> Adam wanted to see something of the industrial North. I must say this enthusiasm for sharing the life of the English working class quickly wilted. After a luxurious night at Cliveden he announced that we must spend the next night in a lodging house, settling however for the Birmingham Station Hotel. On reaching Manchester he wished to call on Mr Vinogradoff, then the foreign editor of the *Manchester Guardian*. As he was by then suffering from a painful boil, my first experience of the lift at the Cross Street building of the *Manchester Guardian* was poor Adam in agony as the usual hordes of passengers bumped into him.[65]

Once Trott had recovered from the boil they travelled on via Glasgow to Jura. Along the way he wrote to Diana Hubback telling her that he wanted to see her friend Stephen Spender, whose poetry he admired, before he left Britain for Germany. From Jura he wrote again. He was working for his *viva voce* or oral examination, 'in a log hut with windows on three sides. Yesterday I went out with a boat and last night walked along the lovely valleys of the island down to the Atlantic bay on the other side.'[66] From Glasgow, on his return, he wrote to Shiela Grant Duff at greater length.

> I have just come back an hour ago from Jura ... where I stayed four days – two at the east and two on the Atlantic coast . . . I walked hours and hours seeing nothing but bare hills, stags and seagulls of most varied types. Part of the time I stalked with a Scottish keeper whom I could hardly understand, he made terrific strides wearing long rubber boots with which he simply walked through bogs and streams leaving me to jump them. I shot a wild billy-goat with fascinating horns about 1½ feet long – it was most exciting in storming rain and clouds on the top of a rocky hill. The sea had become too stormy to return by motor-boat, so we had to sail back with two most delightful fishermen who live in the caves of Jura Island.[67]

Trott's *viva* was on the 25th July. About this time he went down to Lechlade once again to stay with Cripps. Even before the results of his exams had come through he was sceptical of his chances of getting into All Souls. He wrote to Shiela Grant Duff,

> Lord Lothian, who is or was a Fellow of All Souls, and especially concerned with Rhodes Scholars, has told somebody I know that the chances of getting in are nil and Lionel Curtis . . . has said something to the same effect.* I don't take this as ultimate, but I think I must acknowledge it as the prevailing bias. I don't want the argument *pity* to be used in my favour. I would take the fellowship mainly because of then not having to be humiliated by the Hitlerites – but I would not exchange this exemption for another humiliation. It is humiliating to be an emigrant – and this I think I least want to be.[68]

At the time of the *viva*, Trott wrote home to his father about the Oxford that he was about to quit, speaking of the 'wonderful beauty' of the place. 'It has given me more than possibly I can even express – the noblest traditions of Europe, and these, unconscious and taken for granted, live here together, carried on by a simple but truly political race.'[69] Oxford, however, did not find his papers good enough to award him the 'first' he was looking for in order to face the gruelling examination at All Souls, giving him instead a 'good' second in PPE. Diana Hubback went for a walk with him in the woods at Wytham the night the results came out. 'He was bitterly disappointed and there was no way to comfort him.'[70]

Trott had not quite abandoned all hope. He asked Isaiah Berlin if there was no hope with his second. Berlin replied that he should not give up, after all his Oxford degree was mitigated by the *summa cum*

---

* *Lionel Curtis, (1872–1955), Fellow of All Souls and author of* Civitas Dei *(3 vols 1924–1934), in which he set out his 'gospel of Commonwealth' (DNB). He was a sanctimonious figure whom Trott referred to as Lionel the Holy. (Conversation with David Astor and Christabel Bielenberg, April 1988.)*

laude he had obtained from Göttingen.[71] As it later transpired the All Souls Fellows decided to take none of the candidates who presented themselves for the exam that autumn. Berlin wrote to him at the time to tell him that he might yet have succeeded.[72] Trott's tutor Humphrey Sumner wrote to Trott after his *viva* in a comforting manner,

> I have always thought you were really too mature to do these hour written papers up to your real standard. What would have suited you would have been a thesis and a very long oral examination . . . I am sure that if you received from Oxford even half of what you gave, you will have more than justified the Oxford experience.[73]

At the beginning of August 1933 Trott sailed from Southampton to Hamburg, addressing a last letter from England to Diana Hubback from the docks. He consoled himself on his voyage with Swift, a writer who had been introduced to him by Rowse. Before leaving Oxford, he had received a valedictory letter from his friend Christopher Cox, who had been a tutor at New College since 1926, 'There are few undergraduates (if I may say so!) in the last seven years who have contributed as much intellectually and culturally as well as socially to Oxford as you have done; and no one could have vindicated more triumphantly the revival of the German Rhodes Scholarships. To that the accident of a second makes no difference.'[74]

4

An Outsider in Germany

Adam von Trott's boat docked in Hamburg, where he seized the opportunity to visit the Warburg family. The Warburgs were just about the richest Jewish clan in Germany, with wide-ranging banking and shipping interests. At Oxford, Trott had known Ingrid Warburg, who had been sent there with her sister Gisela in order to perfect her English. In the course of her time there she had become a friend of both Diana Hubback and Shiela Grant Duff and through the two girls she had met Trott. In 1933, Ingrid Warburg's father Fritz was on the board of some eighty companies and felt removed from the anxieties which affected poorer Jewish families. At their meeting Trott tried to bring home to Fritz Warburg the dangers of his own position, stressing that his immense wealth would not save him.[1]

From Hamburg, Trott travelled up to Berlin, to see his Balliol uncle Schweinitz. Schweinitz – always on hand with a useful tip – told him not to wait to be summoned but to volunteer immediately for compulsory labour service which the Nazis had introduced in order to shape up German youth and lay in stock for their war machine. Arrangements were therefore made for Trott to attend a camp in September. While he stayed in Berlin he saw something of Shiela Grant Duff's friend, Goronwy Rees the writer and translator and intinerant Fellow of All Souls. He was also in contact with Bley, who later reported that on his return from England, Trott had lost the German accent of his Socialism, changing for a more English form of Fabian Socialism.[2] Bley was still very much bound up with his Socialist Resistance group, the Roter Stosstrupp, which was then in its final three months of existence. His friend Muhle had been pushed out of the Civil Service as a Socialist and was working in a bank.

Another of Trott's friends in Berlin was J.P. Mayer, who was later to become a world authority on the French political scientist and historian Alexis de Tocqueville. At that time Mayer was editing the early humanistic writings of Karl Marx and was also linked to the *Neue Blätter für den Sozialismus*, which had ceased publication as a result of the Nazi *Machtergreifung*. For the time being Mayer was running a bookshop in Berlin which provided a meeting place for Socialists, where they could lay plans for how to deal with the new regime.

Trott did not stay long in Berlin, feeling the need to return to his family in Hessen, where both his Moral Tutor, Humphrey Sumner, and Diana Hubback were due to join him before the end of the month.

Of Imshausen Diana Hopkinson wrote:

> The ochre-washed eighteenth century house was flanked by two small detached wings with long windows wide-open to the summer. From the circular carriage drive broad stone steps led up to the front door above which was carved a coat of arms. The doors gave an ancient creak as Adam pushed them open and from the wide flagged hall a shallow wooden staircase rose between walls embellished with antlers.[3]

It was to prove a relatively untroubled pause before taking up work in the court in the provincial Hessian town of Rotenburg. To Shiela Grant Duff he wrote that the place was 'completely occupied by the "men of trees" (i.e. Nazis)' but that the rest of the intensely rural province was 'in the most promising chaos'.[4] The idyll allowed him to introduce Diana Hubback to his beloved woods, eating cold sausage in a forester's hut while Trott engaged in animated conversation with the forester. Trott also introduced her to his formidable parents. Diana Hubback remembers his mother 'knitting and asking questions about social legislation in England'. Meetings with Eleonore von Trott were conducted in the manner of audiences, terminated by a discreet but unmistakable signal from the lady of the house that she had had enough. For the non-English-speaking father Trott rehearsed her in a different sentence of German to be uttered every evening at the dinner table. The ex-minister 'always replied briefly but politely'.[5]

After Diana Hubback's departure there was a visit to Schloss Boineburg to look at some relics of his earliest Trott ancestors in the company of his father. Then at the beginning of September he went on to the Hessian cathedral city of Marburg to report to the Wehrsportlage. It was to be Trott's first close contact with the new National Socialist Germany and its heavy accent on the physical, outside life. The ordeal lasted for three weeks, during which time he found it comparatively simple to switch off from his surroundings and the political indoctrination meted out by the camp officials. His education and appearance marked him out strongly from the others, especially as his great height meant that he was unable to fit into any part of the uniform other than a green shirt.

On 4 September he wrote to Diana Hubback that his present company was 'very deadening to the mind'. A few days later he wrote again at the end of a forty-two kilometre route march that he had 'heard the others talking at my side, but I didn't listen to their words and they didn't bother me at all'. Letters from his friend came as a considerable relief and diversion from the 'entirely ordinary' people

who were the other trainees at the camp. 'One must get oneself
entirely beyond the danger of being inwardly affected or dulled' by
them.[6] Familiarity with the Nazis in no way endeared him to them; on
the 10th he wrote to say that he would not join the 'children' as he
called the Nazis, even if it was right to attend the camp.[7] Nor had 'the
children' taken to him, seeing him as detached and withdrawn. From
Imshausen, he wrote on, on 22 September, 'Children and grown-ups
belong to different worlds and I to the latter.' He had returned via
Kassel to his cherished Trottenwald. The same detachment he had
adopted for the Wehrsportlage came in useful when he took up his
post as *Referendar* at Rotenburg in November. This was the beginning
of the process of becoming a *Rechtanwalt* which he had begun in the
last few weeks before going up to Oxford. For the next three years he
was obliged to learn the theory and practice of the criminal and civil
laws of Germany, laws which, with Hitler's ideology at the helm, were
rapidly changing their nature. In Berlin Trott's near contemporary,
Helmuth Moltke, who qualified as 'Assessor' at the end of the year,
wrote to his friend Karin Michaelis:

> I may as well give up the law for the time being. The old jurisprudence, which I
> have learnt and which is inspired by the concept of abstract justice and
> humanity, is today only of historical interest because no matter how things
> develop in Germany there is absolutely no chance of bringing back these old
> ways of establishing what is just. Although they have been tested and reinforced
> over the centuries, such drastic inroads have been made in them that it would
> take decades to unearth them again from under the debris.[8]

Starting out on the road to legal practice in the backwater of
Rotenburg, Trott was still able to see some of the positive sides of the
Nazi agricultural policy which, in Hessen and other backward areas,
allowed the peasantry to rise above a level of misery which had
remained unchanged for centuries. In 1968, the German-American
journalist Margret Boveri gave an impartial view of the beneficial
effects of Nazi land reform as it had taken place in her own villiage.

> Children were taught how to wash themselves and how to brush their teeth;
> parents were taught that milk was more wholesome for babies than beer; the
> peasants as a whole, who had been living on a diet of starch . . . [similar to that
> of] villages in India today, were taught to grow vegetables which up to then had
> been enjoyed only in towns.[9]

Unlike Moltke, Trott could see some good in the progressive
codification of jurisprudence, but his approbation was only for the
structure of the reforms, and not for the moral input of Nazi reforms as
some writers have supposed. As for the peasantry and the improve-
ment of their status, Trott's views, for a landowner's son, were radical,
supporting a programme aimed at the break up of the big estates,

especially those east of the Elbe, where the squireens lorded over thousands of acres, living in a semi-feudal relationship with their peasantry. Something of the same policy was inherent in Nazi land-reform projects, although few of them came to fruition as the authorities were frightened of isolating Junker support when it came to the crunch.

In the Rotenburg court, Trott proved the only non-Party member among the officials, with the exception of a single judge. There, in one of the main cities of Hessen, he was able to reap the rewards of his ancient noble lineage. As a von Trott zu Solz he was treated with 'extraordinary, non-interfering loyalty. It is quite clear to them now – so far as I come into contact with them at all – that I do not belong to them or their silly factions, but so far I haven't had a single rebuke.'[10] Although he wrote to Diana Hubback to say that he was getting on 'fairly happily'[11] the calm was no doubt disturbed when he had, for the first time, to defend a Jewish victim of the regime (who had wept over him, causing Trott great shame, when the Jew saw that he was not 'one of his childish enemies'). Trott's refusal to bow down on this score was 'very much appreciated by other members of his [i.e. the Jews'] community already'.[12]

Oxford had not entirely ebbed from his mind. Isaiah Berlin sent him news: 'As I write the usual All Souls scene is going on. By the fire A.L.Rowse and Goronwy Rees are discussing the prospects of politics in Germany. I am unable to listen, Rowse is saying the same things. The conversation rotates in ever recurrent cycles. 3 and 4 are over, the fifth is beginning, the same thing is being said for the fifth time.' To Shiela Grant Duff, Trott wrote that he dared not 'recollect all its beauty and loveliness because I cannot be there any longer.'[13]

Before the year was out he once again became involved in Oxford affairs through the Rhodes Foundation. This involved a further visit to Berlin in December when he was proposed as a member of the selection committee for choosing German scholars. In a letter to the Warden of Rhodes House, Trott went back to the positive aspects of social change in Germany. The new peasant legislation he saw, in Hessian terms, as 'almost wholly beneficial' but added, 'I should not venture to judge things in the big cities and industrial centres.' One fear which he expressed to Shiela Grant Duff was that capitalism and the press would somehow push politicians into starting a new European war before they had come to grips with some of the positive sides of change in Germany. To Allen he wrote, 'I do hope some European settlement may be reached in the near future to set certain anxieties at rest which are naturally almost alarming to an ultimately defenceless country.' However Trott also made it clear in his letter to Allen that the situation for him in Germany was an impossible one for a non-member of the Nazi Party and that it was hopeless to try to continue with his legal studies without interference by the authorities.[14]

One reason for Trott's desire to see positive elements to Nazi legislation lay in his extremely cautious attitude when it came to censors and other Nazi spies. It has already been seen how Trott was adapting his sometimes less-than-lucid English in the anticipation of prying eyes. Compared to Count Helmuth Moltke, who attended an indoctrination camp for Assessors at the beginning of 1934, Trott's utterances might seem unduly sensitive to the danger of denunciation. On the other hand, though he was the scion of a family with as distinguished a past in Hessen, he was no Moltke, the great-nephew of the military genius behind Germany's unificaton who had removed her enemies in a rapid series of decisive wars to lay the foundations of the second Reich. Moltke, unlike Trott, enjoyed seeing how far he could go with the petty officers of the regime. In a letter to Helli Wiegel of the 7 March 1933, Moltke recounted his experience of the camp.

> The lessons in world affairs . . . were a first-class joke. The sort of thing that happened was as follows. We were informed that the Medieval emperors were traitors to the blood of the German people in that instead of satisfying the instinctive urge to colonize the East, they went south. That could only be attributed to racial adulteration of the imperial stock, for, as the instructor rhetorically asked, what true German had ever felt a call to the South? Up shot four hands, one of them mine, followed by at least forty of the fifty-eight. We said that we regarded ourselves as completely Aryan – had we not had a lecture on the previous day about the pedigree of Field Marshal Moltke, which entitled me to give evidence in defence of the German emperors. The man was knocked completely off his balance.
>
> After this splendid initial success we went over to the attack in a lecture about the Jews, and fell on the assertion that Spengler had deliberately skated over the role of the Jews in his book *Decisive Years* so as to increase its circulation. The oldest of us, who had commanded a battery during the war and was thus above challenge, got up and declared that his respect for Spengler was far too great for it to be affected by such a remark on the part of an Assessor Timmermann (loud applause!) and if Spengler had considered the Jewish question to be without historical significance, that carried more weight with him than did Assessor Timmermann saying the opposite (loud applause!).
>
> Thereupon instruction in world affairs was abandoned . . . One more thing. Once when I woke up at night I heard a lot of drunks from another troop singing in the square. And what do you think they were singing? The Internationale.[15]

Trott was not the descendant of one of the triumvirate of German Unification, nor, for the time being, was he resident in a big city like Berlin. Not only was he aware of the gossipy nature of provincial small towns, he also knew the way in which the regime was protecting itself from dissidents by increasingly repressive legislation. In the course of twelve years in power, Hitler promulgated 557 laws by decree, under the terms of the Enabling Act. During that time only seven new laws were passed by the Nazi-dominated Reichstag. 218 new laws were issued in the course of 1933 alone.[16]

The new legislation bit by bit suppressed the civil liberties which had reigned under the Weimar Constitution and repression was effected at every level of society. Chief among the means of repression was the introduction of the notion of *Schutzhaft*, or protective custody, which came into being as a result of the emergency decrees of 4 and 28 February 1933. Under the decree, suspects might be held in prison, or in the new concentration camps for an unspecified period of time. The initial wave of arrests, directed chiefly at Communists after the Reichstag fire, was housed in the infamous 'wild' concentration camps. Most of those arrested were released the following year, when, in a move to remove power from the stormtroopers, the running of the concentration camps was transferred to the hands of the SS.[19]

> After the first disorderly months, however [writes Allan Merson], the Gestapo usually preferred, or was expected, to bring arrested political opponents before the courts for trial. Under laws hitherto in force, a suspect arrested by the police could not be held in custody for longer than twenty-four hours unless an examining magistrate issued a warrant and undertook a preliminary enquiry, which itself must culminate within a definite time in a decision either to drop the case for lack of prima-facie evidence or to proceed on a specific charge to a formal judicial enquiry. This procedure was drastically modified by successive changes after February 1933. Police arrest ceased to be limited to twenty-four hours, and the preliminary judicial investigation was soon dispensed with, and an indictment was drawn up by the state prosecutor, largely on the basis of reports, depositions and other material supplied by the police, without prior judicial sifting.[20]

It was up to the state prosecutor where and with what charge the accused was to be prosecuted. Added to this the range of offences multiplied over the months, categorizing under indictable offences not only violence but also 'infringement of government decrees', malicious criticism of the government and malicious opposition. Charges of this sort were tried under a special court procedure reserved for those who had 'manifested dissent, criticism or opposition'. Most cases of distribution of illicit literature, for example, were interpreted as conspiracy to 'change the constitution of the German Reich by force' and charges were served of 'preparation of treason'. All treasonable offences were originally tried before the higher, Reich, court but after April 1934 they were transferred to the newly created Volksgerichthof or People's Court. The President of the Court was the notorious Dr Roland Freisler, a former Russian prisoner of war and Communist sympathizer, who had observed and admired the Russian purge trials under Vischinsky and merited sufficient admiration from Hitler for the latter to say of him, 'He is our

Vischinsky.' The People's Court was set up in response to the acquittal of the Communists accused of helping van der Lubbe start the Reichstag fire. There was no appeal to a higher jurisdiction.

In the cases of petty 'treasonable acts', however, the Reich Prosecutor delegated the hearing to the higher regional courts of Oberlansgerichte.

> For the convenience of dealing with the large numbers involved, the accused were commonly tried in groups ranging from half a dozen to a hundred or more persons who were suspected of having acted jointly. Sometimes, however, the persons indicted together had little or no connection, except that they had all come to the notice of the police during a particular stage of an investigation.[21]

Another new body to be reckoned with for someone in Trott's position was the Gestapo itself. The Geheime Staatspolizei was set up under the tutelage of the 'Communist expert' Rudolf Diels after Göring took over the Prussian Ministry of the Interior. It formally replaced the old Prussian political police, or Police Department 1A, towards the end of 1933 and later spread to the other German states after the overall responsibility for the German police was given to Heinrich Himmler. As Hessen had been part of Prussia since 1866, the Gestapo became part of everyday life there earlier than in many other states.

> The Gestapo was remarkable, not only for the wide variety of its sources of information, but even more for the wide range of its political interests, which far exceeded those of a conventional police organization ... In the course of time its offices came to have a highly complex structure with specialist sections devoted not only to such major preoccupations as the Communist or 'Marxist' movements, Catholicism or the Jews, but to almost every aspect of economic and social life, not to mention numerous more recondite topics such as Germans returning from the Soviet Union or the French Foreign Legion ... The Gestapo was capable also of taking direct political initiatives over a wide field, beyond the mere detention of opponents. It could ban meetings or publications, dissolve organizations, intervene in appointments or issue warnings which were not meant to be ignored. Its opinion about individuals, confidentially sought out by and given to employers, could result in arbitrary dismissal, even when an alleged offence was still *sub judice*.[22]

The Gestapo used a variety of tactics in order to pinpoint dissidence or sedition, including the usual modern practices of telephone tapping, opening letters and by cultivating denunciation on the part of private citizens who had a grudge to bear against a neighbour, employee or employer. Later on the Hitler Youth was an especially important source of denunciations of this sort, even extending to the children's own parents.

Much more than all these sources, however, the Gestapo relied on regular informers – V-Leute or Vertrauensmänner. Some of this simply kept watch in places of work or blocks of flats, handing in illegal leaflets, reporting gossip and rumours and observing fellow employees and neighbours who had a left-wing past or who had been released from prison or concentration camp. Other V-Leute were deliberately planted in illegal Communist or other organizations. They might be in the service of one of the Nazi Party's own units; or they might be employed directly by the Gestapo. Particulars of the Gestapo's informers were kept in separate files, and these do not seem to have survived; but evidence suggests that, while such V-men must have existed at almost every place of work or residence, and must have totalled a huge number, those who had effectively penetrated anti-Nazi underground organizations were relatively few and therefore of great individual significance. Indeed, most of the mass arrests and trials by which the Gestapo broke up successive clandestine Communist Party organizations were probably the work of a few such individuals in each area.[23]

On 8 December, Trott wrote to Diana Hubback to tell her that the safe and respectful attitude which had earlier reigned in the court at Rotenburg had been replaced by 'a certain pressure' which had set in from a particular direction. This was affecting 'those questions which are at the basis of my future work and existence'.[17] Trott was under pressure to join the Party. At the end of the month he effected a transfer to a bigger court at Hanau, near Frankfurt, where he hoped to find 'a much freer neighbourhood'.[18]

At Christmas Diana Hubback came out to join him in Germany. After a night in Cologne they drove on to Kassel then to Carlshafen where

there was a group of eighteenth century houses round a town square which opened to a quay where the river barges docked. It had been built by the Huguenots to serve as an inland port. Over the door there was a great gilded bunch of grapes hanging up as the inn sign. Inside there was a friendly welcome for us and we dined off silver carp and damson tart.

The couple kept themselves amused playing the latest Cole Porter tunes on a portable gramophone, addicting the hotel staff to the melodies in the process.[24]

From Carlshafen they motored through Hessen, passing a ruined monastery which, Trott explained, had once proved a useful repository for the unmarried or unmarriageable daughters of his Trott ancestors.* His levity caused a temporary rift between them as they argued whether it was the English or the Germans who abused their women the most. At one point they stopped off to visit a castle and in the corridors they passed a custodian who eyed them grimly.

'He is a Nazi,' said Adam.

---

* Possibly the Adliger Damenstift at Wallenstein, or either of the Stifts Kaufungen or Wetter.

'How do you know?'

'Because there is something clod-like and evil about him.'[25]

Trott's short Christmas break did little to resolve his doubts about his present situation. The spreading tentacles of the totalitarian state made it clear that he had to act with extreme caution if he were to succeed in getting to the end of his legal studies, which he needed to do if he was to enter the system and fight it from within. Doubts about his ability to carry it off, especially in the repressive atmosphere of Hanau, led to considerable depression borne of a feeling of political impotence.[26] At the end of 1933 he had even considered becoming a shepherd and retreating into the Trottenwald, an idea which almost certainly sprang from conversation with his elder brother Werner, whose idea of combating the Nazis was a notion of 'inner emigration', turning your back on life around you and cultivating freedom within. Trott was reading *Anna Karenina* at the time and was taken with the character of Levin.

Another frustration was the lack of intellectual activity in his life at the provincial court. If he could not be of any political use to his country, he could surely pick up a project which could occupy his mind at the same time as making a stab at criticizing the regime. In January 1934 he travelled up to Gottingen to see a friend, Clemens Lugowski. Trott described Lugowski as having the 'dignity of a Jesuit and the sensitiveness of St Francis. I love him better every time.' Lugowski was something of an authority on the dramatist and poet Kleist* and it was most probably in the course of his visit that the idea of Trott's doing an anthology of Kleist's journalism and political writings was first mooted.

Trott's new court at Hanau proved no less oppressive in atmosphere then the court at Rotenburg. To Diana Hubback he wrote, 'It seems doubtful at present whether I shall stay long at Hanau, as there are certain adjustments to the service which may make it advisable to move to a different, more important branch.'[28] Hitler had said that he did not expect servility from his civil servants but independence of mind. From his father Trott learnt that he might be able to acquit his law studies as a *Regierungsreferendar* in some branch of the service. Strangely Trott asked his brother Werner to use his influence on Rudolf Diels, founder of the Prussian Gestapo, who had been a contemporary of Werner's at the University of Marburg. Werner Trott not surprisingly opposed the idea.†

---

* *Heinrich von Kleist died at the age of thirty-four in 1811 leaving behind him a clutch of plays and some of the best short stories in the German language; he also founded the* Berliner Abendblatt, *using its columns to attack the French who had routed the Prussian army at the Battle of Jena in 1806.*

† *The idea was not so far-fetched. Diels' contemporary Hans-Bernd Gisevius entered the Gestapo as a result of the Marburg connection and later played an important role in the Resistance through working for the Abwehr. (See* To the

At the beginning of February Trott crossed swords with some National Socialists over the arrest of some local Catholic priests, reporting that he had 'held the field'. Later that evening he drank with a local Nazi leader, an old carpenter, and a young forester. 'I learnt a lot about the district and the political temper of these people. It is soundly nationalist, but also Catholic and not without ironical humour.' Together this ill-assorted trio drank cider which tasted of timber and grass.[29]

Trott was increasingly offended by the attitude of his Oxford contemporaries to events in Germany and their tendency to criticize his decision to return to Germany, 'I want you to understand.' he wrote to Diana Hubback, 'I don't give a damn whether friends in Oxford approve of my actions.'[30] Clearly, however, he did, and was much hurt by their dismissiveness. Another thing which enraged him was the stand taken by the British press on Germany. On the 5th of that month, the *Manchester Guardian* started running a series of articles on the persecution of the Jews in Hessen. Trott thought that the paper was war-mongering by encouraging international hatred. It was for this reason that he responded so strongly to all forms of Germano-phobia. Trott took up his pen in a fury, sending the draft to Diana Hubback to have it typed. He told her, 'The article which made me write it was simply ferocious, you know my attitude on the matter.'[31] To his mother he confessed he might have acted a little rashly in sending it, describing the letter as 'somewhat foolish',[32] and expressed the hope that the paper would decide not to print. But print they did.

Trott's letter asserted that from his own experience, there was as yet little anti-Semitism in the Hessian courts. (Trott's Jewish friend Ingrid Warburg visited him in Hanau at this time and was introduced to a pro-Jewish, anti-Nazi lawyer who worked with Trott.)[33] Throughout his letter he spoke of his own observations.

First and foremost, the charge of partiality of German courts forms an instrument of anti-Semitic persecution. I served for several months on a small county court [Amtsgericht] in Hessen, one of the very parts of Germany mentioned by your correspondent's article as being notorious for persecution. This work at the law brought me in close contact with the business and social life of a small semi-rural district. There was a pretty strong element of Jewish tradesmen in the small Hessian town, small shopkeepers, traders in cattle and corn and artisans. Although the general economic situation makes things difficult for everybody, it was also evident that some of them were not thriving owing to political reasons. A great number of them, however, notably of the

---

Bitter End.) Nor was Diels unimpressed by Werner. One night after the Nazis came to power, Werner had talked to Diels about philosophy and ethics and had succeeded thereby in getting a friend released from Nazi custody. 'This night was something unforgettable for Werner.' (Clarita von Trott, notes to the author, 1989)

60

cattle and grain merchants, were doing the same business as before because of customary connections with Hessian peasants. I have not once during four months heard, as I certainly would have done, working at the court, if it had happened at this time, of any case of active persecution of the kind overheard or of anything corresponding to it.

In the court there was most emphatically no distinction against Jews. I have been present at a great many cases which were brought up by or against Jews, and I can therefore assert this fact from personal observation. Attempts to influence the court by suggestions that the claimant was a Jew were checked with unhesitating firmness.

There is a recent regulation by which the prosecution of a debtor by his creditors can be temporarily suspended if the debtor 'owing to a general deterioration of economic circumstances, and without personal guilt' proves incapable of paying. Now, this regulation was equally applied to such Jewish businesses as had suffered general deterioration, and I have witnessed its being applied with extreme liberality to sustain the very shaky business of a Jewish shopkeeper. As to discrimination on the bench itself – after leaving the first place I continued to work at a district court and there found that my supervising judge was a Jew, and in the first meeting of the court that several of the pleading lawyers were of Jewish extraction.

Hanau, being a bigger town, business life is naturally different. Formerly it was a famous centre of the manufacture and trade of jewellery, a large proportion of which again was being carried out by Jews. Now it is quite clear that a deterioration of their economic position cannot possibly be attributed to local or national, but only to foreign boycotting. Cases of the most appalling come-downs inflicted by the compulsory sale of stocks on a closed market to meet their obligations might easily be related as a striking example for this assumed 'aid' of German Jewry from abroad.

Again and again I have spoken to active storm troopers who feel themselves pledged to the race doctrine of their leaders but would never consider themselves justified to execute it with methods of violence, and who turn with indignation from the suggestion of atrocities being committed in their presence. It is to this effect definitely that the content of their superior orders is directed. And from the very observation of your correspondent that National Socialists are to be found in concentration camps proves that those who do not obey these orders are finding punishments.

The letter was hastily written, and unlikely to be well received by those Britons whose only notion of Nazism was that it was by nature rabidly anti-Semitic. In Oxford his old friends divided into camps, their own loyalty severely tested by what seemed to be a vain attempt to justify Nazi persecution. The changes in attitude are apparent from Diana Hubback's letters to Trott. In January 1934, Rowse was still 'good humoured' if 'slightly mocking' in his description of Trott's philosophic method, while Dick Crossman, 'approved very much'. After the letter's publication the 'golden opinions' were no more, though surprisingly A.L.Rowse came to his defence at the table in All Souls. A rumour went round the university that Trott had joined the Party, a rumour remembered by many of

Trott's contemporaries after the outbreak of war. John Wheeler-Bennett brought up the *Guardian* letter against Trott in his 1943 Foreign Office memorandum.[34]

Trott's contention that there was little persecution of the Jews in Hessen and that the concentration camps contained Nazis, among others, was shot down by the *Manchester Guardian*'s Berlin correspondent, Frederick Voigt.

> These things are known to everyone in Hessen who has eyes to see and ears to hear. If Mr Adam von Trott is blind and deaf to them he will be equally blind and deaf to the less obvious legal victimization of the Jews. As for the Nazis in concentration camps, they are far more likely to have been sent there for persecuting the Jews too little than for persecuting them too much.*[35]

Trott sought by his action to express his belief that the beneficial side of National Socialism, that which was removing injustices in rural communities such as Hessen, should not be tarred with the same brush as the movement's more obviously evil manifestations. To Diana Hubback he explained before the storm had burst in England (a storm which had his old friend Dr Selbie rushing gallantly to his defence), 'If I can be any good at all it is for the future relations between this country and yours, and between this community [i.e. the non-Nazi] and the other one – at present it is hopelessly in a mess unless at least some decent people refuse to "see red" and coolly work for a reasonable settlement.'[36]

In March Trott went up to Berlin to see if there was any hope for his application for a post within the Ministry of the Interior. The trip was not a success, and Trott was told there was no hope of such a position going to one who was not a member of the Party. Trott tried to find some other post which would free him from the law courts. At Göttingen he was offered a research post under Professor Julius Binder. Trott refused, seeing Binder as a 'court philosopher' who had thrown in his lot with the Nazis. Explaining his refusal to his father he wrote that while he agreed with the Nazi view that 'law and ethics should not be strictly differentiated . . .' he would like to go further 'and say that between politics and ethics there may be no inner divergence'. The *immoral* had no place in politics.[37]

One person who encouraged Trott in his desire to enter university teaching was Karl Gottfried Bonhoeffer, Professor of Physical Chemistry at the University of Frankfurt am Main and the brother of Dietrich Bonhoeffer the theologian. Trott had known the Bonhoeffers since his childhood in Berlin.

---

* *At the time the numbers of Jews in the concentration camps would have been small compared to the number of Communists, Socialists and work-shy, as well as other categories of prisoners, which dominated the camps until 1938 and later. (See Krausnick and Broszat, Anatomy of the SS State.)*

An option for Trott was to study at the Kaiser Wilhelm Institute for International Law in order to prepare a thesis comparing Anglo-Saxon and German ideas of international law. As this would have involved transferring his dossier from the Hessian court to the Prussian he engaged the help of his father and his uncle, Eberhard Schweinitz.

Other possible projects were journalism, something opposed by both his brother and his father, and writing. Behind this idea was J.P. Mayer, who encouraged him to write something on Proudhon or Swift. Trott, on the other hand, was keen to try his hand at something on Hegel. After a visit from Mayer and another Berlin Socialist friend, Hasso von Seebach, in Hanau, Trott revived the idea of doing a short book on Kleist. He was chiefly interested in the articles Kleist had written for the Berlin *Abendblätter* and the Prague journal *Germania*, many of which had been attacks on Napoleon during the time that the latter was occupying Prussia. Mayer was still linked to Protte Verlag in Potsdam, which had been responsible for printing the *Neue Blätter für den Sozialismus.*

Mayer and Seebach were on their way to England in order to raise funds for those members of the Roter Stosstrupp who had been imprisoned and to maintain contacts with British Socialists. Trott gave them an introduction to Cripps. In German Socialist circles there was still some optimism that Hindenberg would dismiss Hitler and call back Schleicher with the support of the Social Democrats. To this end Schleicher was already flirting with the Socialists. Mayer and Seebach's mission was therefore designed to tell the British that this should not be seen as a move towards military dictatorship. Mayer returned from a second trip on 1 July 1934 to hear the news of the Night of the Long Knives. The SA leadership, including Hitler's old friend Röhm, had been wiped out along with all other elements who were seen to represent a threat to the regime and who had failed to absent themselves in time. One of these was Schleicher. Far from upbraiding the Chancellor for allowing this to happen, Hindenberg sent Hitler a telegram of congratulation. The army sat by and allowed Hitler to assassinate two of their generals without so much as a protest; this had bitter consequences for them later. Mayer lay low with Trott in Hanau *for a few days. The latter wrote to his mother, 'Es gibt scharfe Luft* [there's a chill in the air],' then, in English, 'They didn't shoot 7 but something between 46 and 100; amongst them the man who wrote Papen's speech and the Catholic leader Klausener and many right-wing people. Saw it in *The Times* . . . Don't write too openly.'[38]

Trott's letter to the *Manchester Guardian* had sent a flurry of rumours through the gossipy city of Oxford. To his closest friends Trott tried to dispel the idea of his embracing nationalist ideas and for the time being, at least, they were prepared to give him the benefit of the doubt. Shiela Grant Duff, who was then preparing for her schools in the University, had expressed a hope that Trott had been right about the comparative absence of Jew-baiting in Hessen and had nervously suggested in her letter to Trott that he was veering in the dangerous direction of aggressive nationalism. Trott wrote back on 7 May,

> No, Shiela, I am not drawn into that curse; and if one has to accept the order of independent nation states, because, as it stands, they are the only means to maintain any order at all, one assents neither to the invidiousness of the Versailles Treaty, nor to rampant nationalism, which are two extremes brought on one by the other.[39]

That same month Trott took time off for a short holiday with Diana Hubback. They started out in Karlsruhe, then travelled across the border to Strasbourg settling at an hotel in the Vosges, Trott having equipped himself with a brace of Balzac novels to read. Walking in the vineyards they encountered a peasant who learned that Trott was German. With a typically Alsatian concern for the material rather than the national consideration, the peasant turned on the stranger: 'We fought the Germans there during the last war, soon we will be fighting you again and the vineyard will be destroyed once more!'

'God forbid,' said Adam.

'Would he could – but it will happen,' replied the peasant.

They returned via Mainz, where Diana Hubback was to take her train. A Nazi rally was taking place in the city and Brownshirts were occupying every available hotel room. They spent the night on a bench.[40]

His legal training and his inability to get clear of the provinces was still frustrating him. Earlier that year he had received some comfort from Ingrid Warburg when she had sent him some sermons of Cardinal Faulhaber, the anti-Nazi Archbishop of Munich. Neither plans to move to Berlin, nor attempts to join the administration in Kassel came to anything, and in the end he was obliged to settle for a transfer to the court at Kassel, where at least he would have the benefit of Imshausen nearby, and the chance to relax in the company of his family at weekends. He took rooms at Wilhelmshöhe, at some distance from the city in the shadow of the Elector's palace with a giant window looking out over the park and fields.

After the schools, Shiela Grant Duff came out to Kassel to stay with Trott. She arrived at night and Trott instantly whisked her off for a tour of the city, pointing out Trott family memorabilia along the way. They went to look at the city from a vantage point; as they watched, the floodlights were turned off at the Palace

> and then below us lay the sleeping town with one brave star hanging in the yellowing sky. Adam roared his great laugh, seized my arm and shouted: 'See how I arrange it all for you.'

This mixture of grandeur and self-mockery was Adam's most engaging quality. He liked the grandeur to be noticed but was happiest when one laughed at it with him.[41]

Trott's position, wrote Shiela Grant Duff at the time, was

> one of unarmed hostility. Could never join it or compromise with it, but he takes his opposition as for granted; he makes no stir about it, he does not plot to overthrow the government, nor makes any secret of his refusal to join the Party. He is the only Referendar in Kassel who has refused to join any Nazi organization. He has been asked his reasons for not joining and answered that the leaders themselves had said no one should join except from conviction. At another time he was saved by the refusal of the older Nazis themselves to allow new and faint principled men into their ranks . . . [42]

In another passage, Shiela Grant Duff noted in her diary something of Trott's despair of finding a way out of his present situation.

> He certainly seemed to think the end was not in sight and had given up all hope of organizing an opposition. It is clear he does not think such a thing exists . . . *
> We walked through the old quarter of Kassel, formerly Communist, and there some of the election notices had been torn down. Adam was full of admiration [,] very glad . . . With the Nazis he can do nothing but wait and perhaps influence his own village. But most of all he wants to make it a real community – Communism, almost, on the land . . .[43]

It is easy to see why Trott was so gloomy about the chances of resistance to Hitler in the summer of 1934. The Communists, who up till then had proved to be the most serious opposition to Nazism, as well as by nature the best trained, had been all but destroyed by the repression which followed the seizure of power and the Reichstag blaze. Their leaders had been murdered, like John Scher, or imprisoned, awaiting murder, like Ernst Thälmann. It would be another year before they could undertake any major activity again. As for the Socialists, there was a small-scale resistance directed from abroad, chiefly Prague, but no signs of activity within Germany itself. The opposition from the right, which had centered its hopes on the uninspiring figure of von Papen, had been largely butchered in the

---

* In a letter to Maria Lazar, Moltke gave a gloomy picture of the non-Nazi camp at the time '. . . the senior Catholic clergy and the lower Catholic clergy in south and west Germany; the Protestant clergy in the Pastors' Emergency League; the large landowners; a few Catholic professors in each faculty; a few private bankers and big industrialists, though the latter are few and far between; and finally a few independent people who have inherited famous names or made their own names well known.' Moltke is poking fun at himself in the last line but the point was well made. (See Balfour and Frisby, Helmuth von Moltke: A Leader against Hitler, 1972.)

bloodbath of 30 June. Moreover any hope of a return to democracy was dished when the aged Hindenburg died on 2 August. Hitler now had his opportunity to combine the offices of President and Chancellor in his person and do away with any niceties which had been preserved for the sake of the old man.

For the most part Shiela Grant Duff's short stay was relaxed. In the afternoons they explored the countryside taking in Trott's old school at Hannoversch-Münden, the Herzwald Lakes and the electoral palaces. Trott sang hunting songs, soldiers' songs, 'even Nazi songs' which Shiela Grant Duff, hearing for the first time, found 'rather stirring.'* Taken up to Imshausen to visit the parents, Miss Grant Duff compared the house to her own home, the Lubbock seat of High Elms in Kent. 'Somehow the trees of the Trottenwald, one felt, were there of their own right, and the Trotts living there was an integral part of the whole neighbourhood where their ancestors had lived for five centuries or more.'[44]

Miss Grant Duff found the Trott parents, 'very impressive, almost alarming.' With the mother however, she crossed swords on German foreign policy. 'Although she despised Hitler as a vulgar upstart, like Adam, she was not entirely averse to what he was doing in foreign policy. Also, like all Germans, she hated the Treaty of Versailles and did not condemn unilateral treaty abrogation as long as it was this hated treaty which was involved.'[45]

Trott was getting into difficulties with the Kleist book. His selection of Kleist's journalism was seen as too *outré* for the Nazi censors. The Protte Verlag dismissed the project making difficulties over small matters but in reality because they were frightened of how the authorities would react to the scarcely veiled criticism of the reigning power. In September Diana Hubback came out to Germany, joining Trott in Düsseldorf where he had gone to get a photograph of Kleist's death-mask to preface the work. The problems with the book lagged on for months.

Professionally Trott was now involved in criminal law and finding it a dispiriting experience. In November, his training required him to visit prisons, in his case Kassel-Wehlheiden. The conditions were dreadful, with 800 convicts crammed into a gaol built for 520. He was stirred by the grimness of prison life and the 'pale men' who lived it. One of these was a Communist called Hans Siebert who had finished two years at a teacher training college before being incarcerated. Trott took a special interest in Siebert and by the end of November, he had visited him three times in his cell. Trott conceived a plan to win over the young Communist, seeing his use in the coming struggle for power.

---

* *Trott was fond of singing; on Jura he had sung David Astor a Russian song. (Conversation with David Astor, February 1988.)*

66

In their discussions, Trott once again reverted to his old standby of Hegel, while Siebert faced him with all the armoury of Marxism. At first Siebert, who was made uncomfortable by the obviously patrician Trott and by his desire to break down his political beliefs, refused to open up. Later the two men formed an embattled friendship. Trott saw the possiblity of a popular front in the fight against Hitler, something which was to be mooted by the Communists themselves the following year. It was an idea to which Trott clung to the end, and one which very few of his fellow conspirators were able to countenance. In order to bring Siebert round, Trott even smuggled a banned book into the prison – Lenin's writings on Hegel! Satisfied that Siebert had a role to play, Trott wrote a report suggesting he be released.

In Kassel too he found means to enjoy himself,

> There's a grand fair on in Kassel at the moment to which we went after coming back [from Imshausen]. It was great fun to take the little street girls over the toboggan railway. From the top you see all the lights moving beneath you, and then diving up and down is wonderfully exciting... After that we went to a very doubtful house in the Altstadt where one of us had a long discussion with the mother-keeper. It was fascinating but horrible to listen. In the end she chucked us out because she took our lack of serious intentions as indication of our being informers. So we went to a Tirolienne Bar whose existence I had forgotten, where we found a lovely peasant girl singing her songs. I had a long discussion with a Roman Catholic who said he was first that and afterwards a German and everything else. He was very excitable and nervous and I remember him claiming at least three times that I had offended him...[46]

On 6 November 1934 he wrote to Diana Hubback summing up his views on Richard Crossman, whom she was seeing at the time. Trott's letters often mentioned Crossman, whom he counted as one of his better Oxford friends and who he eagerly wished to visit him in Germany.

> My view of Dick, I think is not as intimate as yours. Something always seemed to prevent that. But I liked him and thought him a forceful, politically important person – he has a vivid though somewhat restless mind. That may have changed, but I never really felt convinced that he would rely much on his own views. This restlessness is something you are in danger of too, but not of what I think is his other fault, i.e. a certain vulgarity of perception.[47]

Meanwhile, Trott's plans of getting to Berlin had succeeded, through the agency of his friends Karl Friedrich Bonhoeffer and Albrecht von Bernstorff. The former had got his brother Klaus in Berlin and the latter his brother-in-law, Hans von Dohnanyi, to pull strings with the Prussian administration to have Trott's dossier transferred to the capital. As an Oberregierungsrat, Dohnanyi had the status in Germany of a QC, and was assistant to the Minister of Justice. Through

Bernstorff, Trott was able to contact Dr Paul Leverkühn, an international lawyer who had studied at Edinburgh University and had a wide range of contacts in Britain and the United States.[48] Leverkühn gave him a job in his office.

Adam Trott began his five month posting in Leverkühn's firm on 11 December 1934. It was housed in palatial premises by the Brandenburg Gate, within a short step of the major embassies, Unter den Linden, the Tiergarten and the administrative quarter. Trott was also admirably lodged in the apartment of Arnold von Borsig, a scion of the family of leading industrialists who belonged to the circle around Peter Mayer, and who was for the time being away in Italy. The flat, which had often been used for underground meetings of Socialists as well as a storehouse for illegal literature, was in Neu Westend, a forty-minute journey from the centre. Trott quickly settled into a more agreeable and cosmopolitan form of existence that had been possible in Rotenburg, Hanau or Kassel.

Soon after his arrival in Berlin he received a surprise visit from Maurice Bowra, the Oxford don. Since receiving his fellowship in 1922, Bowra had operated a salon within the university for the abler and more exciting undergraduates, drawing his circle from Cambridge as well as Oxford. It was in his rooms, for example, that Guy Burgess met Goronwy Rees and all but convinced him to take the same path to Moscow which he had taken himself.[49] Trott's next visitor was another face from Oxford, 'Do you remember von Oppen,' he wrote to Diana Hubback, 'the Rhodes Scholar who came up the year after me to Queens College? He is sitting on the floor of my room looking at books, while the wireless plays Schumann songs from Belfast!'[50]

Trott's new boss, Paul Leverkühn,[51] was an enigmatic figure from Hamburg. During the Great War he had been a comrade in arms of Scheubner-Richter, the Balt who had been one of Hitler's first enthusiastic supporters until he was shot dead during the Beer-Hall Putsch. (In 1938, Leverkühn put his name to a ghosted biography of the Nazi hero.) After the First War he had lived in New York and Washington where he had served on various international arbitration and finance bodies. During this time in the United States he became a close friend of Colonel, later General, Bill Donovan, the founder of the OSS, the American secret service, at the beginning of the Second World War. Trott had to spend ten minutes of every day with Leverkühn, whom he described as the 'wholly revered, a little stubborn but none the less friendly and clever Hanseat'.[52]

In Berlin, life continued to be social. On 20 December Trott had a party at which the Mayers, Maurice Bowra, Hasso von Seebach and a few others were present. At that stage he was a little doubtful about how he was to spend Christmas, telling Diana Hubback that he intended spending it in the E.T.A. Hoffmann Wine Cellar in the Friedrichstrasse, Berlin. At the last moment, however, he appears to have received a better offer. Writing to Shiela Grant Duff, he told her that he had had 'one of the most interesting experiences' of his life. For the first time Trott had come into contact with the East Elbian squirearchy during a trip to the estate of his friend and corps brother P.C. von Kleist in Pomerania. He had gone there possibly in order to look for the papers of Heinrich von Kleist. Some of Kleist's papers were retained by the family unpublished. Many of these were destroyed or lost when the Russians swarmed over East Prussia in 1945.

> I have met with human greatness in struggle which made my heart jump with joy and pride. And I have met with life 'solid and ordered'* as one does rarely nowadays. Think of infinite planes of acres with hard (no longer sinister) lines of pine-trees along which horses are galloping with the light carriage, my friend explaining to me the cultivation and history of their administering it. Though I was a little ill, I was extrememly happy there.[53]

The man who changed Trott's formerly disparaging views on the East Elbean Junkers was Ewald von Kleist-Schmenzin, one of the bravest and most uncompromising enemies of the National Socialist state. A descendant of the poet, Kleist-Schmenzin was a Lutheran landowner who had alerted German society to the menace of National Socialism before 30 January 1933 in his pamphlet, 'National Socialism, a Danger'. Naturally he was on Hitler's hit list after the *Machtergriefung* and spent some time in custody. Prison merely hardened Kleist-Schmenzin in his resolve. On the eve of the war he undertook a mission on behalf of the Abwehr to seek assurances from Britain that the British would help if the Germans were prepared to remove the tyrant. He saw Lord Lloyd, Sir Robert Vansittart and Winston Churchill in this capacity and took a letter of support from Churchill back to Germany with him. He was arrested after the July Plot, the letter was found and he was sentenced to death by the People's Court. After verdict was pronounced, the vice-president of the court was reported to have said, 'Disagreeable as he was during the trial, he was great in the manner of going to his death.'[54]

Kleist-Schmenzin, who was at this time in trouble for his blunt refusal to fly the swastika emblem from his roof and for his previous attempts to get Hindenburg to see sense about Hitler, took a special liking to Trott and the two began to meet in Berlin on a regular basis. Later Trott wrote to his father at Imshausen, saying that he 'would certainly have heard of him', such was his notoriety after his frequent

---

* *This is presumably a personal code implying some quality of life not easy to find under the Nazi regime.*

attacks on Hitler, and adding that he thought that his father would have liked the man.[55]

As Trott wrote to his mother in March 1935, he wanted 'essential connections'.[56] These were valuable in his desire to build up a circle of people opposed to the regime who might be in the positions of power which would allow them to act effectively. In this the Göttinger Sachsen came in useful time and time again and, for this reason, Trott was prepared to countenance some of the wilder sides of their '*Kommers*' or fraternity meetings. Writing to Diana Hubback in January, he makes this clear.

> Last night I had a big drinking party in my flat to which I invited my rather wild baronial friends from Göttingen and G[erry] Young, whom I like. They got rather drunk and stayed till seven this morning. Since at the moment there is less work to do, I am writing this in bed with a somewhat heavy head. I see various people and find certain lines crystallizing about which I hope to talk to you.[57]

Trott did not have long to wait; later that month Diana Hubback came out to Germany yet again and joined him in Berlin. Soon after her arrival, he told her that he was obliged to give a dinner in the Neu Westend flat for his corps brothers.

> This, he explained to me, was his duty, although it filled him with a contemptuous disgust to think they would literally drink themselves under the table. I could help him buy the wine but must on no account come near the flat while the party was in progress. 'She can't anyway,' said Gerry [Young], who had overheard us, 'she is dining with me that night.'[58]

Gerry Young was a third secretary at the British embassy in Berlin whom Trott had met through Diana Hubback. When they met on the night of the Göttingen reunion, Diana Hubback made an attempt to explain away her German friend's attitude by telling him that Trott was 'not really accustomed to such orgies'.

Gerry Young replied, 'But you know he is living under considerable strain. A night out is positively good for him.'

'Yes, but he does go out quite often. On Saturday night he is taking me to a party at the P—'s house.'

'What!' shouted Gerry. 'I know you are not a typical *jeune fille anglaise* whom it is my duty to protect but Adam goes too far. Last time I went to a party at that house, one of the daughters opened the door and she was completely stark. And after midnight everyone is horizontal. I shall speak to Adam, there are limits!'[59]

Student corps life was conflicting more and more with the ruling Nazi Weltanschauung. In June 1934 a film called *Bei der blonden Kathrein,* depicting a romantic view of student life, was released in Berlin. The Nazi press greeted it in a priggish manner, describing it as an 'antiquated representation of an outmoded lifestyle', which was 'inapplicable and unpalatable' to students who were 'true National Socialists'.[60] In May the following year, when Trott was getting ready to leave Berlin at the end of his stint with Leverkühn, another incident brought the student corps to the attention of Adolf Hitler. This was to prove the final straw. On 21 May the Corps Saxo-Borussia of Heidelberg were celebrating the reception of their new members. Having dispensed with the formalities, they repaired to a local inn and had fun blowing into empty bottles while the insulted customers endeavoured to listen to one of the Führer's portentous speeches on the wireless.

This incident might well have been glossed over were it not for the Saxo-Borussia's next prank. This followed only a few days later when the 'corpsiers' held a dinner to welcome in the new asparagus crop in Heidelberg. As more drink was taken, voices were raised in a light-hearted debate as to how one was supposed to eat asparagus in polite society. The next question was, 'and more especially how would Hitler eat asparagus?'[61] This led to further argument which, according to one version of the story, culminated in one of the drunken students going to the telephone exclaiming that since the Führer knew the answer to everything, he would surely know the answer to their dispute. The call went through to Hitler's adjutant who reported it to his chief.* The Führer was not amused and the Saxo-Borussia was suspended.[62]

Spargelessen – asparagus eating – as this new method of baiting the Reichskanzler was called, caught on in the other Burschenschaften with the result that by the end of the year the corpsiers and Nazis were at daggers drawn. Periods of suspension were meted out throughout the Reich's universities until, by the end of 1935, a general *Verbot* (prohibition) was imposed which lasted until the fall of the Third Reich. From then on the corps and their *Alte Herren* met in secret, becoming a body of bizarre, but powerful, dissidents by so doing. As Trott's subsequent friend and foreign-office colleague, Hasso von Etzdorf, later noted, 'the regular meetings of corps alumni in Berlin during the Third Reich were used as an opportunity to exchange information to aid in efforts against the Nazis.[63]

Although Trott was frequenting Berlin 'high society' during the time that Diana Hubback was in Berlin, he was not neglecting working-

---

* *The story is all the more ironic when one considers the disgustingness of Hitler's table manners. Though asparagus might just have entered into his limited vegetarian diet, the etiquette of whether to use a fork or not would have been beyond him as he uniformly ate with his fingers, bringing his head down to the food rather than the food up to his mouth and shovelling in mixtures of rice and vegetables with both hands. (For Hitler's eating habits, see Schlabrendorff, op. cit., and Terence Prittie,* My Germans, *London 1983.)*

class contacts. Helmut Conrad, stressing the continuity of Trott's resistance activities after 1933, remembered visiting him in Berlin in 1935. 'I clearly recollect,' he wrote in 1957, 'an intense Sunday discussion with a Communist official, whom Adam had invited round in honour of my visit to Berlin.'[64] Diana Hubback was an uncomprehending witness to a *Treff* — meeting — between Trott and a Communist who lived in an allotment hut opposite his flat. The purpose of this visit was an exchange of political literature. Trott, as we have seen before, anticipated the Communist call for a popular front by constantly stressing and working for the unification of all German anti-fascist groups. The German Communists, who by dint of their refusal to protect democracy and the Weimar Constitution had opened the door to the Nazi takeover in the first place, finally saw the light at their Brussels Conference that same year,

> when they came to recognize that war could be prevented and the Nazi regime overthrown – two things which were becoming more and more closely related – only by the broadest unity of anti-fascist forces, and that this unity could only be achieved round a programme for a new democratic republic, leaving the question of the Socialist revolution to the future.[65]

On his way home from work, Trott used to stop off at various U-Bahn stations in order to equip himself with the latest Communist tracts, often making lengthy detours to do so.[66] These tracts had begun to take on ever more ingenious disguises as the repression grew more intense; Dimitrov's closing speech at the Reichstag Fire trial was peddled as 'Home Heating by Electricity', while the Communist Party programme for 1934 was labelled as a 'Cookery Book with Seventy Approved Recipes'. The main resolution of the KPD's Brussels Conference where the popular front was finally decided upon was housed in an innocuous dressing entitled 'The Proper Care of Cactus Plants'.[67]

Trott was playing a dangerous game. In 1936, the Gestapo seized 1,643,200 illegal pamphlets in Berlin alone. Anyone in possession of one of these documents would be liable to prosecution, something that was yet more dangerous for Trott in the light of his still not having finished his legal training. In 1935, a quiet year in Nazi terms, an average of five people were arrested daily in Berlin on charges of membership of left-wing groups.*[68]

While Diana Hubback was with him in Berlin that winter, Trott met a 'wonderfully brave and noble man'[69] in Wilfrid Israel. Israel was to

---

* *The monthly figures are: January 160, February 101, March 345, May 288, August 173, September 162, October 252, December 78. In January and February 1936, a total of 638 dissidents were arrested. (Weissenborn,* Der Lautlose Aufstand.*)*

become one of his greatest friends and supporters. He was at the time general manager of the Kaufhaus Nathan Israel, one of Berlin's largest department stores, which, despite the Nazi persecution of the Jews, still projected its provocative name in lights on to the city's night sky. Israel had been born in 1899, the son of an immensely rich family of Anglo-German Jews. His British passport for the moment allowed him to continue to flout the Nazi terror (though it had not been enough to save him from two spells in 'wild' concentration camps in the course of 1933). His family were cultivated *Hofjuden* – court Jews – who lived a cosmopolitan lifestyle in the great cities of Europe. Wilfrid's mother, Amy Israel, would only allow German to be spoken at the dining table if the guest knew *no* English, 'German is for servants,' she declared.[70]

In the course of 1924–5, Wilfrid Israel spent seven months abroad, during which time he visited India and China. In India he made friends with C.F. Andrews, Gandhi's closest British friend. When he returned he filled his Bendlerstrasse apartment with oriental art. 'He wore a Chinese kimono at home,' writes his biographer, 'set Indo-Chinese Buddhas at his bedside [and] burned Indian incense tapers.' His refined, aesthetic nature struck the English writer Christopher Isherwood during his time in Berlin in the late twenties, and Israel formed the basis for the character of Gustav Landauer in his novel *Goodbye to Berlin.*

Israel had a country villa on the Wannsee, on the outskirts of Berlin. 'Mon Bijou' was built on

one of a dozen or so wooded properties which sloped steeply down to the lakeside. A narrow road, dipping through perpetually damp woods, led into Schwanenwerder, a small peninsula owned almost entirely by wealthy Berlin Jews, past a strange imported ruin – a fragment of the Tuileries masonry, brought back from the Franco-Prussian War. It bore the inscription: 'This stone from the banks of the Seine, planted here in German soil, warns you, passer-by, how quickly luck can change.'

Fortunes were indeed changing for Schwanenwerder's wealthy residents who bit by bit were being driven out and their villas taken over by high ranking Nazis: Goebbels, Speer and Hitler's doubtful doctor, Morell.[71]

One of the other Jewish residents of the peninsula was Lola Hahn-Warburg, a cousin of the Hamburg Warburgs, whom Trott knew through Diana Hubback's Berlin cousin, Lili Melchior. It was in the Hahn-Warburg villa that Trott met Israel. Israel invited Trott to one of his mother's tea parties in the Israel villa and from that moment the men became increasingly close.

In character, the two friends could hardly have been more different. Wilfrid was restrained and found it hard to formulate his thoughts; Trott was exuberant and a fluent talker. Wilfrid had a super-subtle talent for assessing the responses of people he talked to – as one friend commented, 'answering questions that had not been asked'. Trott was often recklessly unaware of the effect he had on his hearers. Trott was at heart a countryman, Wilfrid cultivated 'the weekend idea'. Trott could ignore his surroundings; Wilfrid clung to elegance as to a life-belt.[72]

All his life Jews had held a fascination for Adam von Trott; as a child he had spent time in the Solz house of an old Jew known as 'Binnes' and had occasionally participated in the Sabbath preparations of the household. He would not recognize the half-Jewish Diana Hubback's Gentile side, preferring to see her as something exotic and oriental by virtue of her Jewish mother's ancestry. Through his friend J.P. Mayer, himself a Jew, he met Julie Braun-Vogelstein, the art-historian, widow of the pre-war Socialist leader Heinrich Braun and stepmother of Otto Braun, the young Socialist writer killed on the Western Front whom both Trott and A.L. Rowse held in high esteem.

Julie Braun-Vogelstein lived at Klein-Machow, on the road to Potsdam, with her niece Hertha Vogelstein. At their first meeting in January 1935 Trott had been excited to learn that the Vogelsteins were Hessian Jews. It occured to him that they might have been *Schutzjuden* (protected Jews) of the Trott zu Solz family.* 'Then my family protected yours during the Middle Ages and beyond,' Trott declared enthusiastically, 'Please let me believe it. Hersfeld [where the Vogelsteins had settled] at that time was on our land.' Julie Braun-Vogelstein allowed him to carry on believing this, though there was neither documentary evidence nor oral tradition to justify the claim.[73]

A few months later, when Trott's fragile health had collapsed once again, he went out to live in the Braun-Vogelstein household while he recuperated.[74] Julie Braun-Vogelstein's biography of her late husband had appeared in 1932 but had been rapidly withdrawn from circulation when the Nazis came to power. Before this Trott had got hold of a copy of the book and digested it. When Trott went to stay with the widow he explained to her that before he 'made a decision, he asked himself what would Heinrich [Braun] have done in his place? The frugal existence of my mercurial husband struck Adam, who was not without puritanical traits, as a byword for true Socialism, something which he also aspired to himself.'[75]

At this time, Julie Braun-Vogelstein was beginning to have problems with her servants. One of them, the butler, belonged to the SA and denounced Mayer to the Gestapo. He spent some time in their headquarters in the Prinz Albrechtstrasse as a result. The same butler

---

* '*Another right possessed by many members of the Rittershaft was that of* Judenaufnahme. *Jews who wished to settle in villages under the jurisdiction of these nobles had to obtain permission and pay an annual 'protection' fee* (Judenschutzgeld).' (Pedlow, The Survival of the Hessian Nobility, p. 28.)

proceeded to try to blackmail his mistress. Trott's friend Hasso von Seebach decided that this was the last straw and turfed the servant on to the streets. Over the next few days the SA took their revenge as far as possible by persecuting the widow, but were frustrated in their efforts by Seebach and Trott who mounted guard. The vengeful Brownshirts had to content themselves with wrecking the garden, cutting down the shrubs and trampling the flowers.

The harassment did not stop there. The next person to attempt blackmail was Frau Braun-Vogelstein's maid. When she was sacked she reported the fact to the Arbeitsfront — the National Socialist labour organization. Trott decided to interrogate the maid and found that her testimony was riddled with holes, but Frau Braun-Vogelstein was nonetheless obliged to pay a fine for not consulting the Arbeitsfront before dismissing her. The next ploy was a further trumped-up charge – that the two women were keeping arms in the house. During the search the SA men found a rusting hunting rifle, belonging to the *'Wunderkind'*, Otto Braun's grandfather General von Kretschmar. The very distinguished and deeply Aryan nature of the rifle's owner somewhat deflated the stormtroopers.* Trott and Seebach had remained on the premises throughout, putting themselves at considerable risk by doing so. The women were convinced they had saved their lives.

> When Adam went to a dinner of the Saxo-Borussia [possibly Göttinger Sachsen] he found the contrast presented by the Braun household really amusing. He took a childish pleasure in the fact that he could move in both such different circles. He was, at that time, preparing an edition of Kleist's journalism and political writings. The book represented, behind this mask, a sharp attack on Hitler and the lawless situation in Germany, at the same time as being a call on the people's innate good sense. Later his introduction struck him as too mild. 'Give me something in Greek,' he asked me. 'There must be so many possibilities.' I presented him with several which were both appropriate and which he liked. Suddenly he jumped up and cried: 'No, it would be a fraud, Greece means nothing to me.' Silently we went out into the garden and walked until he came to a halt and with a timid look on his face said to me, 'Otto Braun is also alien, he was a Greek, while with Heinrich Braun I feel in many ways so close.'[76]

Trott continued to make valuable new friends in Berlin. Through Gerry Young he met the British ambassador, Phipps; writing to his mother he said, 'This afternoon, I met the British ambassador and I shall pay him a visit.' Through the Jay connection he also had a cousin at the American embassy as well as an acquaintance with the

---

* *'Once when the people [i.e. the stormtroopers] came, the* Archaeological Yearbook *was lying on the table. "So you're an anarchist too," bawled the Gestapo man, the common syllable "arch" proved everything.' (Julie Braun-Vogelstein,* Was Niemals Stirbt, *Stuttgart 1966.)*

influential American journalist Louis Lochner of the Associated Press Bureau. Increasingly, however, Trott was convinced that only the army was powerful enough to remove Hitler. With this in mind, he dined at the Berlin 'casino', or officers' club, and considered spending part of his Referendar training in the Reichswehr.

In April, Trott went to Kreis Jerichow near Magdeburg to work on the proofs of his Kleist anthology. His hosts were Martin von Katte and his wife, née Anneliese von Bodenhausen. Katte wrote later that Trott was 'the best of guests, his warmth invading the house and garden'. While he was there Katte was able to arrange for Trott to visit Katte's friend, the novelist Ernst Jünger, whose works Trott admired. Sadly, after the war, Katte could remember little of the meeting, except for Jünger's passion for 'old, well-chambréd burgundy.'[77]

Trott recommended Jünger's works to his future wife, Clarita Tiefenbacher, and Jünger became something of a bond between him and Katte in later years. From Peking he wrote to him of both *Blätter und Steine* and *Der Sizilianische Brief an den Mann im Mond*, adding, *à propos* the latter work, that 'we have a lot to learn' fron Jünger.

The meeting between Trott and Jünger gave rise to a later misunderstanding over the character of the young prince in the latter's novel *On the Marble Cliffs*. Later writers have claimed that the character was based on Trott. In reality the inspiration behind the book came from Trott's younger brother Heinrich, who visted Jünger in the company of a friend of Werner Trott called Kütemeier – who was represented in the book as Braquemart. The meeting took place in Jünger's vineyard house at Überlingen. During the war, Heinrich Trott corrresponded with Jünger and saw him in Paris a few days before 20 July 1944.[78]

5
Escape Plans

The Nazi revolution had brought with it renewed problems for the German Rhodes Scholarships which had been revived after such a deal of goodwill and effort on the part of well-meaning Oxonians on both sides of the Channel. By January 1935 the problems had become so acute that it was necessary for the chairman of the trustees, Lord Lothian, who was sympathetic towards Germany,* to fly out to Berlin for interviews with, among others, Bernstorff and Trott. In July 1934, the director of the Deutsche Akademische Austauschdienst (the German Student Exchange Service), Dr Morsbach, had been arrested. Lothian was so incensed that he proposed suspending the awards again until such a time as Morsbach was released. Fortunately this took place the following month. Nevertheless, Lothian issued a stern warning to the British ambassador, Phipps, that any political interference would lead to the immediate suspension of the scholarships.[1]

At the end of 1934 further problems presented themselves when both Trott and Bernstorff were dropped from the selection committee at the instigation of the president, Lindeiner-Waldau. A few weeks later the decision was reversed and Lindeiner-Waldau himself was replaced by the Reich Finance Minister, former Rhodes scholar Lutz Graf von Schwerin-Krosigk. The new committee elected Trott to one of the three executive posts – which he put down to the benign influence of Lord Lothian who had always had a high regard for Trott's talents. The position, in providing Trott with the cover under which to travel to Britain and the United States without arousing suspicion, possessed enormous advantages. Despite Lothian's admonitions, the rot was not entirely cured. Bernstorff, writing in November 1935, gave Lothian a dismal picture of the problems as he saw them from Berlin:

Things are not going smoothly this year . . . The danger that I have always tried to eliminate is growing stronger and stronger – that of the committee becoming

---

* Lothian's attitude was not 'pro-German' as some believed at the time, but based on an acute feeling that the post-war settlement had been unjust. '. . . he was obsessively pre-occupied with Germany because of his direct personal involvement in the punitive clauses of the Versailles Treaty, which haunted him'. (David Astor, notes written for the author, 1989)

'governmental' . . . Ultimately the only solution will be to leave the selection exclusively to the former Rhodes Scholars – they are the only people in this country who understand the aims of the founder and who can be trusted to select the right man without taking political or Party influences into account.[2]

In May 1935, it had been almost two years since Adam von Trott had set foot on English soil or spoken to the many Oxford friends who had not yet travelled out to Germany. On 11 May, winding up his appointment with Leverkühn, Trott flew to London. He had been planning the trip for some time, getting Diana Hubback to make arrangements for a small drinks party to which his better friends were to be invited. He was careful to stipulate that only in a very few cases should his own name figure on the invitation. Miss Hubback had instructions to drop a hint of his visit to David Astor, while he himself would undertake to write to Professor Tawney, Isaiah Berlin and 'of course Rowse'. Two weeks later, in another letter, Trott added some more names to the guest list, including his Communist friend Jack Dunman, the music critic Philip Hope Wallace and Charles Collins.[3]

After a few days in London, Trott travelled up to Oxford. Very few of his undergraduate friends were still up at the university and Trott moved in an essentially donnish world, staying first in Balliol and then moving to All Souls as the guest of the Warden, Adams. After leaving Oxford Trott paid a call on Cripps at Lechlade. Elsewhere in England he had conversations with David Astor, Tawney, Collingwood and Isobel Henderson. It was with the latter that he appears first to have mooted the idea of travelling in the East for an extended period.

Trott was disappointed with the reception he received in England but he was far more aggrieved by the increasing tendency of his closest English friends to see him as a representative of the aggressive Nationalism which was corrupting his country. In December 1934, Shiela Grant Duff had been asked to cover the Saar plebiscite for the *Observer*. Trott distrusted the easy judgements of journalists and their story-mongering, and was unhappy that his friend should fall into that world. He was even more unhappy at her partisan view that the Saar should vote against reunification with Germany, from which it had been detached under the clauses of the Versailles Treaty so that France could exploit its coal resources during the period of post-war recovery.

Shiela Grant Duff saw the issue in black-and-white terms, i.e. that the Saar should vote against reunification in protest against the present German government. Trott, as a patriot, saw the area as an inalienable part of Germany. Furthermore, Trott considered the Western attitude hypocritical and too closely aligned to capitalist interests. In his turn Trott criticized the English, pointing to the repression going on in their own Empire. The crystallization of these points of view drove a wedge between the two friends which, in time, destroyed their friendship. Shiela Grant Duff wrote to him in June 1935,

> Let's make a pact and fix it all up? Dear Adam – I want to see you again not in the rain after a long journey – let's meet in China – Puff! for your moral tyranny. Goronwy [Rees] and I decided last week you were governed entirely by intelligent self-interest – so am I – and I like you because you laugh at yourself with me . . . I like your attitude to presents and girls and everything else. You ought to have been a Red Indian rather than a German. Let's chuck our nationalities – it's all bunkum anyway. Man's a man for all that . . .*[4]

Trott now had thirteen more months of training before qualifying. He returned to Kassell where the work of looking after drunks, lunatics and vagabonds was dull and dispiriting. Trott amused himself from time to time by going out on the town with his fellow lawyers. He wrote to Shiela Grant Duff,

> I took them [the lawyers] to drink in the place where we once danced — you remember: the semi-underworld place. It's now called the 'Neue Welt' and we had great fun encouraging people to dance faster and drink more. These fellows I am with sometimes (working at the law to make up for my abominable gaps of legal knowledge) are extraordinarily crude, but good natured. You would probably dislike them.[5]

Trott's mind was turning increasingly to the idea of China and the East, encouraged by Wilfrid Israel. He had written to his old Wandervogel leader Gösta Ecke in Peking to ask his advice and received an encouraging letter. With currency control in Germany linked to the idea of *Autarkie* — economic self-sufficiency, which was one of the flimsiest planks of Nazi economic theory — it was necessary for him to find the money for this project from elsewhere. The ideal solution was the postponed third year of his Rhodes Scholarship, but there was the professional law exam to get out of the way.

Another project which was proving difficult was his Kleist anthology. He wrote to Diana Hubback to express his frustrations on that account.

> My publisher has got into some kind of trouble and does not at present dare to let Kleist come out which is very annoying. This kind of thing – of which there have been many in the last few weeks and more serious in nature – makes my wish to carry out the China plan all the more urgent.[6]

---

* *Earlier in the letter, Shiela Grant Duff reminded Trott of what he had said to her on Bebra station: 'In the coming struggle for power we must be in the right places'. In her diary she had noted, 'I think he is in the right place.' (Klemens von Klemperer,* A Noble Combat.*)*

The book did, however, come out at the end of June. Entitled *Heinrich von Kleist, politische und journalistische Schriften*, it uses Kleist's veiled but recognizable attacks on 'the foreigner', Napoleon, as a metaphor for attacking the 'foreigner' who at that time was in charge of German destiny. In his introduction, Trott defined Kleist's concept of freedom in the light of the Napoleonic invasion of Prussia. The political Kleist fought for human rights, a free independent form of life and the removal of the foreign emperor. He pressed for the actual liberation of his country, not for a liberal constitution.*7

Kleist's anti-French journalism came as the result of acute frustration at his inability to deal with the conquering zeal of 'that damned Consul' (Napoleon). His first attempts stemmed from the patriotic drama *The Battle of the Teutoburg Forest*. In this he was following his own dictum, that 'a man must throw his whole weight . . . into the scales of the times'. He was particularly sensitive to the Bonapartist scourge and created a literary resistance movement in Berlin in 1810, the fruit of which was the daily *Berliner Abendblätter* with its veiled attacks on the French. The paper was destroyed by the interference of the *Prussian* censors, and Kleist committed suicide the following year.8

Resistance to despotism and the fight for Christian self-determination 'determines Kleist's life until his suicide, which, despite all its sadness, was glorious,' Trott wrote. In his selection from the writings, Trott quotes from Kleist's *Guidebook to French Journalism* using it as a vehicle to attack Nazi journalism of the Goebbels' school, ' "French journalism is the art of making people believe what the government believes to be good," wrote Kleist. "It's purpose is to protect the government from all outward changes in the situation, and to keep men's minds under silent subjection to its yoke . . ." '9

Trott wrote to Diana Hubback expressing his doubts about the book. During production he had thought the Introduction too mild, while the publishers, the Protte Verlag, thought it too uncompromising.

> I am sending you *Kleist* by the same post. I am not happy about it – as I fear your instinct about the preface is true regarding the general reader, who will not understand the qualitative character of the protest which Kleist put up against Napoleon – as I try to disclose in the latter pages of my preface, the picture and the choice itself. What do you think?10

---

* *'The relevance of the poet's attacks on Napoleon's tyranny to contemporary events was obvious. And Trott's introduction established beyond any possibility of misunderstanding that Kleist became a rebel because he saw the 'divine destiny' of man trodden in the dust and that he set his hopes on the 'sense of uprightness of the individual citizen' who would rise against 'an immoral and demoralizing despotism.' (Rothfels,* The German Opposition to Hitler.*)*

Lost as the protest was on the general reader, it was not lost on Trott's German friends who appreciated how much Trott had in common with the German romantics. Helmut Conrad wrote to him on 21 June 1936, 'You were right when you said not only is Kleist's development to be found in your introduction, but that it also reflects an important stage in your own . . . to a certain degree it is an essay in self-justification, in a state of oppressive isolation, reluctantly borne.'[11]

Shiela Grant Duff also got a copy and promised to learn German, 'if only to read it'.[12] Public interest was aroused in the book, as was that of the Nazi state, the publisher being asked to forward a copy to the 'Commission for Total Spiritual and Ideological Education'. Despite their 'interest' they clearly did not believe the volume constituted a danger to the regime and it was not banned – probably because the subject was not of sufficiently wide interest to allow for it to be treated as subversive. Trott, on the other hand, was pleased to have made some sort of public protest, however slight.

In July, Trott was cheered up by a visit to Kassel by Richard Crossman and his fiancée, Zita Baker. Crossman found him unhappy about the future. While he was in Kassell, Crossman confined himself to intellectual skirmishing – largely teasing Trott about Hegel, philosophy and politics. When Crossman's baiting got too much for him Trott would suggest they go out and get drunk in the same *louche* bar which he had mentioned to Shiela Grant Duff. Crossman recalled that this meant getting very drunk indeed.[13] Trott summed up the visit in a letter to Diana Hubback: 'Dick was nice to have, vulgar as he may be in many ways.'[14]

Diana Hubback visited him in Kassel and lodged with Hans Siebert's fiancée's mother in Waldsruhe. While she was there Trott succeeded in having the young Communist liberated from Torgau concentration camp, with himself acting as guarantor. Trott had conceived of Siebert as a protégé to use in the coming struggle. He intended that he should emigrate to the United States and be of use there as a contact man. In the end Siebert remained in London, an embarrassment to Trott's friends and upsetting Trott's plans. While Diana Hubback was in Kassel, Trott took her to visit some Jews. When they got to the house they found to their dismay that it was daubed with the slogan, '*Juden heraus*'.[15]

In August 1935, Trott had to face the forbidding local Nazi boss responsible for the assessment of Referendars. The Gemeinschafts-leiter (literally 'community leader'), Dr Edmund Kessler, tore him off a strip. Trott was aware that this was a potentially damaging judgement in the light of his final examination. He wrote to Diana Hubback:

It seems ironical that I should attribute to you lack of energy in essential adjustment when this is the very charge with which I was dismissed by a testimonial in my last hour in Kassel. The chieftain in charge of my ideological and political education read me the statement which he had handed in about me to the authorities. He stated in so many words that not only was my attitude to the ruling tendency a sceptical one, but also that this was due to my weakness in not being able to arrive at a new departure . . . and to the fact that I had a rather more scholarly than a fighting nature, lacking – though gifted in various respects – fundamental integration. I hope to demonstrate to him one day what *I* consider a fighting nature.[16]

Trott's next Referendarstation was three to five months in commerce or administration, with an option on two months' military training. Despite his earlier interest in the latter for the contacts it might yield within the general staff, he decided to spend the full time at the law. The reason for this change of heart was probably to do with Siebert. At first he had looked for a post in Göttingen which would be near home and in an atmosphere that he knew and liked. No such position was available for the moment and Trott was obliged to look elsewhere. Finally, through another former Rhodes Scholar, Dr Harald Mandt, he found work in Hamburg, with the Hamburg-Levant shipping line.

Trott liked Hamburg from the first. To Martin von Katte he wrote that the old Hanseatic port was 'a freer, a humanly stronger city than Berlin, I could well live here.'[17] He even thought of staying on there as a lawyer after his exams. To his mother he wrote, 'I like the kind of people I meet much better than the Berliners . . . One gets to know people here much more easily than one does in Berlin and there is generally a much higher standard of taste, education and political judgement.'[18]

Trott found pleasant, inexpensive quarters and renewed his friendship with another former member of the Nibelungenbund, Helmuth Boehncke, with whom he went sailing on the Alster, watching the 'play of clouds over the spires'.[19] At first the antics of the merchants puzzled him, as he wondered how they managed to work in such noisy surroundings, among the clatter of typewriters and adding machines. His work involved commercial law in the Mediterranean, which meant reading the newspapers with an eye to potential trouble spots for the shipping firm. He found the job pleasant enough and later managed to get a half-day off to work for his exams in which he hoped to do well despite 'vindictive hands'. From Berlin, Leverkühn offered him a job on completion, but Trott was sceptical, possibly as a result of Leverkühn's distinct lack of enthusiasm when he had been told about the harassment of Julie Braun-Vogelstein and her niece.[20]

On his father's advice, Trott set out to get to know the patrician families of the port. On his arrival he had known only the paediatrician Boehncke, Ingrid Warburg and Graf Bernstorff, whose estate was nearby. The Warburgs had remained in Hamburg, though it was 'most unpleasant' for them now. Ingrid, he told Diana Hubback, he particularly admired, 'for her pluck and freshness.'[21] Through the Warburgs he met another Referendar, Peter Bielenberg and his English wife Christabel. Peter Bielenberg had done part of his legal training attached to the German embassy in London, when he had taken the opportunity to attend lectures at the London School of Economics. It was there that he had married Christabel Burton, who had been a pupil in Hamburg of the singer Alma Schadow, who had also been the teacher of the great sopranos Lotte Lehmann and Elizabeth Schumann. The couple lived at Reinbek, thirty kilometres to the south-east.

With Peter Bielenberg, Trott arranged to get together for study sessions for their exams. Bielenberg had two years to go as opposed to Trott's one. For Christabel Bielenberg, Trott was a surprise. In the heavily commercial world of Hamburg she had not met this combination of aristocracy and idealism before. In German terms Hamburg was a world of its own, bowing to no one and immensely proud of its traditions as a free city. For the Hamburg patricians, there was no temptation to enter the army or the bureaucracy; they

served their apprenticeships in far-flung overseas trading posts before returning to occupy comfortable seats on the City Council, and rather less comfortable ones in the massive sombre mansions they had built for themselves around the larger of the Alster Lakes, or along the east bank of the Elbe. There, they were accustomed to live out their lives in frugal solidity, until the next generation grew up to carry on the family business. Sieveking, Brödermann, Kellinghusen: these were the names to conjure with in Hamburg society. The little prefix 'von', significant of some aristocratic blood throughout the rest of Germny, not only failed to cut any ice in Hamburg, but carried with it a faint aura of irresponsibility, even degeneracy, which made it highly suspect. To be 'accepted' was definitely easier if one was English rather than Prussian or Bavarian, and although the goings on in the rest of Germany could not be completely ignored, there were other matters (such as the sugar and coffee plantations in Central and South America or the Corn and Stock Exchanges) which demanded more attention.[22]

At the end of September Shiela Grant Duff came to join Trott in Hamburg. She was on her way back to England where she intended to marry her long-standing lover Goronwy Rees. Trott drove her out to Bernstorff's estate at Schloss Stintenberg on an island in the Schallsee. As Miss Grant Duff later noted,

Stintenberg seemed a place apart, huge and ancient, and still untouched by the Nazis. The other guests there that weekend were Basil Newton, the British minister in Berlin, whom one of the party described as 'bone from the collar-stud upwards'. Conversation was boringly confined till late into the night to the ancient pedigrees as witnessed by their tombstones of the Trotts and the Bernstorffs.*[23]

Another guest was the historian John Wheeler-Bennett who later denied meeting Trott that weekend, claiming that he had not visited Germany between the Night of the Long Knives and the Fall of the Third Reich. The evidence certainly points to the contrary. Trott writing to his father on 18 October 1935 says, 'There was an especially interesting English author there who is currently writing a book on Hindenberg.' Wheeler-Bennett's book *Hindenberg, the Wooden Titan* was published in 1936.[24] In the course of writing the book Wheeler-Bennett had made contact with a number of anti-Nazis, both in the army and elsewhere. His contacts with this group came in useful when he became adviser to Lord Lothian, who put him on his staff when he was appointed ambassador to Washington in 1939.

The following weekend, Trott took Shiela Grant Duff to Travemünde on the Baltic Coast. 'In the evening, after walking together along the sand, we returned to the little sitting room in the house where we were staying. Adam asked me what my plans were and when I answered, "to marry Goronwy" he flung himself down beside me and said, "Marry me." ' In her account of events Shiela Grant Duff confessed to being 'completely flabbergasted' by the proposal, which she saw not only as a betrayal of Rees, but also of Diana Hubback. She rejected him.[25] At the end of that year he wrote to his mother, who was aware of his feelings towards the Englishwoman, in English: 'What worries me most about Shiela at the moment is not so much her refusal but the fact that she has doubted my general honesty about things . . . It hurts my pride and general peace to disappear in a cloud of confusion and suspicion. I must therefore remedy this before I can concentrate on any new difficulties.'[26] Shiela Grant Duff's doubting of Trott is one of the more heart-rending aspects of their extraordinary correspondence.

While Shiela Grant Duff was in Hamburg, the Nuremberg Laws were pushed through at the Nazi Rally. The German Jews had been progessively losing their civil rights since the Nazis came to power, with their being barred from an increasing number of professions. The Nuremberg laws imposed a code – in itself too moderate for the extremist wing of the Party – which regulated inter-racial marriages, forbade 'miscegenation' and imposed restrictions on Jews keeping Aryan servants (Aryan female servants had to be over forty to prevent the likelihood of their bearing their masters' children!)[27] Although the measures merely codified an existing repression – and were to a degree milder than one might have been led to expect – the fat was in the fire and a number of prominent Jews, who had held on in the hope of a relaxation of racial policy, now cut their losses and prepared to

---

* *It seems surprising in view of Miss Grant Duff's background and similar social milieu in Britain that she had not been bored by this sort of conversation before.*

leave. For the time being the Warburgs clung to Hamburg. Ingrid was still seeing Trott at the end of that year, but Julie Braun-Vogelstein had definitely had enough. Before leaving she showed her gratitude to her protectors by pressing gifts on Siebert, Helmut Conrad and Werner Trott. Hasso von Seebach incurred Trott's anger by deciding to leave for America with her. Trott thought that it was a duty for all Germans to remain as long as possible to act as a moderating influence and to be ready to serve any new government once the present regime fell. If all the good elements left the country there would be no one left to fight against the regime.* The party was escorted to Berlin station by Seebach's friend Werner von Haeften, the brother of Hans-Bernd and later adjutant to Stauffenberg. He died at the latter's side in the courtyard of the Bendlerstrasse building on the night of 20 July 1944.

That November, Trott received a visitor from his corps brother von Rumohr. Since the dissolution of the Göttinger Sachsen in October of that year, the Corps brothers had moved closer to one another. Rumohr worked in the Reichsnährstand (food supply) office in Berlin and convinced Trott that with Kessler's report still on file, there was a serious chance that he would fail the Assessor's examination. He advised his friend to do something positive to alter the situation. Trott sought advice from Hans von Dohnanyi; he travelled up to Berlin to see Dohnanyi on 23 November and as a result succeeded in having his dossier replaced by a more favourable report. In his dealings with Dohnanyi in 1934 and 1935, Trott was at the very heart of the German resistance to Hitler as it existed in conservative circles before the war. Dohnanyi was later removed from the Ministry of Justice as a result of his antipathy to Nazism. At the time he was compiling a list of Nazi crimes. This he was to continue to do when drafted into the Abwehr by his friends Canaris and Oster at the beginning of the war.†

The idea of a job in business now crossed Trott's mind. A senior director of the firm of I.G. Farben was Ministerialrat Dr Buhl who, as it happened, was keen to get his son into Oxford. Trott, however was not tempted by this sort of *quid pro quo*, and when the awards were announced that winter, Dr Buhl's son's name was not among them.‡

---

* *In October 1936 Trott had a similar fight with his Oxford friend Schumacher.*
† *Arrested after 20 July 1944, Dohnanyi swallowed a diphtheria bacillus which had been slipped him by his wife in the hope of postponing his trial and execution. He succeeded in paralysing himself but was executed all the same. (Schlabrendorff, Officers Against Hitler, 1966.)*
‡ *As Trott wrote to Shiela Grant Duff, '... before I left Frankfurt [where I.G. Farben was based] the chief legal director of the chemical concern, whose son wants to become a Rhodes Scholar, gave me a princely lunch. They have a monster building of sandy stone with thousands of large glass windows, millions of busy clerks like ants crawling about it, and – evidently in order to flatter me and show his importance – he discussed the legal aspects of setting up a huge*

Trott had in fact put some weight behind a candidate called Captain Otto Hans Winterer, a Luftwaffe pilot whom he had known in the Nibelungenbund, who had perfected a new process of dive bombing. Winterer had lived as a child with the family of Trott's Hamburg friend, Helmut Boehncke. The Rhodes selectors in England took a dim view of this serving officer, excusing themselves to Trott on the grounds that he was too old to benefit from the award.[28] 'A candidate I should very much liked to have sent has been ruled out on grounds of age. I wrote to Allen in Oxford and Bernstorff and to Lord Lothian, but there seems little chance for him,' he wrote to Diana Hubback that Christmas.[29]

Trott was still working on Siebert who was proving somewhat unreceptive to his lessons in political theory despite long walks and boating trips with Boehncke on the Alster Lakes. Siebert went home with Trott that Christmas to Imshausen. There he was a witness to Frau von Trott's struggle with the local SA who were insisting that she hang the Swastika from the roof of the manor. The Swastika had been declared the national flag in September of that year, but Trott discovered on examining the decree, that the old national flag might legitimately be flown instead. Legal niceties were lost on the local stormtroopers who were encouraged by a denunciation from one of Eleonore Trott's friends. For a while it looked as if the Trott home would be subjected to the full rigmarole of a search. Trott wrote to his mother in a codified English, 'You might remove those [books] of a conspicuously Jewish or Marxist origin. But please look after them well – they are indeed necessary for anybody who is seriously interested in their refutation.' In the end the house was spared the search as the Landrat for the area was well known to the family.[30]

Trott's relations with his English friends were at a low ebb. He had tried to distance himself from Diana Hubback, both for her sake and his own, and his offer of marriage to Shiela Grant Duff had been spurned. In both cases the correspondence (which flowed at remarkably frequent intervals) continued; with Shiela Grant Duff, however, it occasionally descended into acrimony both as a result of his unhappiness at her refusal to countenance marriage and at her insistence on seeing Germany as a monolith in which all its citizens were responsible for the actions of its leaders. This last drove Trott to exasperation. 'If some of the things you say or imply were really true I would be a little ashamed of your not despairing of our friendship once and for all,' he wrote to her on 29 November. 'You say them with

plant for the manufacture of artificial rubber, with fabulous sums of money. But he is a thorough crook, and when he glanced at me with his dead fishlike eyes I felt he must know I knew it. No chin at all, and flat ears like a fiend.'
(Letter, November 1936.)

very little knowledge of the facts of my existence, and with an extraordinary readiness to imagine the worst.'[31]

Another factor which filled Trott with justifiable depression was the need to spend the best part of January 1936 at the Referendar *lager*, the indoctrination camp which Moltke had enjoyed sending up a couple of years before. He had hoped to be able to get to England before this began, travelling on one of the Levant Line's ships. The chance of this brief respite fell through and after spending a last weekend with the Bielenbergs in Reinbek, Trott took the train up to Berlin and on to the camp at Jüterbog, seventy-two kilometres south of the capital. He wrote to Shiela Grant Duff from the train between conversations with a greengrocer who ate huge ham sandwiches and quizzed him on Catholicism. 'The greengrocer had just discovered I am writing in a foreign language and asks me with a twinkle in his eye whether I am writing everything I think. No, I answered, perfectly candidly.'[32]

Trott had expected a camp of some 150 lawyers and dentists – 'some of them will look at least as funny as I will in uniform.'[33] On arriving, however, he discovered that the camp was to be graced with only about a third that number, confined to large rooms twenty-eight a piece. Both Trott's bed and uniform proved too small. Having decided that he had to enjoy the camp, he did not find the eight weeks too arduous. From the camp Trott sent Shiela Grant Duff photographs in which he looked like 'a condemned convict'.[34] In a further letter to her Trott described a half-term break:

It was pleasant to walk freely on a pavement, to smoke and drink leisurely. You begin to enjoy the simple things again . . . We drank a very great deal with two young plumbers who seemed to me more intelligent and fresh in their outlook than most people here. The one called Paul was very grand explaining to me with extreme subtlety that you must never talk politics in a pub nowadays – he called me 'my little boy' in the end, and to my grief stood me drink after drink . . . which I could not have refused without hurting him deeply. I also had to smoke his tobacco. He earns a guinea a week. His friend Emil was a sarcastic wit who explained the relation of feeling and intellect – he said, 'You will have to hurry if you still want to win our hearts.' Personally, I seemed to have won them all right, and they mine. I shall meet them again . . .

Later on I seemed to have won the admiration of an overcrowded café for dancing well in my big boots. I danced many waltzes and tangos. One of my friends found the ground too slippery to remain on his feet and offered to box the ears of one of our superiors who was there in civilian clothes. We had a very gay time . . . I am very happy at the moment – perhaps because of yesterday which has made me feel strongly how necessary people like myself will be to this country – this I realize with no arrogance, but with a glad certainty (I have doubted it painfully and often enough and will do so again to be sure – if only I can keep heart now). Perhaps it is better to be trusted than to be loved . . .[35]

Trott's participation in the camp gave rise to fresh rumours in Oxford. The year before, Trott's friend Patricia Spence, later Countess

Russell, had heard a story that Trott had joined the party. She had defended Trott, saying that had he done such a thing it would have been in order to fight from within. The story got back to Trott who sent her a postcard on which he expressed the hope that she had not changed the colour of her hair – which was red – and that she should know that he had not changed the colour of his either.[36] A German Rhodes Scholar, Alexander Böker, pressed Trott to answer his critics. Isobel Henderson confirmed to Trott that it was Isaiah Berlin who was gossiping; however, it appears that Richard Crossman was also responsible for the rumours. To Diana Hubback he wrote, 'Sometimes I feel I never want to go to England again, whatever kind of homesickness I might feel towards it. Happily the world that I love is not moved by these squabbles.'[37]

While Trott was in the Jüterbog camp, his friend Siebert was once again arrested for distributing Communist literature in Berlin. Trott was powerless to act in his present position. That autumn, Trott finally got Siebert out of Germany to England. Eventually he married an Englishwoman and remained in Britain throughout the war. Trott last saw him in the Egyptian rooms of the British Museum in 1939.

On 7 March 1936, Hitler denounced the Treaty of Locarno and reoccupied the demilitarized zone. The moment had come for the dictator to go over to the attack and to put into action a forceful revision of the Treaty of Versailles. To many, war became a inevitability from that moment onwards.

Trott had reached the final station before his Assessor's examination, that of the Higher Provincial Court. For this part of the training he returned to Kassel, living out at Göttingen as his work in the court only amounted to three days a week. In the university city he worked with a fellow member of the Jüterbog camp until a heavier workload in Kassel forced him to move back to the provincial capital. In the Kassel court he witnessed one of the mass dissident trials which were taking place at the time. He much admired the courage of the eleven defendants and said he had no desire to forget the bravery of these men in the face of such injustice.*

As ever Trott was looking beyond Nazism to the future and Germany's place in a new European order which would come about after its fall, a European order that would involve deep changes in the structure of all nations. He wrote to Shiela Grant Duff,

---

* Up until the beginning of the war, the ordinary – as opposed to People's – courts sentenced around 225,000 men and women to roughly 600,000 years imprisonment. There were at least eighty-six mass trails against members of Socialist parties. (Weisenborn, op. cit.)

My trouble is rather that I cannot take too seriously that soulless monster 'Europe' which is agitating you so much. I can and want only to work for the new order of labour which I know will come about whatever our bad fate will be in the near future. I also know that my country has a very essential, if not the most vital, contribution to make in that order, whatever its façade is now. To share in this contributon has been the object which I have never quite lost hold of all these years, and though it may look like fatalism it makes me certain and tranquil in view of the dangers which shatter people's nerves so much – that certainly makes them no more effective when it comes to really vindicate the position for which they claimed to stand all the time. I think that [Stafford] Cripps is more realistic than he knows himself. In the meantime one must hope that other side will consider the bloody thing too costly for all and themselves . . .[38]

Trott was still concerned with the need to find a group with the necessary moral and physical strength to bring about the change in power. The English were no help; their 'flexibility' and 'polite scepticism' were inadequate weapons 'in a world where things clash badly'. The Communists lacked the 'courage and moral concentration which is needed if you want to strike beyond the sphere of moral welfare. Stafford [Cripps] in a way has it, but that type of courage is possible ônly in a democratic community and beyond those borders his striving for a brotherhood of nations seems untimely enough.'[39]

That June Shiela Grant Duff came to stay. The difficulties which had beset their friendship in Hamburg and afterwards were temporarily shelved and a 'new phase had opened in their friendship'. Trott lived in the Mozartstrasse, 'in a spacious first-floor room with a balcony. He had a charming newly painted attic for me on the fourth floor, whose two windows were like eyes looking out over the rooftops to the park.' Trott was hard at work on his law finals but at lunchtime found a moment for a picnic in the park or a drive in the country. 'Gradually the charm of each other's presence took over. I loved Adam's alternative moods of gaiety and solemnity. Today, more than anything else about him, I remember his laugh,' wrote Shiela Grant Duff in 1982.[40] Trott still resented her criticisms of the non-Nazi Germany, taking personally her attacks on the weakness of the opposition, but this was not enough seriously to upset the idyll.

The next months were dominated by exams: legal theory at the end of July, a written practical in Berlin taking up most of August and an oral in late October.* Trott went to Berlin to work with a tutor, staying

---

* Trott's exams gave him no time to follow the Olympic games which took place in Berlin that August. Moltke, writing to Freya, found them a vulgar spectacle. 'Berlin is frightful. A solid mass is pushing its way down the Unter den Linden to look at the decorations. And what people! I never knew the likes of them existed. Probably these are the people who are National Socialists because I don't know them either!' (Balfour and Frisby, op. cit.)

with Wilfrid Israel in the Bendlerstrasse. His mind still turned on the possibility of working in industry in order to escape the Nazi net, but negotiations with I.G. Farben broke down when Ernst von Simson, a relation who was on the board, informed him that the firm was anything but apolitical,* and advised him to go the East instead. On 6 October, Trott appeared to have made up his mind, writing to his father that there was simply 'no other way'.[41]

Trott's oral was on 22 October, chaired by an unsympathetic young *Ministerialrat*. Among the more sinister members of the panel was the *Senatspräsident* of the newly created People's Court. Trott was judged *befriedigend* or 'satisfactory' only. He had done poorly in his written papers, which had been marked down for their lack of National Socialist ideology. The marks meant he could not join the administration but he had the consolation of at last being free of the Ministry of Justice. To Diana Hubback he wrote of the examiners, 'They behaved very severely and told me that I wasn't at all good really and deserved neither the first nor the second class and gave me something between a second and a third and added a lot of rude things before I quitted.'[42]

After the oral, Trott went to Prague where Shiela Grant Duff had been posted as a journalist. The visit was a mixed success. Trott was introduced to her new guru, the Czech politican and journalist Hubert Ripka; the meeting did not work out well. On the other hand Trott was interested to meet Otto Strasser who was in exile in Prague. Strasser, whose brother Gregor had been murdered on the Night of the Long Knives, had formerly represented the left-wing of the Nazi Party which had taken the 'Socialist' aspect of National Socialism seriously. After coming to power, Hitler had played down the radical elements in the Party's programme in order to please conservatives, big business and the army. Their remaining influence in the Party was largely destroyed on 30 June 1934. The Strasser brothers' synthesis of nationalism and socialism was to some degree based on Spengler's book, '*Preussentum und Sozialismus*', and it is not surprising that the few elements of Nazi policy which Trott found positive were the work of the Strasserite wing.[43]† Otto Strasser himself had split from the Party as early as 1930 when he founded the Union of Revolutionary National Socialists. Trott made an impression on Strasser and for his own part he admitted Strasser had been 'important for me to meet, for whatever his detail [*sic*] qualities are, his will is determined and he will not make mistakes out of fear, though perhaps out of lack of thought.'[44] While he was in Prague, Shiela Grant Duff also introduced him to Wenzel Jaksch, the Sudeten Socialist leader.

---

* *During the war I.G. Farben benefited enormously from concentration-camp labour in its factories, especially at Auschwitz. (Krausnick and Broszat, op. cit.)*
† *Joseph Goebbels had originally been with the Strasserite wing of National Socialism and to some degree maintained 'left-wing' Nazi ideas to the end.*

After Trott's return from Prague he went to Berlin, where he was joined by Shiela Grant Duff. The latter was busy with a journalistic assignment and Trott wrote to Diana Hubback to say that they had scarcely seen one another during the two days she was there. On 8 November Trott went to England, staying in London for five days before going up to Oxford. Before he left Berlin, he told Diana Hubback to arrange meetings with a number of people, mentioning '[R.H.] Tawney and Mr Wheeler-Bennett' by name.[45] He also saw Ellen Wilkinson, the firebrand Labour MP who in May 1937 was to kick up such a fuss about Göring attending the Coronation of King George VI that he was forced to retire humiliated into the German Embassy, only emerging twelve hours later to catch a plane back to Berlin.

The primary purpose of Trott's Oxford visit was to arrange to spend the postponed third year of his Rhodes Scholarship in China. This was unconventional; Rhodes Scholarships were intended – by the founder's wish – for use in Oxford itself. But Trott had powerful friends in the university – not only Lothian but also the Warden of New College H.A.L. Fisher, the Master of Balliol and E.L. Woodward, the Germanist whose views on Germany Trott had so much disliked. In recommending Trott warmly to Allen, Woodward took the chance to put the world to rights. 'What a mess the Germans are making of the world,' he wrote, something he put down to the neglect of 'principles laid down by Bismarck.'[46]

Woodward was sensitive to Trott's dilemma, understanding the problems caused by his non-membership of the Party in Germany. 'I know he feels awkward to put this fact down on his application; but, as you can understand, it exists and there is no way out of it.'[47] Lothian too stressed Trott's problems at home. 'His sympathies are not with the present regime,' he wrote on 27 November (the day he had unofficially told Trott he would get the grant).[48] To Ned Carter of the Institute of Pacific Relations in the United States, Lothian spelled out Trott's problem. 'He is an extremely good man, but his refusal to identify himself with the Nazi Party has prejudiced his prospects of getting the kind of diplomatic or legal employment for which he was originally trained.'[49] Lothian's enthusiasm was such that Allen's considerable reservations were easily swept aside. While he was in Oxford, he stayed as a guest of the Warden of All Souls, staying up to the early hours of the morning talking to Isaiah Berlin and the philosopher Stuart Hampshire, then a recently elected fellow who had come from Balliol.

From Oxford, Trott went down to London and then on to stay with Lord Percy at Catfield Hall near Great Yarmouth. He had been asked to fill out a written statement about his Chinese venture which Diana Hubback was going to type out for him. 'I sit long times [*sic*] in a room with large windows on the ground floor and can't think what to write – [he wrote to Shiela Grant-Duff] because (at the moment) I'd much rather stay and save Europe with you.' Lord Percy, on the other hand, was trying to convince him that China was a *far* better idea. On his way back to Berlin, he dropped in to see Lothian in London, who gave him an unofficial indication that the trustees were in favour of the trip. Trott was overjoyed. The German apprenticeship was finished and with it the mental torture of life in Nazi Germany could be put off to another day. To Shiela Grant Duff he wrote, 'I shall get any amount of splendid introductions, starting from Roosevelt and several Chinese cabinet ministers to Chinese intellectuals and commercial attachés in Tokyo . . .'[50] In Berlin Shiela Grant Duff joined Trott, both staying in Wilfrid Israel's flat before Trott returned to Imshausen to spend a family Christmas.

6
Wanderjahre

Preparations for Trott's Chinese study year and its American prelude preoccupied him from the end of 1936. His spirits were considerably raised by the notion of a period of repose and meditation after the years of political impotence in Germany. China not only afforded time to pull his thoughts together in order to work out how to deal with the German dilemma, but also the time to work on combating the influence of Hegel on philosophy and on himself in particular. In order to effect this he had the idea that some elements of Confucian political science might might provide a useful antidote, in an attempt to find a common denominator in answer to the question, 'why do subjects obey?' This was to be the basis of a *Habilitationsschrift* (the second German 'doctoral' thesis) which would gain him entry to the faculty of a German university. In the winter of 1936–7 Trott therefore set about making as many contacts as he could who might provide him with letters of introduction in America and China. Some of these were to come in useful in the fight against Hitler.

On the Feast of the Epiphany in 1937, Trott went to stay with one of his most important contacts, Ambassador von Dirksen, at his house in Bavaria near the town of Ansbach. Dirksen had been stationed in China until recently when he had been replaced by another old-school diplomat, Trautmann. He had been shifted to London to replace the crass Ribbentrop who had become the laughing stock of British social and political circles as a result of the many gaffes he made in this unfamiliar social and diplomatic world. Trott was not best pleased with the accommodation provided by Dirksen:

> the most extraordinary castle I ever was in . . . in the Middle Ages it used to belong to the Hohenzollerns, and was never conquered in the Thirty Years War – unlike humble Solz which was burnt to ashes – and now belongs to a man who has filled it with Chinese vases and pictures – a slightly bogus performance. Good God, I spent the most uncomfortable night of my life in that vast medieval room they gave me and never attempted to heat.[1]

From the chilly *schloss* of the former German ambassador to China, Trott went later that January to stay with his corps-brother Münch-hausen. Exceptionally for one of his class (although this was true to some extent of Trott's brother Werner), Münchhausen was a Communist sympathizer, 'one of Jack's friends in his mind and some degree heart', but 'very wild and hard and brave'. They seem to have made a merry night of it, perhaps making up for the Bavarian visit which had made Trott so ill; 'we drank a few bottles of 1893 Rhine wine', he wrote to Diana Hubback, 'and French champagne (you won't know that there is such a thing as German champagne) and I am very glad of this friend.'[2]

From Münchhausen, Trott went on to Leipzig to stay with Dr Wolfram Eberhard, a sinologist to whom he had received a letter of introduction from Ecke and who had agreed to accompany Trott on his Chinese expedition. Eberhard was to teach Trott Chinese as well as initiating him into Chinese culture and philosophy. Julie Braun-Vogelstein had agreed to pay his fares. In mid-February Trott travelled to Paris, theoretically in order to meet Shiela Grant Duff there. She, however, had left for Spain on an assignment to cover the alleged Malaga massacres and to obtain the release of the writer Arthur Koestler who had been thrown into a Nationalist gaol. During her absence he stayed in the rue de l'Université living 'on rolls and coffee at stalls and sponging on the people I have introductions to.'[3]

Despite the poverty imposed on him by the ramifications of Göring's Four-Year Plan and German *Autarkie*, Trott managed to keep himself amused in Paris, and would have been happy to stay longer as that visit in the winter of 1937 was his first. An active tourist, he went to the Chambre des Deputés and crossed the river to the Place de la Concorde. He rode in the Bois de Boulogne with Ulrich Schmidt-Ott and took a trip out to Versailles. At the Sorbonne he attended a lecture and spent his evenings at the theatre or the music hall watching André Siegfried and Josephine Baker. Finally, after three days of waiting, Shiela Grant Duff appeared and together they travelled to England.

His first host in London was his Göttingen friend Alexander Werth, who had left Germany in 1934 with his Jewish stepfather after a longish spell in the Colombiahaus, one of the SA's more notorious torture chambers in Berlin-Tempelhof.[4] Once again he went up to Oxford where he finally took his BA on 27 February. 'I saw Maurice Bowra,' he wrote to Shiela Grant Duff from the boat, '. . . we had a very friendly parting. Same with Shaiah Berlin although he had the cheek to say that I was now "worming my way in with all the crook-humanists of the world". He is a nice but not very loyal friend to us, you know.'[5]

Another person he saw was Rowse, who, as chance would have it, was able to introduce him to Count Helmuth Moltke. 'It seems somehow symbolic,' wrote Rowse later, 'that these two, who were to die together in July 1944,* should have first met in the Hall at the

---

* *Arrested in January 1944, Moltke was not executed until January 1945, five months after Trott.*

fireside before dinner. I shall not forget the mutually appraising, slightly suspicious look those two gave each other in the increasing danger of the late thirties.'[6] Moltke had been brought to All Souls by Lionel Curtis.

Helmuth James von Moltke was a couple of years older than Trott. The great-nephew of the Field Marshal, he had been born at the estate at Kreisau in Silesia in 1907. His mother, née Dorothy Rose-Innes, was South African, the daughter of the Chief Justice of the Supreme Court in Pretoria. Moltke studied law at the Universities of Breslau and Berlin. During his university years he formed, with Paulus van Husen, Carl-Dietrich von Trotha, Hans Peters and Horst von Einsiedel, the nucleus of what was to become the Kreisau Circle during the war. In the late twenties he and some friends had started a series of labour camps. Ironically these went some way to inspiring the Nazi training camps which had proved so dire to both Trott and himself.[7]

Moltke tried and failed to win a Rhodes bursary in 1930 and therefore committed himself to finishing his legal studies in Germany. Through his grandfather, Moltke had a large circle in Britain, exclaiming that he had 'more friends in London than I have in Berlin'. Most of these, like Lord Lothian and Moltke's close mentor Lionel Curtis, had been members of Lord Milner's 'Kindergarten', a bright group of colonial civil servants who had gathered around Milner in South Africa at the beginning of the century.

Moltke had a strong streak of natural arrogance; asked by the Kaiser at Doorn what his father's regiment had been, he replied, 'No idea, Your Majesty'. Like Lord Lothian and Nancy Astor, Moltke's parents were Christian Scientists, and throughout his life Moltke combined deep piety with an austere, overbearing and sometimes haughty manner. Margert Boveri found him a 'rather rigid and unapproachable person'.[8] He could be eccentric, dressing like an undertaker, carrying a brief-case under each arm, one for urgent business and the other for not-so-urgent business, or filing one nail a day in order to average the time spent doing the lot. With Nazism he was uncompromising; he described discussing economics with the National Socialists Gregor Strasser and Gottfried Feder as being 'like discussing astronomy with someone who believes that the sun is not the centre of our system but, say, Saturn'.[9] In the 1932 presidential elections he voted, somewhat perversely, for the Communist Thälmann.

In 1936 Moltke decided to read for the English Bar. The Rose-Innes family were in a position to surmount the currency problems involved, and for the next three years Moltke travelled backwards and forwards from Kreisau to Berlin and from Berlin to London. When Rowse met him he was much struck by his aristocratic bearing and his immense height – he was six foot seven – 'dark and glittering, he

95

looked like a sword'.[10] Moltke's English biographers point out that the comment 'might have applied almost as well to Adam'.[11]

The same source, however, stresses the total difference in character between the two men. 'Adam's love for the good things in life would have been likely to upset Moltke's streak of asceticism, just as the talkativeness of the one would have jarred the reticence of the other.' Trott and Moltke's attitudes were so much at variance that 'they did not become firm friends until the circumstances of wartime gave them an end in common and led them to work closely together in its pursuit.'[12] Rowse had decided which one of the two he favoured, and from that moment he resolved to sport the oak during Trott's visits to All Souls.[13] Before going down to London, Trott went to stay with his friend and benefactor H.N. Spalding who allotted him further funds for his American and Chinese expeditions.*

On his return to London, the Astors put Trott up at their palatial home in Saint James's Square. For the first time he came into close contact with Nancy Astor, the formidable mother of his friend David.

> I really liked Lady Astor for all her wiry liveliness – she said the last day, 'I am sorry the little Trott is leaving,' and I am about twice as big as she is, and I told her so – she gave me a letter to Charlie Chaplin, and money to buy riding boots and a trench coat which she thought I ought to have when I went to the Virginian horse farm of my cousin.[14]

England had proved a pleasant and rewarding trip,

> In Oxford I met a lot of Chinese, including their ambassador, whom I saw again in London. I also saw [Lord] Halifax, whom I had so much wanted to meet, but [had] hardly a word with him. He seems in many ways a person one should try [to] ... become like. On that Saturday evening I met a remarkable man called Sir John Hope Simpson,† who rescued [several] ... million people's lives with flood relief in the Yangtze valley – he told me all about it, and what one must do to get great masses of people working together.[15]

When he left England in early March 1937, Trott had gathered dozens of introductions from important people in Germany and Britain, the most important of them being from the Astors, Cripps and Lothian. With a Rhodes grant of £350, as well as support from Spalding, Cripps and Mrs Braun-Vogelstein, Trott was on a firm footing to spend a long period away from a troubled and troubling Europe.

---

* *In a letter to* The Times *of 15 December 1949, Spalding described Trott as 'the greatest and best German I have known'.*
† *Sir John's son, John Frederic, had been a near contemporary of Trott's at Balliol.*

The preparation for Trott's Chinese trip was to start when he reached the East Coast of America, but his mission was twofold in that it had an underlying interest, that of making contacts which would be useful later. On the East Coast he had a variety of introductions to public figures, as well as a number of members of his own influential family to look up. From his travels in America Trott was going to write a paper, 'American Impressions', which could possibly be used in order to get him in on the 'inside' of German public life. As his widow writes, 'Basically, Adam's trip had much in common with the travels of the journeyman. He wished to learn his trade, despite the multiple impediments which lay in the way of state service.'[16]

The transatlantic voyage had a poor effect on Trott's fragile health at first, but his spirits rallied, especially after he met an amusing American library builder at his table. This man had worked at the Vatican, and told dirty stories ('they aren't dirty at all really,' wrote Trott) to the Pope. 'He also told me of a cardinal who – borrowing an ordinary suit from him – went to see Josephine Baker one evening with him in Paris.' The engineer gave Trott advice.

> He said I could do some real good in the world if I kept in touch with the underdog! Introduced him to a diplomat friend I have in first class, he said to me he thought "that was a shit of a man" – grown up like a protected industry. When I refused a cigar from him the first evening, he said would I rather have the money? . . . I never saw anybody so little of a snob at this ruffian, I have to look out to keep on my feet in talking with him. But we like each other, he has shown me pictures of his wife and asked me to his house. And we have big contests of who can eat more at meals, and sometimes he and sometimes I win. I am afraid we are rather shocking to other people. Yesterday he was feeling sick, and I triumphant.[17]

Trott's boat docked in New York on 12 March and he was met on the quay by Ingrid Warburg and Josias von Rantzau. The latter was working at the Consulate in New York. In New York he stayed with his cousin Dr William Schieffelin and his wife. Like Eleonore von Trott, Schieffelin was a direct descendant of John Jay. One of Trott's most momentous introductions in New York was to the former Attorney General, now Colonel, 'Wild Bill' Donovan to whom he had an introduction through Paul Leverkühn. Donovan was now a partner in a firm of lawyers, but in civil life his mind was still taken up with issues of military intelligence in an inevitable European war. In this he had collaborators in the German Consul General, Otto Kiep and also Leverkühn, who made frequent trips to New York.[18]

> During his term with the Justice Department in Washington, Colonel Donovan had taken the opportunity to talk with European diplomats and visiting businessmen and scholars who had just arrived from abroad. Fitting their remarks together, he saw a pattern that disturbed him, and he made it his

business to cultivate every foreigner who might be useful now or in the future. His home in Georgetown became an official clearing house for intelligence.[19]

The American colonel seems immediately to have made his Washington home available to Trott. Donovan himself, who had been part of the previous Republican administration, remained at his practice in New York where he had already extended the hand of hospitality.[20] The house in Washington was 'very much like one of those English houses which envelop one at once [in] . . . a sort of gentle and rational peacefulness . . . the old Viennese butler was the only person in the house . . .'[21]

The butler turned out to be a considerable find, as Trott wrote in his essay, 'Amerikanische Eindrücke' (American Impressions'). 'My landlord was a clever old Austrian servant, who was able to teach me about all of Washington's big-wigs, whom he knew from serving at their elbows. Apart from Roosevelt himself, he [i.e. the butler] had few enough friends in the present administration even if he had helped to entertain most of the high-ranking Republicans. But he knew the others too . . .!'[22] One evening Trott had dinner with Donovan's brother, a 'charming Dominican Father' (sic),[23] but with the colonel himself, he does not seem to have had a long talk.* In the light of the attitude which Washington, and indeed Donovan, took to Trott during the war, this was a great pity.†

Trott was looking for contacts within the administration and with this in mind he made use of a number of former Rhodes Scholars, including the Editor of the Washington Post, Felix Morley, another friend of Leverkühn's. He wrote to Shiela Grant Duff describing Morley: 'Saturday I lunched with a he-man of a journalist, the editor of the Washington Post, [a] good fatherly friend he might be. He walks down the street like a ranch-owner, broad stepped as though the place belonged to him.'[24] Morley confided in his diary for 31 March his impressions of the young German:

Von Trott, Leverkühn's German Rhodes Scholar friend, proved a thoroughly delightful young fellow and I was glad to pay back some of the past hospitality

---

* See below, pp 159–161.

† 'Have been given very varied and interesting letters of introduction. I made the mistake of reading all the names to my host in NY the other day, because he is somewhat at the top of the opposite faction [i.e. Donovan]. He is in with the big business world, though himself a kind, humble, Catholic lawyer now. I was trying not to trespass on his time when I first met him – there was a queue of business waiting – but he said, now you stop and sit down quietly because I would seriously like to help you. He then sent me to the president of the second biggest bank [in] . . . the world – across Wall Street [from] where his office is – to give me introductions to China!' (Letter to Shiela Grant Duff, about 26 March 1937.)

98

in that country [*sic*]. He spoke with exceeding frankness of the repression of the Nazi regime and he regards a popular uprising as by no means impossible, it will be a ghastly business if it comes.[25]

Trott's great-uncle Schieffelin had given him a letter to Cordell Hull, the Secretary of State, but the minister was sadly absent from Washington.[26] Trott was, however, able to visit ex-Secretary of State Henry Stimson, in his 'wonderful house'. Stimson, who was brought back as Secretary for War during the Second World War, had earlier in the 1930s made a strong stand against the Japanese; Trott described him as a 'wise and beautiful old man who was most encouraging about China.'[27] In the administration itself, Trott spoke to the Secretary for Labour, Frances Perkins, for two hours in her office. 'We completely charmed each other, I thought – anyhow she me – and she seemed to go on talking quite willingly – on sit-down strikes, religion and that politics are only such a small part of life – she was very nice. A big warm, stable perceptive mind she brings to play on things.'[28] Trott also met another Rhodes Scholar in the State Department, Dr Stanley Hornbeck, who ran the Chinese department and his assistant, Herbert Feis. He also had interviews with the 'great senators', Robert la Follette and Robert Wagner.[29]

In Washington, his time was also taken up with Jay memorabilia and night-time trips to 'negro cafés'.[30] There was also his American family, which consisted of a great many well-placed cousins. Returning to his great-uncle's apartment in Park Avenue in New York, he was drawn into the American season – walking in Central Park by moonlight with his cousins, hating the New York streets 'numbered like files', admiring the 'skyscapers and their aspect by night.'[31] One group of cousins he was drawn to were the Osborns.

> I stayed with them in the country last weekend and they have a house in the middle of the woods and six dogs and three horses on which we galloped through the country . . . they have a house in New York and go out for the weekends. They are all over six foot tall and really very charming and innocent and quite intelligent. Others are in business and very eager patricians – i.e. very much one of the '800 families' – running all sorts of useful and useless enterprises, functions, balls and charities.[32]

With Margery Osborn, one of General Osborn's daughters, Trott fell in love. This worried the father, engendering a 'distrust' which Trott thought 'only natural in the present international situation'.[33] Margery Osborn was 'very tall and very young and beautiful in her way'.[34] He described her as belonging to 'a more sensitive type of the New England aristocracy which is fighting a defensive battle against the absolute supremacy of the vulgarians.'[35] When Trott was not hob-nobbing with the 800, he was indulging his fascination for the

American blacks. 'I like the blacks the more I see of them and I like the coarse primeval independence of the ruffians in the streets.'[36]

While in New York, Trott met Roger Baldwin, the head of the American Civil Liberties Union, a brave man who had suffered imprisonment for his views and who took to Trott immediately. Trott had had an introduction to Baldwin from Sir Stafford Cripps. His wife and children also liked Trott, who fought a prolonged pillow battle with the younger Baldwins, during which 'they got quite wild'.[37] After Trott left for China Baldwin wrote him an encouraging letter:

> You are, I think, doing the only thing a Westerner can do in China, cultivating your own outlook and loyalties in a world that demands the hardest kind of decision of any of us. And for a young man confronting a life in Germany of all places, your decisions are vastly more painful than ours here in a country where democracy and capitalism still function with enough power to give us what passes for freedom. We need have no reservations anyhow, however little any of us can do to effect historical processes. You have an unusual independence of thought and feeling and the courage to follow where your mind leads. Whatever you do, whatever direction you take I shall respect it and know it is right for you. Honour is a great asset in understanding; and you belong to that universal class, found in all lands, who see things whole, historically, with vision. Nationalism to us is an illusion for the masses, a tragic and terrible force, to be transformed one of these days into an internationalism of the sort we sense and live . . .[38]

From New York Trott travelled on to Canada, stopping off at Harvard on the way. At the university, Trott had an introduction from Isaiah Berlin to Felix Frankfurter, Byrne Professor of Administrative Law and an intimate adviser to President Roosevelt. Frankfurter had been at Balliol and Trott and he were able to dwell on past experiences in common, even if Mrs Frankfurter found him, 'too darned good looking'.[39] Among the other jurists Trott found an air of pessimism or indifference; 'It is not far-fetched to suppose that this is attributable to the relationship of the universities to business circles.'[40]

In Ottawa Trott stayed with Lord Tweedsmuir, the Governor General of Canada who, as John Buchan, had written the great adventure stories which featured Richard Hannay. To Tweedsmuir, Trott communicated something of the current feeling of people in his circle in Germany. Tweedsmuir wrote about Trott to the Prime Minister of Canada, Mackenzie King. 'There are thousands of people like himself,' he said, referring to those opposed to Nazism. Trott gave Tweedsmuir some of the thinking current in Resistance circles of the time, with its belief that the National Socialist movement had somehow been captured by extremists, 'His own feeling is that Hitler himself is fairly reasonable and that even Göring is not without elements of common sense, and that the influence of Goebbels and his type is rapidly decreasing.'[41] The view of Hitler as a moderate is

100

surprising in the light of what we know today. He was an enigmatic figure to most Germans, presumably because of the difficulty they had in penetrating the Messiah image which had been invented for him by the Nazi media. That Göring was a reasonable man was a view held in many high-ranking circles, even after the beginning of the war.

The readiness to treat Göring apart from the Nazi leadership in general may at first sight seem a trifle surprising . . . Several contemporaries had their own facetious explanations. The British liked Göring, Rauschning suggested, because he did not pick his teeth during diplomatic conversations. A British diplomat at the Hague told his Swedish colleague that the Reichmarshal was preferable because, unlike Hitler, he ate, drank, and slept with women just like a normal human being.[42]

While Trott was in Canada most of this time was spent in the 'royal household' of the governor general.

I bowed dutifully whenever they came in or out of a door, led by a (rather nice) young naval officer shouting: THEIR EXCELLENCIES! There was another aide-de-camp . . . a charming, apple-cheeked smiling, uncertain youngster who agreed with most things I said, and shaking his head ponderously would repeat: 'You know I believe you Germans are in many ways not unlike ourselves.' But he wasn't at all arrogant, and enjoyed court life like an eighteenth-century page. I liked him too. But best of all I liked the 'Comptroller of the Household', a heavy, beautiful big colonel with a blond moustache and the most British physiognomy I have ever seen. Whenever he said something very difficult like how far away some spot on the mountain was, or who was coming to dinner, he had to shut his eyes and lean his head back on his strong neck. We took a great mutual liking for each other, I think. His girl told me he had said to her, 'I don't usually like his Exc's guest but . . .'[43]

After his success with the colonel, Trott's odyssey took him on to Chicago, where he wished to consult one or two heads of department at the university. During his stay he indulged his new passion for Negro bars. One of these boasted

Negro men dressed as women, and performing wild and exotic dances alone and in groups. Really beautiful creatures in build and even in features. The place packed with a discriminating coloured public hurling dollar bills at their favourite singers and dancers. They are wonderful, these Negroes – so uninhibited and gentle, full of natural vitality and yet very vulnerable to our type of civilization. They all have an expression of passionate suffering somehow, I mean the finer ones have.[44]

Trott liked the Midwest in general: 'I found too, that the real magic of America lay out here in this wide-open unpopulated region with its simple, unspoilt people.'[45]

Adam von Trott's objective for the time being was Julie Braun-Vogelstein's house in Carmel, California, where several strands of his existence were to coalesce for a period of calm, before his going on to China. With Julie Braun-Vogelstein and her niece was Hasso von Seebach with whom relations had become difficult in New York. There was to be a reconcilation in California. Dr Wolfram Eberhard was also there in the capacity of Trott's Chinese tutor. In nearby Taft was Miriam Dyer-Bennet, Trott's love from Göttingen days and for whom he had, to a greater or lesser degree, maintained the same affection throughout the years since their parting.

Mrs Braun-Vogelstein was devoted to Trott. Trott on the other hand was not so certain about her, occasionally reserving a harsh word for his benefactress in his letters. This possibly had much to do with Hasso Seebach's defection to the United States, something which Trott felt strongly about. In one of the rare letters he sent her from Germany, he touched on this issue. 'How do you find things? Are you flourishing away from your home soil? Or is it the more Christian notion of "home is where your heart is"? If I could say that of myself then it would be easier to go on.'[46]

Once in California he became reconciled to 'Hasso's *Pflegemutter*' (foster-mother, but also 'nurse')[47] and in the relaxed atmosphere of those days, he opened out as if he had been

> released from imprisonment . . . he often said to me that he had never before felt so much at one with his work. The gloomy puritanical lines vanished from his face, the tension lifted. Every afternoon we walked along the coast relaxing on the cliffs or in a meadow surrounded with wild flowers. In those hours he would open his heart to me. He spoke of his childhood and the conflicts of his youth, his hopes and fears, his doubts and beliefs. As we wandered on he would tell funny stories, but for the most part he interrupted himself as he broached a philosophical or political problem. On one of these digressions he fell into a prolonged silence and then exclaimed, 'There is no way out but Socialism . . .' Then, after a moment, very shyly as if aware of some fallacy, 'If I were in England, of course, I would join the Conservative Party.' 'Tory Socialism,' I laughed and he brightened, as he always did when he felt himself understood.[48]

In his 'little *Gelehrtenrepublik*' (republic of letters)[49] Trott's relations with Seebach began to improve. As the latter wrote after the war,

> . . . In California, Adam used to amuse himself by comparing me to the seals which gathered in packs in the fish-rich waters and on the cliffs on Carmel's coastline. At that time Adam's criticism was always kind and well disposed towards me, and we often laughed together. At the time he wanted to make his relations with friends and acquaintances as friendly as possible . . .

Later he became difficult and occasionally harsh. 'The reigning prince casts aside his kid gloves' was his Hessian slogan and his warning.

In this manner we lay on the beach of China Cove on Point Lobos – him, Miriam, her son Fred and I, on a stretch of deep snow-white sand only a few feet wide, at the foot of the most beautiful, narrow, cliff-hanging, enclosed creek on the Pacific Ocean. All the while, he went this way and that, making jokes, plans or light-hearted reflections about me. 'Really, there is scarcely any difference between you and the seals; you cavort around in the sun, wind, beach and water'; and later, something reproachful, 'For me the head has always been the most important part of the body' . . . As he spoke to us in this way and pranced around us along those beach walks, he and his Gothic air seemed alien to the beauty of nature as we found it. He was all intellect, yet he never lost his romantic love of nature; he was rooted in the hills and forests of his ancestral Hessian homeland, which was forever calling him back . . .[50]

Trott's teasing of Seebach seems to have had the right effect, and the 'profound grudge'[51] he had felt on his arrival gradually disappeared, especially after the arrival of Eberhard from whom he took daily Chinese lessons. To Diana Hubback he promised 'soon I shall write you a Chinese letter'.[52] With Miriam Dyer-Bennet he also effected a reconciliation. He went over to the town of Taft to stay with her. From Taft he went to stay in Los Angeles, where he visited a film studio in Hollywood. While he was there he hoped to meet both Charlie Chaplin and the novelist Upton Sinclair. There is no evidence that he saw either.

Trott was still worried by the situation in Germany and the possibility of a European war which was all that he sought to stave off. He admitted that the means at the Germans' disposal to deal with their internal problems were few, but that his people should not be castigated for that alone; 'If a man uses a wooden axe to rescue something from the fire and (offering no other tool) somebody else argues that a wooden axe is not good enough – he has no claim to be heard.'[53] As for his own role in the process, he still saw himself as politically impotent, something that his Chinese apprenticeship would possibly solve. 'I left Germany with the conviction that powerful processes making for peace were at work there – but that I could not substantially contribute anything to them myself.'[54]

Increasingly he realized that the Americans were unlikely to want to be drawn into a European peace-keeping exercise and that he could not bank on them. This was the gist of his essay 'Amerikanische Eindrücke', where he compared America to a country whose foreign policy was in dry-dock, the people having lost interest in foreign policy after the First World War. His hope lay in an Anglo-German friendship which might eventually result in a German-American friendship. Their political naiveté later caused him to lose his temper on the boat to China: 'I sometimes think we Huns are really better people [than

Anglo-Saxons]. I had to listen to a lot of rubbish on this boat and finally behaved very badly myself by telling the good Americans more or less diplomatically what I thought of their barbarism.'[55]

With the theme for his Chinese work being settled as 'Why Subjects Obey', Trott was returning to the issues of political philosophy which had always entranced him. In Kierkegaard he saw a means of renouncing Hegel. 'I have read some Kierkegaard again on this trip,' he wrote from the boat. 'He answers some of my profoundest dissatisfactions with Hegel and he will enter into my final criticism of his political philosophy which is taking me so many years.'[56] In a letter to Shiela Grant Duff he emphasized the danger of Nietzsche. 'N is good, in parts most noble and encouraging stuff too, but I believe we will have to fight him tooth and nail.'[57]

After a number of hitches, stemming partially from the late arrival of funds from Britain, Trott finally boarded a Chinese ship on 16 July 1937. Writing to his English friends, he emphasized the need to carry on with the elaborate codes used in previous correspondence. The war had started up again between the Japanese and the Chinese and German spies were bound to be crawling all over the sub-continent. The Japanese from now on were to be 'barons' and the Chinese, 'peasants'.[58]

The purpose of Trott's stay in China was to prepare his *Habilitationsschrift*, the thesis which would partly qualify him to enter a German university, and thus avoid the pressures to join the Nazi party incumbent on him in other walks of life. The subject postulated to the Rhodes Trust in 1936 had been on the old theme of international law and how Chinese law slotted into the framework existing in Germany and the West. From his exchange of letters with Gösta Ecke that year he was aware of the possibility of teaching work at Yenching University in Peking for the time he was there. He also knew Ecke was prepared to lodge him.

The university idea greatly appealed to the Rhodes trustees, who distrusted the idea of his being a roaming scholar. It also went some way to placate Allen. Another force who had added his voice to those in favour was Edward Carter of the Institute of Pacific Relations in New York, which had already encouraged Rhodes House to take a wider view on the discretionary third-year grants.

Ecke was delighted with the plan, he was himself writing a book on Chinese history and was just the man Trott needed to explain the Chinese state 'at all levels'. As Ecke wrote in 1957, 'the thought of a responsible young German and future statesman coming into contact with the Confucian idea seemed excellent to me.' In addition, the thought of getting Trott out of Germany must have appealed to Ecke who had returned in 1933 after an absence of ten years to find the

Nazis in power. At that moment he had made the decision to return to China for an indefinite period.

As Ecke observed, Trott's problem was that Japan was destroying his project by eliminating the Chinese state. Trott became aware of this before even reaching China, when, as a result of the newly flared-up conflict, he was forced to disembark at Hong Kong. Shanghai was 'flooded by Japanese ships and troops',[59] and he made use of his time in the Crown Colony by contacting Sir William Hornell, the President of Hong Kong University. Hornell suggested Trott visit Canton. Taking up the idea, Trott stayed at Lingnan University where he learned that his great-uncle, Dr Schieffelin was chairman of the trustees. The Provost of Lingnan, Dr Henry, thought that Trott's best plan was to explore Kwangsi province, using Lingnan as his base. In the event of Peking being cut off by the Japanese, Kwangsi was one of the most developed provinces in China. Trott returned to Hong Kong to contact Eberhard, who had arrived in Tokyo, cabling Eberhard to join him.

Despite mishaps, Adam von Trott was happy to be within reach of his goals.

China is amazing. The soldiers of Kwantung look like children, but one of our generals who was returning from leave in Java to Nanking told me the central government troops are good stuff. Peasant boys, quick on the uptake, brave and loyal. I also met a Chinese general – an American or Canadian gunman originally, they say – who conveyed a little of what is in the Chinese fighting spirit this time. And yesterday I spoke to someone who had just come down from Shanghai – it must be hell.[60]

The German general whom Trott had met was possibly von Falkenhausen, the head of the Germany Military Mission to China. Falkenhausen was politically anathema to the Nazis and had been pushed out of Germany to China before the Night of the Long Knives,[61] which might well have included him in its victims. As a subaltern at the turn of the century, the general had served in China and he knew the country and its people well. Trott was later to have contact with him in Germany. While he waited for Eberhard and tried to decide what he must do in the changed circumstances, he stayed in a German-run hostel in Hong Kong, 'luckily clean'[62] in view of the cholera epidemic which was making its way from Shanghai in the company of refugees from the war. Life in Hong Kong, a semi-colonial society in which he was obliged to drink too much in the company of English people, became increasingly onerous. He lacked introductions to those parts of China as yet unaffected by the war and asked Shiela Grant Duff if she might not be able to procure some through her friend Peter Fleming of *The Times*. He toyed with the idea of scrapping the subject altogether and going to South Africa via India.

Eberhard, however, finally arrived from Japan and, armed with introductions from Lord Lothian, the two went up to Canton to see the Governor and Marshal of Kwangsi. There they experienced their first air-raid, wakened during the night by the visit of nine Japanese bombers – a rude foretaste of life during the war in Germany. Two of the marauding planes were shot down.

> It was a beautiful sight seeing three of the attackers disappear into the dawning sun with a silhouette of a pagoda looming up sharply on the horizon, the bamboo hedges of our garden in the foreground, and all the incredible wealth of unheard-of tropical flowers and bushes . . . At every corner you see soldiers with mounted bayonets, and even coolies with guns. Everybody is terribly excited and half Canton is evacuated.[63]

A German alliance with Japan was becoming increasingly likely. In 1936, Japan had been brought into the Anti-Comintern Pact, effective from the following year. The drift of German policy in the Far East was clear to see. For Trott a Germano-Japanese alliance would have put an end to his projects, something which filled him with unhappiness,

> It's damn hard to give up the north and Peking, but it would have been awful to be there under the Japanese auspices – it will probably work out that, if we get out of these bombardments all right, we'll travel through Kwangsi and go back to Hong Kong from where Eberhard will reimbark for Europe and I for Japan, India and South Africa – if I make the Rhodes trustees see my point.[64]

Trott and Eberhard continued their journey despite the mounting dangers, travelling up the Si-kiang river to Wuchow, the Kwei river to Kweilin and the Losing river to Nanning. On 21 September he wrote from the Kwei river:

> We have been on a sampan for five days, and will be for another two. You must imagine a middle-size wooden boat – looking, as a Chinese writer put it, 'like an upturned egg-shell with a roof over it' – in which we dwell under the mat-roofed middle part while two men row in front and one man at the back. There is also the wife of the man at the back – he's the owner of the boat – and two very nice little daughters and all that on a bottom of wood of probably less than twenty square metres. It's like travelling in a gipsy cart only that they are much cleaner and entirely adapted to the river which they never leave . . . They are supposed to be the most ignorant and lowest race and caste around here and knowing this may add to their extreme modesty. The little girls do nothing but stare at us all day and try to bring things when we appear to be wanting something – it's an experience which is entirely out of the ordinary for them as few Europeans travel round here. The mother cooks our meals on a space of three square feet and it tastes quite nice once it's ready.[65]

Trott grew rapidly disillusioned about learning Chinese – Cantonese or Mandarin, 'You cannot get very far without the language . . . and in

106

the language you cannot get very far within one year – so perhaps providence with this bloody war has really spared me an impossible attempt.'[66] In Wuchow, Eberhard laughed and joked with officials while Trott was frustrated, 'having to stand aside like a bore.'[67] On the Si-Kiang river they were received by a young Chinese banker. 'The entertainment consisted of music played on cymbals, bells, drums, singing girls, rice wine, a delicious menu of shark's fin, swallows' nests and doves' eggs, and the gaiety of their companions all of which seemed as unreal as a fairy tale.'[68]

They took a bus cross-country to Liuchow, learning about local arts and crafts, and proceeding to Kweilin, the seat of a provincial governor and the former seat of the Imperial provincial administration. The place had taken on the appearance of a garrison city and it was deemed inadvisable to stay long. From a Roman Catholic priest they learned that Japanese propaganda was using the new Japano-German friendship as a plank in their campaign against the Chinese. Antagonism towards Germans seemed to be on the cards. In addition, there were rumours of a plot to overthrow the provincial government by either the Japanese or the Communists. The presence of two strange Germans must have looked very odd indeed. The day after they arrived seventy-two people were shot as 'Japanese spies'. Trott and Eberhard decided that the prudent solution was to leave as soon as possible and so they took a sampan to Wuchow, arriving in Hong Kong on 24 September. From Tokyo, Trott wrote that he had had a miraculous number of escapes from disaster: 'earthquake in Manila, epidemic here, bombing in Canton, shooting and arrest in Kwangsi, running into mines on the Canton River and being shot at by Japanese warships when we passed them, and last and by no means least the typhoon here which cost some 10,000 lives.'[69]

Trott was in Tokyo from a 'sense of duty', otherwise unexplained, but probably motivated by the need to get the Embassy's clearance to go to Peking. Before leaving China, an argument had broken out between him and Eberhard. Trott persisted in his project to go on to Peking which had fallen to the Japanese. Eberhard maintained that being in the city under Japanese occupation would be like living in National Socialist Germany, with the German 'friends' (i.e. Nazis) being able to discipline their own subjects from Berlin through their close ties with the invaders. Trott chose to overlook the problem – probably realizing that he would have to abandon his project otherwise. As it transpired Eberhard had no desire to return to Germany. He had already taken the decision to emigrate and encouraged Trott to do the same. This was not a sympathetic argument for Trott who maintained that it was the 'citizen's obligation to remove the ruling authority'.* In early October Eberhard decided to

---

* *John Locke called a revolution to remove a tyrant 'an appeal to Heaven.'*

take up the offer of a teaching post at the University of Ankara, and Trott proceeded to Peking.

Having received a cable from Ecke – 'Welcome beginning October, own risk' – Trott sailed to Tientsin, arriving by train in Peking on 20 October 1937.[70] Ecke met him at the station bringing him to his house in 'a mixture of palace and peasant quarter outside the inner city and surrounded by trees'.[71] The following morning he made his first tour of Peking.

> It is all very strange. The huge imperial city with a dead life. The Europeans seem like dwarfs in it all – persevering tenaciously with their petty habits from home. But we live so far out that I shall see little of them. My host [Ecke] is a very peculiar man – a little like a magician. Our household will not be very easy. Imagine yourself being suddenly surrounded by [a] huge, cold calmness, ancient and solemn, looking down on you, as it were, and waiting with an ironic smile which turn you're going to take next. The deadness and forlorn beauty of it all is bewitching and one feels like a fool outfooled.[72]

To his father Trott wrote, '. . . In spite of the war, this town emanates an atmosphere of superior calm for which it is famous. It is this which attracted me here, and I have not been disappointed.'[73] Apart from trips to Japan, Manchuria, Shantung and Shanghai, Trott remained in the city for a year, concentrating on Confucian political philosophy, to which end he had discussions with Confucian scholars and Ecke in Peking wine houses. At Yenching University, the President, Leighton Stuart, made him a 'special student', and on the advice of Professor W. Hing he 'buried himself in ancient Chinese political philosophy.'[74] Gradually he was coming round to a more solid object for his *Habilitationsschrift*: 'The Classical Concept of Sovereignty in China.'

Trott was still worried about his ability to master Chinese in the time. He was equally worried by Anglo-German discord. In the growing atmosphere of suspicion between the two countries, Trott with his love of Britain felt particularly torn, not wishing to show any outward antagonism towards Germany on the one hand and not wishing to lose his English friends on the other. Something of this comes across in a passage from Harold Acton's memoirs. Acton met Trott in the house of one Leopold von Plessen in Peking in 1938 and found him 'a suave international figure'. They talked about Oxford and Maurice Bowra but did not get to know one another well. Acton thought Trott was a member of the German legation.[75] In his memoirs Acton gives a picture of the Peking German colony in the period.

> The manifest signs and symptons pointed to another war in Europe. A German acquaintance of mine had urged me to read *Mein Kampf*: surely that was clear enough. He could not help being dazzled by Hitler. Germans of Jewish blood were losing their posts in Chinese universities and even in firms and hospitals, owing to persistent intrigues of their Aryan rivals. Most of them attached

108

Swastika flags to their private rickshaws. Even with the seemingly anglicized Adam von Trott I never felt sure of his intimate convictions. The German Embassy was a hotbed of sinister denunciations and the amiable Ambassador Trautmann, an old-fashioned diplomatist, was eyed askance by his subordinates as insufficiently Nazi.[76]

Trott had sunk into the discreet persona which years of Nazi rule had made second nature to him. He had not abandoned the idea of returning to Germany and was aware all the time of how Nazi officials in China and their contact men were measuring him up, observing his meetings with non-Germans. Even the 'hermit'[77] Ecke noticed how buttoned up Trott had become, but never sought to challenge him about it. 'I often had the distinct feeling that there were many things he had no wish to speak about and for my part I never put any pressure on him to talk. All the time I had the impression that whatever he had in his head was both good and responsible.'[78]

Besides the need not to be seen to be against the regime, Trott was making use of the German Embassy library for his sources on German philosophy. Given what Acton says about the Nazis in the German diplomatic corps it would have been a mistake to be too open there. Their distrust of Trott was evident enough to him: 'I have a bad reputation with them [the local Germans]. They think me baronial and conceited and perhaps politically undesirable.' The poor impression he was making was not confined to the Germans: 'The Americans here have been told about certain deprecating remarks which I made in the wrong company about their country, and they dislike me.' As regards the British, 'I have said a little too boastfully that I don't wish to be invited and the world fashion [for] . . . being anti-German adds to it all, so that all in all I am very much out of favour with European Peking.'[79]

Trott's feeling about the Westerners in Peking may smack of persecution mania, but it is true that with one or two exceptions he remained aloof from Europeans, refusing to enter into discussions on Nazism and the current state of Germany.* 'With the representatives of urbane elegance,' wrote Ecke, 'he happily took part in equestrian events, while giving nothing of his private existence away.'[80] From his letters to friends, however, this appears to have been a deliberate policy, both to keep out of the way of the Nazis and in order to complete the work he came to China to do.

I am going to take French lessons from a White Russian former diplomat probably, or from a Chinese girl who was brought up in Paris. I shall be neither social nor flirtatious and I am meeting 'old China hands' in preference to the legation quarter where Gerry Young has risen to some prominence and treats

* He did none the less give a speech to the German club on Anglo-German relations since 1870, praising Bismarck for keeping the peace.

me with friendliest hospitality. Our home is our castle though – it is run [in] . . . the slow and dignified style of Imperial Peking, with even the children of the servants playing their part . . . Actually it is not aesthetic spleen, but an ingenious design to rescue a calm retreat for thought and work. You and I know that this is a hard secret . . .[81]

His friendship with Gerry Young notwithstanding, the British were also watching Trott in China, officially or unofficially. Later when Cripps sought to defend his friend to Eden in the Cabinet, the latter told him of damaging material going back to Trott's time in China. John Fulton, Trott's philosophy tutor from Balliol also heard something suspicious and reported it to Warden Adams of All Souls. The story in Oxford was helped on its way by the presence in Peking of Michael Lindsay, the son of the Master of Balliol, who was perplexed by Trott's desire to go to Tokyo.* Yenching University was a warren of anti-Japanese activity and Trott was seen as a possible spy. Once again the cloudiness of the man – brought on by the need for extreme prudence – gave rise to a great many rumours which ultimately harmed him in the quarters which would be of most use to him later, like the British Foreign Office, where he acquired a reputation as a 'trimmer'. His interest in practical politics and fascination for guerilla warfare were also misinterpreted by Western observers more and more inclined to see him as a bad element.

To be distant from diplomatic and commercial circles Trott retired to a house in a Chinese garden near Yenching where he was attended by a native servant while he pored over the necessary books for his task. If he was immune from the pleasures of cosmopolitan society, he was not oblivious to the charms of the city. He wrote to Martin von Katte:

Peking and its common people, and above all its gorgeous landscape, spreads itself out uninterrupted before me. I am writing you this from an old Lama temple outside the city, where hundreds of Christians were slaughtered at the time of the Boxer Rebellion. Even today you can still see the dent in the stone where their famous broadswords were sharpened.[82]

Something of his lack of interest in the European community is expressed in his letter to the Secretary to the Rhodes trustees, Millar, in London. 'The merchants are gloomy and the Western aesthetes cluster around their antiquarian interests and try to forget the trouble which is only too visible on the streets.'[83] Totalitarianism, occupation and repression were not new to Trott, and though they must have considerably detracted from the pleasure of his 'retreat', he knew enough about 'inner emigration' to be able to deal with it.

---

* Michael Lindsay, later 2nd Baron Lindsay of Birker, was a lecturer at Yenching University 1937–41.

Increasingly, Trott's inability to get to grips with Chinese in the limited time available to him proved a stumbling block in his desire to construct a political system in which a common denominator could be found between Eastern and Western ideas. The idea underlying this ambitious reinterpretation of political philosophy was a need to find an ideal for the reconstruction of Germany and ultimately Europe on a more stable and less dangerous framework. If, however, the project has a slightly far-fetched air, it should be borne in mind that this was exactly what the Kreisau Circle were trying to effect in their discussions during the war, as indeed were those circles centring on Popitz and Goerdeler.[84]

Even if they were unlikely to bear fruit, these 'meditations in tranquillity' had the beneficial effect of allowing Trott's mind to breathe in an atmosphere removed (though perhaps not far enough) from Germany. To his father he wrote describing the impasse he was in:

> ... I am more and more convinced that my original plan to analyse the Chinese concept of the state, not knowing Chinese characters, will not rise above the level of an experiment conducted with insufficient means. Working on my subject every day in this tranquillity – now in complete solitude in an ancient, walled-in temple outside the city – is a cure and a strengthening preparation for whatever course I shall have to take on my return home.[85]

Still, if Trott was not able to make any large-scale progress in this project, he was able to return to the original idea of international law and international relations and this was expressed in his paper, 'East Asian Possibilities'. As he wrote to his cousin Adelbert von Unruh, 'What seems to me essential in contemporary international relations and politics is the question of how the various sovereign powers justify their claim to impose the ultimate jurisdiction within their boundaries, while in their relations with each other they accept no mutually binding legal yardstick.'[86]

The catalyst behind Trott's paper was the change in direction in Nazi foreign policy which was signalled by the replacement of Neurath by Ribbentrop in February 1938. Neurath had been a throwback to the old National-Socialist-Conservative alliance which had come to power in 1933; he was not the man to put forward the 'revolutionary' Nazi foreign policy which would lead to a new order in Europe. That mission was entrusted to Ribbentrop, who had been in charge of the Nazi foreign policy bureau since Hitler's coming to power. Ribbentrop's appointment gave the go-ahead to *Gleichschaltung* (bringing into line with Nazi ideology) in the Foreign Office which was still very much dominated by traditional diplomats of the old school. It is a measure of Ribbentrop's incapacity as a new broom that Goebbels was still complaining in the spring of 1945 that the Foreign Office had not accepted Nazi ideas.

111

One of Ribbentrop's earliest moves was to recall Falkenhausen's military mision, announcing a closer rapport with the Japanese and turning Anglo-German relations on to a collision course in the Far East. Trott was fascinated by the idea of an Anglo-German *rapprochement* being worked out over China and this was behind the essay written in early July 1938. The original was in German and was sent to Trott's father and mother to have fifty copies made and circulated among influential figures in Germany. These included the former Ambassador to China and Ambassador to London Dirksen, Minister Schacht, Ambassadors Ott in Tokyo and Trautmann in Peking, Minister Schwerin von Krosigk, Hans von Dohnanyi, Wilfrid Israel, Peter Bielenberg, Professor Herbert Kraus, Gottfried von Nostitz, Hans Muhle and Göring's respectable cousin Herbert, the friend of Ambassador Hassell who acted as a liaison between the conservative resisters and the clownish Hermann.

Peter Fleming of the *The Times* took the paper to London, where Trott managed to prevail upon Millar in the Rhodes Trust offices to have it retyped and copied. The essence of the paper is in the covering note to Lord Lothian, where he suggests that there was a

> . . . constructive way out of the mess in which China, Japan, England and Germany are finding themselves in the Far East. Could it be found in Anglo-German political co-operation and possibly as joint move for peace? . . . British and German interests were equally threatened and the expansion of the Japanese empire would lead to still more intensified conflict with the major world powers.
>
> Japan needs Germany's military and [to] some extent moral support – she needs England economically. Her soldiers would listen to Germany, her politicans and businessmen to England's representatives. A joint move would probably be irresistible.[87]

Appended to the English translation of 'Far Eastern Possibilities' was a short list of people to whom Trott wished the report to be circulated: H.N. Spalding, Dr Allen, Lord Lothian and Lord Astor. Trott's earlier reports had come under the gaze of leading conservatives who acted as Rhodes trustees; in February Millar had forwarded a pile of them to the Colonial Secretary Amery – 'Lord Lothian thinks you might like to see the enclosed reports he has had from von Trott (Germany 1931). Will you please circulate them with this letter to Mr Dawson [i.e. the Editor of *The Times*, Geoffrey Dawson], Sir Edward Peacock and Sir Sothern Holland. We shall be pleased to have the papers back after the trustees have had the opportunity of seeing them.'[88]

On his own initiative Lothian sent the paper to Lord Halifax, adding that Trott was 'suffocated in the Third Reich' and suggesting that 'Halifax and his office would like to read it.'[89] Halifax had taken over at the Foreign Office after Eden's resignation that February. His department, noting Lothian's recommendation that it 'might pave the way for better relations in Europe', read Trott's essay with interest. One official jotted in the margin, 'This is an interesting paper, it is written in a thoroughly German idiom but the underlying argument and the common sense behind it is clear enough. Personally, I have always thought it would be politic to encourage the Germans to collaborate with us whenever possible in the Far East.'[90] The same anonymous hand added that the best course would be to get in touch with Ambassador Dirksen on his return.

The paper then passed through the hands of various minor officials in the department who duly minuted approval. (one wonders how many of these were later to add their facetious comments to Trott's memoranda during the war years). Two things, however, proved insuperable obstacles to Anglo-German co-operation in the summer of 1938: one was the worsening situation in Czechoslovakia where tension had been mounting since the full-scale war scare in March and the other was the German refusal to appreciate economic arguments in the face of military ones. The paper disappeared in the wake of Munich.

At the beginning of March 1938, Trott set out for Japan, reaching the coast at Tientsin and sailing from Tangku to Moji. From Beppu he wrote to Shiela Grant Duff, of his climb to the summit of Mount Aso,

> the largest volcano in the world. It may seem strange to you that while the face of Europe is being changed I should idle in this wilderness. I infinitely prefer it to humiliating inactivity at home, and to cut loose and free from all attachments that are not essential and independent of periodical reassurances makes me better inside.[91]

His mind was already turning on a longer escape to the East, with a new conception of the Chinese work as a magnum opus.

> I don't know quite how long I am going to stay in the East. I have started to work seriously on their political philosophy and the collection of this material may take longer than my intended stay. So far it seems probable that I shall sail in October, pass through India and possibly stay a while in Turkey on my way home. The question is financial more than anything else but my chief concern is the book I want to bring [with me].[92]

On 11 March Germany annexed Austria. Trott had never approved the Versailles solution when it came to Austria (or anywhere else) and had no reason to lament the Anschluss any more than did the vast majority of Austrians. For the moment he glossed over the development a little unthinkingly in his correspondence with Shiela Grant Duff who had taken the Czech cause to her bosom and saw the annexation of Austria as a means of encircling Czechoslovakia. Trott wrote somewhat airily from Japan, 'I wonder where you were when we took Austria. You will probably have to revise a good number of your premises – though your experiences of the countries concerned will be specially valuable for digesting these new developments.'[93] In truth, in his isolation, it took a while before Trott was able to appreciate fully what had happened on 11 March, and to differentiate between a legitimate alteration of what he believed to be an unjust treaty, and a step towards world domination on the part of a criminal adventurer.

While in Tokyo, Trott's movements were observed by the British Embassy. He was seen in the company of Generalmajor Ott whom the British obviously took for a Nazi. Ott was a friend of the 'red general', Hammerstein-Equord, the former chief of the armed forces who had been relieved of his command in 1934. Hammerstein was a fierce critic of Hitler and his replacement by Fritsch was meant to render him harmless. It was Hammerstein in conjunction with another friend, Schleicher, who had contrived to get Ott out of Germany before the Night of the Long Knives. In Japan he survived while Schleicher perished in Germany. Trott probably had an introduction to him from Hammerstein's son-in-law, his friend and kinsman Münchhausen. On 1 April Ott was promoted ambassador.

At the end of April Trott sailed from Hiroshima to Korea, travelling north to Manchuria. In mid May he visited Mukden and the Russian-leased city of Harbin. In the latter he was taken round a German firm and expressed an interest in the work they were doing. Writing to his mother, he said, 'Father would be happy to hear that I am putting his advice into practice, and keeping two professional irons in the fire.'[94] He returned to Peking at the end of May.

During Trott's time away from Europe, both in America and in the Far East, he had progessively drifted away from his emotional attachments in the West. While letters to his old friend Diana Hubback are factual and descriptive, his correspondence with Shiela Grant Duff plunges ever deeper into an unfathomable abyss. From her side she was witnessing the collapse of Europe into war, from a seat in London or Prague, while he was cultivating a Chinese garden in the East. Their letters make sad reading: seldom can a correspondence have been so wracked with misunderstanding. They never listen to one another's arguments. From Miss Grant Duff's point of view it seems that her fondness for Trott is entirely dependent upon the progress of Hitler's expansionist foreign policy. Trott *was* Germany, and as long as Germany was oppressing the smaller nations of Eastern Europe, Trott was going to have a hard time.*

---

* *For example: 'Last night we listened to Harold Nicolson on the Foreign Office, a very good, interesting lecture. Everybody was obviously expecting it to be just funny, and not when it was. He attacked* your friend *Brick and Drop* [i.e.

Trott still clung to the idea of preserving peace – not through classic appeasement (in the sense of throwing the dictator tit-bits in the hope he'd go away), but by trying to bring about an equitable solution to a *European* problem through the working out of a new European settlement. Shiela Grant Duff was an anti-appeaser, believing a firm stand on the Czech issue would result in an explosion in Germany in which Hitler would be removed. In this her views were not so far removed from those of the generals and opposition politicans who, under the leadership of General Beck, hoped to use the advent of war against Czechoslovakia as a pretext for removing Hitler and his henchmen. Shiela Grant Duff had already decided that the only hope lay in Winston Churchill. For Trott, Churchill had something of the aura of Bismarck in 1862 – 'only to be used when the bayonet reigns triumphant'. 'Isn't he a warmonger?' he asked her, 'Don't make yourself a wire in a cynical game of Central European power politics.'[95]

In the spring of that year, Shiela Grant Duff began to put together her book on the European crisis, *Europe and the Czechs.** The idea was to alert the British to the dangers of abandoning Czechoslovakia to the Nazis who were using the alleged victimization of Sudeten Germans in the north of the country in order to provoke a crisis which would lead to the cession of Sudetenland to Germany – if not the complete emasculation of Czechoslovakia. The Sudeten Germans, who had previously formed part of the Austro-Hungarian Empire, had been shabbily treated in the Versailles settlement which had refused them the right to 'national self-determination'. In the 1920s the new Czech republic had behaved in an over-lordly manner towards them and though by the 1930s it had made necessary concessions the Sudeteners, under their leader Henlein, had already pinned their hopes on the aggressive Nazi regime which had come to power across the border in Germany.

Once again, as a German, Trott can hardly have been expected to approve whole-heartedly the isolation of the Sudeten Germans, but he was none the less aware that Prague had become, after 1933, the refuge for *emigré* German socialist leaders like Friedrich Stampfer and renegade National Socialists like Strasser. As Miss Grant Duff herself put it in her book, 'For the persecuted Germans, Czechoslovakia has become a refuge . . . Prague has become the home of "the other Germany" – the Germany of Goethe and Kleist, of the poets and musicians.'[96] Trott was no doubt cheered by the reference to Kleist. On the other hand he was unlikely to be too thrilled by some of the more blatant partisanship of the little volume which postulated that, within Germany itself, a German was a Nazi and vice versa.

Ribbentrop] *very forcefully and met with complete silence.' (Letter from Shiela Grant Duff to Trott, about 5 October 1937. Author's italics.)*

* *The book was published on 30 September 1938.*

Shiela Grant Duff set out to prove her point by quoting Henlein himself, who had it that 'National Socialism corresponds with the manners and character of the German.'*⁹⁷ The book, a Penguin Special, is journalese, and good journalese, but to Trott, who despised the easy conclusions of journalists and who had a hundred times told his friend how much he resented her becoming one, this sort of line was a red rag to a bull. If the book was not to appear till the autumn, the tenor of its conclusions found its way into virtually every letter he received, the result being that Trott began to doubt his ability to go on with 'the best friendship in Europe'.⁹⁸

Trott for his part was still enjoying the inner contentment of the East.

> Sometimes I come home at night [he wrote from Peking], driven, or rather pulled by a gentle, barefooted coolie through the wide, deserted street leading north from the Palace, or, with my bicycle, ride through the moist and hot summer fields with their many groves and ups and downs. It's a completely new kind of solitude I enjoy away from all and everybody and . . . which I know is passing as fast as a dream.⁹⁹

On 20 July he wrote,

> I have just been up to Shansi and Suiyuan, lovely but miserably unhappy countries. I saw the upper reaches of the Yellow River, China's sorrow, and the Mongols and Turks who up there intermix with the Chinese. I wish fate had permitted your having come with me there and – as I did in Paotow [–] approach under a clear evening sky the far outlying pale brown mudwalls of that city which made it look like a fairy castle in [the] *Arabian Nights*. It is so far from the heat and bitterness of European family quarrels, so solemn, eternally oriental though held under martial law and only ten miles from enemy terrority. We were welcomed hospitably by an old Chinese merchant and another very scholastic but rather beautiful young dealer who offered me his girl for the night. I made her acquaintance, she came from Suiyan province while he had all the culture of the old capital. I did not sleep with her but she was nice and her little sister sang Chinese songs to us. In the streets, Mongol soldiers were galloping on their little horses, and bought their things in the bazaar-like open shops where donkeys were tied to poles as in the Bible. Later I made the acquaintance of a charming old Mongol prince and his lady and heard all the ideas which they inherited from Jenghis Khan. The great issues of the present international situation met most vitally in that region . . . Japanese, Mongol, Chinese, Russian, Western influences fighting it out on the back of the peasant

---

* In the light of Miss Grant Duff's attitude to Trott, certain passages seem distinctly illogical. 'If a Reich German ever used journeys abroad for the purpose of agitation against his government, as Henlein does in this country against the Czechoslovak Government, he would be arrested and shot on his return.' (Europe and the Czechs, p. 26) 'My book is terribly aggressive and I have written some things about the G[erman] mentality which you will not like but I am so convinced that it is anti-European and must change absolutely.' (To Trott, 23 June 1938.)

who mostly turns bandit or starves or survives in more sheltered areas after his own fashion.[100]

Enjoying the colour of the Orient, Trott accuses his correspondent of humour failure[101] in her persistent, irate letters from England – 'I think your proper attitude would be shame and to ask forgiveness,' she wrote.[102] In September he was off on his travels again, visiting Tientsin, Shantung province and Tsintao before repairing to Shanghai. On 24 September he wrote to his mother in Germany describing his return from the Temple of Chüfu in Shantung:

> I am not yet so accustomed to the horror of poverty and filth which reigns on the streets here that I am not further upset at each new visitation. The faces of the people here reveal for their part something more extreme than the continuing danger of attacks and so on. Their gaze is at once stiff and wild – no smile breaks through – even the children, it struck me, were tense. It has to be said that here we are dealing with a different race to the people of Peking – who are more used to foreigners. The Shantung peasant gives the impression of being especially hard, stubborn and industrious. Perhaps this land is China's Hessen.[103]

Trott was feeling a trifle homesick. Tsientsin, for example, put him in mind of 'a small German country town'.[104] The area was chaotic, with the Japanese in partial control. Writing to the Rhodes trustees, Trott was able to report one or two encouraging noises from Germany as a result of his paper 'Far Eastern Possibilities': Hjalmar Schacht had written encouragement from Berlin and Ambassador Dirksen had also voiced his approbation. For the time being, Trott, like most Germans, saw Munich as a victory for peace. 'Mr Chamberlain's courageous stand has made a strong impression on my countrymen,' he wrote to Lothian, 'lingering spite suddenly changed [to] . . . an unmistakable revival of respect after the Munich accord . . . I am convinced that if we stand together we shall be able to shape the peace in the rest of the world.'[105]

At the end of September, Trott was getting ready to leave China, planning a long route back to Europe through Rangoon, Calcutta, Bombay and Port Said. In India he hoped to see his friend Kabir and talk to him about Indian independence, a subject which had interested him since meeting Freer Andrews in Geneva. Earlier plans had envisaged a stop over in Ankara, where Trott hoped to work on his Chinese with Eberhard who was teaching there. After Munich, however, the strong possibility of a European war began to dawn on him and he even thought again of emigrating:

> I am strongly tempted to go via America . . . to look for a place to work if our continent is really going to be what we both feel threatening . . . It is a damned hard choice, but I'd rather be a beggar than a slave and I am not too old to start all over again and I have good friends in America.[106]

117

In Tsingtao, Trott began to think more closely about the significance of what was happening in Europe, conceding to Shiela Grant Duff that 'It proves that you were right in many respects where I was foolhardy and optimistic.'[107] A few days later the fateful agreement was signed:

> We have now heard of the Munich accord, a solution which is no doubt very painful to you in many respects. I wish I could weigh together its probable outcome: I don't feel at all easy about it yet. Anyway the thing seems to be settled as a *European* and not as a German-Czech issue, which, if people had sense, might lead to something really more satisfactory – but I participate in the fears you have previously expressed about exactly this contingency and I agree with you in your present apprehensions.[108]

> I confess that I failed to realize the intrinsic turning point which came about with the Anschluss and which opened up the path for a coercive settlement of the Central European problem – which I had never considered possible with the power, prestige and commitments of the Western Democracies in that area. Though I did realize that there was in England a large body of opinion that favoured a negotiated settlement of the Sudeten question in Germany's favour, I believed that France and Russia would remain intransigent on the matter and that your country would back [them] up . . .[109]

On 28 October, Trott received a cable from Germany to inform him that his father had died of a stroke. Complicated travel plans had to be abandoned and Trott decided to leave immediately for Europe. He sailed the next day on the SS *Ranchi.* The journey via Singapore, Ceylon and Suez, took four weeks. To Shiela Grant Duff he wrote, 'This ship is like a big black coffin carrying me back to Europe to be buried there.'[110] At one of the ports he heard the news of the anti-Jewish pogroms of the night of 9 November which had been whipped up by Goebbels and the Party in response to the assassination of the German diplomat vom Rath in Paris. At the end of November, he wrote to Diana Hubback expressing his concern for Wilfrid Israel.

> My thoughts have been with him very much these last weeks – do you know where he is? . . . you know it is we who are humiliated by what has passed and it is for us to wonder whether our former friends wish to have anything more to do with one who – after all – (in my case through my very absence) has to accept his full share of responsibilty.
>   This I think will be my hardest discovery on my returning to Europe after these eventful months. I shall have to face it and set to work in other directions . . . I don't return with any tactics or doctrine but I am determined to hold my own.

Unknown to Trott at the time, his mother had taken her own stand in response to the Kristallnacht; driving into the local town and leaving her driver at a safe distance, she had gone from Jewish shopkeeper to Jewish shopkeeper and personally apologised for the damage which had been done to their property.[111]

Trott's emotions as the boat made its way towards Europe were mixed indeed; to his friend Martin von Katte he wrote, 'It honestly will be enough just to hear the sound of our language and to enjoy home and friends.'[112] To Allen at Rhodes House he reported his father's death as the reason for his precipitate return. Allen posted a copy of the letter on to Trott's benefactor, Spalding, adding, 'I'm afraid he's returning to a very uncongenial Germany.'[113]

7
Failure in Peacekeeping

The SS *Ranchi* docked in Marseilles at the end of November 1938. Trott had wanted Shiela Grant Duff to meet him on the quay, but the latter quite reasonably pointed out that unless Trott wished to spend some time in that unappetizing port, it would be wiser to meet in Paris, thus saving her a long, tiresome and unnecessary journey. Provocatively, however, she sent off *Europe and the Czechs* to the offices of the shipping line, so that he might have something to think about on the train. Trott would have been further distressed to learn that she was following up her study of the Czech problem with a contribution to another Penguin Special entitled *Germany: What Next?*

They stayed together in a hotel on the Palais Royal, but the reconciliation was not a success, being 'thwarted by shyness and embarrassment'.[1] On 27 November Trott left Paris for Germany and Imshausen. The family home was gloomy after August von Trott's death; 'I miss my father, who kept the peace of our home.'[2] Trott's brother Werner was being difficult again. He had conceived an idea of his brother as a 'Don Quixote' figure, resenting his trips abroad, especially his fraternization with the English. Werner Trott had managed during his brother's absence to bring Heinrich, the Benjamin of the family, into his camp. 'Werner,' wrote Trott, 'disapproves of my attitude, my philosophy of life, etc., etc., and has completely turned Heini his way'.[3] Werner resented the importance attributed to Adam Trott within the family circle, something which continued to rankle even after his death. Friends may well have put their finger on the problem when they described the brothers as 'unconscious rivals'.[4]

Once back in Germany the perennial problem was not slow to seize his mind: How was he to enter the corridors of power? 'I spoke to a cousin in Frankfurt [Adelbert von Unruh], a friend from Hamburg [Peter Bielenberg] and an uncle from Berlin [Eberhard von Schweinitz]. They all think nothing can be done without bowing to the formula. The field after that is wide and full of opportunities but the starting point is evil . . .'[5] Later, in Berlin, he also canvassed the opinion of his Socialist friend Helmut Conrad. Conrad does not say how he answered but it seems likely that he too saw the logic behind entering some branch of the administration.[6]

In the aftermath of Munich and the Kristallnacht the atmosphere of Imshausen was one of 'sterile despair';[7] 'behind any sense of peace there is a deeper one of guilt and shame. But I do care intensely for my home and its people.' The anti-Jewish pogrom had not been popular with the German people; the British chargé d'affaires in Berlin noted on 16 November,

I have not yet met a single German from any walk of life who does not disapprove to some degree of what has occurred. But I fear that not even the unequivocal condemnation of professed National Socialists and senior officers in the armed forces will have any effect on the gang of madmen who are at present in control in Nazi Germany.[8]

The moderate nationalist Ulrich von Hassell, who had been removed from his post as ambassador to Rome in the shake-up which accompanied the attempted *Gleichschaltung* of the Foreign Office, confided in his diary on 25 November,

I am writing under crushing emotions evoked by the vile persecution of the Jews after the murder of vom Rath. Not since the world war have we lost so much credit in the world . . . I am most deeply troubled about the effect on our national life, which is dominated ever more inexorably by a system capable of such things . . . There is probably nothing more distasteful in life than to have to acknowledge the justice of attacks made by foreigners on one's own people.[9]

Anxious to have news of political developments in Germany during his absence, Trott left for Berlin. To Shiela Grant Duff he sent his impressions, including a veiled account of the 'Generals' Plot' which had planned to remove Hitler at the time of Munich and which had been foiled by Chamberlain's 'peace in our time'.

I was surprised when I got to Berlin. Instead of the triumphant capital of the future Empire of Europe, I found a sulky, disgruntled, demoralized mess. Few if any see the Czech business as you do and I tend to: as the entry into unlimited economic and political possibilities.*

The attempt to couple the venture with a general overhaul and readjustment of the inner gears of the machine was frustrated by your clever Neville and the only alternative is another 'venture' or an overhauling in the garage in which many chaps only disguised as mechanics would have to be squeezed out of the door as the engine is neither big nor tough enough to stand all their clumsy hands. At present the door is shut, the engine stinks and puffs the evilest poisons, suffocating all the more sensitive lungs while everybody gets more and more uneasy. Although some will still not believe that the gas is poisonous, all seem

---

* *Possibly Trott's meaning is – 'few people agree with you and me, that the Czech business has opened the way to German economic and political domination of Eastern Europe.'*

121

to agree that something must happen soon – push some men out or let the whole engine crash its way out so that all of them may remain under cover a little while longer. Schacht whom I saw said there is no chance at all of a European war . . . as clever Neville had been forging ahead with the other hand while holding out the one, and that the other with all that it could pull with it was ever ready and probably stronger already than both of ours.[10]

Shiela Grant Duff did not understand this convoluted letter. This was not only a great pity in view of their troubled personal relations, but also because the passage represents, behind its code, a full-ish picture of the state of play in resistance to Hitler.*[11] The 'overhaul' refers to the attempt to assassinate Hitler which was to take place at the order of mobilization in the Germano-Czechoslovak war and which was thwarted by Chamberlain – 'clever Neville' – preserving peace. Another 'venture' had now to be prepared. The 'overhauling in the garage', seems to point to the idea of a revolution from within the Party – perhaps a reference to the confidence that people had at that time in the 'reasonableness' of Göring. The simile of the stinking, poisonous engine refers presumably to the increasing desertion of the more conservative elements who had remained with the regime.

Trott had known Schacht for a number of years through the German Rhodes Committee of which the former minister was a member. Schacht had also been a recipient of 'Far Eastern Possibilities'. Trott had visited him in order to obtain information to convey to his friend Curt Bley, who was in contact with the socialist underground. Schacht had agreed to provide what help he could. For the next few months Schacht and Trott met at regular intervals for discussions. When Trott left for America in September 1939, Peter Bielenberg stepped into the breach, himself meeting Schacht and obtaining information to pass on to Bley. 'After Trott's return from the United States in the spring of 1940, Trott himself once again undertook the maintenance of liaison with Schacht.'[12]

Schacht had been able to give Trott the details of the plot. In the Auswärtige Amt, Weizsäcker and the brothers Erich and Theo Kordt had been involved in a scheme to arrest Hitler, planned to coincide with the outbreak of hostilities against Czechoslovakia. This scheme had been communicated to Lord Halifax in London by the German chargé d'affaires – none other than Theo Kordt. In the army opinions had differed as to what to do with the captive Hitler; Beck was for trial,

---

* In fact the letter offered Trott the chance to be far more frank than usual as he was not sending it by post but giving it to R.T. Latham to deliver it for him. Latham was a friend of Diana Hubback's, a lawyer and fellow of All Souls who had become involved with Wilfrid Israel in the latter's determination to promote the mass emigration of German Jews. (Latham had been a recipient of 'Far Eastern Possibilities'.)

while Halder, his successor as Chief of Staff, advocated having him quietly killed. Through Gisevius, the Berlin police had been brought into the plot, with Count Helldorf, the police chief, pledging support. It was eventually resolved that Hitler would be handed over to the psychiatrist, Professor Karl Bonhoeffer of the Charité Hospital, to have him certified insane. Hitler's removal would have provided the cue for a restoration of the monarchy. Trott was overawed by what he heard, the story filled him with an enthusiasm which he immediately communicated to friends like Bielenberg and Astor; the latter said later, 'The people involved were of a status that astonished Adam.'

Wilfred Israel was still in Berlin, and it was with him that Trott stayed in the Bendlerstrasse. Once again, Trott was keen to make contacts with members of the armed forces, all the more so, one imagines, after what he had learned from Schacht, and possibly Bernstorff, whom he also saw while he was in Berlin. A contact in this was his friend and kinsman Münchhausen, with whom he renewed acquaintance at a 'corps evening' at which one Pappenheim began his speech with Henrich Heine's verse,

Denk Ich an Deutschland in der Nacht,
So hat's mich um den Schlaf gebracht.*

At Trott's wish, Münchhausen later engineered a meeting between him and Colonel General Beck in the house of Münchhausen's father-in-law, Colonel-General von Hammerstein-Equord.[13] (See below, p. 210)

Trott also got in touch with Alexander von Falkenhausen, who had now returned from China. A correspondence grew up between the two and one day Trott went down to see him in his home, accompanied by his friend Albrecht von Kessel of the Foreign Office. Having told Kessel how well he knew the General,

Trott declared himself prepared to take me to him. One Sunday we travelled together to Dresden. Taking the danger into account we naturally made no appointment. As it turned out there was only half an hour available for our discussion, but what with Falkenhausen's interest in political issues and his wide-reaching knowledge of the world this was enough. It was clear enough after a few sentences that Hitler was a political and military catastrophe who must be confronted and removed.[14]

One of the younger men then suggested that Falkenhausen should get him down to inspect the troops under his command and then assassinate him. Falkenhausen was not so keen on the idea of killing

---

* *'Whenever I think of Germany in the night/the thought robs me of my sleep.' Heine, as a Jew, was banned in Nazi Germany.*

him himself, and proposed offering Hitler two minutes to choose between suicide and being shot.

A third colonel-general with whom Trott became acquainted was the unfortunate Freiherr von Fritsch, who had replaced Hammerstein as chief of the armed forces in Germany in 1934. In 1938 Fritsch had fallen victim to Hitler's desire to have men personally subservient to him at the head of the army, but the means used, a trumped-up charge of homosexuality – which in reality had been the sin of a certain Colonel von *Frisch* – administered the *coup-de-grâce* to this old-fashioned Prussian career officer. Although his name was finally cleared by a court of honour, Fritsch was not given back anything other than an honorary colonelcy. At the beginning of the Polish campaign in 1939, he followed his regiment into action and seems to have sought death in battle.

Over the Christmas lull, Trott was visited at Imshausen by his Hamburg friend Peter Bielenberg. The Bielenbergs had grown rather sick of life in the Third Reich and had been making plans to emigrate. Christabel Bielenberg was even then in Ireland looking for a country house where they could live by breeding horses. As Christabel Bielenberg remembers,

Peter visited him [Trott] in Hesse, and when he returned all thought of turning his back on what I had learned from my *Times* to call 'the German question' had faded from his mind . . .[15]

Adam was now back. Adam had been to Berlin and the news which Peter brought home with him after his visit was exhilarating enough and also promising enough to have convinced him that we had been wrong to think of leaving Germany at a moment when the tide was on the turn. At long last the isolated dissident voices of some years back had become a chorus; with a possible world war on their hands, the generals who commanded the only weapon capable of overthrowing the regime were sufficiently alarmed to be ready to act.* The nucleus of a civilian government capable of taking over after Hitler's arrest was forming. It would be presented with no easy task, for much had happened since 1933, and it would be in need of reliable support in every grade of the Civil Service.[16]

From that moment Peter Bielenberg needed little prompting. He set about winding up his legal practice and made moves to get into some branch of the Civil Service.

---

* Cf Hassell's diary for 16 December 1938: 'The situation [Danzig, Memel, etc.] is so threatening that we must now begin to prepare for action. But how? That is the big question. There is no chance of creating an organization. The one positive approach in this direction, which has already been made, is the surveillance of the entire Party through the intelligence section of the army [i.e. the Abwehr].'

124

In February Trott paid his first visit to England for two years. This was made possible by some remaining Rhodes Trust money: German citizens were not allowed to take more than 10 Reichsmarks out of the country. He repeated the programme of previous years, going up to Oxford soon after his arrival and staying as a guest of the Warden of All Souls. Everywhere on this trip Trott noticed among his friends 'a severe frostiness which I have not met with before'. Oxford 'was . . . somewhat disappointing',[17] though he saw the heads of Balliol, All Souls, New College and Wadham (the newly elevated Maurice Bowra). In London he stayed with the Astors, Nancy Astor once again taking sartorial matters in hand and sending him off to have a suit made at her expense. One person he possibly saw then (or in June) was Hugh Montgomery, who reported coming across him in the Travellers' Club. 'He did not disguise his intense disapproval of the Nazi regime and I remember he said something to the effect that he and some friends of his might have to do something about it (clearly something drastic).'*[18]

Trott also appears to have had a meeting with someone at the Foreign Office. He spent the weekend at Shiela Grant Duff's home in Kent, meeting Diana Hubback's husband to be, David Hopkinson, for the first time as well as Miss Grant Duff's Czech friend, the journalist Hubert Ripka. Trott had, in his letters from China, confessed his jealousy towards Ripka in his special relationship with Shiela Grant Duff. In the first days of March Trott returned by air to Berlin. Two weeks later Hitler's armies invaded 'rump-Czechoslovakia' and all chance of rescuing the friendship with Shiela Grant Duff was lost. In a lucid passage from a letter written that spring, Trott put his finger on the difficulties between them at the same time giving a clue to his current activities in Germany:

> If we relate all elements of friendship to the whirlpool of public events we will certainly be lost to each other in no time: it would be the Devil's triumph to see us both dance to his pipe. When you address me in the collective 'You' I have no case to defend against you and I agree that serenity, kindliness etc. in an asylum are not only unbecoming but disgusting. Actually 'serenity' is utterly impossible and something else is more and more rapidly taking its place which you would find hard to attack, though possibly equally difficult to share. You see, darling, I am back in that pool, and from the first moment (that's why I said that your attack came at an ill-chosen moment) I was soaked right through, skin and all and the question is whether we have some common dry bank anywhere or not.[19]

The letter's openness is partly explained by the fact that it was

---

* Montgomery, who later became a Monsignor in the Roman Catholic Church, compared Trott to the martyrs Campion and More. (Letter to Christopher Sykes, 1964.)

125

delivered by hand by a friend travelling to England. Possibly the date of the letter is April (there is no date at the top) and the carrier was Trott's old Geneva and Oxford friend Geoffrey Wilson who had become secretary to Sir Stafford Cripps.

Trott had seen Wilson in England and they had made an arrangement to meet in Germany that spring. The purpose of this trip was clearly intended to give Cripps and his circle an inside view of the state of the opposition in Hitler's Germany. Starting out from Imshausen, where Wilson had an audience with Frau von Trott, the two of them drove first to Heidelberg, then through Baden and Bavaria to Munich and then continued up through Franconia and Saxony to Berlin. During the journey, Trott gave Wilson his ideas on how to remove Hitler in order to prevent at all costs a war which, if victorious, would add to the dictator's prestige, above all in the army. At their stopovers, Trott met people by appointment in hotel rooms 'with the radio set turned up loud in case the room had been bugged by the Gestapo'.[20] In the Black Forest they met Trott's younger brother Heinrich, who also had a role to play in the conspiracy in liaising with exiles in Switzerland. In Freiburg-im-Breisgau they had a meeting, possibly with Professor Ritter or some other member of the resistance circle in the university there. In Berlin, Wilson was introduced to Wilfrid Israel, then on the point of leaving Germany in order to continue his work for Jewish refugees from London.

By the late spring of 1939, Trott had made some progress in his desire to enter the Nazi administration. Through a cousin, Hubertus von Weyrauch, Trott had been introduced to Walter Hewel,* a failed businessman and old friend of Hitler's who served as the latter's liaison with the Foreign Office. Despite being one of the earliest of the *Alte Kämpfer* who had taken part in the Beer Hall putsch and had been gaoled with his leader afterwards, Hewel had the reputation of being civilized by Nazi standards. He had started a mineral water company in Australia, which had gone bankrupt when the bottle capsules had popped off in the heat. He spoke English fluently with an Australian accent.[21] Trott met Hewel at the Garde-Kavallerie Club, to which Hewel had been elected by Weyrauch. Later Weyrauch gave a dinner to which six couples were invited, including Peter and Christabel Bielenberg. The latter was put next to Hewel to probe him.

After that more meetings were arranged in the course of which Adam provoked Hewel into confessing that he was also worried by the political developments. He seemed genuinely Anglophile and showed interest in what could be done

---

* *1900–45. Hewel was with Hitler in the bunker to the end, and is thought to have died there. (See Trevor-Roper,* Last Days of Hitler.*)*

to avert the war and promised to help Adam within his means, in particular to bypass Ribbentrop who was known to distort British views in his reports to Hitler.[22]

With Hewel, Trott also discussed the idea of representing Germany at the meeting of the Institute for Pacific Relations ('Pacific' as in the Ocean) at Virginia Beach that autumn. He must also have let him know how well connected he was in British Government circles. Already by 29 April Trott was able to report something of a major breakthrough to his mother (before he had had the chance to get to know Hewel); writing in English he said, 'The Foreign [Auswärtige] "Amt" has offered me – conditional on the minister's approval, which is highly doubtful for Party reasons – the post of a secretary [Legationsekretär – the equivalent of third secretary] which would mean skipping the rank of attaché and open a prospect for a relatively favourable promotion.'*[23] In the final event, however, he was right in thinking that his non-membership of the Party would be an insuperable obstacle.

Trott's contacts in the Auswärtige Amt were good. His friend Kessel was now secretary to Ernst von Weizsäcker, the permanent under-secretary, and there were also Trott's friends Gottfried Nostitz and Josias Rantzau, who were willing to speak in his favour. Trott also had the support of both Count Bernstorff and Minister Schacht in getting the ear of Weizsäcker, a former Swabian naval officer turned career diplomat.[24] Weizsäcker, like many non-Nazi members of the AA, was still obsessed with the idea of preserving peace by whatever means. His chief method was obstruction, scrambling Hitler's instructions in their execution and advising foreign diplomats on their best tactics with the dictator. He had been made state secretary in April 1938 in the shake-up which was supposed to breathe some Nazi air into the Wilhelmsstrasse. Part of the Nazification process was to ensure that all high-ranking officials were dressed in Party colours.

One of the first consequences of this, though only a superficial one, was that I was made a member of the NSDAP, 'for decorative reasons', as they said, and was also given a fairly high 'honorary rank' in the so-called SS, without this implying the receipt of any special information or having to perform any special official tasks or duties.[25]

Honorary SS rank was given to prominent officials, aristocrats and businessmen with the idea of making Himmler's army into the élite of Nazi Germany. It also had the effect later on of tarring the recipients of these 'honours' with the same brush as some of the more repulsive SS

---

* *The probable origin of this offer was Kriebel, the head of the Foreign Office. (See below, pp. 177–8)*

units such as the 'Death's Head' squads which ran the concentration camps. Weizsäcker's conception of peace-keeping is clear from the following passage, recorded by Carl Burckhardt, the Swiss historian and High Commissioner for the League of Nations, in Danzig on 22 August 1938:

> Something has to happen; we are now standing on the furthest edge, the English have got to send someone we can talk to as soon as possible. But no highly placed personage, no prime minister, no all-too-polite Englishman of the old school; when Chamberlain comes the fellow [Hitler] triumphs over him saying, 'The Englishman eats out of my hand, I've made him eat humble pie.'. Chamberlain is too good for these people, they ought to send some forceful soldier who can also scream and beat the table with his riding crop when he needs to, preferably a Field Marshal with a whole string of decorations and war-wounds, a man without too much consideration . . . It is only reasonable transactions and at the same time strength of character that he [Hitler] is able to foil, outwardly you must play the same dangerous game that he has applied inwardly with so much success. I beg of you, go back to Switzerland as quickly as possible and get in touch with London; if we don't get round a table we risk seeing Prague bombed and Bohemia invaded.[26]

In those final months before the outbreak of war, Weizsäcker was continuing his attempts to diffuse the international situation by maintaining secret contacts with Britain through Theo Kordt in London. The Auswärtige Amt was not alone in its attempt to interest British diplomats and politicians in taking positive steps to avoid a conflagration in Central Europe, nor was it the only institution in Germany interested in the idea of seeking help in getting rid of Hitler. The indefatigable Carl Goerdeler had been in Britain trying to drum up support for the opposition in Germany. To this end he led the British to believe that Brauchitsch, the army's Commander-in-Chief, was prepared to act.[27] Back in Germany, Brauchitsch was quick to deny the fact and made serious moves towards denouncing Goerdeler to the Gestapo. Through the Abwehr, Ewald von Kleist-Schmenzin and Fabian von Schlabrendorff made their separate visits to Britain, pinning their hopes on Churchill rather than Chamberlain – Chamberlain had said that the German resisters put him in mind of the Jacobites at the court of Louis XIV. Schlabrendorff brought news of the possibility of the Germans signing a pact with the Soviet Union and met Churchill at Chartwell. 'I am not a Nazi,' he told Churchill, 'but a good patriot.' A broad smile lit up Churchill's face and he said, 'So am I.'*[28]

Trott's mission to England, in the summer of 1939, should be seen in the context of these other German attempts to give information to the British. Extreme secrecy was above all necessary, as it might be

---

* When Erich Kordt told Vansittart about the Russian Pact, the latter replied, 'Keep calm, it is we who will sign an agreement with Russia.'

said that these envoys were committing treasonable acts. This goes some way to explain the action of different agencies like the Auswärtige Amt and the Abwehr. Trott discussed the mission with Weizsäcker and received his blessing, but he also went under the protection of Hewel, who agreed with him that Hitler should be dissuaded from going to war. This was where Trott's report came in, intended for the Führer's eyes and therefore dressed up as much as possible in the sort of Nazi garb which might be thought to appeal to him.

While Hewel facilitated Trott's mission, he gave Trott no orders as such. While for Hitler's sake Trott would be suggesting that there was still room for agreement and that war could be avoided, his actual mission was to stress points central to resistance thinking of the time which he wished to press home with leading English figures he saw; one theme was that war should be seen as the last resort; once the fighting started loyalties would become confused and the likelihood of the army participating in the plot would be slim. If war was inevitable it should be staved off for as long as possible in order to give the opposition more time to prepare – in a police state you cannot plot in letters or on the telephone. The British government should be careful to create the right appearances; it had to be clear who was recklessly fomenting war, that way the plot would gain in popularity and the idea of Hitler's removal would not be seen as a 'stab in the back'. Finally, account should be taken of the fact that Danzig was a legitimate grievance; a concession, possibly a motorway or the establishment of a German-Polish condominium to govern the city, would deflate the situation. As Peter Bielenberg wrote later of the British guarantee, 'They were completely intransigent on Danzig's future, making war all the more likely. Czechoslovakia, on the other hand, should be restored; a return to pre-Munich frontiers would be all the more likely to rid the Germans of their infatuation with Hitler.'[29]

For the month of May, Trott was involved in organizing his British mission. On the English side the Astors were the key as they had access to those members of the government who comprised the so-called 'Cliveden Set' – with which Trott was connected by his friend David Astor and the fondness the latter's mother had developed for him. Many of his English friends had simply ceased to be friendly towards him, something which saddened him. Writing to Diana Hubback, he said,

I have a growing suspicion that a number of my friends identify the evils of Europe with Germany as such and base their continued relationship with me only to the degree that I happen to fit into your English life. I consider that verdict profoundly untrue and unjust and I do not wish to compromise with this kind of acceptance . . . It is my primary duty to offer my hand here and only if I fail, to leave again.[30]

Trott arrived in England on 1 June. On the 3rd he went to Cliveden for the weekend. David Astor had received a letter from China in which Trott had expressed his resolve to become active in the opposition and his need for contacts with high-ranking officials in London. Astor was therefore aware of the precise nature of Trott's business and he in turn had informed his father Lord Astor.[31] Halifax was coming to dinner on the 3rd as well as Trott's friend and benefactor, Lord Lothian. A description of the scene has been left by William Douglas Home, who was present at dinner that night.

> ... over the port (and because Lord Astor was a man of personality as well, there *was* port), I sat between Michael and Jakie [Astor] and heard, at the far end of the table, a discussion about international politics between a British cabinet minister [Halifax] and a young German called von Trott. Between them, a more dispassionate and, as it seemed to me, more understanding figure than the minister, sat Lord Astor, turning his kindly, gentle eyes from one speaker to the other, as they ranged around the problems of the world.
>
> Von Trott, as passionate an anti-Nazi as he was a patriot, spoke, with a perfect mastery of English, of the aspirations of the German nation as a whole. While allowing for the mistrust engendered in the British mind by the activities of the Nazi leaders – a mistrust which he fully shared – he seemed to be trying to impress upon the minister the necessity for an immediate adjustment to the status quo. He argued that some gesture of goodwill, not only verbal but actual, should be made towards Germany, not only to satisfy her just desire for a revision of the Versailles Treaty, but also – and this might be decisive – to remove some of the planks from Hitler's dangerously popular political platform and thus pave the way to power for those who had the interests of the world, as well as Germany, at heart ... This young man, who a few years later was to die a martyr's death in opposition to the Nazi regime, spoke with a deep sincerity and a sense of urgency. Listening to him, I understood how it was that so many Germans, loathing and despising Hitler as they did, yet felt that, in his insistence on the rights of Germany, he was voicing the wishes of his people ...
>
> ... It was the future and not the past, with which von Trott concerned himself that night. He saw the disaster ahead, and he felt that, with mutual co-operation and sacrifice, the danger might yet be averted and the problem solved by peaceful means. Implicit in this was the essential qualification that the status quo should be revised.
>
> When he had finished speaking, the minister stubbed out his cigar in an ashtray and said, 'Yes, it's a fascinating problem,' and it seemed to me, sitting at the other end of the table, that, in the hopelessness of that answer and that gesture, he stubbed out Germany, and Europe too, for many years ahead.*[32]

Halifax was not as unsympathetic as Douglas Home made out.

---

* *That evening had a profound effect on William Douglas Home, who, convinced of Germany's internal opposition, visited the country with a friend. His conviction later made him strongly opposed to 'unconditional surrender'. Later his attempt to stop the bombing of civilians in Le Havre landed him in Wormwood Scrubs Prison.*

Through Dr Thomas Jones it was arranged that Trott should have an interview with the prime minister, Neville Chamberlain. In a speech delivered at Chatham House on 29 June, Halifax alluded to Trott's visit when he referred to 'patriotic Germans who deplored the excesses of National Socialism yet felt Germany's legitimate aspirations should be fulfilled'.[33] Trott saw Chamberlain on 7 June in the presence of William Douglas Home's brother, Lord Dunglass (later prime minister as Alec Douglas Home). In all probability he repeated to him what he had told Halifax, *sotto voce*, at Cliveden – that the Germans were 'up to something' with the Russians (something he must have learned from Weizsäcker).[34] On the constructive side, Trott continued to urge that the Polish guarantee, signed earlier that year, left no room for manoeuvre over Danzig. He explained the existence of the opposition in Germany and emphasised the need to use 'rump Czechosolovakia' as a pawn over Danzig.[35] Trott reported later to his friends that Chamberlain listened politely but was 'ice-cold' in his reaction. To David Astor he used terms like 'remote', 'seemed a bit tired', and that he thought the Prime Minister was unable to grasp what he (Trott) meant.[36]

During his time in London, Trott had the opportunity to explain himself at length to David Astor. It was then that Trott first mentioned the name of Carl Goerdeler, the man most like to become chancellor in the event of a successful *coup d'état*. He also encouraged him to meet Helmut Moltke, demonstrating his knowledge of the two sides of the resistance movement in Germany. To Astor, Trott explained the problem of getting rid of Hitler by means of two analogies:

> You could imagine Hitler as a heavily armed village drunkard. His wild behaviour is endangering the lives of his own family and his neighbours. The best way to deal with him might be for two people to take him, one by each arm. One would be taken by his strongest relative (the German plotters) and the other by his strongest neighbour (Britain). These two should then persuade him to come for a long walk, with much pretence at helpfulness (negotiations on Danzig, colonies, anything at all). Having got him into a quiet field, they should then hit him on the head with his own revolver (the German Army) ... I asked him once how he could possibly imagine that Catholics and Communists could work together within the German opposition. He compared them to tennis players suddenly threatened by a gunman. The players would co-operate to deal somehow with the gunman and then return to their game – meaning they had a common interest in restoring the conditions of their own more civil.zed rivalry.[37]

Possibly on the same evening that he had met the British prime minister, Trott dined at Shiela Grant Duff's Chelsea home and there met Hubert Ripka. After dinner Trott asked that he might be able to have a talk with Ripka alone as there was something that he wished to tell him. As it transpired, Trott was in possession of a German opposition plan for a solution to the German-Czech problem which involved a withdrawal of German forces from Bohemia and Moravia in exchange for Czech acquiescence to German demands for Danzig and the corridor. The idea was once again to gain time during which a means might be found to remove Hitler. Naturally Trott could not dwell on the idea of overthrowing the regime, as this would have put many lives in jeopardy. In the light of the Polish annexation of Teschen in 1938 when the Poles took advantage of the Sudeten settlement to further their own desire to revise the Versailles Treaty, it was believed the Czechs would accept the German opposition plan. Ripka, who was foreign-policy advisor to Beneš, was furious and would hear nothing of it. The result of the private discussion was a scene and a furious letter from Ripka to Shiela Grant Duff. Ripka in his fury forgot that the proposals had not been Trott's own, but transmitted through him from circles in Germany. The Czech informed Winston Churchill of the meeting, but did not mention Trott by name.

On 9 June Trott flew back to Berlin to write his report on the English trip. The paper was drawn up in the Bielenberg household in Dahlem and eventually typed by Rita Lüdecke, who had been Wilfrid Israel's secretary up to the time of the latter's leaving Germany. Peter Bielenberg's special role was to supply the sort of language which would appeal to the Nazis. In order to protect some of the public figures, their words were put into the mouths of others; all anti-German remarks were omitted from the text while the two of them enjoyed 'good laughs at writing a lot of the Goebbels language'.[38]

The purpose of the report, however, was not in the least bit comic: 'Every sentence of Trott's original report . . . [had the] . . . object of trying to delay the outbreak of war.'[39] British Germanophiles were scattered throughout the text to impress Hitler. Nonetheless the latter was shown that Britain would fight if he continued with his present policies towards his neighbours. Czech national independence, the report postulated, would humiliate Britain as it would deprive her of the role of protector which she had assumed at the time of Munich. Lord Lothian was given considerable space, possibly as a result of his known willingness to negotiate with Germany, and the idea that the independence of Moravia and Bohemia would have a marked effect on British public opinion was attributed to him.* As Lothian's biographer carefully adds, 'We have no direct evidence that Lothian knew and approved the purpose of the report. But in view of the long-standing confidential relations between the two men it can hardly be doubted that he did, though he probably did not know exactly how it would be worded.'[40]

Trott's memorandum was presented to the Foreign Office at a time

---

* *Once Lothian had good-humouredly allowed himself to be photographed reading* Mein Kampf.

when Nazi foreign policy was in a state of total disarray. An enormous problem was caused by the multiplicity of different foreign policy agencies which concealed themselves behind the still bland exterior of German diplomacy. Ribbentrop based his policy on a Russian alliance, something which ran counter to Hitler's wishes as expressed in *Mein Kampf*. The Führer himself remained faithful to his projected alliance to his 'cousins' across the Channel, whose interests 'did not conflict' with those of Germany. Himmler's policy was based on little more than racialism though, as the war wore on, he became an increasingly convinced 'Westerner'. Goebbels took the opposite line, believing that there was a need for a *rapprochement* with the Soviet Union, but blaming Ribbentrop for bungling the business. Göring and Schacht were for a peaceful expansion of Germany by economic means. At any given moment it was not clear which of these variants was being expressed. As one historian put it,

The conservative, moderate right associates of Hitler manning the government offices in the Third Reich helped, *nolens volens*, to conceal the true policy of the Führer. The diplomatic activities of a well-trained, trustworthy and distinguished body of career diplomats went on apparently undisturbed against the background of a planned utopia of world conquest.[41]

Trott had reason to have high hopes for his memorandum, but he underestimated Ribbentrop's mean-mindedness regarding policy towards Britain, his desire to become the sole person with access to the Führer on foreign-policy matters and his determination to see the Russian pact become a reality.

On his return to Berlin Trott dashed off an optimistic note to his mother at Imshausen: 'A week ago today I had a four-hour conversation with Lord Halifax and on Wednesday half an hour with Mr Chamberlain. In the meantime I have not been idle: tonight I worked till three; in a few hours I have a meeting with Herr von Ribbentrop, and perhaps with Hitler too.'[42] In the end, Ribbentrop ducked out of the meeting and later thwarted Trott's chance to have a discussion with Göring on the same lines: no one was going to get in his way, least of all an 'amateur' presenting ideas for a new rapprochement with Britain.

Frustrated in his attempts to reach the fount of power in Germany, Trott flew back to England on 11 or 12 June. Once again he stayed with the Astors, both in their St James's Square house and at Cliveden. In the intervening period he went up to Oxford to stay at All Souls. The Oxford trip was a disastrous failure for Trott and one which contributed enormously to the attitude taken towards him in official British circles during the war. Despite Rowse's resolution to spurn Trott should he appear in the college again, they do appear to have met as Rowse recalls that it was Trott who informed him of Hitler's coarse epithet for Neville Chamberlain.* Elsewhere he accepts the version of Trott's mission given by Dr Thomas Jones, that Trott was on a mission from the German General Staff. Jones, however, had confused Trott with a certain Colonel (later General) Count Schwerin who had been in contact with various people in Britain in an attempt to prevent the war, and who had arrived at much the same time as Trott.†[43]

Trott had several meetings with Isaiah Berlin in his rooms, and appears to have spoken more frankly to him than he did to many other Oxford friends during that fateful visit. From some writings in *Horizon* printed at the beginning of the war, it would appear that the poet Stephen Spender was also present. As a contribution to the war effort, perhaps, Spender made a caricature of Trott mocking his behaviour at the time; for greater effect in *Horizon* Trott is divided into two characters, one called Werner and the other called Jobst:

> When I first met him, he was an ardent Social Democrat, in fact he was literally holding up in his rooms at Oxford a red banner which a Jewish girl with whom he lived had embroidered for a peace procession. When the Nazis came to power he took the complicated view that this after all was perhaps the Socialism he had been fighting for. He was a law student and pretended to admire the legal code which the Nazis introduced with their revolution. He forced, rather cruelly, the Jewish girl (who still used to visit him and camp in the woods) to admire this masterpiece. She told me that although she did not agree with the treatment of the Jews, etc., nevertheless, the documents in which the new laws were codified were marvellous. It was pathetic. I showed my lack of understanding again by fulminating.‡

> . . . the most remarkable case was that of a young aristocrat I met in Shyah's [i.e. Berlin's] rooms only a few months ago. He was a Prussian and his name was Jobst. He had the fine looks of all those well-bred Germans, though in his case something seemed to have gone wrong. There were the blonde hair, the blue eyes, the well-defined bones and the strong jaw, and yet in spite of its fine structure, his face seemed to have collapsed. Perhaps his mouth when in repose was almost too rich and well formed, and when he moved it, it seemed to

---

* *'Der Arschloch'* – *'the arsehole'*.

† *Schwerin had an introduction to David Astor through Lazards Bank where Astor was working at the time. Astor introduced him to certain people in Naval Intelligence to whom the colonel set out his plans for avoiding war (i.e. naval exercises off Danzig and the RAF transferred to bases on the Franco-German border, etc.). A tough military man should be sent to negotiate. Schwerin had apparently been sent by the General Staff. In general, the British took a dim view of this sort of emissary, believing that in some way they were not playing the game. (See Thomas Jones,* A Diary with Letters, *London 1954; also Sykes, op. cit. For Schwerin, see Astor in* Bull, The Challenge of the Third Reich. *)*

‡ *The 'Jewish girl' was Diana Hubback, who later told the author that the flag mentioned belonged to another Balliol undergraduate, Tristan Jones (the son of Dr Tom Jones).*

become distorted and his lips to disappear inside his mouth. He was tall and strongly built, but his movements were so nervous, and the veins of his hands stood out so much and were yet so fine, that he seemed to be pulled the whole time by hundreds of fine threads . . .

We stayed up till 3 a.m., Shyah and Jobst talking without ceasing. I got very sleepy, so sleepy that I lay down on the sofa and attempted to doze off from time to time . . . He did not really attempt to apologize when he said, 'Excuse me for keeping you up but we shall never meet again.' 'Oh nonsense,' said Shyah. 'No, no, it is not nonsense. I know it, we shall never meet again. This is our last day of peace together.' He did not mention Germany. He only said 'It is very sad to leave Oxford. I shall never see anything of this again . . .'

Next morning he turned up again before breakfast. 'I have not slept,' he said. 'I went to bed at three, lay down for three hours and got up at six.' 'Why did you get up so early?' 'Because it is my last morning and I shall never see Oxford again.' He held out his long, expressive, conductor's right hand. Other people called, but even when Jobst was silent it was impossible to escape from his drama. He did not rest. When he stopped pacing round the room, he knelt down, with those speaking hands of his touching the carpet. The worst of it was that he was not an actor, he was by nature a quiet scholarly person, with a rich inner life. Seeing him act was as unexpected as, say, seeing one's father cry.[44]

Spender's conclusions look rather silly in the long run but this sort of ill-conceived and essentially racialist writing was common enough at the outset of the new war. Trott's Oxford trip in the June of 1939 does appear to have been an unmitigated disaster from start to finish, which those who loved him tried hard to forget and those who were spoiling for a fight with anyone German elected to remember throughout the war years. Some people have not even forgotten to this day. Rowse locked him out, Berlin argued with him all night, the Balliol don, and later Master, Christopher Hill reasoned with him in private but found to his dismay that Trott was preaching nationalism, and Bowra showed him the door.[45]

What, then, was Trott doing to annoy the Oxford dons so much? His basic fault appears to have been a lack of frankness in dealing with those issues which underlay the menacing crisis. Hill, for example, expected that once he had got him on his own over a whisky Trott would reveal himself to him; but Trott, nervous of what might get out in a gossip-heaven like Oxford, continued to push the nationalist line. With Bowra, on the other hand, who was more aware of Trott's activities in Germany, Trott unwisely dropped his guard, and, thinking he was in the presence of a real friend, revealed that he was playing a double game, working for both the resistance and the Auswärtige Amt at the same time. Speaking openly, Trott told Bowra that Germany would have to retain some of her new-found acquisitions (the Sudetenland) in order to enlist the support of those right-wing elements (the Generals) who were the only ones capable of bringing

135

off the *coup*. 'I then decided that von Trott was really on the side of the Nazis and asked him to leave the house.'[46]

Bowra did not stop there. 'Knowing he was going to the United States, I wrote to influential friends there and warned them against him, thinking that his plausibility might deceive friendly Americans.'[47] The 'influential friends' were the Frankfurters, whom Trott had visited in Boston in 1937. Felix Frankfurter was a judge in the Supreme Court and a close friend and adviser to President Roosevelt. 'What I overestimated,' wrote Bowra in his memoirs, 'was the competence of the Gestapo, who could be extraordinarily blind.' Bowra's letter was to have a monumental effect. It scuttled Trott's American trip, undertaken on behalf of the German opposition, and it left an indelible impression on those Americans who would later be responsible for wartime policy towards the Resistance.

Sadly for every one, Trott was just a little too taken in by Oxford 'with its serene medieval walls' which were, that June of peace, 'more beautiful than ever'.[48] He underestimated the bitchery and back-biting which pervaded its senior common rooms and the self-importance of dons like Maurice Bowra.

From Oxford, Trott travelled to Kent and Shiela Grant Duff's home, the Avebury seat of High Elms, where he spent the weekend. Also staying with Shiela Grant Duff were Churchill's daughter Diana and her husband Duncan Sandys. It was perhaps hoped that through them Trott would agree to meet Winston Churchill, but Trott remained impervious to attempts to get him before the future prime minister, whom he regarded as 'too much of a hot potato'.[49] A meeting with Churchill would only have added to his difficulties at a time when he was trying to avert war by talking directly to the British Government. On the Monday, Trott left for Cliveden. Writing to thank Miss Grant Duff for the weekend, it is clear that there was no hope of patching up their friendship, '. . . since you *are*, darling, so fundamentally sure (much more than I am) that we are after different things and since neither verbal or other intimacy can dispel the clouds between us, we must I think let deeds speak for themselves later on . . . Love and *Auf Wiedersehen*'. It was their last meeting.[50]

Some of Trott's mood of the time is expressed in a letter he wrote to Diana Hubback at the time. She was then in hospital recovering from an operation. 'S[hiela] . . . tells me that there is an infinite suspicion spreading about me – nice fools. The Thames near Cliveden reminded me of old days, punts, meadows and flowers. Pray that we may keep this peace – precarious as it may be, it is better than another wholesale return to collective crime. This is what I am working for now.'[51] The letter was written from the Astor's London home. This begs the question of whether Trott had not backed the wrong horse with Cliveden and the out-going appeasing administration. This was in no way his fault, but when the Churchill party achieved power the following year, he lost all the clout he had gained through his energetic soliciting of the appeasers.

In London, in the week following the 19th, Trott had a number of meetings with various old friends of his. One of these was with Richard Crossman who had left his job at Oxford in order to become the assistant editor of the *New Statesman*. Trott once again advanced the idea of bargaining in a last-moment attempt to maintain peace. Crossman, however, expressed the new-found unity which had seized Britain in the wake of its invasion of Rump-Czechoslovakia; he had completely abandoned faith in an appeasement policy and told Trott,

> You come along with all this damned peace of yours, but you don't realize we don't want peace with the Nazis. We've tried it and it doesn't do. We're out for war. That's our interest. If it can be a bloodless war, so much the better, but we don't want to make pacts and alliances and agreements with any more Nazis. We are hostile to the Nazis. We think they're a lot of bastards. We want to defeat them, push them down, smash them.[52]

There was further disagreement with Peter Mayer and with Professor Tawney, whom Trott regarded very highly indeed. However, to his cousin Barbara Bosanquet he made things clear enough, in fact clearer than he was to any of his other London friends and acquaintances on that fateful trip. Referring to the purges and persecutions of Jews, which he called 'poisons which seem to rise to the top', he declared, 'they are bad and they must be eliminated'. His cousin asked if that meant eliminating Hitler. After a moment's reflection Trott replied, 'Yes, that means getting rid of Hitler.'[53]

Trott returned to Germany some time after 21 June. Back in Berlin he was anxious to hear of any positive results arising from his English mission. On 29 June, Halifax made a speech at Chatham House which appeared to allude to the matter of Trott's arguments.

> Whatever may be the difficulties of the colonial problem, or of any other, I would not despair of finding ways of settlement, once everybody has got the will to settle. But unless all countries do in fact desire a settlement, discussion will do more harm than good. It is impossible to negotiate with a country the leaders of which brand a friendly country thieves and blackmailers and indulge in daily and monstrous slanders of British policy in all parts of the world. But if this spirit gave way to something different, His Majesty's Government would be ready to pool their best thought with others in order to end the present state of political and economic insecurity, and if we could get so far what an immense stride in the world we would have made.[54]

When Trott and Peter Bielenberg read this speech the following day they were overjoyed to see an echo of Trott's arguments. Perhaps, they thought, something would come of it after all.

Positive signs continued to materialize, signs that the war might be staved off or postponed. Hitler for his own part had resolved upon a course, one set out in the famous Hossbach Memorandum,* which would solve Germany's 'living-space' problem as soon as possible. Ideally, as he made clear later, he would have gone to war in September 1938, but the British and French governments' insistence upon negotiations prevented him from setting in motion his plans for world domination.[55] Hitler's enemies in this were not just those foreign statesmen who still clung to the idea of preserving peace, but also those members of his own administration who, though not exactly 'doves' (it would be hard to conceive of Göring as a dove), were far less anxious than he was to set in motion an operatic life-and-death struggle for the German race.

The Auswärtige Amt still contained old-school diplomatists whose loyalty to the National Socialist state was doubtful, even after the shake-up of 1938 which had dealt the Foreign Office to Ribbentrop. The minister physically divorced himself from the institution, avoiding contact by maintaining himself and his staff in a separate building and allowing most of the department to carry on functioning as before, under the benevolent eye of its head, Weizsäcker.[56] Only a few months before, Weizsäcker had threatened to resign in the face of the growing menace to peace, but had had his hand stayed by General Beck, the former Chief of the General Staff and with Carl Goerdeler, the leader of the opposition to Hitler. Beck rightly surmised that Weizsäcker would be replaced by someone far less well disposed towards his own group.

Apart from the Auswärtige Amt, the other unlikely thorn in Hitler's side was Reichsmarschal Göring, who despite the swagger and bluff, or indeed the frank brutality of his character, was reluctant to lead Germany into another war when the expansion he desired could be won by other means. It was Göring, with his conception of Sweden as his second home (it was the country of his beloved first wife, Karin), who set in motion the peace missions of Dahlerus who rocketed between Berlin and London in those tense last months of peace. Another factor which recommended Göring to the conspirators was the existence of his reasonable, civil-servant cousin Herbert Göring; older resisters, like Hassell, were in close contact with Herbert Göring who lent credence to the now unlikely notion that Hermann Göring might have made a civilized successor to Hitler after a *Putsch*.

---

* *In the Hossbach Memorandum, Colonel Hossbach set down the views expressed by Hitler during a conference on 5 November 1937 in the presence of Blomberg, Fritsch, Raeder, Göring and Neurath. These included his resolution to acquire* Lebensraum *by use of force. (See Bullock,* Hitler – A Study in Tyranny, *p. 367 ff.)*

Trott continued in his last-ditch attempts to prevent or at least to localize hostilities. In July he made a further trip to England where he appears to have seen only the Astors and Cripps.* While staying at Astor's Regent's Park home, Trott spoke frankly of his doubts over the sense of war. He agreed with Astor on the issue of the evil of Hitler, saying

> ... he is a fanatic nationalist, because he's cruel and guilty of the murder of his fellow men, because he is blind with hate. I agree with you in all that – but can't you see that if we have war, then everyone will become a nationalist fanatic, everyone will become cruel, and you and I will kill our fellow men and perhaps each other. We will do all the things we condemn in the Nazis, and the Nazi outlook will not be suppressed but will spread. Is that really the solution?[57]

Trott was right. The Nazi regime was vile in July 1939, but its leaders were as new-born lambs compared to what they were to become in the thick of war. Nor were the barbarities confined to the Axis side.

In Trott's arguments with Astor, Göring was once again suggested as a moderate influence.† Before Trott's last visit to England that mid-July 1939, David Astor had been out to Berlin to see his friend there. One of the few positive things to come out of the curious Count Schwerin episode (see note on page 134) was Astor's being able to discover that the General Staff had no plans to move against Poland before August. It was safe for him to make his planned visit to Berlin in July.[58] Trott wished to introduce him to Hewel as an important political contact in Britain. Astor, for friendship's sake, played the part at a specially arranged cocktail party. Astor succeeded in impressing Hewel, who arrived with his son, and with a rose in his button-hole; 'obviously he thought he was meeting someone grand.' While he was in Berlin Trott took Astor to dine with the Bielenbergs.[59] On his last day, Trott drove Astor out to a concentration camp — possibly Sachsenhausen or Oranienburg — to 'remind his friend what he was fighting against'.[60] They stayed watching the camp until a guard began to take an interest in them. When Astor got back to Britain he submitted a report on his trip to the Foreign Office.

Trott had projected a further trip to England in September, possibly with his socialist disciple, Curt Bley, in the hope of being able to get

---

* *Though David Astor now believes that it was in July that Trott had his disastrous interview with Maurice Bowra. If so possibly the meeting with Spender occurred at this time too.*

† *'Light on the link between Göring and those normally considered to be within the opposition camp is provided by FO 800/316, a memo by David Astor of 9 July 39 conveying the views of Adam von Trott. The latter urged the British to work directly on Göring as an attempt was being made to align moderate forces behind him in an endeavour to oust Ribbentrop.'* (Kettenacker, Das andere Deutschland im Zweiten Weltkrieg.)

another interview with someone in the Cabinet. For the time being he was happy with the British firm stand against Germany. There would be no repeat of Munich, he thought – though perhaps he saw the chance of bending the British over the Danzig issue, a prize which could be earned in exchange for an independent state in Bohemia. To this end he tried to get Diana Hopkinson to find him a flat where he and a friend might lodge during the negotiations. At the beginning of August he wrote again from Falkenried 30, Berlin-Dahlem, the Bielenbergs' home, this time giving a telephone number to emphasize the urgency.

> I am told that England is now seething with Germanophobia. Has it caught our and Dick's friend [i.e. (Dick) Crossman, therefore a Socialist. The friend is perhaps Stafford Cripps], do you think? And what about our own little circles and the old man at the bottom of your house? [This was Tawney, who lived in the same house in Mecklenburgh Square as Diana and David Hopkinson.] If at all possible, at the beginning of September a friend of mine and I would be particularly anxious to come and see him. Would you ask him and tell me whether he'd be prepared to give us a bit of his time then.[61]

The crisis flared up again sooner than Trott thought and it was decided that Peter Bielenberg should go at once.

> We heard that behind the scenes several emissaries were hustling back and forth betweeen England and Germany in a last-minute effort to pierce this fog of misconception. One such proposal involved a journey for Peter. Perhaps the British Government could be persuaded to make some dramatic move, to by-pass diplomatic channels and therefore von Ribbentrop, to send some uncompromising figure, such as Lord Gort, direct to Hitler and bearing a message from the King, warning him that by crossing the Polish border he would be launching Germany into world war. If the visit were to take place in a blaze of publicity, it would convey to the German people exactly what Hitler was letting them in for and might also persuade the generals to act.*[62]

Bielenberg set off for London at a disastrous moment, the week following the 'glorious twelfth', when few contemporary Cabinet ministers could be expected to resist the call of the grouse. War loomed and with it would come Bielenberg's call-up papers. He had no formal permission for his London trip. He stayed at David Astor's house and Astor sent off a note to Lord Halifax explaining that Trott had not been able to come in person but had sent 'his closest friend' to explain the mission, one dear to the heart of Weizsäcker and others in the Auswärtige Amt. When Halifax, though not absent, could not see Bielenberg, Bielenberg and Astor drew up a memorandum which

---

* It appears that the General ear-marked for speaking man-to-man to Hitler was not Gort but General Sir Edmund Ironside.

improvised Trott's views. In fact, Halifax was involved in discussing this very issue, not only of sending a military man for Hitler but also finding a similar gentleman to deal with Mussolini. For one reason or another he opted not to see Bielenberg who returned to Germany on 20 August.

On 24 August, Trott tried another attempt to get through to the British government, using a friend in the Embassy to transmit a short paper on the aims of the German resistance.* This he addressed to David Astor. 'The new opposition in Germany,' he wrote, 'is a) developing on the ground of unity and organization, b) on the basis of political unity, not only in the negative sense of the fight against Fascism, but also in a positive sense.'[63] What Trott meant was that the movement – then under the leadership of Beck and Goerdeler – was attempting to find a political basis for a state in which extremism of the Fascist sort could no longer find a voice: not reactionary but something wholly new. Writing of their political thinking, one German historian has said, 'We should now be speaking of a German "renewal movement" as opposed to a simple resistance movement. This was the essence of the goals of Beck and Goerdeler. Their thinking centred on moral and political reform.'[64] That Trott was expressing these views shows that he was deeply 'back in the pool'.[65]

---

* *Later a goodbye party was thrown for the British diplomat in a Russian restaurant and everyone drank more than their fill of vodka. (information from Peter and Christabel Bielenberg, July 1989.)*

8
Mission to America

On 17–18 August 1939, Ambassador Ulrich von Hassell wrote in his diary:

> Some people believe we must go through the catastrophe of a world war, in which the chances of defeat are eighty per cent, in order to achieve healthy conditions at home. I cannot share this view and consider the whole business an irresponsible adventure, both from the National Socialist point of view and that of an enemy of the Nazi regime. *All clear-headed people should do everything in their power to prevent war.** The only question is what one can do. The ideal moment for a coup would come directly before or at the moment of the outbreak of war. But, practically speaking, simply to wait for that moment means taking a terrible risk, the more so since apparently not much is to be expected from the present leaders of the army. The last speeches of Brauchitsch and Raeder† vie with each other in Byzantine expansiveness.[1]

The Polish campaign which began on 1 September 1939 confirmed the worst fears of the conspirators. Originally it was hoped that those generals who were involved in the conspiracy, the Chief of the General Staff, Halder, the Head of the Office for Economic Warfare, General Thomas, and Admiral Canaris of the Abwehr, would be able to stage-manage a *coup* similar to that planned in September 1938. Halder, however, got cold feet, feeling that the massive expansion of the army which had transformed the Weimar force of 100,000 men into a war-weapon of over thirty-five divisions had also succeeded in 'politicizing' the institution. No longer was it a basically 'Prussian' army, ruled by Prussian traditions, but one which owed its very existence to National Socialism. The younger officers were simply not to be trusted in any move to remove the tyrant. Not even Colonel-General Beck, 'the successor to Moltke', with whom Hassell dined on

---

* *Author's italics.*
† *Colonel-General Brauchitsch, the Commander-in-Chief of the Wehrmacht, had been thought a possible collaborator in moves to rid Germany of Hitler, but the latter had showered him with gifts and facilitated a tricky divorce allowing him to marry a 'rabid' Nazi. Grand Admiral Raeder was Admiral of the Fleet.*

the 14th was able to see a glimmer of hope; '. , . he sees no place where we could gain a foothold'.²

Another factor which stood in the way of a military conspiracy was Hitler's *Fingerspitzengefühl*, his famous intuition, which led him, for example, to push away those generals most likely to want his downfall — keeping Rundstedt and Manstein on separate fronts, for instance, in order to prevent this powerful combination from challenging his position as Commander-in-Chief later on in the war. At the time of the Eight Weeks War of September/October 1939, this was especially true of some of those Prussian generals like Witzleben in whom he sensed an antipathy. Hammerstein-Equord was another general he distrusted and he had been given a command on the Western Front, out of the way of the activities in the east. Earlier that year, Hammerstein had told Rudolf Pechel, the editor of the *Deutsche Rundschau*, 'Just give me some troops and I'll not fail you.'³

After the news came through of the massacres against Polish civilians – aristocrats, priests, intellectuals and Jews – by special SS squads behind the lines (protests against these led to the dismissal of the Commander-in-Chief, General Blaskowitz), Hammerstein told the journalist, 'Doctor Pechel, I am an old soldier but these people [his fellow officers] have turned me into an anti-militarist.'⁴ As soon as Hammerstein was appointed to a command, on 9 September, plans went ahead for a *coup*, linking Schlabrendorff and his friends in Berlin with Hammerstein by means of Nikolaus von Halem and Colonel Stern von Gwiazdowski. The plan was to assassinate Hitler and restore sovereignty to Poland and Czechoslovakia. Hitler was to be invited to review the troops under Hammerstein's command and the deed was then to be carried out. However, only a little while later, Hammerstein was, for no apparent reason, relieved of his command.*

Meanwhile, Hitler's racialist war for the mastery of Europe and the world had not produced any great enthusiasm in the population. There were none of the scenes of patriotism and glorification which had greeted the outbreak of hostilities in August 1914, and even the remarkably swift victory over the Poles failed to produce much enthusiasm among the public as a whole. In Dresden, the former Saxon capital, General Falkenhausen summed up the mood of the ordinary citizens in a light-hearted passage:

---

* *'Until his death in 1943, the general lived in Berlin without the power or the possibility to impede the merciless fate which was befalling Germany and the world.' Count Schwerin-Krosigk observed that, apart from himself, not one member of the Nazi hierarchy attended the funeral of the former Commander-in-Chief. (Schwerin-Krosigk, Es geschah in Deutschland, Tübingen and Stuttgart 1952.) One of the last people to see him was Hassell, on 28 March 1943; 'Above all don't make it a Kapp Putsch,' Hammerstein told the diplomat. 'Tell that to Goerdeler too.' Hammerstein had been responsible for suppressing the Kapp Putsch. (Hassell, op. cit.)*

143

An event of little importance which took place a few days after the British and French declarations of war . . . accurately depicts the mood at the time. I was travelling on a tram. An elderly man dressed in overalls worked his way to the centre of the packed carriage and cried out loudly: *'Heil Hitler!'* No reponse: one or two people pretended to be asleep, others looked out of the windows or lurked behind their newspapers. The man called out in a threatening tone, 'When I say *Heil Hitler*, I'm speaking to all of you.' Once again total silence reigned. The man, looking around him with a smile on his face, said: 'All right, I see that we all think alike,' and the passengers heaved a sigh of relief.[5]

In Berlin, Adam von Trott was preparing to leave Germany for the United States to attend the Institute of Pacific Relations Conference in Virginia Beach. Trott's attendance at the conference had been organized as far back as December 1938 when Ned Carter had written to Lord Lothian to tell him that he was 'profoundly impressed with the use that von Trott has made of his year in the Far East'.[6] The letter backed up an earlier communication in which Carter had proposed the idea. Lothian, for his part, had ensured that Trott would receive a further grant of £250 to cover expenses in the United States.[6] By September 1939, there was not unnaturally some anxiety as to whether or not he would make it to America but on 18 September Carter was able to cable Rhodes House to say that Trott was taking the first available steamer.[7] Unbeknown to Rhodes House, the German Foreign Office was also taking an interest in Trott's American trip, for the same reasons that they had been inclined to support his journeys to England in June. This time the Auswärtige Amt was even paying Trott's fares as Trott's making a speech at the IPR Conference was 'tantamount to a considerable prestige victory for the German government'.[8] This had been arranged during conversations with the 'Sea-lion', as Trott called Hewel, and also with Weizsäcker.[9] Trott could be of considerable use in America if he could get Roosevelt to put on the mantle of Europe's saviour and end the war at the culmination of the Polish campaign. Trott had had contacts with other members of the Resistance – Schacht certainly, but possibly Beck and Goerdeler too. He was also carrying a letter from Moltke to Brüning.

Trott was not entirely sanguine about the American trip. This was something he voiced in a letter to Clarita Tiefenbacher in July, informing her at the same time of Hewel and the minister (Ribbentrop)'s approval of the project. Clarita Tiefenbacher was the daughter of Max Tiefenbacher, a prominent Hamburg lawyer. Trott had met Clarita at a party in 1935. The Tiefenbachers lived at Reinbek and were thus neighbours of the Bielenbergs. They were an old patrician Hamburg family. Trott had recently seen much more of Clarita Tiefenbacher in Berlin and had asked his mother to send her a copy of his edition of Kleist.

At the beginning of September, Trott enlisted in the German army, even though he knew at the time that his temporary attachment to the Auswärtige Amt was likely to be made permanent on his return. On 19 September he travelled to Genoa to board the SS *Vulcania*, an Italian ship which would be sailing to America on the 22nd. On the quay he ran into an old friend and fellow German Rhodes Scholar, Fritz Caspari, who was travelling back to the United States to take up a university teaching post there. It was clear from what the captain of the vessel had told Caspari that morning that there was some doubt as to the fate of the German passengers in the event of the ship being boarded at Gibraltar.[10]

Trott told Caspari that he was not worried. He had influential friends in Britain and hoped to avoid internment. Among the passengers, however, was a Nazi *Apparatschik* who became distinctly nervous as the ship neared the Balearic Islands. Approaching Trott for advice he told Trott, who was gleeful at the other's difficulty, that he had thrown his Party badge overboard. 'You did quite right to throw away your badge,' he said, 'and all you have to do now is to keep up the act. Don't let them think you are a Nazi. If they ask; you say, "No, certainly not, Hitler's an absolute bastard." ' When the *Apparatschik* expressed shock and inability to take such an extreme step towards apostasy, Trott further reassured him of the ease of the operation. 'Look you want to do it like this,' he said. A British officer comes to me and says, "Are you a Nazi?" I reply like this, "Me, a Nazi?! Good God — I should think not! Hitler's an absolute bastard!" ' Trott then told the man what to say if that proved insufficient, giving him even grosser descriptions of the Führer and 'putting him through a rehearsal'.[11]

As it turned out the captain of the *Vulcania* outmanoeuvred the Royal Navy, which was indeed waiting to intercept the ship, and managed to steer her into neutral waters before a search could take place. Once they got to Lisbon, the British were no longer a threat.* By this stage the Nazi had recovered his nerve and was lamenting the loss of his Party badge. He also felt distinctly sore towards the person who had made him abjure his Führer with such obvious relish. The Nazi therefore approached Caspari and asked him about Trott, saying that he fully intended to report the incident to his superiors in Germany. Caspari managed to calm him and suggested that he have it out with Trott himself. Trott managed to charm the Nazi, telling him that he was a devoted admirer of the regime. Caspari nevertheless believed that the Nazi did file a report. If he did, it had no obvious effect.

On 21 October 1939 Ned Carter wrote to Lord Elton, who had replaced Lothian as chairman of the Rhodes trustees on the latter's nomination as His Majesty's Ambassador to Washington.

---

* *It is here that Wheeler-Bennett airs the fantastic story about Trott facing the British officers with his Balliol tie. (*Nemesis of Power.*)*

I myself was surprised that von Trott got through. He arrived on the morning of 2 October on the *Vulcania*, which came through unvisited by any unit of the French or British fleet! He has gone to work in his usual intense fashion and I think will very shortly have justified his coming. I have given Lord Lothian privately a general picture of his activities. When his work here is finished it is likely he will return to his home by way of the Far East.[12]

Trott spent the month of October in New York. When not busy with his secret work, he saw old friends now to be found on that side of the water. Very soon after his arrival he became aware of the fact that he was being tailed by agents of the FBI, which he found little more than irritating. Christopher Sykes, citing an anonymous source, attributes the FBI's suspicion to a message left for Caspari at Trott's hotel which they interpreted as meaning that Trott was communicating with his Nazi masters by means of a concealed wireless transmitter. It is possible, as Sykes suggests, that some of the British Secret Service's reservations about Trott had been passed on to the Americans at the beginning of the war, or – and this seems eminently plausible – that the Americans were simply tailing any strange German who washed up on their shores. Even Jewish refugees were treated with extraordinary suspicion by the FBI once America had entered the war. The dossier is now, in theory at least, open for inspection, but all pages concerning relations with the British have obviously been removed. The American authorities did not relax their surveillance for a moment during the three months of the German's visit.[13]

Apart from his time spent with Ned Carter of the IPR, Roger Baldwin of the Civil Liberties Union and John Wheeler-Bennett, then on Lord Lothian's staff in Washington, Trott was also able to relax a little in the company of Mrs Braun-Vogelstein and Hasso von Seebach, who had travelled all the way from California to see him. He was also in close contact with his Oxford and Hamburg friend Ingrid Warburg, who had settled in New York. In a rather dotty passage referring to Trott's activities at the time, Countess Spinelli tells us that Trott took refuge in her flat from the attentions of 'the FBI, the Gestapo and William Bennett [*sic*] of the English Secret Service'.[14] As a result of the bitter experience of having been forced to quit their fortunes and positions in Germany, the Warburg family had become understandably wary of Germans; 'My Aunt Friede reproached me for having brought into her house what she defined as a German.'[15]

Ingrid Warburg proved useful to Trott in more ways than one as she had contacts with other German Resistance groups then based in New York. One of these was 'Neubeginnen'. This was a group with cells in England and America which had been set up in Berlin in 1936.[16] Her contact was 'Paul Hagen' – Karl Franck – and she was able to introduce him to Trott, who she knew wanted to of build up a far broader base

146

to the Resistance with more than just a military dimension; this was also the aim of Neubeginnen. Above all they were not out for a simple transfer of power from Hitler to Göring or even a more responsible military figure. They wanted rather a complete reform of German society from the bottom upwards. Sadly, however, 'Hagen' did not feel he could go on talking to Trott, given that the latter was in America under official auspices. Later, Frank wrote to Ingrid Warburg to tell her that Trott must not return to Germany. Ingrid Warburg also introduced Trott to the First Lady, who was later very indiscreet about Trott's reasons for coming to the USA.[17]

The most important gathering point for democratic German exile groups in the United States was the circle around former chancellor, Heinrich Brüning. Brüning had been forced to leave Germany for his own safety as the Nazis had kept a close watch on him from the moment they came to power. From his hospital bed in 1933, he had told Schlabrendorff that 'people have to choose between the Swastika and the Cross of Christ . . .'[18] Trott got in touch with Brüning through the former Rhodes Scholar Alexander Böker, who acted as his private secretary under the name of Alex B. Maley. Another person who was in close touch with Brüning at that time was John Wheeler-Bennett, who had not yet shaken off the pro-German Opposition stance he had maintained up until the outbreak of war or exchanged it for the more contemporary and acceptable Vansittartist position – which he was to retain throughout the latter years of the conflict.[19]

After an initial moment of distrust, clearly borne of Trott's double mission to the United States, the former chancellor took him to his bosom and from that moment onwards set about clearing the way for Trott's meetings with high-ranking members of the administration in Washington. Despite having to make regular appearances at the German consulate, Trott was able to make contact with figures like Brüning without arousing the suspicion of the Gestapo. On the other hand, J. Edgar Hoover had an idea of what he was up to and clearly did not approve. In a letter to President Roosevelt's secretary, General Watson, Hoover wrote that Trott had come to America only 'ostensibly' to attend the conference at Virginia Beach; in reality, he was 'soliciting the assistance of a number of prominent individuals in the US in supporting a movement involving the overthrow of the present regime in Germany.[20]

Other data on the subject are given in other letters between the FBI chief and the president's secretary. For example, Trott was travelling under a couple of very cunning aliases – 'von Tropp zu Solz' was one and the other, 'von Trott zu Sole'. He was carrying introductions from people in London, clearly suspicious characters both of them: one was Professor C.W.K. Webster, the biographer of Castlereagh and expert on the history of diplomacy, the other was Henry Brooke, later British

Home Secretary.* Hoover notes with some distaste that Trott was advocating a military *Putsch* as a prelude to a Socialist government in Germany, Socialism being the most untrustworthy part of his demands. No Hitlerian peace had a chance of surviving and sooner or later the situation in Poland and Austria (!) would lead to an uprising. Elsewhere these amusing documents reveal meetings with 'Arthur' Seebach – who was also 'apparently at odds with Nazism'.

Trott had travelled down to Washington on 18 December with Seebach, Paul Scheffer and Witney Shephardson, with whom he had made plans for a peace programme to show why the League of Nations had failed. Witney Shephardson was another former Rhodes Scholar who was connected with the Foreign Policy Association and the Council on Foreign Relations. Paul Scheffer was the American correspondent of the *Deutsche Allgemeine Zeitung.*[21]

It was through his contacts with Paul Scheffer that Trott came closest to effecting the change in American policy for which he had crossed the Atlantic. Trott had first met Scheffer in Berlin in 1935. The latter had been a friend of Leverkühn's and they had met when Trott was working there as a pupil. Scheffer was initially cautious towards Trott, as a result of the official nature of Trott's mission and it was not until their second meeting that they were able to discuss issues openly. The idea was to exploit the calm in Europe as it existed between the end of the Polish campaign and the beginning of the offensive in the West. Scheffer, as a result of their talks, drew up a plan for an article for the *Atlantic Monthly* in which he suggested that if it came to a choice, the Opposition would support Hitler rather than face military defeat. Trott did not agree with that, but found the rest of the paper convincing.

For two reasons it was decided that the paper which Scheffer subsequently penned should be seen as Trott's work. Scheffer was known to be virulently anti-Bolshevik, which was not thought to be an advantage at the time. It was also thought that Trott's signature would carry more weight in Washington. Trott made some modifications to the paper and some of the points which he had made in conversation with Scheffer had their echoes in it, but it was Scheffer's memorandum, something which has only fairly recently come to be generally known.[22]

The intrinsic contention of the memorandum was that nothing could be done to encourage the positive elements in Germany until the Allies came out with a statement of war aims. As long as it appeared that the Allies intended to destroy Germany, the good elements of that country would continue to throw in their lot with Hitler. It was therefore necessary to make clear that with the removal of the National

---

* *He was also carrying letters from Schacht. (see* Account Settled, *London 1949.)*

148

Socialist regime the Allies would look on Germany in a different light and ensure for it a future in a newly defined Europe. In that light the memorandum encouraged the Americans to put pressure on the British and the French. Scheffer stressed the danger of 'National Bolshevism'; this was one of the main planks of his argument. 'National Bolshevism' was likely to spread beyond Germany if not checked now. Germany, the memorandum went on, would revert to the Versailles frontiers, and the only requirement they should need beyond that was a recognition of social and economic conditions, which would be necessary for them if they were to play a part in a future Europe. 'Above all,' the memorandum declared bluntly, 'Germany must be placed in a position which fulfils the wishes of all European people by excluding the possibility of new wars between them.'[23]

Before being taken to Washington, the paper was shown to a number of *emigré* Germans, including Brüning, Hans Simons, a former Regierungspräsident and Rector of the Berlin College of Politics, whom Trott knew from the *Neue Blätter* group, Hans Muhle and Kurt Rietzler. The latter was a former secretary to the Chancellor Bethmann-Hollweg who had in the years prior to the First World War advanced some views which had a distinctly Nazi ring to them. In the 1920s, however, he recanted and was so horrified by the advent of National Socialism that he went into exile in the United States. Trott's contact with Witney Shephardson was useful in getting the memorandum taken to Washington by W.T. Stone, another member of the Washington Foreign Policy Association.

Stone got George Messersmith, Assistant Secretary of State in the State Department to read the paper. He was clearly impressed and that same day he gave a copy to Cordell Hull, the Secretary of State, who spoke about it to his assistant, Sumner Welles, the following day. Welles had already seen it; possibly he had been shown it by Lord Lothian, who had also been given a copy. Trott had one or possibly two secret meetings with the British Ambassador during the time he was in Washington as the latter's biographer makes clear; 'Lothian had known him long enough to justify his trust in him.'[24] Scheffer later recalled twenty-four copies being duplicated in all.

When Trott went to see Messersmith on 20 December, he took a slightly modified stance, one perhaps closer to his own thinking than that Scheffer expressed in the paper. Trott told the minister that it was as yet too early for a public declaration of war aims of which the present régime might reap the benefits. This would be a tragedy. On the other hand it was highly important that the Conservative opposition be made aware of Allied aims as their efforts for the time being were hampered by uncertainty. Messersmith continued to be enthusiastic about the paper, urging Sumner Welles once again to read it. However, over the coming weeks doubts about

Trott began to be expressed in Washington, despite Brüning's endorsement that Trott was an 'honest man' who could be taken to represent those elements of Germany from which a future non-Nazi government would be taken.[25]

Despite the 'good impression' that Trott had made on the State Department, initial doubts as to his credentials *vis-à-vis* the Resistance had been created as a result of his contacts with German diplomatic circles. Questions were asked as to how it was that Trott was able to come and go from Germany with such apparent ease – the same suspicions which had been voiced by Bowra in England. No one seems to have understood then that Trott's official backing was the price he paid for the liberty of action he enjoyed on that American trip. A further meeting was held between Trott and Messersmith during which Trott told the minister that discretion was vital as his statements 'in effect ... put a noose around his neck'. It was at this stage that the FBI file was opened on Trott – 'Subject: Espionate Activities: Adam von Trott in the United States (case no 862 20211).'[26]

While he was in Washington, Trott had a meeting with Felix Morley, the 'he-man' editor of the *Washington Post.* Morley wrote in his diary the next day,

> Adam von Trott, who left Germany three weeks after the declaration of war, had tea with me yesterday, and today I arranged lunch for him with [Eugene] Meyer [the publisher of the *Washington Post*] and me at the office. He is over as a Far Eastern expert, to attend the conference of the Institute of Pacific Relations at Virginia Beach, but is devoting most of his time to developing a receptive attitude here towards the big change which he thinks is coming in Germany... It is an heroic work in which this noble and idealistic young German is engaged ... The chief problem is how to ensure that a war of extermination against the Nazis will not force behind them all the elements beginning to cohere for Hitler's overthrow. And here von Trott confirms my feeling that if a Danzig formula could have been found there would have been no further aggression – because of the coalescing of anti-Hitler sentiment in Germany. Now it is far more difficult.[27]

The views expressed to Morley were also contained in a memorandum written for Lord Halifax and delivered to him by Trott's cousin, Charles Bosanquet. The theme was also expressed in the Scheffer/Trott memorandum:

> If the theory is accepted that Germany is bound to remain a nefarious element in the family of nations, any proclamation of war aims on this basis can only do harm. Such an act could only contribute to the prolongation of war. Even though the German people are increasingly opposed to the National Socialist government and embittered by its policies, it is clear that only a negligible minority of Germans will deny support to the present regime if the preservation of the German nation is at stake.[28]

In December or early January 1940, another memorandum found its way to London, this time sent by Wheeler-Bennett. Wheeler-Bennett had participated in a number of discussions with Trott and German *emigré* groups and Trott had written to David Astor to tell him how well the Englishman understood the situation in Germany and how his views should be heeded in the circumstances. Wheeler-Bennett's memo contained ideas similar to Trott's, advocating a clear definition of war aims stressing that the British were not fighting the German people but their leaders.

> A declaration should be made as soon as possible by Britain, France, Poland and the British Dominions at war with Germany guaranteeing that there would be no political division or dismemberment of Germany; that there would be collaboration with a new Germany, large-scale trading facilities, access to raw-materials, economic agreements and limitation of armaments.[29]

Trott's Washington contacts had been building up for a meeting with the President himself, during which Trott would doubtless have outlined his role for him as the saviour of Europe. In the event, however, suspicion against Trott had grown so intense that his lines of communication with the administration were gradually closed. The reason for this appears to stem from Trott's unwise action in sending one of the twenty-four copies of the memorandum to Judge Frankfurter at Harvard. Frankfurter had been warned by Maurice Bowra that Trott was really a Nazi pretending to represent the views of the German Resistance. Frankfurter asked to see Trott, who was keen to have such a meeting and who was unaware of Bowra's actions. They argued, chiefly about Trott's contention that Hitler's ascendancy had come about as a result of the Treaty of Versailles. Trott also felt that Frankfurter, as a Zionist, was not wholly impartial. Frankfurter decided to write to the President telling him not to see Trott.

Roosevelt wrote back in a light-hearted vein on 7 January 1940. 'For Heaven's sake! Surely you did not let your friend Trott get trotted out of the country without having him searched by Edgar Hoover. Think of the battleship plans and other secrets he may be carrying back. This is the height of indiscretion and carelessness on your part!'[30] Frankfurter was clearly restored to his sense of humour by this ribbing. He replied on 23 January,

> Dear Mr President,
>
> So little of the world manages to enter these narrow, impervious confines that I learnt for the first time from your memorandum of the 17th that the responsibility for the administration of the FBI has impliedly been transferred to me. Here I have been labouring under the foolish notion that somebody else is Edgar Hoover's boss! That he is under my authority opens up a vista of possibilities that I had not heretofore suspected in this job. And so I say, life begins after fifty.[31]

As Christopher Sykes observed, Adam von Trott's American mission followed the pattern of his June trips to England; both began promisingly and thereafter collapsed into suspicion and recrimination. Aware of the growing attitude towards him, he put on a brave face while accepting that, for one reason or another, the mission was doomed to failure. He did not at the time know of Frankfurter's role in this. His bravery and commitment were not called into question, however, by those who had some understanding of his goals. After the war, Scheffer told Countess Moltke, 'Adam came to America at Christmas 1939 [*sic*] saying that the English had abandoned him. In the United States he spoke with reckless bravery about the National Socialist regime and put himself in grave danger.'[32] Two examples of his recklessness stand out – his using his great uncle Schieffelin's New York flat to address meetings of German *emigrés* and his giving an address to some thirty guests of Ned Carter at the Yale Club at which he made no secret of his views. The usual FBI monitors were also – it seems – Yale alumni for the course of the evening.

Acts like these, typical enough of the man, somehow lent credence to the idea that Trott was a spy or an *agent provocateur*, an idea which was gaining ground every moment he spent in the United States and which was still extant in American official circles in the 1960s. Trott had an inkling of the dilemma. He wrote to Diana Hopkinson in England expressing something of his frustration: 'Doubts, at this moment, as to what one fundamentally cares for, seem to me fantastic and evil.' [33] Later, from Connecticut (where he was staying with his cousins), he wrote to her of the 'unfavourable general circumstances' which reigned in the USA, where informed opinion was less than neutral as regards the European conflict. 'Suspicion is rife everywhere and human contacts unless they are intimate or casual become a burden.' Once again his mind turned to Oxford. 'It is a pity Oxford is so hostile. It is a lack of imagination and also of realism.'[34]

The Conference of the Institute of Pacific Relations took place at the Cavalier Hotel in Virginia Beach from 22 November to 3 December 1939. Trott was billed as an expert on the Far East by virtue of a year or more in the field. He was also seen as the German representative, despite his official membership of the Secretariat. Lord Lothian, who was following Trott's American venture, had despatched John Wheeler-Bennett to the conference and the two of them travelled down to Virginia Beach together. Despite the suspicions against Trott, he appears to have made an impression on the other participants. He spoke against the menace of Communism and the need to regard Germany as a Western nation. He warned against Japanese militarism and the danger it threatened to peace in the Pacific and made a plea for the United States and Britain to join hands in the struggle to save civilization from brutality. This was Trott speaking, and not the voice of Hitler's Germany.

On 8 November a strange event had taken place in Germany which remains even to this day the source of a good deal of controversy: the attempt on Hitler's life which took place on the occasion of the Führer's annual address to the *Alte Kämpfer* in the Löwenbrau – formerly Burgerbräu – Keller in Munich. The address commemorated the abortive *coup* of 1923 and gathered together the old soldiers of the Nazi movement. For one reason or another, Hitler cut short his speech that evening and thereby missed death by a 'hair's breadth'. A carpenter and former Communist, Georg Elser, had packed one of the columns of the hall with explosive which detonated a few minutes after Hitler's departure and succeeded in wiping out a number of his most loyal supporters.[35]

Elser was later caught trying to cross the border into Switzerland. Despite torture and all other methods of persuasion available to the Gestapo, they never succeeded in uncovering the names of any of Elser's accomplices and today German historians tend to the theory that Elser acted on his own. He was kept in solitary confinement in Dachau till 5 April 1945 when, either fearing that this valuable prisoner would fall into the hands of the approaching enemy or out of sheer spite, his captors quietly put him to death.

Elser's assassination attempt had an exceptional significance even if at the time it was generally interpreted in opposition circles to be a put-up job by the SS with the aim of increasing the Führer's popularity. In Hitler's terms, it meant that security surrounding his person was increased to an enormous degree and that further attempts on his life would be far more difficult as a result. One of these was actually being planned at the time the bomb exploded; Major-General Oster of the Abwehr was in the process of locating the explosive necessary for Dr Erich Kordt of the Auswärtige Amt, who had volunteered to perform the deed. Naturally after the Bürgerbräu Keller incident this could no longer go ahead. The most important repercussions, however, were linked to the Venlo Incident which took place the next night, 9 November.

Two British intelligence officers, Captain Payne Best and Major Stevens had been establishing links with German *emigrés* from their base in the Hague. At the time, British Intelligence was following up Resistance leads during the 'Sitzkrieg' or Phoney War, as in Westminster a genuine desire to find a settlement for a compromise peace still existed, chiefly channelled through Josef Müller's contacts with the British in the Vatican and Switzerland, where Ambassador von Hassell was conducting secret negotiations with an unofficial envoy of the British government called James Lonsdale Bryans. The *emigrés* in contact with Stevens and Payne Best, however, were German secret agents, and their master was none other than Walter Schellenberg, Himmler's mythomaniac, but none the less highly intelligent, foreign-policy expert.[36]

153

Lured by the idea that they were going to meet one of the anti-Nazi Generals so often mentioned in the course of the Resistance's overtures to the Allies, the two British officers agreed to travel down to the Dutch-German border. In their confusion, they were easily abducted by Schellenberg's men and eventually thrown into the same concentration camp as the unfortunate Elser. For the German press at least the kidnapping of the two Britons was to prove of immense usefulness in explaining away the Burgerbräu Keller incident which was from now on attributed to the nefarious British Secret Service. In Whitehall, the kidnapping of Stevens and Payne Best added fuel to the already blazing fire that wanted to stop contacts with the German opposition and poured water on the notion that there were indeed generals who wanted to put an end to the National Socialist regime. Relations with the Resistance entered a new phase which finally crystallized when Churchill came to power the following year. In future any overture was to be treated with 'absolute silence'.[37]

In London, Wilfrid Israel heard of the Burgerbräu Keller incident and was heartened by the news, which he saw as proof that a wider plot against the regime was in operation. Hearing at the same time that Trott was in America, he saw that this too was a sign that 'the opposition had some plan of action'. He wrote to Trott, 'How grateful I am to know that you are in the USA. I pray that you will be prompted to stay there. I am absolutely convinced that you will be constructive in your present surroundings. It is essential to carry on and be ready to strike at the critical moment.' At another time Israel would have counselled his staying in Germany as an ambassador for all that was good in that country; but now, 'You are an ambassador of all those within who are of good will and at the present moment . . . they need a permanent intermediary and interpreter of their attitudes and motives . . . You know, I feel responsibility towards the future; that is the reason I have a clear conscience in writing you this letter.'[38]

Trott was not convinced. He was filled with a horror of emigration. If everyone were to leave the burning ship, who would be left to put out the fire? It was a point that came up many times in discussions between *emigrés* in New York that December after the close of the IPR Conference.

> Trott argued forcefully that there were already enough *emigrés* who might some day serve Germany usefully from their vantage, but that in Germany itself the need for men willing to fight the regime was far greater. Besides, he felt certain that if Germany were ever to return to its place within the community of civilized nations, the leadership would have to be drawn from men who had stayed in Germany during the terror . . .[39]

For his own part, Trott was maturing in adversity, learning lessons from the salutory experiences of England in June and America that winter. Writing to David Astor at the end of December, Trott saw that the solution lay away from mass politics:

> ... One essential lesson we must clearly draw from the tremendous failure of the purely popular approach in European politics during the past ten years is that no amorphous trust in the wisdom of the masses can help. I think that both the democratic and the totalitarian playing down to the instincts of the mass mind have resulted in this barren and cynical defeatism which underlies the spiritual chaos of Europe. Popular movement has ended in some form or other of despotism. To prevent their self-destruction and to save their progressive and legitimate elements, I feel it is indispensable that certain conservative traditions should be emphatically reasserted, for instance, the necessity of constitutional authority to protect and guarantee lawful processes and existence, the rehabilitation of Europe's common Christian tradition with its moral values in personal integrity (in character, conscience and freedom of worship) in family and educational life. As yet the longing back to such 'normal' orientations of life is not exhausted among those in the countryside – impending destruction may drive them into forms of desperation in which they will no longer listen to terms like these ... [40]

Although Trott had to a large extent lost his religious faith in his late teens when he confessed as much to Visser't Hooft in Geneva, he remained interested in the positive aspects of religious teaching and had a certain fascination with the Catholic Church – to which both his brothers converted in 1942.* In 1929, he had attended mass with Hugh Montgomery. Ten years later, however, perhaps in a gesture towards his elder brother, he showed that he was not about to retreat into religion.

> People begin to think in a strangely intense, though I believe somewhat false way of the Catholic Church as a shelter of peace. I can understand that, though I wouldn't follow the call for such reasons. I think God would prefer us to be honest pagans and die a brave death in our irresponsible folly and the failure to get a grip somewhere on our sliding fortunes. [41]

Like many people at the time, Trott must have seen religion not only as an important force for good in the face of the 'new morality' of Nazism; it represented a tie with civilization as well as a call for love when so much hatred was being spouted by those in charge. He must also, like many Germans, have conceived of Christianity as a form of resistance in itself. Apart from the doubtful institution of the state church under National Socialist control, the churches, both Catholic and Protestant,

---

* The horrors of the war may have led to any number of such conversions – the moving example given in Ursula von Kardorff's diary is a case in point. (See Ursula von Kardorff, Diary of a Nightmare, Berlin 1942–1945, translated from the German by Ewan Butler, London 1965. I am very grateful to Simon Wallis for directing me to this excellent and neglected book.)

were not slow to show their opposition to the regime and to rally round them those disoriented elements who would later fight hard to rid Germany of Nazism. In the confessing Church, one third of the pastors subscribed to the Pfarrernotbund, the Pastors' Emergency League, which assembled to protect the Church from Nazism. Several Catholic bishops and priests made courageous stands against the regime. After 20 July 1944 nearly all those interrogated said that the persecution of the Churches had been to some degree behind their actions. Trott was not one of these but he saw Christian morality as a bulwark against the operation of tyranny.[42]

In the depression he felt as a result of the growing sense of failure of his American mission, Trott turned increasingly to Mrs Braun-Vogelstein, with whom he was able to laugh off his FBI tail from time to time. She remembered that in November, 'He came into my hotel room one evening. "You will have been seen coming in," I told him as he entered. "Yes," he laughed, "the fellows followed me right up to your threshold." ' Trott kept his visits to Mrs Braun-Vogelstein for night-time; during the days he was too busy.

> Whom he met and what he was planning, he wouldn't tell me as it might have incriminated or endangered me. Not occasionally he called on me towards midnight: 'Am I disturbing you?' Every time he got the answer, 'I wait up for you happily.' He spoke to me about his inner loneliness in a country where the air was poisoned for him.'[43]

> On another occasion he complained to me that now the real purpose of his American trip had been thwarted he would have to return to Germany. Despite the monstrous things being perpetrated there, yet more heinous acts were being planned. At this moment he seemed to harden. 'Stay here in America and show the people here another Germany', I implored him. 'This is what my English friends are asking me to do.' . . . But he had to try to prevent further mischief from taking place. In vain I tried to convince him how pointless this would be after what was being mapped out after the Polish campaign. He should listen to his friends not only from motives of self-preservation, but also so that he could later be employed in the resurrection of a rule of law. Adam leapt up angrily, 'You would be the first to drive me back, if you knew what it meant. If it had been Heinrich Braun, he would not have hesitated an instant.'
>
> The next evening he came again. In the light of our pressing farewell he was calm and composed. We spoke but little. Suddenly he met my gaze in a way I had not seen before, silently looking deep into my eyes. We remained like this until he asked me in an insistent way, 'Will you trust me, no matter what you hear about me?' His stare remained firmly judging me while I frankly replied: 'Perhaps I will not approve of what you do, but I will always believe that your motives and your views were pure.' His face brightened. With a handshake we parted. The next morning he called me from the airport; 'Leben Sie wohl, auf Wiedersehen, until the next time.' I gave him a blessing for the journey and I was then overcome with sadness. That was farewell for ever. I could feel it.[44]*

---

* *Dietrich Bonhoeffer also had to face a difficult decision in returning to Germany at the outbreak of war. 'I must live through this difficult period of our national history, with the Christian people of my own country . . . Christians in*

Trott flew to California leaving behind him in the care of Mrs Braun-Vogelstein a packet full of documents which would certainly have incriminated him had they been found by the German authorities. They included the memorandum entitled 'A Practical Vision of the Future Peace as an Integral Part of the Present Conduct of War' and a translation of it into German, together with a letter from Roger Baldwin giving Trott addresses in Moscow, including that of Maxim Gorky's widow,[45] the memorandum of John Wheeler-Bennett*, as well as a letter from the same, affectionately signed Jack and transmitting his 'warmest greetings' to Helmuth (Moltke) and Albrecht (Bernstorff). There were, in addition to these, letters from David Astor containing some irreverent pen portraits of leading figures of the time and telling Trott not to go back to Germany. There was also the letter from Wilfrid Israel with the same object, mentioned above. The packet also contained notes from Cripps, Geoffrey Wilson, Miriam Dyer-Bennet, Eleonore von Trott, Scheffer and Caspari.[46]

When Trott's plane landed in California, it was Caspari who met him at the airport. Trott confided in him that the mission had been a terrible failure, a fact he put down to his conversation with Frankfurter, when he suggested that it would be wrong for Jews to contribute to anti-Nazi propaganda.† Together they drove down to Taft to see Miriam Dyer-Bennet. There was a brief reconciliation before Trott and Caspari motored north again to San Francisco. The car was being followed, and Trott explained the reason. Finally giving in to a mischievous temptation, Trott resolved to have some 'sport at the expense of the FBI'. Asking Caspari the details of his car – registration and make – Trott steered the vehicle into a dark turning and allowed the FBI car to coast by. Sure enough it returned some moments later when the agents realized they had lost their tail. To their surprise, the

---

Germany will face the terrible alternative of either willing the defeat of their nation in order that Christian civilization may survive, or willing the victory of their nation and thereby destroying civilization. I know which of these alternatives I must choose; but I cannot make the choice in security.' (Quoted in Bishop Bell, A Letter to my Friends in the Evangelical Church in Germany, 1946) In returning to Germany, Pastor Bonhoeffer suffered the same tragic fate as Adam von Trott.

* *Wheeler Bennett's protector Lord Lothian died in December 1940. His life might have been saved by an operation but, as a Christian Scientist, Lothian would not submit to one. When Churchill came to power, attitudes towards the German Opposition had changed dramatically (see below pp. 225–6). In order to maintain his position within the Foreign Office, Wheeler-Bennett was obliged to adopt a more anti-German stance which is witnessed in the memoranda he wrote during the war, as well as in his book,* The Nemesis of Power, The German Army in Politics, *London 1953.*

† *Sykes reveals that later Frankfurter was known to advocate just such a policy and to try to restrain Jews from being too outspoken about Nazism.*

G-men found Trott waiting in the road with a torch in his hand. Signalling them to stop, Trott informed them of the details of the car and gave them his address in San Francisco, telling them that if they found his speed too slow they might care to go on ahead. Caspari, in the car, tried hard to suppress his laughter.

From San Francisco, Trott drove out to visit another German *emigré*, Professor Karl Brandt, who taught at the University of Stanford. Brandt, who had gone into exile early in 1933, was Walter Hewel's brother-in-law, though that does not appear to have influenced his political thinking. Trott was shown into his office by an Englishwoman who had been present at the IPR Conference and was therefore *au fait* with the conference tittle-tattle that Trott was a German master spy. This she indicated to Brandt by means of gestures behind the unfortunate Trott's back. Brandt, however, soon became aware that the rumour lacked foundation and invited him to dinner at his home. After dinner they had another talk during which Brandt lost his temper, shouting so much that his wife had to intervene, admonishing him for his rudeness towards a guest. The bone of contention was not that Brandt had begun to believe in the Nazi credentials of his guest, only that he had no faith in the ability of the German Resistance to deal with Hitler.

Trott left America soon after, travelling via Hawaii. Just before landing he penned a letter to Diana Hopkinson giving his final impressions of the American trip. He had 'left America with a sigh of relief – they don't really partake in anyone's troubles and – apart from certain confirmed circles – will act unmoved by any kind of spirit.' Light entertainment on the voyage was provided by Trott's cabin mate, a Brazilian-Indian-Portuguese-German-and-English Honolulan who was married to a Chinese woman.

> In his best of moods he stands in the little cabin and imitates the speech of a certain Central European politician, clenching his fists, rolling his eyes, shouting – in Russian – till all [the] people in the corridor come and think someone has gone mad... He is an optician, was a cowboy, owns land, is a milk inspector and was a member of the legislature of Hawaii.[47]

In Hawaii, Trott stopped off to visit Klaus Mehnert, a Russian German who was resident on the island. Mehnert gave Trott a letter of introduction to Gustav Hilger in Moscow.[48] Hilger was another German Russian who was councillor in the German Embassy and a long standing collaborator with Ambassador Graf von der Schulenburg.[49] Hilger doubled up as Ribbentrop's interpreter at the time of the Ribbentrop–Molotov Pact.[50] At the end of the war it was Hilger who had to tell Ribbentrop the bitter news that the Russians were no longer interested in concluding a peace agreement with Germany as long as he, Ribbentrop, remained Foreign Minister.

From Hawaii, Trott went on to China, travelling to Peking, where once again he was lodged by Ecke. It was to be a brief and valued moment of calm before stepping back into Europe. While he was in Peking he picked up a sickness which got worse as his journey went on, making the meetings he had arranged in Moscow difficult to keep. Somewhere between Moscow and Königsberg the symptoms of jaundice set in and Trott, too ill to continue, was forced to leave the train at Kant's city, Königsberg, where he knew he would find a sympathetic nurse in his friend Götz von Selle.

When Trott left America in the second week of January 1940, official attitudes towards him, though menaced by the strong suspicions engendered by Frankfurter and others, had not yet gelled into the rabid distrust which was to attach to his name after the United States' entry into the war in December 1941. (At that time Trott's attempts to forestall American involvement were easily construed as those of a Nazi agent on an official mission.) For the time being George Messersmith gave Trott the benefit of the doubt, writing to Alexander Kirk at the Embassy in Berlin instructing him to keep channels open. 'I am inclined to think he is an honest man who is deeply concerned over the future of his country.'*[51] On 9 January Kirk replied, 'I shall be glad to see him when he reaches Berlin. We occasionally meet persons of his persuasion and have already indicated to the department the kind of view they are prone to express.'[52]

Once the Americans had decided that Trott was a master spy the reasonableness of the Messersmith–Kirk correspondence is replaced by a more conspiratorial tone which later gives way to an intriguing form of loopiness. On 31 October 1941, George Gordon, Under Secretary of State at the Department wrote to Sumner Welles,

> A meeting was held in Colonel Donovan's office this afternoon, attended by Colonel Donovan, Mr Edward Tamm, Colonel Ross of the MID, Commander Smith of ONI, and myself. After brief discussion it was agreed that it would be preferable to have von Trott go to Switzerland to make the communication in question to our minister, or other duly appointed American representative, in that country. It was further agreed that if, for some reason, the matter could not be transacted in Switzerland, it could be in Portugal, but it was felt that von Trott should be told of the conditions under which his communcation would be received – i.e. by our representative in Switzerland – and if he were not

---

* 'Sein Schmerz um Deutschland sei so tief, dass er nur mit dem lieben Gott darüber reden könnte.' (*So profound was his agony over Germany that he could discuss it only with God on high.*) This is how Ecke, paraphrasing the Baron vom Stein, summed up Trott's mood in China. (Ecke to Clarita von Trott.)

prepared to meet those conditions it would, in the absence of a very good explanation, reflect adversely upon the good faith of his intentions.[53]

This strange document was probably occasioned by one of Trott's frequent visits to Switzerland and his attempts to interest the Allies in various peace initiatives. The next entries in the file are not so easily explained, unless somewhere along the line there was a case of mistaken identity; once again George Gordon is writing to Sumner Welles; the date is the same, 31 October. 'With reference to your query concerning von Trott: I called this morning on Colonel Donovan and one Mr Edward Tamm, who, in the absence of Mr Hoover, said that he was entirely competent to speak for the latter.' The subject of these conversations was Trott's presence in Brazil (!). Neither Donovan of the COI (later OSS) or Tamm of the FBI had any objection to Trott getting in touch with their representatives in that country;

> both felt, however, that von Trott should not be encouraged, or in fact allowed, to come to the United States – certainly not until there has been ample chance to digest whatever communication he may have made in Brazil and to ensure his activities' being entirely innocuous should he be allowed to come here. Donovan was even more sceptical than Tamm as to the advisability of his coming here under any conditions; as he put it, von Trott should not be allowed to come unless and until he has been properly 'vetted', and that is not always an operation of precision.[54]

The mysterious Brazilian affair continued to draw ink in the State Department for a few days to come. On the very day of the Donovan/Tamm conversation the FBI files were re-examined and a full report drawn up on Trott's activities in America over the three months from October 1939 to January 1940. The paper alluded to his American relatives and connections and stated that he was a 'professed anti-Nazi' who was striving for a 'more lenient peace than Versailles'. During that time he had seen a large variety of people 'running from Dr Brüning down to professors on the Pacific Coast and Hawaii', some of whom were now under FBI investigation. 'Since von Trott's return to Germany via the Far East in January 1940 he has been continuously in the German Foreign Office.'[55]

On 21 November 1941, a new element enters this curious drama – British Intelligence. George Gordon is once again writing to Sumner Welles.

> Mr Tamm has telephoned to inform me that this morning Colonel Donovan telephoned Mr Hoover stating that the British Intelligence had asked him if one of their men might interview von Trott, who is now in Brazil. Aside from the fact that I thought von Trott was to be dissuaded from going to Brazil, it is not clear why British Intelligence should be asking Donovan for permission for one of their men to talk to von Trott, but Tamm stated that this was exactly what Donovan told Hoover.[56]

At Göttingen University

At Göttingen University, Trott is on the extreme left

Trott at Oxford. New College is in the background

The Marquess of Lothian

Sir Stafford Cripps

Richard Crossman

Wilfrid Israel

At the Referendar Camp, Jüterbog, 1936

With his Chinese servants, Peking, 1938

Felix Morley, Editor of the *Washington Post*

Willem-Adolf Visser't Hooft, Secretary to the World Council of Churches

At the Institute for Pacific Relations Conference in the autumn of 1939. Trott is second from the right, front row; Ned Carter is on Trott's left. John Wheeler-Bennett wearing a trenchcoat is in the centre of the front row

Lord Halifax

Revd George Bell, Bishop of Chichester

Julius Leber on trial, January 1945

Helmut James, Count Moltke, before the People's Court, January 1945

Eugen Gerstenmaier on trial, January 1945. Moltke is seated behind him

At his wedding to Clarita Tiefenbacher in the summer of 1940. He is wearing Peter Bielenberg's suit

With his eldest daughter Verena

With members of the Informationsabteilung of the German Foreign Office. From left to right 'Judgie' Richter, Trump, 'Alex' Werth and Leipholdt

On a visit to Reichsführer Himmler's headquarters in 1942. Subhas Bose is second from the right. Trott is wearing glasses

Ivar Andersson, Editor of the *Svenska Dagbladet*

Claus Schenk, Graf von Stauffenberg, in North Africa (right)

Willy Brandt as Mayor of Berlin (1960). He is with President Theodor Heuss who was on the fringes of the conspiracy

Before the People's Court, 15 August 1944. Hans-Bernd von Haeften is on the right of the picture

Dr Roland Freisler, President of the People's Court. 'Our Vishinsky' (Hitler)

After the death sentence, 15 August 1944

Trott's monument at the highest point in the Trottenwald. 'Adam von Trott zu Solz 9.8.1909–26.8.1944. Executed with his friends in the struggle against the despoiler of our homeland. Pray for him. Heed their example.'

A letter was sent to Donovan on 24 November, presumably giving him leave to tell British Intelligence that neither Brazil or Trott was in any way sensitive to the State Department. On the 25th Welles asked Stone (was this the W.T. Stone whom Trott knew?) 'to go down to Brazil and interview von Trott'. On that same day Gordon wrote another memo to Welles:

> I immediately informed Mr Tamm by telephone of the foregoing, and told him I would be glad to write him a letter for the record if he desired. He replied that the telephone message was quite sufficient, and by the way of keeping me informed said that Donovan had called up Hoover yesterday afternoon and said that if Mr Hoover had no objection Donovan thought, and would suggest, that someone go down to Brazil to interview von Trott. Hoover replied that as the matter had come from the State Department he thought that Donovan should seek an expression of the Department's views on the premises. The phone call from Colonel Donovan to Mr Welles was apparently the result.[57]

It is tantalizing to try to imagine what, if anything, the British and American Intelligence Services found once they got to Brazil. What is incontestable is that they did not find Trott who after his return to Germany never again ventured further than Turkey. The letters leave little room for doubt that someone calling himself von Trott was in Brazil and anxious to get in touch with the Americans. Who he could be and what happened to him is not made clear by the file.

9
Foreign Office and a New Circle of Friends

Failure in America, the Chinese flu, jaundice contracted in Moscow – where he 'lost three well-prepared days'[1] – proved a cathartic experience for Trott who mended slowly in the care of Götz von Selle and his wife in Königsberg. The convalescence allowed him to take stock of his work so far and to plot a path for the future. He wanted to bring his mind to bear on those decisions which would save Germany from the fate proposed for her by Hitler and his crew. Like those of his hero Heinrich von Kleist, Trott's illnesses almost seem to have been brought on by mental frustration.

From his sickbed he began to realize for the first time the need to act in concert with other people which the independence of his mind had so far prevented him from doing.[2] His budding friendship with Moltke was one opportunity for him to participate in a forum resolved to plan for a future Germany – the circle later called the Kreisauer Kreis, after the Moltke family seat in Silesia. The strong strain of pacifism, however, which underlay the Kreisau Circle was not wholly congenial to Trott who had early on realized that the only way to remove the evil was *physically* to eliminate the men behind it. As a result Trott kept up contacts with most of the Resistance groups, acting as a liaison between Kreisau and the *Alte Herren* – Beck, Goerdeler, Popitz, Hassell and the other older conservatives – as well as maintaining contact with the Churches through Drs Eugen Gerstenmaier, and Hans Schönfeld and Willem-Adolf Visser't Hooft in Geneva. Trott was also particularly keen to include forces from the left, especially trades unionists, in the group. This brought him into contact with Julius Leber, the former Socialist defence expert in the Reichstag. Except in isolated cases such as that of Falkenhausen, Trott's contacts with the military resistance were few at this stage, full collaboration only coming after he had met and befriended Claus Stauffenberg.

From Königsberg, Trott got in touch with Otto John, with a view to joining Lufthansa. Trott had met John before the war in Berlin, but their friendship began only after his return from America. Trott's mind had turned to marriage during his absence from Germany. In his conversations with John, the latter had 'warned him against marriage' in the circumstances.[3] John was as aware as Trott of the slim chances of surviving the war. Trott chose not to take John's advice. Marriage removed the last means of escape after the failure of the bomb plot; as a single man John had had no fears of the Gestapo abducting his family. In the end, however, the Gestapo made no distinction between those who fled and those who stayed – their families were rounded up anyhow. By marriage Trott was to benefit from what his cousin Achim von Arnim described as an 'extremely happy and harmonious' union during those vital last years.[4]

On 18 March 1940, Trott wrote to Clarita Tiefenbacher from Königsberg expressing his relief at being back in Germany after the disappointment of the American trip. Although he was aware of the failure of the mission, he had, however, something to work on. In the course of the year following his return from the Far East, their friendship had grown closer. By the time he had recovered from the worst of his illness he had resolved that they should wed. Writing to his mother on 9 April Trott revealed that his intention to marry Clarita had been with him throughout his American trip. 'She has a humble but brave character; refined and cheerful . . .'[5]

In April he travelled to Hamburg, staying in town as a maxillary sinusitis still required him to be close to a doctor. On the 26th he wrote to his mother again, this time in English.

Her parents and people are very much like this town and different from people you know, but nice and dignified, though a bit set in their patrician environment. I always liked Hamburg and even appreciate this quasi-stability. Her father is considered perhaps the best lawyer here and he and his wife are different from the rest, finer and he extremely intelligent. I have only met them once, as I had to stay in town because of the doctor – but I shall visit them this afternoon . . . C's brothers are charming – simple in the good sense, candid, upright and good-looking. The father is not so good-looking, but a hard-worked perhaps slightly grave man and very concerned about everything, as indeed one may well be these days – I found myself in considerably deep agreement with his views . . .[6]

The marriage was celebrated in Reinbek on 8 June, just eight days after Trott officially entered the Foreign Service.[7] The ceremony took place at the house of Clarita's grandparents. In his speech, Trott alluded to his friends across the Channel and to the fears he had for them in the course of the German bombardment of British cities. Clarita Tiefenbacher was eight years younger than her husband. Two children were born of their short marriage, Verena in March 1942 and Clarita in November 1943.[7]

While he was still convalescing from jaundice, Trott was obliged to write his report for the German Foreign Office which had sponsored his American adventure. It had to be carefully written, as his entry into the service depended on it. Christabel Bielenberg remembers the scene when her husband, a self-appointed expert on Goebbels-type German helped his friend out with the phrasing:

> Sitting near the door, as far from the bugs as possible, I watched Adam's yellow face as Peter, supremely confident of his ability to withstand any bug, sat by his bedside helping him compose the report on his journey for the German Foreign Office. They were having some fun with the official jargon. A sudden burst of laughter;
> 'All right Peter if you think so, but isn't it laying it on a bit thick?'
> 'You can't lay it on thick enough, dear boy!'[8]

Trott was casting around too for contacts who might offer renewed hope of Allied support for its German opposition. In the third week of May he used Josias von Rantzau in order to get in touch with Hans von Dohnanyi, the man whom the Kaltenbrünner reports were later to dub the 'instigator and guiding spirit of the movement to eliminate the Führer', in Berlin.[9] Closely connected to the crucially important Bonhoeffer clan, Dohnanyi had got to know Beck and Major-General Oster of the Abwehr in the course of the shameful trial of General Fritsch. His refusal to join the Rechtswahrerbund — the Nazi lawyers' association — had led to his dismissal from the Ministry of Justice. Posted as a Reichsgerichtstrat to Leipzig in 1938, his contacts meant that he was able to slip into the Abwehr. Another person he saw again was Schacht, whose conception of a non-Nazi Germany was broadly monarchist. During Trott's absence in America Schacht had given Peter Bielenberg some ideas on how to avoid civil war in the event of a Putsch.[10]

In April 1940, Trott was in correspondence with General Falken-hausen. It has been suggested that the General leaked the invasion plans to Colonel Goethals, the Belgian military attaché in Berlin. There is perhaps an allusion to this in his letter to Trott of 5 April. 'Many developments are contrary to my wishes, and I have my own thoughts about them; but all this is better said orally. In any case, I believe that we have done everything possible. This, at any rate is a consolation however slight.'[11] After the fall of France, Falkenhausen was to become the military governor of Belgium and Northern France, and as such a focus for the Resisters.

Trott continued to see Otto John, who was, despite everything, the best man at his wedding. John was closely linked to the Bonhoeffer clan, and in politics, a convinced monarchist. His job as legal adviser to Lufthansa had the advantage of allowing him to travel to neutral countries and its basically non-political nature meant that, unlike Trott, he had no need to join the Party.[12] Trott was still trying to avoid the stigma of the Party badge by getting a job outside the civil service, and for a time he thought of Lufthansa. John made enquiries on his behalf but his Resistance friends in the airline thought that Trott would serve the opposition better in the Auswärtige Amt.* There was therefore no alternative but to apply for Party membership. Trott applied through the Bebra branch, where his family was well-known. His acceptance would therefore have been swift.[13]

It was in 1940 that Trott began to see eye to eye with Moltke over the structure of a future Germany after the Nazis. The two were never to agree on the wisdom of assassination[14] but, with their mutual connections with and respect for the Anglo-Saxon world, they were to find much common ground in the memoranda they drew up in connection with Kreisau discussions. The war had effectively altered Moltke's plans in much the same way as it had changed those of the Bielenbergs; like the latter, Moltke had planned to emigrate in the autumn of 1939; he hoped to practise at the English Bar, to which he had been called. Although the war nipped his project in the bud, Moltke successfully got out of service in the army by taking a job as *Kriegsverwaltungsrat* (war administration adviser) to the foreign countries division of the Abwehr. He was engaged as an expert on International Law to advise the German armies in their administration of occupied territories. Although this kept Moltke from the front line, it nevertheless involved him in first-hand knowledge of the atrocities committed by the SS and others in these conquered lands. Through Moltke, others opposed to the regime would receive a thorough description of what was going on – at least in the earlier stages of the war, before the SS tightened up their security and started putting their victims to death more clinically within the confines of extermination camps.

Another vital sideline, allowed for by Moltke's work, was the chance to travel abroad which was so important for contacts with the Allies. Moltke had, to some degree, become the spokesman for Germany's observance of international law, and could speak directly to a military commander when ever an infringement was suspected. His illustrious Prussian name must have served him well when it came to addressing the still preponderantly noble and Prussian generals. Even in 1943, when Hitler had cause to be disappointed with the 'Prussian' war machine under his control, eleven out of seventeen field marshals were from these traditionally military families.[15] Even after 20 July, 1944, which convinced Goebbels and others that it had been a mistake to build Nazi armies on the base of the traditional German officer class, the higher echelons still contained a high proportion of Prussian nobles.[16]

By his position, Moltke had become a member of the armed forces, still one of the few places where one could be guaranteed protection from the Nazi Party. By joining the Abwehr, he was '. . . going into the

---

* *Trott had got to know John through Otto-Hans Winterer, the Luftwaffe pilot he had tried to put forward for the Rhodes Scholarship in 1936.*

the nerve centre of the group seeking to deprive Hitler of power, an organization which General Jodl in his trial at Nuremberg was to describe as a "nest of conspirators" . . .'[17] The Abwehr was under the command of Admiral Canaris, an enigmatic figure who allowed the organization to fill up with anti-Nazi elements as a result of his own disgust at the regime and its leaders.[18] So strong were his feelings towards the latter that he could not bring himself to shake Himmler's hand, 'Whoever shook hands with a "*Schweinehund*" like Himmler, could no longer be touched without befouling one's self.'[19]

The strongly anti-Nazi character of the Abwehr came as a surprise to those who came into contact with it for the first time. Colonel Lahousen, who was drafted into the institution from Austrian Military Intelligence after the Anschluss, experienced the effect of making the 'Hitler-grüss' in front of Canaris and his assistant:

> When Lahousen had first entered Canaris' presence, he had acted very formally, clicking his heels and giving the Hitler salute. Canaris merely smiled; then he reached out and gently drew his visitor's arm down to a more normal position and motioned him to sit. When Lahousen repeated the salute on entering Oster's office, Oster laughed loudly and, unguarded as ever, cried, 'No Hitler salute here, please!'[20]

After 1938, the Abwehr was divided into three parts: 1) The Foreign Countries division under the command of Admiral Leopold Bürkner; 2) Division Z, which handled personnel, finance and administration and was run by Oster; and 3) the Abwehr proper in its three sub-sections, a) Intelligence Procurement, b) Sabotage and Subversion and c) Counter-Intelligence. Moltke was attached to 1), of which International Law was the sixth of seven branches. Conveniently for his work and for the meetings of the circle in its early days, Moltke had the use of his brother-in-law Carl Deichmann's house in the Derflingerstrasse, which was only 600 yards away from Canaris' headquarters on the Tirpitzufer. Deichmann's house was destroyed during an Allied air raid in 1943 and Moltke then moved out to Lichtenfelde to stay with his friend and cousin, Peter Yorck, Graf von Wartenburg. Remarkably the Abwehr headquarters survived the bombing and are still there to this day.

Although Moltke's cousin, Peter Yorck, Graf von Wartenburg, was three years older than the Lord of Kreisau and had only become a close friend in January 1940, from that time onwards he became the most faithful and assiduous member of the Kreisau Circle.[21] Yorck enjoyed the patronage of the Gauleiter of Silesia, and later Price Commissioner, Joseph Wagner. Wagner was one of those early Nazis who had been attracted into the movement by the genuinely reformist Strasserite wing. He had been drummed into active resistance by the merchant Nikolaus von Halem, and had been one of those who had

166

played an active role in 1938, at the time of the Munich crisis.[22] Under his rule in Silesia, a number of anti-Nazis were employed in the administration of the province, including Fritz-Dietlof, Graf von der Schulenburg. Schulenburg was another enthusiastic Nazi of the Strasserite wing, but had become disillusioned with the Party after the Night of the Long Knives. He no longer wore his gold Party badge. While Wagner was in charge he had been vice-president of the Silesian Administration but at the Gauleiter's recall he had thought it wise to slip into the army, where he could be more easily protected from the Party.[23]

Schulenburg, Yorck, Moltke and Trott became the mainstay of the younger civilian resistance, when it began to coalesce in the wake of Hitler's remarkable victories in 1940. Trott's collaboration with Moltke, right up to the latter's arrest at the beginning of 1944, was to be close and fruitful, and it was initiated by their first meeting after Trott's return from America on 27 May, when Trott, Moltke and Hans Peters met in the Derflingerstrasse for a 'general exchange of views'.[24] One thing that Trott and Moltke also had in common was their love of Britain and their despair at the war which existed between that country and Germany. On 18 April Moltke wrote to his wife Freya of a dream he had had in which he had seen his friends Michael Balfour and Lionel Curtis. At the end of the dream he was forced to choose between two alternatives, 'either to be shot in England as a spy or in Germany as a traitor'.[25]

Although Adam von Trott had stood on the fringes of the Auswärtige Amt since his meetings with Walter Hewel and Ernst von Weizsäcker in the late spring of 1939, he was not formally admitted – and then onlv to the Informationsabteilung (the IA, or Foreign Office information service) – till 1 June 1940. The two lengthy reports he had drawn up, both as regards his Cliveden experiences and his trip to America, had contributed something towards his getting the job of Wissenschaftliche Hilfsarbeiter or technical assistant, as had the goodwill of Hewel and Weizsäcker. But Trott had faced insuperable difficulties when it came to the minister himself, who had not taken it well when the former had presumed to come between him and his Führer the previous year. Matters of policy towards Great Britain were Ribbentrop's special domain and one in which he exercised the extreme bitterness which he had harvested from the snubs and ridicule which had dogged his London years. Until 1943, Ribbentrop put an effective stop to Trott's entering the Foreign Office proper, even though he had taken the trouble to put in his application for Party membership at the same time as pressing his application with the AA.

Even before he and Bielenberg got together to draft the report of the American venture, Trott had sought to influence Foreign Office thinking when it came to the United States. Learning of Sumner Welles' projected fact-finding mission to Berlin in the spring of 1940, Trott had written to Hewel from Tokyo to warn him that if Welles were to form the opinion that Germany was a threat to American interests, it would lead to a strengthening of Roosevelt's hard line towards Germany. So far the president had had little success, as the American people had been disinclined to become involved in a second European war. The same argument forms the essence of his '*Bericht über eine Kriegsreise nach Nordamerika im Winter 1939/40*' (Report on a Wartime Journey to North America in the Winter of 1939–40), in which he shows which factors would in all probability lead the Americans into war: English propaganda, the American Jews and President Roosevelt – who had political reasons for wanting to involve America. The only hope lay in the American people who, though equally antipathetic to Nazism and Communism, would call for war if America's interests were threatened; 'effective support for German interests in America depends solely on the actual course of events in Europe'.[26] Trott was once again trying to put a brake on further escalation.

Hindered by the minister himself, Trott was finally conscripted into the Civil Service by his friend and Corps-brother Josias von Rantzau. Rantzau worked in the Informatsionsabteilung of the Auswärtige Amt, Ribbentrop's own propaganda machine. In the chaos of Nazi government all the top Nazi brass were allowed to indulge their petty jealousies to the full. Hitler thrived on the inability of his ministers to act in concert. The distrust and animosity which existed between Goebbels and Göring, between Göring and Ribbentrop and between Ribbentrop and Goebbels is one of the great tragi-comic features of the Third Reich. As Ribbentrop could not conceivably have been expected to accept Goebbels' assistance in questions of foreign propaganda, he insisted on having his own propaganda department.

Information departments or ministries of information in general are a great boon to the educated in time of war. In these enormous circuses the cerebral are set to work on ludicrous projects in the vain hope of helping the war effort. There can be no better picture of such an institution than that contained in Evelyn Waugh's *Put Out More Flags* which is a merciless send up of the Ministry of Information in London at the beginning of the Second World War. By all accounts, the Informationsabteilung of the German Foreign Office was every bit as chaotic and inexplicable as ours, and would, one imagines, have proved no less an inspiration for the comic novelist.

One person who came into contact with Trott for the first time in the summer of 1940 was Tatiana Vassiltchikov, later Princess Metternich, who had fled to Berlin from Estonia, after the Russians who had been assigned that old stamping-ground of the Teutonic Knights in the aftermath of the Ribbentrop-Molotov Pact. She came penniless to Berlin in the company of her younger sister Marie ('Missie') and they both immediately set about finding jobs where they could use their many languages. Tatiana Vassiltchikov was put into the public relations department of the AA, where later her sister joined her. It was there that they first ran into Trott, who with Alexander Werth ('Worthy') and Hans Richter ('Judgie') were 'more friends than colleagues'. 'Newcomers were observed with microscopic care. If undesirable, whenever possible they were shunted on elsewhere'.[27]

Tatiana Vassiltchikov gives a portrait of Trott at the time of their meeting.

He could not accept the fact that the Allies had embarked on a crusade against Germany without making any distinction between Nazis and non-Nazis. Of course, we didn't know this at the time, but we realized that the personality of Adam Trott, quite apart from his striking looks, stood out in stark relief beside all those around him, for he was such a many-sided man in search of a challenge and a meaning in all things.

He was always happier when speaking English, as if it brought on pleasant, lighter memories. He had studied in England and had many friends there, but although he spoke the language perfectly, the rhythm of his thought was German.

He usually sat, lazily draped in easy grace over his hard office armchair, dictating at a leisurely pace. But he could suddenly switch to immense concentration, for he had an untiring capacity for work. His brows drew together, his eyes seemed shadowed, his face hardened, while incisive sentences formed in his mind.

Although perhaps at times his total unselfconsciousness could be mistaken for arrogance, wherever he was one felt at ease, but also somehow on one's mettle. Always direct (but not obvious) in his dealings with people, he would listen with great attention, feeling for the colour of their thoughts. If no headway could be made, he asked ironic questions in a gentle voice. He treated his chiefs with condescension, and was never afraid of speaking his mind . . .*

* Tatiana Metternich's sister Missie, whose diaries reveal what it was like to work with Trott. 'Wednesday, 22nd January First day on my new job with the Information Department of the Foreign Ministry. I feel depressed as everything is unfamiliar. Adam Trott has installed me temporarily in a kind of research institute attached to his India Office as his bosses might get wary were we not only to hold similar political views, but also to work together. My immediate chief is an elderly woman journalist (Frau Kretschmar) who is a specialist in Indian affairs. Adam seems to hope that once I know more about the work, I will eventually influence her in a way useful to him; but I fear he overrates my capacities . . . Monday, 17th February Since last week Adam Trott has taken me into his section. I am very glad, as the atmosphere is much more congenial. Adam has one room; then comes an office for me and two secretaries; then another large room for Alex Werth and a man called Hans Richter, whom everybody calls Judgie . . . For the moment Adam drowns me in translations and book reviews. I have one to do right now for which I have been given only two

169

Alexander Werth – Trott's friend from Göttingen – had only recently joined him in the IA, his cooption being part of a conscious policy on Trott's behalf to fill the offices with like-minded opponents to the Hitler regime. Once or twice people failed to match up to his standards, as was the case with Josias Rantzau, who, while supporting the idea of a Putsch, stopped short at the advocacy of assassination. Trott's relations with Rantzau were strained as a result. Werth had returned from exile in Britain just before the war and after quickly passing his Assessor's examination he had joined the army, serving in the French campaign.[28] The German conquests of Poland, Holland, Belgium, Norway, Denmark and France had brought about a need to expand the information services of the AA and Trott seized this moment to get Werth away from the army – as he was to do with another old Socialist friend, Curt Bley. 'Werth is a '*Teufelskerl*' (a devil of a fellow), he said, 'but he needs friends.' Werth, it seems, had volunteered for one of the most dangerous branches of military service.[29] 'Judgie' Richter was a former export merchant who had been drummed into the AA, his expertise when it came to Anglo-Saxon countries being considered invaluable to the service.

Another man with whom Trott came into close contact through the IA was the veteran trade unionist, Franz-Josef Furtwängler. Until 1933,[30] Furtwängler had worked in the administration of the Berlin unions. When the Nazis came to power he had moved to Hungary and worked in the petrol industry. In 1940 he had got to know Helmuth Moltke and through him became a fringe member of the Kreisau Circle, providing extremely important contacts for that still basically

---

days. Sometimes I must fill in by taking German dictation. I horrify the entourage with my grammatical mistakes. Tuesday, 22nd April *I am still sweating away at translations. Adam Trott wants me to take all his routine work in hand so that he can retire to more Olympian heights and not be bothered by red tape. I started by trying to clean up his writing table while he was away at lunch. I sat on the floor scooping out drawer after drawer and nearly cried at the mess. His little secretary, who is devoted to him, came in and comforted me:* "Herr von Trott ist ein Genie und von einem Genie kann man so etwas wie Ordnung gar nicht verlangen" *(Herr von Trott is a genius and you can't possibly demand that a genius is tidy as well!) I repeated this to him on his return and he was visibly touched . . . we usually speak English together. I feel more at home with him that way. When he speaks German he becomes so intellectual that I cannot always follow, or rather I cannot do so when he dictates. He throws the beginning of a sentence into the air, pauses for a second, and then the rest comes tumbling after it. Later, when I am faced with my hieroglyphs, I usually seem to have missed half. My German is simply not yet good enough. Judgie Richter and Alex Werth also often speak English to me – Judgie having spent much of his life in Australia. We are sometimes referred to as the "House of Lords".'* (Missie Vassiltchikov, Berlin Diaries 1940–1945.)

aristocratic group with former Socialist Reichstag deputies like Julius Leber and Carlo Mierendorff. Under Trott's initiative, Furtwängler made a trip to the Far East, where he got in touch with Ecke. Another result of Trott's Chinese expertise had been the establishment of a German Information Office in Shanghai, which could also be used as a base for anti-Nazi operations in the Far East and source of contact with sympathetic German exiles.

Werth's first meeting with Trott since the London days had taken place on 20 April in the Bethanien Hospital in Berlin when he was turning his thoughts to the organization of the resistance in the Auswärtige Amt. Werth was only involved with Trott in certain aspects of his work – notably the India Office; on the other hand Trott had no secrets from Werth even if he played little part in the resistance and they did not always see eye to eye on things.

After Dunkirk, Trott had been genuinely worried that the victorious German advance might well take in Britain and that he would need to do the maximum to protect his friends there in the event of a German puppet government – most probably under Mosely – being set up. At that time Trott had also brought Peter Bielenberg into the Foreign Office for those very reasons. Once Göring's Luftwaffe, however, had proved itself unequal to the task, it was clear to most people that the invasion would not take place. Peter Bielenberg therefore left the AA and took up managing a fish paste factory instead. Hitler had never had more than a passing interest in Operation Sea-Lion, (or the invasion of Britain) hoping after Dunkirk that the British would come to their senses and reach an agreement or conclude an alliance with the Germans.

As the Germans settled down to administer the vast bulk of Europe, the offices of the IA at Kurfürstenstrasse 137 began to expand with the necessary personnel required for the exercise. This was the great moment for Trott and his collaborators to seize the departments which would be vital in order to ensure the maximum freedom of movement – especially those of Great Britain and the Empire, the United States and the Far East. Neutral countries were the focal points for the collection and dissemination of information in connection with the propaganda war which was being waged against the British and the numerous sections of the American population who were now increasingly inclined to support them. The occupation of these departments and the journeys connected with them were from the very first the basis for Trott's 'unofficial' work or, to use Werth's words, his 'illegal responsibilities'[31] Strangely enough the Allies were never able to grasp how Trott managed to travel with such apparent ease, possibly because Trott would have been embarrassed to let his contacts know how much he was involved in propaganda as part of his 'double-game'. Even long after the war it was suggested that the 'Gestapo must have known' of his work, because otherwise such freedom of movement would never have been permitted. It is a tribute to Trott's organizational ability that he was to see so early how to exploit the situation to pursue his anti-Nazi ends.

Not everyone was prepared to go along with the Janus-featured chicanery which the double game involved. Peter Bielenberg's decision to quit the service at the end of the year was due to his 'almost Biblical directness which could not get used to our practices in that so often murky atmosphere'.[32] Part of the more light-hearted work was connected with the operation of foreign writers and artists and the business of getting them to act counter to the interests of their own countries. The most famous of these was Lord Haw-Haw – William Joyce – the Irish American who became a figure of fun in war-torn Britain[33] and whom the British, clouding over the nationality of the man, were able to have hanged at the end of the conflict. Another (but this time British) victim was John Amery, the son of the then Colonial Secretary Leo Amery. In theory Amery was raising a British SS legion to fight Communism in the East but in practice his propaganda worth was too great. High-ranking officials were constantly employed to provide for his person and his complicated love life.[34] Another who fared a little better after the war was the writer P.G. Wodehouse; as with the others, the job of the department was 'to keep them sweet'.[35]

As the office was necessarily staffed with linguists, a good part of their business was taken up in the translation of useful gobbets from pro-German writers and artists which could be used either through the foreign service or through Goebbels' propaganda machine. Another role was influencing neutral states and presenting the blackest possible picture of British practices and atrocities. In this the man they called 'mass-murderer Harris',[36] Arthur Harris the head of British Bomber Command, proved a godsend in neutral countries where his civilian bombing campaign was seen as a distinct counter-balance to British propaganda directed against Nazi atrocities. It is regrettably true that although the relentless bombing campaign waged by the British and later by the Americans against German towns and cities played a considerable role in destroying morale and bringing the war home to German citizens, the cost was the death of hundreds of thousands of civilians and the quasi-total destruction of the monuments of Central European civilization.*

---

* At Nuremberg the Allied atrocities were necessarily glossed over. As Speer noted after the trials had finished: 'And then this beastly way of talking. How was it I never really felt revolted by it, never flared up when Hitler – as he did almost all the time in the last few years – spoke of "annihilation" or "extermination"? Certainly those who would charge me with opportunism or cowardice are being too simplistic. The terrible thing, the thing which disturbs me much more, is that I did not really notice this vocabulary, that it never upset me. Only now, in

While Trott was convalescing in Berlin, he wrote to his mother at Imshausen, 'I am very anxious to get in touch with our friend Tracey [Strong].'[37] The American clergyman was part of the house-party that Whitsun. Strong was based in Geneva where Trott had got to know him as a young student. Now, with his links with the United States and his proximity in a vital neutral state, Trott could conceive of a new use for Strong. For his friends in the United States, like Edward Carter, Strong could be used as a letterbox for compromising material, while tamer missives could be passed through vetted diplomatic channels. '. . . while you might make use of this same channel for letters to me,' he wrote to Carter, 'you could very well use Tracey's address for more bulky stuff. I might go there from time to time and collect it in person.'[38]

At Imshausen that May, Trott had a number of private conversations with Strong. Clarita Tiefenbacher, who was then making her first visit to the Trott home, remembers a talk with Tracey Strong, during which he expressed his considerable fears for her future husband.

> . . . the old gentleman asked me on leaving whether I would not accompany him in the coach as far as Bebra [the local railway station]. In the course of the journey he said to me as discreetly as possible that I should take care not to let Adam get involved in any dangerous undertakings, he was both too honourable and too direct for any good to come of it. However, this view did not in any way present an impediment to his willingness to help which did not diminish in the course of the war . . . At the time he was often in Germany on behalf of the Geneva Convention, helping Allied prisoners as much as possible by making use of its clauses to alleviate their conditions as well he might.[39]

Despite his scepticism when it came to religion, Trott's honesty endeared him to churchmen. In Switzerland men like Strong, Visser't Hooft and Schönfeld proved his staunchest supporters during the war years. Through his work in Berlin, he came into contact with other churchmen who had been drafted into the AA or the Abwehr at the beginning of the war, like Dietrich Bonhoeffer who had seen Trott prior to the latter's American trip and had discussed the situation with him. For Bonhoeffer it was not enough just to pray that the anti-Christian regime of the Nazis be brought to a speedy end. He was convinced that action must be taken too to hasten a German defeat, for only in defeat would God's judgement on the Germans become clear.[38]

---

retrospect, am I horrified. Certainly part of the reason was that we lived in a tightly shut world of delusion isolated from the outside world (and perhaps from our respectable selves). I wonder whether in Allied headquarters, as in ours, the talk was not of victory over the enemy but of his "extinction" or "annihilation". How, for example, did Air Marshal Harris express himself?' (Albert Speer, Spandau Diaries, *entry for 21 December 1946.)*

The militant wing of Protestant opposition to Hitler lay in the Pfarrernotbund and its leader, the former submarine commander turned pastor, Martin Niemöller. Niemöller had railed against Nazism from his pulpit in the Berlin suburb of Dahlem, attracting a congregation in such numbers that the tiny medieval church was quite unable to accommodate them.[41] In 1937 Hitler had had him arrested and tried but despite acquittal he was dragged away by the Gestapo and thrown into a concentration camp.*

Another churchman who played a part in the Resistance and survived the war to become President of the Bundestag was Eugen Gerstenmaier. Gerstenmaier was born in Württemberg in 1906, the son of an artisan. He started work as a merchant but continued to study at the local gymnasium and later, read theology and philosophy at Tübingen, Zurich and Rostock universities. Gerstenmaier was an Evangelical and an enemy of National Socialism from the outset which he branded 'political Messianism'. In Geneva he became friendly with Visser't Hooft.[42]

With the Nazi takeover of power, Gerstenmaier's attacks on Hitlerian and Rosenbergian racial and religious policy became more outspoken. The Nazis responded by forbidding him to teach. He found work instead in the Church foreign office under Bishop Heckel. Travel was part of his duties and he attended an ecumenical conference in Oxford in 1937 where he became acquainted with Bishop Bell of Chichester.[43] Links with Bell, through Gerstenmaier, Bonhoeffer and Vissert's Hooft, provided an excellent channel to a more compassionate England, though one which was sadly impotent after the fall of Chamberlain and the later posting of Halifax to Washington at the end of 1940.[44]

In 1940, Gerstenmaier was yet another intellectual with an anti-Nazi track record who slipped into the AA as a 'technical assistant' in the Information Service. There he came across Trott. Gerstenmaier was introduced to Trott in the latter's office soon after he joined the department by Dr Heinz Simon, 'a young attaché with a silver Hitler Youth badge on his lapel, a rapid understanding in his head and an overwhelming readiness to help in his heart'.[45] At this time Gerstenmaier was looking for very much the same thing as Trott, a means of keeping foreign channels open in the struggle against Nazi ideology.

Looking for men who might be able to help in this work by virtue of their position, I became acquainted with a group of young officials of the Foreign Ministry. Outstanding among these was a young legation counsellor, Hans von

---

* By some miracle he survived to become an equally vociferous opponent of evil and bad government in the post-war years. (James Bentley, Martin Niemöller, Oxford 1984.)

174

Haeften, the son of a Prussian general. Hans was a devout Christian and an unswerving opponent of the Nazi regime, but he was so competent in his job that he was entrusted with important work. He rendered great service to the creation of a German opposition. We were joined later by Adam von Trott zu Solz, [a] former Rhodes Scholar who combined superb education with a social conscience and a knowledge of the world.[46]

Through his meetings with Haeften and Trott, Gerstenmaier was beginning to piece together the Resistance cell of the AA. Later he met Georg Federer and Trott's old friends Gottfried von Nostitz and Albrecht von Kessel. Through Trott and Haeften, Gerstenmaier made the acquaintance of Moltke and from that moment became the spokesman for Protestant religious affairs within that Kreisauer group. Later, Gerstenmaier and Moltke lived together in Peter Yorck's house in Lichterfelde.

As a Christian, Gerstenmaier was annoyed that people within the department believed it somehow 'chic' to be ill-informed on Church questions. Both Haeften and 'der Staats' (Weizsäcker)* were exceptions here; as for the rest, Christian sympathizers could be numbered on the fingers of both hands.[47] Trott's religious position has been discussed many times. Gerstenmaier's testimony is interesting, given that they were extremely close at the time.

Adam von Trott had travelled widely. He had submitted a doctorate on Hegel's legal theories without going further to examine his theological interests. In China he had been impressed by the great religions of the Far East and the effects they had on their people. When we met for the first time he displayed a religious thinking which was the cherished bequest of his cultivated family home. His father had been Prussian Kultusminister at a time when Adolf von Harnack had been the brightest star in the firmament of German science. The relatively neutral and conventional relationship which Adam von Trott had with Christian belief became more profound, developing in its own way the longer we worked together in the Kreisau Circle. I shall never forget his pensive response to my question, what did he understand by Christianity? He said, 'Enlightenment and brotherhood.'[48]

---

* The AA was a congenial place for anti-Nazis. 'In the Foreign Office there was no group at all which would seriously have supported Hitler; and there was, on the other hand, a group of men who were working with inner conviction for the overthrow of the regime. Not many of them are alive today. With the exception of the brothers Kordt, Albrecht von Kessel, Hasso von Etzdorf, Gottfried von Nostitz and a few others, they are all among the dead of 20 July 1944 ... I myself was not a registered member of any such group. My permanent work was to carry out obstruction in foreign policy. I did not aim at being given any post when the change should come, and I spoke openly about it to only a very few friends ... After the late summer of 1938 I never gave any other advice but that Hitler should be removed.' (Weizsäcker, Memoirs.)

It was through Franz-Josef Furtwängler that Trott received his introductions to leading Socialists and in particular to Julius Leber. Leber was born in Alsace in 1891, the illegitimate son of a peasant woman. The unnamed father, however, was rich enough to set his mistress up in a house, and later arrange for her to be married. Too poor to continue his studies beyond middle-school, Leber received a grant enabling him to complete his education in Freiburg and to study history at Strasbourg University. He was already a member of the SPD when he volunteered for service in the army in 1914 and he soon became a front-line officer. Later he described the conflict in fierce terms which were typical of his style; the war was the result of

> the lies and folly, the passions and fears of thirty diplomats, princes and generals, who from *raisons d'etat* transformed the peaceful millions for four long years into murderers, robbers and arsonists, only to leave them brutalized, contaminated and impoverished hundreds of miles from their houses. No people made any lasting gains. Everyone lost and the decades have not been able to redeem them. The European people have been obliged to pay the reckoning with nine million corpses.[49]

Highly decorated for bravery during the war, Leber did not leave the army until 1920, when he was involved in the suppression of the Kapp Putsch. That same year he submitted his doctorate at Freiburg University and moved to the Baltic city of Lübeck. In Lübeck, he became a journalist on, and later editor of *Lübecker Volksboten*. It was not long before he was a respected figure in the city and the leader of its SPD. He was elected to the Reichstag in 1924, rapidly becoming the Party's spokesman on military matters, an experience which 'inspired him later in his Resistance work to seek out contacts with politically minded officers'.[50]

Even before the Nazi takeover, Leber was a marked man. On the night of 30 January 1933, he was set upon and badly wounded by five SA thugs. Though he was rescued by a group of Socialist 'Reichsbanner' men, he was arrested and imprisoned. The Lübeck Socialists responded with a massive protest strike which succeeded in getting him released from prison. On 23 March however, he was incarcerated once again and later transferred to a concentration camp where a long attempt was made to break his spirit. He was released only in 1937. As he was forbidden to work as a journalist, his friend Gustav Dahrendorff found him work as a coal merchant in Berlin-Schöneberg. This discreet and unlikely occupation became an ideal cover for his Resistance activities.

Among the sacks of coal, Leber continued to gather together his old party comrades, introducing them to arrivals in an off-hand way, 'This here is an old SPD member, who has spent time in a camp, and here is the daughter of a comrade whom they murdered in a KZ.'[51] It was in the coal depot that Franz-Josef Furtwängler introduced Trott to Leber.

In the first half of 1940, Adam von Trott zu Solz came back from America and immediately became an active member of the Resistance movement within the Foreign Office. It was then that I introduced them for the first time. Within a little while Leber became one of the best friends of the unforgettable, genial Trott. It came as no surprise as Leber too brought together heart, courage and temperament with spirit and intelligence. Nor was Leber a mere intellectual, possessing that rare capacity for self-irony.[52]

Schöneberg – at least at that time – seems to have been somewhat misnamed. Leber's coal depot lay in the shadow of a vast gasworks, 'a sad environment with the black gasometer, the black coal-heaps, the grey wooden hoardings behind which was located the shed which served as Leber's office.'[53] Once Furtwängler had effected his introduction, he left the two men to deliberate alone. 'In the underground movement, people were advisedly sparing when it came to meetings and assemblies, the more close the friendship between Trott and Leber became, the more seldom was there any necessity for my visits to the latter.'[54]

Furtwängler has left us with a portrait of Trott in 1940. Contemporary photographs confirm that Trott had aged rapidly, his receding hair line giving the impression that he was older than his thirty-one years; losing his hair had given Trott a look reminiscent of the Droeshout engraving of Shakespeare. 'Only when he laughed in a boyish, high-spirited way, which he did often, did he radiate total youthfulness.'[55] A dangerous game which Trott enjoyed playing at the time, and one which had echoes in Canaris' Abwehr, was getting Jews out of prisons on the pretext that they were required for some higher political use, or possessed an expertise indispensable to the German Foreign Office. Furtwängler remembers one occasion soon after the fall of France when he caught Trott in the act of packing a huge briefcase. "I'm off to Paris again today," he told me. "They have locked up some Jews whom I know; I have attributed to all of them indispensable special knowledge, with which they can be drafted into the Foreign Office. That way they can be pulled out of the paws of the Gestapo."[56] Furtwängler noted that the trick made Trott 'quake with pleasure'.[57]

Trott was extremely quick to learn how best to use the chaos of the IA to his advantage. He had no qualms about using his charm in order to achieve his ends, often making his friends uncomfortable as a result.[58] For a terrible four weeks, the Bielenberg household had been saddled with Wolf Kriebel.

He was a rather limp young man, the more than harmless son of Alter Kämpfer

177

Parteigenosse Kriebel, head of the personnel department of the Foreign Office and bearer of the Party badge in gold. Such birds were rare, unique in fact in our acquaintanceship, and Adam, having met son Wolf when he was in China, had decided that he must be cultivated. When Adam came to such decisions he was charmingly ruthless, and usually had little difficulty in persuading his friends to co-operate. Four weeks, though, had seemed a long time not to be able to speak openly even within one's own four walls, and I had heaved a sigh of relief when Wolf told us that he was taking a job in Bohemia. It was surely not too soon, for my never very patient Peter had almost ceased bothering to be polite to him any more.[59]

Furtwängler, too, describes his 'bending' of officials in order to gain precious advantages for foreign travel and authority within the IA.

'The 'bending' of his superiors and opponents, even the most dangerous ones, was his speciality. With an almost feminine intuition he was able to read the thoughts of interlocuters and to shape himself to their manner of speaking. It did not matter whether the person in question was a typist, a Communist chauffeur, an army general or a Party chief; in each case he displayed his characteristic excellence in the understanding of the person involved.

It was an aesthetic pleasure to listen to him when he spoke to a State Secretary, who was also a high Party functionary, suggesting a decision be made but all the time giving the other the impression that he had taken the decision himself. Only in this way was it possible for him, throughout the years of the Third Reich, to travel abroad on official missions which were also his own – for which the end was the overthrow of the regime. All the time it should be stated that this diplomatic jobbery and adversity had as little effect on the warmth and purity of his character as a glass splinter does on a diamond.[60]

On 11 September, Trott and Bielenberg turned up to see Helmuth Moltke in Berlin. Moltke in his impatient and high-handed way was unimpressed with what they had to offer. 'Trott turned up yesterday with Bielenberg less to exchange news as I had expected, than to be told what attitude to adopt. They too, have lost their sense of direction and allow themselves to be influenced by external events and expect those events to provide solutions which they don't think they can discover on their own.'[61] Moltke himself had been to Brussels the month before to meet Falkenhausen, whom he saw as an 'outstanding and courageous man'. He had gone in the company of Under Secretary Woermann from the AA and former Consul General Otto Kiep.

We had a fantastic dinner in a restaurant in a park: caviare, ham in burgundy, duck, crêpes. The drink was obviously out of this world; vodka, a claret[,] 'Enfant Jésus', champagne and armagnac. I didn't touch any of it, but the others seemed blissfully happy. Afterwards at about 11.30 we went back to

178

Falkenhausen's hotel, where whisky and beer were laid on. Woermann was thoroughly tight and most of the rest, including Kiep, distinctly jolly. So that the only people really sober were Falkenhausen and myself and for the most of the time between 11.30 and 1.30 we entertained one another. I welcomed this because at dinner I was inevitably too far away to talk to him.*[62]

Despite the apparent aimlessness which Moltke found in Trott on the 11 September, that same month Trott made another bid to keep the lines open between Germany and Britain. Trott travelled to Geneva where he got in touch with his old friend Visser't Hooft. The Battle of Britain had failed. 'It was clear that Sea-Lion was no longer on the cards. Steel was being given to the army for tanks. So Russia was the enemy.'[63] The change in the situation *vis-à-vis* Britain appealed to Trott as an opportunity to restart negotiations now that Britain's back was no longer against the wall. Trott gave the Dutchman a report on the situation in Germany which he asked him to transmit to David Astor through a Mrs Gladys Bretherton, who was involved at the British end of the World Council of Churches.[64]

The picture Trott painted for Visser't Hooft was very gloomy. The Nazi regime was immensely successful and no one foresaw the possibility of a revolt being carried out by the German army. Trott believed in the circumstances that people should work for peace based on a settlement in which Germany should be as much as possible restricted to her ethnographical borders. The Germans believed that the ultimate battle was a spiritual one. Christians had fundamental ideals in common; there was a need for a spiritual mission to Europe after the end of hostilities in order to link up the peoples of Europe. Only governments were at odds with one another, the Christian peoples were not.[65]

Visser't Hooft fully concurred. Perhaps Trott was playing the game of bringing the Dutchman round to the mission by putting his own thoughts into the other's head. Trott wanted to appeal to the clergyman on the grounds that the Resistance desired a common Christian mission which lay one hundred per cent in Visser't Hooft's parish. Some of the discussion appears to have covered a less nebulous terrain: Astor was informed of the state of the Resistance in Germany which united all religious groups – Catholics and Protestants as well as Socialists and conservatives – behind its banner. The latter,

---

* *Falkenhausen's sobriety was not for want of drinking. 'Physically Falken-hausen is a phenomenon. He is able to drink enormous amounts in the evening without ever showing the slightest after-effects, and he is at his office shortly after eight o'clock in the morning. Eleven years in China have stamped out in him any tendencies towards a drill-ground mentality and dull mechanical obedience he might have had and pumped some adventurous blood into his veins. It is a pity he is not at a more central spot.' (Hassell, Diaries entry for 2 August 1941.)*

he said, were 'troubled by the brutalities and excesses of the Nazi leaders'. Trott considered neither the Pope nor Roosevelt trustworthy mediators; a settlement 'should aim at securing to Germany, as far as possible, her ethnographical frontiers. If it shows any sign of wishing to "do Germany down" the nation will rally behind Hitler.' Lastly, in the version which Astor received, Trott spoke of the need to find some co-operation with the 'other' Germany in the event of an invasion of Britain. In the Auswärtige Amt it was current that Sir Oswald Mosely would be made Gauleiter.

Trott made at least one other visit to Switzerland that year, as is evident from a short note he penned to Diana Hopkinson in London on 5 December from Zurich. The letter, which dwells on his wife's virtues and speaks of 'stretches of hectic activity, of little use but no harm', is signed 'E'. Trott had a number of Swiss friends in Zurich whom he visited during the war years. He had contacts with the publisher Martin Hurlimann over a planned book involving the Swiss scholar and diplomat Carl Burckhardt. Geneva was much more a 'home from home' even then as both his friends Kessel and Nostitz were posted to the consulate there and the latter had a large residence where Trott could lodge on his visits. Naturally there were also the churchmen – Visser't Hooft, Tracey Strong and Dr Schönfeld.

Apart from Trott's foreign contacts there is a hint of an involvement with one of the shadier figures of the Nazi resistance, Beppo Römer. Captain Dr Josef Römer, retired, a former World War I officer, was the erstwhile leader of the Freikorps Oberland, one of the paramilitary groups which had sprung up at the anarchic beginnings of Weimar modelled on the famous Freikorps which had waged war against the Napoleonic invaders after Prussia's crushing defeat at Jena in 1806. In 1930 he had started a newspaper in Berlin called *Der Aufbruch* (the *Departure*) which declared war on National Socialism.[66] Sometime before Hitler's takeover, he joined the Communist Party and from that moment onwards maintained close contacts with working-class groups, particularly in factories. One such was the enormous Osram group where a Communist network was established by Robert Uhrig. Römer had the advantage after 1935 of friends in high places which the Communist rank and file lacked. 'The alliance with Römer gave the Uhrig organization a new social dimension. At the same time Uhrig had been working to extend its connections geographically as well.'[67]

Römer's passionate hatred of National Socialism probably owed something to the fact that his beliefs had once been akin to theirs. He made little secret of his opposition and as a result spent several spells in concentration camps over the peacetime Nazi years. Trott very probably met him through his brother Werner, as later Römer became attached to Herbert Mumm von Schwarzenstein and Nikolaus von Halem. Werner may have met Römer through a Communist contact

180

and then introduced him to Halem, who was one of Trott's brother's closest friends. Through Werner, Halem was able to lodge his wife and children at Imshausen throughout the later stages of the war.

Römer's group was the best-organized broad-based Resistance cell in Germany, and no other was to come anywhere near it until the Saefkow-Jacob group began operations later on in the war. Römer himself possessed the advantage of wide-ranging contacts from his army days and officers were ready to communicate with him in a way that they might not have been with a working-class Communist. Indeed, Römer's release from Dachau in July 1939 had been 'swung' by General Ritter von Greim, a regimental fellow officer who was later to become the last chief of the Luftwaffe.[68] The details of Römer's activities are 'necessarily obscure'. We know that he was receiving important material from the Foreign Office, communicated by, among others, Geheimrat (Privy Councillor) Kuenzer of the Solf circle. He also had links with Peter Yorck and therefore with Kreisau.[69]

Through Count Ballestrem and his wife (née Solf), Halem and Mumm engineered a job for Römer in the Ballestrem coal business while they set to work to find a means of assassinating Hitler. Halem was of the conviction that no good would come from contacts with the military; that what was needed was something approximating to a 'professional hangman'. Over this he had fallen out with his schoolfriends Yorck, Botho von Wussow and Albrecht von Kessel. Through the Foreign Office, Halem and Mumm received details of Hitler's trips and travels as well as the closely guarded dates for his increasingly rare public performances. Hitler was well aware that there was a risk of assassination – 'In the future there will never be a man who wields as much as authority as me. My existence is therefore of enormous importance. At any moment I could be slain by some criminal or some idiot.' Römer was not to get his chance to have a go; he was sadly betrayed, and his arrest on 4 February 1942 led to the incarceration and appalling torture of both Mumm and Halem.[70] None of the three was executed till after the bomb plot of 20 July 1944. Herbert Mumm was part of the group the SS executed by shots in the head after the Russians had entered Berlin.

After their meeting in Oxford in 1933, Hans-Bernd Haeften had written to Trott: 'From our very fleeting acquaintance I have the impression that an occasional, full exchange of views would be worthwhile.' Clarita von Trott recalls the first occasion upon which Haeften telephoned his colleague in their Dahlem home. Trott held out the receiver exclaiming, 'Just to hear the voice of this man does me good!' Haeften possessed a deep faith, anchored in Evangelical Protestantism, and at one time thought of studying to become a pastor. His faith made him feel crime and evil personally, to the degree, writes, Frau von Trott, that it 'threatened physically to annihilate him.'

At first Trott was reticent about bringing Haeften in on his Resistance activities. He was, however, to play a full role as a member of the Kreisau Circle, later maintaining the bond through his brother Werner, who became adjutant to Claus Stauffenberg. Tatiana Metternich remembers an occasion soon after she joined the IA, in the summer of 1940.

> One day Trott invited me to dinner to his house, saying, 'I particularly want you to tell me what you think of a friend of mine, who will be there.'
> We were only four: his friend von Haeften, Adam, his charming wife Clarita and me. Adam, taking the talk in hand as usual, touched on a variety of subjects.
> As he drove me home, he asked, 'Well, what did you think of him?'
> 'But what can it matter what I think of him? He is an old friend of yours. A charming and cultivated person. How can one say more after one meeting?'
> 'I would like to know what impression he makes when one doesn't know him.'
> Rather exasperated at his insistence, I said, 'Well, I wouldn't like to steal horses with him: one would get caught sitting on the fence.'
> To my great surprise, he was stunned. 'Why should you say that?'
> 'I don't know really. Unrealistic, perhaps too much theory about his views. He loses touch with the main issue.'
> Only much later did I realize why Adam had minded so much what I had said quite thoughtlessly, for he was on the verge of associating Haeften closely with his plans.

Tatiana's sister, Missie Vassiltchikov, who also worked closely with Trott, did not join the IA until the end of 1940. Her first meeting with Trott took place in the Bielenberg house near the Trott home in Dahlem on 12 July 1940. 'An old friend of Peter's since university days [sic], Adam von Trott zu Solz was also there. I had seen him once before in Josias Rantzau's office. He has remarkable eyes.'[71]

Trott's looks continued to 'fascinate' Missie Vassiltchikov on subsequent meetings in and around the AA.[72] On 10 November the Trotts asked her to a cocktail party with her sister.

> Drove with Luisa Welczek,* Tatania and Josias Rantzau out to Adam Trott's in Dahlem. He married Clarita Tiefenbach [sic] recently. He is a former Rhodes Scholar and there is something very special about him. Hitler's private secretary and liaison man to the AA, Gesandter Walther Hewel, was there ... He is clumsy, but is said to be relatively harmless and is the only member of the 'inner establishment' who occasionally surfaces in other circles. Some people seem to hope they can acquire a positive influence through him.[73]

Just before Christmas, Trott announced to Tatiana Vassiltchikov that

---

* *The daughter of the last German ambassador to Paris before the Nazi takeover.*

he had plans for her sister and he wanted to draw her in under the umbrella of the IA as his private secretary.[74] For her part Missie Vassiltchikov was excited about the idea because it would mean that she could quit the uncongenial job she had at the time. 'The job seems interesting, though difficult to define. He evidently would like to turn me into a kind of confidential factotum. He is doing many things at a time, the whole of it under the official cover of "Free India".'[75] This is the first mention of Trott's later work for the 'Sonderreferat Indien' which for two years would bring him into close contact with Subhas Chandra Bose, the most hated man in the British Empire and a man even today seen as a sort of Quisling when the subject of the last days of British India is introduced.

10
Bose and the India Office

An interest in India was by no means new to Adam Trott. In 1927, in
Geneva, he had been introduced to the idea of Indian independence
for the first time. Later, in his single term at Mansfield, he had struck up
a close friendship with Humayun Kabir, an Indian who later served as
a minister in an independent Indian government. Again at Oxford,
and this time at Balliol, he met and even questioned Gandhi, who had
visited the college as the guest of its radical Master, A.D. Lindsay. From
that meeting Trott treasured a group photograph showing him in the
company of the Mahatma with a number of other undergraduates and
dons sympathetic to his cause.

In the later 1930s Trott's enthusiasm for Indian independence did
not diminish. British India he saw as an abomination. When riled by
his correspondents he would happily cite the behaviour of His
Majesty's administration as a comparison to Nazi brutality at home
– though this was mainly a reaction to his friends' criticisms of
Germany, which were always guaranteed to stir up in him furious
anger. In this instance his correspondents, Diana Hubback and Shiela
Grant Duff, might well have agreed with his savage condemnation of
British atrocities in the Subcontinent; at one stage in the 1930s
both were working for the charismatic Nehru and warmly recommending the latter to their German friend.[1] Several times in the early
days of his Far Eastern expedition he had thought of studying
the Indian situation at first hand, planning not only to visit the Oxford
don Humphrey House who was then teaching at the Presidency
College in Calcutta, but also Kabir, who had extended a warm
invitation to him to stay. Only August von Trott's death had put an end
to these projects.[2]

When the King of England declared war on Germany on 3
September 1939, the Marquis of Linlithgow, the Viceroy of India
responded for the subjects of the Emperor of India. On that day,
Subhas Chandra Bose, leader of the Forward Bloc and the fire-brand
among Nationalist politicians, veteran of nearly a dozen spells in
British detention, was addressing a meeting of 200,000 supporters on
the beach in Madras when 'somebody thrust a newspaper into his
hand. The headline told the story: Britain was now at war with
Germany, and India had followed. Within hours of Chamberlain's

broadcast Lord Linlithgow had, without consulting a single Indian, plunged four hundred million into a European war.'[3]

Bose was born in Bengal in 1897, the son of a well-off lawyer.[4] He was a Kayastha, a caste which had risen to being second only to the Brahmins in Bengal. After school he attended the famous Presidency College in Calcutta. While he was there, however, he became involved in a disturbance which led to a violent outburst against a British teacher. Bose was sacked as a ringleader. Hunting around for another institution, Bose sought refuge in the Scottish Church College and it was there that he took his BA examination.

Having finished his degree, Bose sailed for England, ostensibly to take the Indian Civil Service exam. Hearing from a friend on arrival that there was a chance of his studying for a couple of years at Cambridge, he seized the opportunity and entered Fitzwilliam Hall, (then not strictly speaking a college of the university but a body taking in students who could take university examinations). Bose shows no sign of having developed any fondness for Britain and its institutions while at Cambridge and seems to have been equally immune to the beauty of the place. While he was studying in England he took the ICS examination and was placed fourth. Nevertheless he decided against entering the Civil Service of the Raj and resolved to devote himself to the cause of Indian independence.

On the boat back to India he travelled with Rabindranath Tagore, the Indian poet and philosopher, and together they discussed the significance of Gandhi. Bose was then an enthusiastic supporter of the Mahatma, though their paths were soon to diverge. In contrast with the approach of Gandhi, there was no hint of romanticism in Bose's proposals, no return to India's golden past. Bose did not simply want to take India into the twentieth century. He wished to make her a world power. In this he firmly rejected non-violence from the beginning: 'The days of the bullock cart are gone for ever, Free India must arm herself for any eventuality as long as the whole world does not accept wholeheartedly the policy of disarmament.'

With his attacks on Gandhi went a rejection of the halfway house of dominion status which the latter was campaigning for. 'If you want to overcome the slave mentality you will do so by encouraging our countrymen to stand for complete independence.' Despite an early espousal of democracy and even the contention that it had been an historic Indian system of government, Bose was increasingly attracted by authoritarian regimes. During the war, both Trott and Alexander Werth tried to instil in the man a feeling for a British-style bicameral system for an independent India; perhaps the mention of Britain was unwise. Bose countered that the government which came closest to his requirements was that of Atatürk in Turkey.[5]

From early on, Bose adopted Mussolini-style paramilitary artefacts for his movement. He was attracted by the outward image of fascism with its weapon training and marching and the total subordination of the state to one man. This later led him to style himself the 'Netaji,' after the models of 'Il Duce,' 'Der Führer', 'El Caudillo', etc. He sought to synthesize Fascism and Communism as he had earlier tried to bring together strains of Fascism and Socialism. In his inaugural speech as mayor of Calcutta on 24 September 1930, Bose said, 'I would say that we have here in this policy and programme a synthesis of what Modern Europe calls Socialism and Fascism. We have here the justice, the equality, the love which is the basis of Socialism, and combined with that we have the efficiency and the discipline of Fascism as it stands in Europe today.'

At that time Hitler had yet to attract his attention, but when, three years later, he was recuperating in Europe from one of his eleven unhealthy sojourns in British gaols, he applied for a visa to visit Germany in order to observe the youthful National Socialist regime at first hand. At first the British were reluctant to grant his request, either because they feared Hitler's co-operation with the Nationalist leader or because they had grave misgivings about the effects his visit might have on the Indians studying in Germany (Bose had not been granted a visa to enter Britain). The India Office finally gave way in May 1933, but Bose overestimated the welcome he would receive from Hitler – just as he was to overestimate it in 1941. Bose was nothing if not an opportunist and in this instance he had not bothered to ask himself, like Gandhi or Nehru, which was the greater evil, the Nazis or the British?

Hitler, for the time being, showed no interest in seeing him, and later in that decade, in a conversation with Lord Halifax, suggested to the scandalized British minister that he should have him shot. He did meet the 'Nazi philosopher' Rosenberg, and possibly Göring. The possibility of a fruitful discussion between the former and Bose would seem unlikely. Rosenberg uttered his usual racialist gibberish, suggesting that, as a Nordic race, the British were the best thing for India, a view which Hitler certainly shared with his 'learned Theban'. Bose did, however, find some common ground with the Nazis, particularly with the younger Strasserite National Socialists on the left wing of the Party. In the early days of National Socialism the Strassers and the north-west German Working Group had called for a federation of oppressed nationalities in the pages of the *Kampf Verlag*. This anti-British stance was unpopular with Hitler.

Bose's chief contact with the Party was Lothar Frank; through him Bose began to find many attractive details in the Party organization. The co-operation with Frank led to a promise of arms being shipped to India for the revolution, but in the end the Night of the Long Knives removed this source of support in Germany as it wiped out the left-wing influence in the Party. As far as Fascist leaders went, Bose had better luck and was better treated by Mussolini. Hitler shocked him with his dependence on capitalist funding, by what Bose assumed to be a pro-British imperial policy and by his racialism. When Bose came to read *Mein Kampf*, the following passage (which he later made an unsuccessful bid to have deleted) rankled:

England will never lose India unless she admits racial disruption in the machinery of her administration (which at present is entirely out of the question in India) or unless she is overcome by the sword of some powerful enemy. But Indian risings will never bring this about. We Germans have had sufficient experience to know how hard it is to coerce England. And, apart from all this, I as a German would far rather see India under British domination than under that of any other nation.[6]

After his return to India, Subhas Bose became President of the Congress Party on two occasions, in 1938 and 1939. His policies, however, led to fighting between him and Gandhi, who started a campaign to have him removed. At the end of 1937, he had made his second and last visit to England, meeting a number of Labour leaders who were known to support Indian independence. One of these was Trott's friend and benefactor Sir Stafford Cripps who 'evidently didn't like him'. When war broke out a little more than eighteen months later few Socialists in Britain would have been sympathetic towards an Indian campaign of civil disobedience or rebellion – issues of that sort would have to be shelved till the end of the war. This policy was accepted by the moderate Indian nationalists who could see concessions being granted in exchange for acquiescence. Bose, however, felt that the time had come to seek a partner in the battle with Britain.

At first Bose conceived of Russia as a potential friend, but the Russians spurned his overtures. After the Allied defeats in the early stages of the war, Bose could not control his enthusiasm, his grave and humourless demeanour fairly melting at news of the fall of France.

I remember how Subhas' face lit up with joy [wrote a friend later]. He hugged some of us and danced round the room like a merry schoolboy. To him the Fall of France was his victory, the victory of his people – as with France prostrate, the day of reckoning for Britain was close at hand. He was sure that Britain could not avoid abject surrender and equally confident that the mighty Empire would melt like snow on a hot day.

A few days later Bose led a march through Calcutta towards the monument consecrated to the memory of the British who perished in the 'Black Hole'. His avowed intention was to destroy it – an action that even his closest supporters found in bad taste. It was then that Bose was arrested for the last time. He was kept under house-arrest pending trial. Six months later he took the chance he was waiting for, fleeing from Calcutta under cover of darkness dressed in broad pyjamas, a long coat and a black fez. He had now decided that the Russians would be most sympathetic to his interesting blend of totalitarian thinking. His chosen destination was Moscow.

Bose left Bombay in the early hours of 17 January 1941, travelling via Peshawar to the Afghan border. On the 22nd, his Afghan guide informed him that they were no longer in British India. Bose, though weary from days of walking, was suddenly overwhelmed with joyful energy; jumping in the air, he exclaimed. 'Here I kick George VI,' then, gurgling with happiness, 'Here I spit on the face of the Viceroy.' Once they reached the road, they were able to hitch lifts to Kabul, then little more than a collection of mud huts around a royal palace with a few embassy compounds dotted around in the chaos.

From the first Bose had no luck with the Russians, who would not open their gates to him. Even when he alighted upon the Soviet ambassador's car stuck in some mud, the ambassador was not keen to get involved, believing that Bose had probably been released intentionally by the British in order to stir up trouble on the Russo-Afghan border. He had better luck at the German embassy where he not only met an enthusiastic attaché, who was busy reading the exploits of his escape in a German newspaper, but also the ambassador, Pilger, who consented to telegraph Berlin even though he felt much the same way as his Soviet counterpart. Before he did so, however, he contacted the Italian embassy where the case came up before a diplomat called Pietro Quaroni who saw an immediate propaganda use for Subhas Bose. Although Bose was still maintaining his 'absolute preference for Moscow', to Quaroni he expounded his view that the Germans should encourage the founding of governments in exile, 'paying England back in her own coin'.[7] As a result of a joint German and Italian initiative, their governments were able to find the funds necessary to transport Bose by car to the Russian border, by train to Moscow, and finally by plane to Berlin. In the meantime he had gained a new identity as 'Orlando Mazzotta', an Italian diplomat.

In Berlin, the Auswärtige Amt was posted as to the movements of this curious 'Italian' envoy.[8] At the end of 1940, Trott had already laid the foundations for a separate Indian Department within the Far Eastern section of the IA. This was to be another fief for himself and his friends, hence his recruiting of Missie Vassiltchikov the previous December. Within the department, Trott's advocacy of attacks on Britain's Achilles' heel in India was one of his major claims to fame. In the early months of its existence the department was maintained through his initiative and managed by his enthusiasm – all of which raises the question of how Trott could exploit this British weakness while at the same time professing a love for Britain and her people?

The answer is twofold. On the one hand Trott needed to impress his bosses with his efficiency in order to get the freedom to travel vital to his underground work; the Indian project, which involved collecting Indian nationals from European cities and spreading propaganda in neutral states, was excellent cover. On the other hand, Trott had no love for the British Empire. As he told Christabel Bielenberg:

> Nothing can be the same after this war . . . Your little island will just have to change its role. It won't be so important, it may not be so smug. It will have to loosen the reins, cease exploiting and start to educate, and allow those pink blobs on the map to change to any colour they please. I could believe it will be done gracefully, England is a pastmaster at seeing the light just in time; and I could believe too, that she will be helped by all the richer countries having to provide massive support to the poorer ones in order to help them to their nationhood. No charity about it; it is dangerous as well as unethical to be rich in a poor world.[9]

Although Trott saw nothing unethical in promoting independence in the Subcontinent, in time he began to wonder whether Bose would be a suitable leader for the new state. In his heart Trott remained loyal to the same Gandhi who had fired his youthful imagination at Oxford;[10] he was scarcely impressed by Bose's frankly unimpressive character.

The day after Bose's escape from Calcutta, the German Foreign Office had gone into action. Alexander Werth, for whom Bose became something of a *cause célèbre* in the latter years if his life, tells the story:

> . . . Rome, Berlin and the German legation in Kabul were informed. The telephones were kept busy. Thus a small number of competent staff members of the Foreign Office in Berlin, including Adam von Trott zu Solz . . . and myself learnt about the project 'Orlando Mazzotta'. Netaji could reach Rome or Berlin only via Moscow. At the Italian legation in Kabul there happened to be a vacant position for an official wireless operator with diplomatic status. This position including a diplomatic passport in the name of Orlando Mazzotta was taken over by Netaji. A German courier, Dr Weller, was sent off by plane to meet him. On 18 March 1941 he continued on his route to Moscow via Bokhara and Samarkand. Netaji left Moscow by plane on 28 March 1941. The Soviet Union did not hinder Netaji crossing her territory on his way to Berlin where he arrived on 3 April 1941.[11]

At that time, continues Werth, both he and Trott were Referatsleiter – or heads of division, for all those countries which came under the British or American sphere of influence. The department in 136/137 Kurfürstenstrasse contained a quantity of experts and a few routine officials; 'there were only very few National Socialists among them'. Members of the IA, adds Werth, had no civil service status, though Trott entered the Foreign Office proper when he was elevated to the rank of Legationssekretär, or third secretary. 'We were practically our own masters in our relatively vast working sphere.'[12]

As for the Foreign Minister, he had cut himself off from the day-to-day working operations of the Foreign Office and his interest in the running of the IA was virtually non-existent.

Contact between the officials of the Foreign Office of the India division and the Foreign Minister was actually restricted to a teleprinter message once a year from the Foreign Minister who usually had his headquarters on a special train in Westphalia. The Foreign Minister never gave any regular or definite instructions to his officers who worked in the India division because Ribbentrop had no personal contact with them and he remained always very distrustful and sceptical about the civil servants who worked for him.[13]

Liberty of action within the India department was assured by the lack-lustre Nazi *Apparatschik* who was nominally in charge — Wilhem Keppler. Keppler was an old Party time-server, an Alter Parteigenosse and SS Gruppenführer (the equivalent of a Generalleutnant in the Wehrmacht or a Gauleiter in the Party hierarchy)* whose chief claim to fame was that it was he — as a failed businessman with important contacts — who was able to bring together Hitler and Papen in January 1933. This meeting, *unter vier Augen* (one to one), resulted in the electoral pact which brought the Nazis to power.[14]

Despite the momentous import of Keppler's diplomacy, he was slow to find himself a role in the Nazi hierarchy and remained to the end in the second rank. This was perhaps due to his credulous admiration for his chief, one day he went so far as to tell an English visitor, *'Der Führer hat eine Draht direkt zum lieben Gott'* (The Führer has a private line to God the Father).[15] At first, in the years following the *Machtergreifung*, Keppler played the role of liaison between Hitler and Himmler. His earlier capacity as head of the Studienkreis für Wirtschaftsfragen (Study Group on Economic Issues), in which he brought together sympathetic economists such as Hjalmar Schacht, had failed to get him the job which he desired – that of Economic Minister. Instead he turned his mind to foreign politics. Seconded to the embassy in Austria at the beginning of 1938, Keppler played a key role in organizing the political disruption which brought about the Anschluss. As the AA's chief trouble shooter he was off again on his travels at the beginning of 1939, this time to Slovakia to prepare the Slovakian leader, Father Tiso, for the stab in the back of 'rump Czechoslovakia' which was brought off with the invasion of Prague in March. On his return from Slovakia he was made State Secretary at the Foreign Office, with special responsibility for Far Eastern affairs as a reward for his endeavours.

Trott's Far Eastern experience and knowledge made him an

---

* *Wehrmacht general officers' ranks are complicated by the fact that a* 'general-major' *is the equivalent of brigadier in the British army.*

essential second-in-command to this uninspiring figure. It was, as one writer has said, 'a bitter irony of fate' that the two should be thus thrown together in partnership, 'incorporating in Second World War Germany two worlds which no bridge could span'.[16] Trott's assistants were his friends Alexander Werth and Franz-Josef Furtwängler, both of whom had widely differing views on India and more especially on Bose himself. Werth – perhaps as a result of strong Socialist principles – was the hardliner and most enthusiastic Bose supporter in the office. As he was to say years later in a Bose commemorative address, Netaji's flight

opened a new front for a psychological warfare against Great Britain. Besides, it appealed to our personal feelings of sympathy for India and her fight for freedom, not counting the notorious German admiration for Indian philosophy and art. This was our first reaction to Netaji's arrival *before we had any personal contact with him.*[17] [Werth's italics]

Furtwängler was less taken with 'Orlando Mazzotta' than Werth. Werth later went on to write at length about Bose, becoming something of a celebrity in post-independence India (though he was careful to say that if Trott had survived the war he would have been the honoured German guest in the newly independent country). Like Trott, Furtwängler was to some degree disappointed with this Indian windfall, having grown up with the cause as presented by the more acceptable Gandhi and Nehru (although Gandhi was to change his tune towards Bose when he realized the power the latter had to disrupt India at the time of the Cripps Mission). Furtwängler also had a habit of telling Bose what to do which the Indian resented. Furtwängler points out, however, that in the circumstances of the Nazi control of Germany, Bose had little to hope for during nearly two years based in Berlin: 'His up-till-then unambiguous political role became tragi-comic . . . but I should not like to maintain that this was entirely his fault. The atmosphere of the National Socialist psychopathic tyranny with its intrigues and prattling chaos was for him a permanent strain on his nerves.'[18]

On 3 April, the day of his arrival, Bose was ushered in to meet Woermann of the Foreign Office's Far Eastern desk. Bose immediately pressed for the setting up of an Indian government-in-exile. Woermann gave him a cautious response; for the moment he 'wasn't buying'. A week later Bose began to puzzle the sober diplomat; in the week following their first meeting in the Wilhelmstrasse, Bose managed to halve the strength of the British army in India from some 140,000 to 70,000 men. He also expressed the wish to remain Signor Orlando Mazzotta (Bose had a fondness for subterfuge) which Woermann found hard to understand. Bose did not see Woermann's chief, Ribbentrop, until 19 April in Vienna. Ribbentrop was doing his usual imitation of 'his master's voice,' telling Bose that the war was won, 'England finished', and that Hitler had great plans for Europe. Bose tried to encourage Ribbentrop to organize an Indian army from the prisoners taken in North Africa. He also expressed his reservations about the inherent racialism of the Third Reich. Ribbentrop riposted that the regime was not opposed to any race, seeking merely to preserve 'racial purity'.[19]

A few days later in Berlin, Bose called on Woermann once again. Encouraged by Rommel's great sweep across North Africa, Bose wanted a German declaration of support for Indian independence after the war. He also wanted German armies to launch an attack on India. Finally he urged the Germans to sponsor a *coup d'etat* in Afghanistan to remove the pro-British government there. Again Woermann was unmoved and on 24 April all plans *vis-à-vis* India were indefinitely postponed. It was in mid-May, however, that Bose met Trott for the first time. Perhaps this was on Woermann's initiative or Trott suggested the idea to Keppler. Given the way that he had been thinking at the end of 1940, it is probable that Trott himself was behind it.

As Werth enthused in 1969,

> It was great luck for Netaji and his cause that Adam von Trott zu Solz happened to be the head of the office in charge of all matters concerning Netaji's activities in Germany, a man who had the power to act politically in accordance with Netaji's way of thinking and who had the personality to be able to tie Netaji to Berlin at least for a certain time despite Netaji's criticism of the political structure and the political leaders of Germany . . . without Trott, his circle and his friends and his devoted working team, Netaji would not have remained in Berlin. He most probably would have worn himself out in a continuous fight with Party authorities and Party functionaries, who in spite of their temporary power, could not, by nature and due to their lack of education, culturally and intellectually, come up anywhere near the same level as Netaji. Trott – with his particular talent for organizing and also for camouflaging if necessary – was able to influence, by means of *the vast power extended to him in the spring of 1941*, [Werth's italics] all political authorities concerned, specially the Foreign Minister and State Secretary Wilhelm Keppler and other competent authorities in such a manner that they collaborated with us, and what is more important, they did not disturb us. Netaji and we were strong, because the circle around Trott, which included Netaji and his people, could trust one another as far as defence against outside danger was concerned, while internally we spoke *one* [Werth's italics] language. The working team under Trott could count from the beginning on the support of the Political Department of the German Foreign Office, specially the Division Pol VII under Dr Melchers who later became German Ambassador to India.[20]

It should be borne in mind that Werth's gush was destined for the annual Netaji Oration which still unites his supporters in India and holds mystic significance for those who to this day refuse to believe that Bose was killed in 1945. Werth was then not quite as enamoured of Netaji as his account would suggest and Trott's misgivings seem, in the end, to have finally disillusioned him about the Indian Nationalist leader. Trott's doubts were not reciprocated by the Indian. From that first meeting Bose certainly believed that he had struck up a firm friendship based on Trott's understanding and charm, and their mutual interest in the philosophy of Hegel. Trott was, it was said, 'the sole friend [Bose] found within the Auswärtige Amt'.[21]

The failure of Bose's *démarche* in Berlin took him to Rome where he hoped for an audience with Mussolini. The Duce had, after all, been sympathetic in the past, and Bose was perhaps right in thinking that he had a greater interest in bringing about the collapse of the British Empire as it conflicted more with Italian territorial ambitions than it did with Hitler's which were still for the time being geared to European supremacy. The Duce, however, was looking over his shoulder to Germany and would not allow the visit. Ciano, his son-in-law and foreign minister, did, however, see Bose twice.

Some mystery surrounds an event which may or may not have taken place at the end of May or beginning of June; Bose's supposed marriage to Emilie Schenkel, an Austrian girl whom he had known from his earlier European stay. According to one report Trott would have been a witness at the ceremony, as someone later stated that they had seen his name on the certificate.[22] Whether married or not, Fraulein Schenkel and Bose did indeed live together in Berlin and a daughter was born later.[23] In India, Bose had always maintained the image of a celibate but it is interesting to read a privately circulated report of Alexander Werth's which suggests that Bose's celibacy was for Indian consumption only. Werth did not believe that Bose had married Fraulein Schenkel nor is any evidence to be found to prove that he did. As for celibacy, Trott recalled to Werth that 'whenever, for example, Bose went into a brothel, he did so with the greatest pleasure, becoming, the later it got, ever more taciturn and aristocratic in his bearing. Finally he became so grand that we could – without insulting him – make our way home. As for the rest, "the singers fall courteously silent".'[24]

Fraulein Schenkel was brought over to Berlin by Bose's old Austrian friend Kapp, who had set up the Austro-Indian Press and Information Institute in Vienna after Bose's last European sojourn. Werth suggests that he did so 'in order to improve his own relations with Bose.

Fraulein Schenkel remained in Berlin long enough for the old Kempner Villa at no 7 Sophienstrasse, earmarked for Bose and his household (including Fraulein Schenkel), to be decorated. Trott and I ourselves bought the furniture together and we took an exceptionally malicious pleasure in making Fraulein Schenkel's bedroom as ugly as possible. She was the typical product of the Second World War, the baggage in fact of any war. She got permanently on our nerves with her risible desires which we, and later Bose, had to satisfy with such regularity. As a result of Indian sensitivity in personal affairs, and especially in erotic matters, we had to take care that in all things the wishes of Fraulein Schenkel be fulfilled for the first month of their Berlin existence. What we took amiss, though never let on to them, was the fact, that they were well aware of too, that we were in no position to refuse.[25]

The generous amounts of money made available to Trott's office for these ends must have come in handy.

The German offensive against Russia, code-named 'Barbarossa', came as a 'hard blow'.[26] On the afternoon of 22 June the writer Giselher Wirsing found Bose sitting cross-legged in front of a map muttering 'that won't be good'.[27] With the end of the Ribbentrop-Molotov Pact went the lynchpin of Bose's European policy. As Furtwängler recalled, 'We left him in his household to reflect on his grotesque position.'[28] The pact had been the physical demonstration of his weird synthesis and while the two countries were bound together the path to India through Russia was ensured. With the Russian-English Alliance there came confirmation of Bose's worst fears. Strategically, too, Bose's plans had become considerably more difficult – in fact irreconcilable with his position in Germany. Sensibly Bose should have sought Japanese assistance from that point onwards, on the other hand it was extremely unlikely he would receive the hoped-for assurance of Indian independence from the Japanese. Another result of Germany's declaration of war against Russia was that from now on Indian Communists would turn against him and brand him a 'Quisling'.[29]

On 9 July he went to Vienna, returning to Berlin on the 14th; he went to see his friends Kapp and Otto Faltis, the Viennese Police Commissioner. On his return he was accommodated in a series of luxury hotels – the Exzelsior (which he left as a result of a *contretemps* with a National Socialist-minded *Kellner* who would not call him '*Exzellenz*' as he required)[30], the Esplanade and the Kaiserhof. By that time his 'palatial'[31] villa in Charlottenburg – decorated by Trott and Werth – was ready for him and his mistress. It was there that he kept his court, insisting on a degree of protocol which was compounded by German bureaucracy. At this point Trott's minding work became a nightmare. On 14 August 1941, he wrote to his wife, 'The office work drives me to distraction.'[32]

Bose clearly much enjoyed the princely lifestyle which made up in some ways for political impotence in Germany. 'Bose,' Werth wrote later, 'liked to be called "Excellency" and in the end extended this to Trott and me when there were others present.' However, 'Bose was fundamentally lacking in respect for his own people',[33] with the exception of the veteran Indian journalist A.C.N. Nambiar,* who was

---

* *Later Indian ambassador to Bonn.*

then living in France. Bose wanted Nambiar to assist him in Berlin but none of Boses's entreaties could get Nambiar to come to him.

Finally Bose went to France in person and still had no success in convincing Nambiar to join his movement. As Trott had no time to get involved with the Nambiar business it was Werth who travelled with Bose instead. Werth managed to convince Nambiar, and after an *intermezzo* with the German authorities there, Nambiar was brought to Berlin where he proved a much more popular figure with Germans and Indians alike than Bose. When Bose left for Japan, Nambiar took on his functions at the head of the Free India Committee.*

In a letter to Clarita written on 8 August 1941, Trott summed up his views on Bose at that time: 'He is highly gifted but, despite everything, on a human level we remain definitely cool. It is as if every time we have to start again at the beginning.'[34] A week later he returned to the subject of Bose in another letter to Clarita: 'It is high time that I break loose from him, I am beginning to be indispensable to him, his fundamental beliefs are too negative for a rewarding relationship.'[35] At the beginning of the month Bose had had an unfortunate meeting with Trott's boss, Keppler. Keppler had been distinctly haughty with the Indian and had not allowed him to get a word in edgeways while he expounded at length on the glories of the Führer. It was a style of interview Bose was to get used to but never to appreciate.

The result of the meeting was nevertheless positive. From that moment onwards the Arbeitskreis Indien, the forerunner to Trott's Sonderreferat, was given powers and funds and a limited recognition – without the vital recognition of Indian independence or even a declaration of German war aims in India. The Arbeitskreis was also showered with money for propaganda uses and also in order to keep the 'bird in the gilded cage' happy in his idle existence in Berlin. Trott's office had a hundred per cent call on the special 'war funds' allotted to Keppler, an inexhaustible supply of money which could just as easily be channelled into Trott's 'illegal' work as fed into the business of managing Bose.

As a result of the Keppler monologue, some of Bose's aims could now be pursued. The first of these was a 'Free India Centre', a gathering place for those people working for Indian independence which would bring together the press, publishing and radio functions of Bose's propaganda machine. The building, in the Liechtenstein

---

* *Nambiar remained unconvinced when it came to Subhas Bose. When the Indian leader left for Japan he told Trott, 'I believe you are just as happy that he is finally going.' He had been reluctant to get involved in politics, once telling Clarita von Trott he would have wished 'to be able to sit on a tree and watch the political scene from there'. He must have had some idea of the game Trott was playing as he once told him, 'You will either end up an ambassador or a criminal.' (Clarita von Trott, notes for the author, 1989)*

Allee of the Tiergarten, became the meeting place for the thirty or so Indians then in Germany.[36] A newspaper, *Azad Hind*, was started under the auspices of Hans-Georg von Studnitz, the ministry's press attaché. A further organization was set up to mobilize all Indians in exile in Europe. A German-Japanese-Indian liaison committee was to look into military aspects of co-operation, uniting the Japanese military attaché and representatives of the German High Command. This last body was to examine such ideas as sabotage in India and the building of an airstrip inside Afghanistan so that Indians could be incited to action from just across the border. It was a start even if it fell far short of what Bose demanded.

Despite the limited concessions which had been made by Keppler and the luxurious existence in which he languished, Bose was not happy with his lot. For one thing, he was convinced he was being spied on. He was probably right. When he travelled abroad, he remarked that people followed him, and he was quite certain that his telephone was being tapped.* Bose's suspicions settled on the 'elderly female journalist' of the office, Fraulein Dr Kretschmar, who was almost certainly innocent of the charge. With his natural tendency to paranoia, life in Berlin can only have been *extremely* difficult for Bose.[37] He would have been happier in Rome where there was less suspicion and less racialism and where his projects had more appeal. To his frustration it was the Italians, with their own Indian, Schedai, who in September 1941 were the first to set up a proper Indian Bureau.

On 10 September, Furtwängler (who was keeping his head low in Bangkok after one or two rumours had got about concerning his

---

* *In reality telephone tapping under the Third Reich was made difficult by the fact that it was one of Göring's fiefs and that the Sicherheitsdienst and Gestapo had to get permission from the Reichsmarschal's Research Office before they could fix a bug. 'It was Diels who introduced him to new machines to record telephone conversations which were manufactured in Switzerland. Göring decided to create a "research department" of the Air Ministry – "research" meaning supervision of the internal enemy, including the highest ranking personalities in the state. Everybody was a potential enemy. A special staff prepared a daily dossier of "interesting" telephone conversations: extracts in the form of "Brown Sheets" were submitted to the Air Minister [i.e. Göring] personally every morning. It was Göring's jolliest hour of the day. Robert [his valet] brought his coffee, turned on the gramophone to play a soft record and Göring studied the Brown Sheets, roaring with laughter one minute, raving with fury the next, as he read what people said about him, Hitler and the Nazi regime. The Brown Sheets helped him to become the best informed man in Germany, an ever-present witness to his friends' and enemies' most intimate conversations.' (Frischauer, Göring.)*

196

continuing friendship with known Socialists) suggested German policy should be to attack Gandhi in favour of Bose.[38] The reason behind this was the belief that Gandhi's non-violent resistance was not sufficiently damaging to the British war effort and that what was required was the fomenting of a revolution. It was a queer card for the Gandhian Trott to play. It also brought about a strong attack from the ministry's press attaché, Hans-Georg von Studnitz, who, without being exactly a Nazi, was not the sort of person who would have officiously striven to oppose the regime. Studnitz wrote:

> I have vigorously opposed the chairman [of the Indian Committee], Secretary of State Keppler, and his general factotum, Adam von Trott zu Solz. The latter insists that our propaganda should attack Gandhi and make him look ridiculous in the eyes of the Indian people. As an ex-Rhodes Scholar, he ought to know better, but he is, of course, completely under the influence of Bose, who hates Gandhi. Melchers and I know that any German policy towards India which fails to accept Gandhi as the most potent factor in the Indian independence movement would be devoid of all reality. But Trott is quite incorrigible, and he is supported in his fanatical outlook by Keppler who usually ends our arguments with: 'Let us keep our tempers, gentlemen. No one for a moment believed the Anschluss would materialize, but, in his own time, the Führer will solve the Indian question in the same way as he solved the Austrian question.'[39]

Studnitz was, of course, unaware of the paramount importance of Bose to the German Resistance movement and had little or no idea why Trott should be so perverse as to advance him and not Gandhi.

On 29 November 1941, Bose was granted another interview with the Reich Foreign Minister, Ribbentrop. The meeting was the result of a letter written with Trott's assistance which the latter considered to be 'not a bad' a piece of work.[40] The interview was, however, so long in coming about that Bose resolved not to see Ribbentrop even if he were asked. Finally he was called before the minister at his headquarters but even then the summons into Ribbentrop's presence did not take place until midnight, when the Indian was already in his pyjamas, in bed and asleep. Bose was in an understandably evil temper when he was ushered in, immediately demanding that the offending passage in *Mein Kampf* belittling the Indian independence movement be removed. Ribbentrop had no answer for him there and then. To Trott's immense embarrassment, the whole thing was over in the twinkling of an eye. As Furtwängler put it, 'The National Socialists, the foolish Ribbentrop in particular, had not a clue where to begin with this strange oriental – whether he should be shown to the people as an allied oriental prince in order to strengthen morale, or whether he should be kept on ice as the Gauleiter for a conquered India.'[41]

In December of that year the decisions of the summer were being gradually put into action. Azad Hind Radio was broadcasting daily in English, Hindustani, Bengali, Persian, Tamil, Telegu and Pushti. These

197

broadcasts in so many languages took all of three hours fifty minutes to perform. In order to attract listeners, the programmes were prefaced with the same music as the BBC used for their Indian transmissions. It was in December that recruitment started for the Indian Legion which was to form the core of Bose's Indian national army. Early on, Bose had seen the potential of propaganda directed at Indian troops fighting with the British – particularly those of them who were now prisoners of war. With the propaganda literature being churned out by Trott's department he hoped to bring over whole divisions to the cause. As early as 1941, a German officer, Walter Harbich, had been assigned to training.

The training took place in East Prussia. The soldiers swore an oath to both Hitler and Bose, who stipulated that they should never be used on the Eastern front – only against the British. The strength of this Indian Legion was fixed at 3,000 men, largely staffed by Wehrmacht officers, in addition to which there was formed a reserve division of a further 7,000. Recruits were drawn from among prisoners of war. The fascist-style trimmings so dear to Bose were also worked into the decoration of his army. A flag was created with a leaping tiger superimposed on a tricolour. A hymn by Tagore became the regimental song and national anthem. 'Heil Hitler!' was echoed in the greeting 'Jai Hind'. The whole performance was dismissed by Furtwängler as 'a piece of comic opera which no one took seriously'; it was on Furtwängler's copy of the Koran that the Muslim soldiers swore their oath. Later Trott found a use for the Legion – as a handy means of removing his friends, and family, from the Eastern front and despatching them to France where they were relatively safe.[42]

Another benefit for Trott and his team was an increase in the amount of travel they were permitted to undertake. Often these trips involved accompanying Bose, or retrieving him from one of his sulks, as was the case when Trott went to fetch him from Bad Gastein in September. These journeys often took Trott or Werth to Rome, Paris or Prague, and made a considerable change from the normal war-time atmosphere of Berlin. Werth remembers in particular a journey to Rome with Nambiar after Bose's departure for Japan which provided the chance to lounge about in cafés in the Via Veneto while the Italians made exaggerated claims as to their victories at sea.

It clearly made a change from the day-to-day routine of the office as recounted by Werth:

Yesterday it had been a demand to strengthen the Indian Legion to 20,000 men, today a girl had to be located for this and that fellow, and the next day a house for some working group or other. Proper officers' quarters had to be found for more Indian officers or the rations augmented for colleagues in France or other

198

occupied countries. Shortly afterwards came the call for new quarters as the bombing in Germany or the west had wiped out the old ones. Then came the journeys with Bose, chiefly to Rome, Paris, Brussels and the Hague. As it turned out, whoever accompanied Bose, landed with a *laissez passer* for the embassy or consulate and fifteen trunks full of alcohol, cigarettes, food and cigars, etc., all for the ten or so colleagues who were not reluctant to accept it. Understandably, Bose took responsibility for all this, but thank God, there was always something in it for us.[43]

The largesse also extended to Bose's Austrian friends, who on the pretext of an important meeting with the Indian leader came up to Berlin to relieve him of some of the contents of his well-stocked cellar.

It was a cruel irony for Adam Trott that the crowning achievement of his Indian work was the civil disobedience campaign which greeted the so-called 'Cripps Mission' to India in March 1942. Stafford Cripps had been one of the last people he had seen in Britain on that short visit to England in July 1939, and to his death he still believed (and had every reason to believe) that Cripps had faith in him. Cripps was seen as the man to deal with the situation in India as his reputation was that of an anti-imperialist and a committed Socialist.[44] His first war-time trip to the Sub-continent was in November 1939, when he was accompanied by his secretary, Geoffrey Wilson, Trott's friend from Oxford and before. The situation had been worsening as a result of India's enforced participation in what was seen as a European war.

Westminster was sufficiently worried by 17 October 1939 for a White Paper to be issued promising dominion status. This was not enough for the Congress leaders who promptly withdrew from the Council. The following March, the Congress leaders had made it clear they would have nothing short of complete independence. When, that August, Linlithgow had offered them seats on a 'War Advisory Council' they had once again refused their co-operation. In September a new campaign of civil disobedience had led to mass arrests and the setting up of what German propaganda was happy to call 'concentration camps'.[45]

In March 1941 there were false hopes of a breakthrough when the moderate leaders proposed a solution which would reconstruct the Viceroy's Council and give Indians a voice on defence and finance. Imperial and international matters would be handled as for a dominion. At a specified date after the end of the war India would receive dominion status. This move, however, failed to receive adequate backing from the Indians themselves. In July the Viceroy's Council was expanded to include a majority of Indians. Any good odour created by the last move was dispelled in September of that year when Churchill's speech appeared to exclude India from the provisions of the Atlantic Charter.

On 2 February, Trott tabled a lengthy memorandum outlining the German support for a campaign of civil disobedience, subversion and sabotage. From Bangkok, the German consul, Thomas, also reported on the gathering of the elements of an Indian national army in Thailand. Already in January, Linlithgow had expressed his fears *vis-à-vis* Bose; the Fall of Singapore on 15 February had added substantially to the British feeling of insecurity in India while giving no end of encouragement to Bose himself who on 26 February established his own eleven-point programme for the liberation of his motherland. The Germans would, according to Bose, advance through the Caucasus to invade India while, at the same time, the Japanese would start the invasion of the coastal cities. To some extent the proposals (which yet again called for a meeting between Bose and Hitler) were scuttled by the Japanese refusal to countenance an early strike at India and by the Cripps Mission which began in earnest on the 22nd March.

As Cripps made his way out to India, Bose left to sulk in Bad Gastein, where once again Trott had to comfort him. Bose was increasingly disillusioned by the unreadiness of the German government to make a declaration of support for the Indian independence movement. He strongly suspected that India's role was to be as a pawn in a game of *rapprochement* between Hitler and the British. Trott had once again to promise to try to effect a meeting with the Führer at which this issue might be ironed out. Meanwhile in India the talks on Indian dominion status were breaking down either as a result of Cripps or of Gandhi. The latter was changing his tune about Bose, sensing the effect of his more violent methods and clearly aware that the British now had their backs to the wall over India. Gandhi became a fan of the Azad Hind broadcasts.

Azad Hind was of course preaching the total rejection of any proposals which might have retained India for the British Empire as a dominion. It called for revolt. After the war those elements of the German Foreign Office who had been involved in Indian policy prided themselves on the spurning of Cripps' proposals. They had become in some way the 'fathers' of Indian independence; a fine action in German foreign policy among so many evil ones. In their view, they were pursuing a legitimate strategic aim in attacking the heart of the Empire. India was one area where the German Foreign Office at least might be said to have fought a just war. Sadly for them, perhaps, their unjust leader took little interest in their endeavours.

Werth, outlining the successes of the movement, runs the disturbances at the time of the Cripps Mission into the longer upheaval caused by the 'Quit India Movement',

For three months the militarily most important parts of India – Bombay and

Calcutta – were shaken with heavy unrest, trains were derailed, bridges blown up, etc. In other words, this situation was the fruit of seeds sown in Bose's systematic struggle and the continuation of his fight in Berlin. The English were forced to throw in divisions from other theatres of war and thus through Bose was the German military leadership able to succeed momentarily through essentially pure psychological means. For our labours both Trott and I received the Service Cross [Verdienstkreuz] First Class, of which we were very proud, notwithstanding the signature of our not very beloved Führer.[46]

The Quit India Movement resulted in the burning of 318 police stations, the raiding of 945 post offices, the derailing of 59 trains and the arrest of 60,000 Indians. It has been described as the 'biggest threat' to British rule in India since 1857.[47] Trott, despite his medal, had less clear feelings about the destruction of the Cripps Mission than Werth and others in the Foreign Office, finding it hard to reconcile his actions with his friendship for Cripps. His widow remembers her husband's moral quandary at the time, 'Werth's *Bericht* does not make it clear how bitterly hard he [Trott] found it to praise the failure . . . of the mission of a man who was such an important friend and who in many respects shared his aspirations.'[48] Even on 15 July 1944, when Trott was in the thick of preparations for the *putsch*, his mind turned to the British politician and he exclaimed to Furtwängler, 'What must Cripps think of me?'[49]

The success of German-backed propaganda in India was impressing the authorities who gave Trott and Werth their gongs. On 2 April an enthusiastic Keppler wrote, 'We must from now on do everything possible to "revolutionize" India.'[50] More and more propaganda exercises were drawn up, involving leaflets and posters (these were also distributed in North Africa and the prisoner-of-war camps), the planting of agents in India and Afghanistan and the encouragement of a go-slow campaign in war industries. However, because of Japanese territorial ambitions there was 'absolute silence' on the demand for an assurance of independence for India. Ironically, Hitler himself was more than sceptical about the idea of the Japanese succeeding in India – something sensed by Bose. Hassell noted in his diary, 'It is said that Hitler himself is not entirely enthusiastic over the gigantic successes of the Japanese, and has said that he would gladly send the English twenty divisions to help throw back the yellow men.'[51]

Once again lured to Italy by the thought of better reception there, Bose finally got his chance to talk to Mussolini on 5 May 1941. Sometime in April of that year both he and Trott had been for a three-day stay with Reichsprotektor Heydrich in Prague. They were to spend another three days with him in October of that year. As Trott's widow recounts, Trott was fascinated by the sinister Heydrich — the head of the Reichsicherheitsdienst and the probable architect of the 'final solution' for the extermination of the European Jews. 'The thought preoccupied him, when he confronted this extraordinarily skilful fiend become such a fearsome adventurer, what enormously richly faceted possibilities he might otherwise have espoused.'[52]

The success of the propaganda operation in India and Ribbentrop's intervention finally managed to achieve the long-awaited meeting between Bose and the Führer which took place at the Wolfsschanze at Rastenburg in East Prussia on 29 May 1942. A photograph of their meeting shows Bose and Hitler smiling broadly for the occasion.* The meeting, however, was anything but cordial. Trott who accompanied Bose as interpreter as Hitler spoke no English, recounted his version of the events – presumably soon after – to both Furtwängler and Werth. It was to be Trott's one and only meeting with the Führer.

According to Furtwängler's version:

> Bose opened the conversation with the usual assurances of what a portentous day it was for him to find himself face to face with the great Führer of the German Reich. At this point his contribution to the conversation was cut short. The rest was taken up with one of Hitler's celebrated monologues. He didn't wish to begin a premature propaganda campaign in India. In Iraq he had had a bad experience in this line. Then he treated the worthy Brahmin [sic] to a long lecture on the cultural achievements of the English saying, word for word, 'It is my conviction that it will take about 150 years before India is ripe for self-government.[53]

According to Werth, who, as we have seen, was a great deal less jaundiced in his attitude to Bose than Furtwängler, the conversation began wholly differently, and it rings true only in that it mirrors the abortive conversation with Ribbentrop earlier that year. According to Werth, Bose launched into an immediate demand for the insulting passages from *Mein Kampf* to be expunged. Hitler, however, refused 'point blank' to discuss them. Then, in response to Bose's demand for a recognition of India's independence after the war, the Führer exclaimed that such an assurance was of 'little practical significance' and with that led Bose over to a map of the world in order to show the Indian how far the German armies were from his country.[54]

The Indian then asked once again – still through Trott – for a confirmation of his political freedom in India, something which had been agreed with Ribbentrop only a year before.

> ... the Chancellor in this connection asked what kind of political concept Netaji actually had in mind. Netaji became impatient and asked Trott to give the Chancellor the following reply: 'Tell his Excellency that I have been in politics all my life and that I don't need advice from any side.' Trott translated this reply in a more diplomatic form, but yet the meeting was not successful.[55]

---

* *The British press had countered the Bose-inspired campaign in India with a show of malicious humour. The* Daily Express *ran an old picture of Bose at the Berlin Zoo over the legend, 'Indian Leader Plans Invasion 5th Column'.*

The meeting proved a turning point for Bose, who from that moment onwards chose to look for a more committed assistance from the Japanese.

Of course it might be added that Hitler was, indeed, in no position to drive his armies through to India; his supply lines in Russia were already overstretched as would be proved in not so many months at Stalingrad. Nor had India ever been a priority for him, as Bose should have recognized from reading *Mein Kampf.* Hitler was not, after all, a statesman with a pragmatic and changing view of his aims and objectives, but a man who saw his mission in concrete terms. Bose may well have realized this after his visit to Rastenburg. As Hassell cynically put it, in India Hitler was British, he 'never seriously thought of allowing India – which according to . . . [world partition] would fall to Japan – to break off from the British Empire.'[56]

Although Bose believed that the meeting with Hitler had been a failure, there were positive results as far as Trott's team were concerned. Bose, ever proud, had told the Führer that all moneys made available to him in Germany were in the form of a 'permanent loan', which ensured that Bose had no problems when he wished to dip further into the resources of the Reichsbank.[57] On 13 October 1942, Trott's Arbeitskreis was finally upgraded into a Sonderreferat (special department) with Trott at its head, Alexander Werth as his deputy and six Wissenschaftlicher Hilfsarbeiter attached (including Richter and Furtwängler), all of whom had 'a special knowledge of the land'.[58] The office was based at 75 Wilhelmstrasse, adjacent to the Foreign Office proper, meaning that for Werth and Trott there was a further duplication of their functions, another office which allowed for even greater obfuscation when it came to accounting for time. It also meant for Trott personally the possibility of a change in status as Luther, the AA's SA man, had put his name forward for promotion to Legationssekretär (third secretary) on the basis of his successful leaflet campaign in North Africa among Indian troops.[59]

Ribbentrop, despite a warm commendation from Keppler, wanted to see further evidence of Trott's work before making him a Beamte and a member of the AA proper. On 19 October, Ribbentrop agreed to Trott's promotion to the higher rank of Legationsrat. However, progress was slow, and the official stamp was not set on the appointment until 28 April 1943, when Trott was gazetted Legations-sekretär. Ribbentrop further procrastinated over Trott's position in the ministry, despite the responsibilities and offices he held; he was only finally posted as Legationsrat on 19 November 1943.[60]

On 11 June 1942, Trott, Werth and Bose travelled to Paris to open a French branch of the Indian Propaganda Office. This was no doubt the occasion on which Bose met the French Prime Minister, Pierre Laval.

Nambiar was also present as was Trott's old friend Gottfried von Nostitz who acted as interpreter. Nostitz later wrote of Trott and Bose that the former 'had soon recognized the absolute nullity of his job and carried on only from the point of view of camouflaging and protecting his real work . . .' When the episode came to an end with Bose's departure, he was 'visibly relieved'.[61]

The purpose of Bose's meeting with Laval was to discuss Axis war aims involving India, the Near East, the Mediterranean, Afghanistan and North Africa. Laval advanced the view that whatever the outcome of the war, both France and India would regain their independence. At this Bose told Laval, 'Were the British to come to France again, you would not be able to maintain your optimistic prognosis'. At this point Bose asked Laval about the future of French North Africa, and whether the Germans would not alter the status quo there. Laval replied that he did not exclude the possibility. Finally, Bose said, 'I too have my worries about Berlin, I still don't know how correctly it will deal with India after the war.' Trott and the others, says Werth, were only silent witnesses to this conversation.[62]

From 14 to 16 July Bose and Trott visited Himmler's headquarters. According to Himmler's foreign-policy expert Walter Schellenberg, 'Bose's outstanding intelligence and his mastery of modern propaganda methods had made a deep impression on Himmler, and we were therefore considering whether we should not shift our support to him [from their own Far Eastern stooge, Sidi Khan].'[63] Despite Himmler's warming to Bose, he began once again to be frustrated by his treatment in Germany and to take an interest in some Italian experiments in long-range flight which might be useful in getting him to India and back. On 23 July he wrote to Keppler to ask permission to avail himself of one of these trips in order to visit his motherland once again.

For the Indian Legion, things were not going smoothly. The Germans were only beginners when it came to managing a multi-racial force and made a number of elementary mistakes. They had succeeded in bring out 4,000 prisoners of war by sifting through the camps and working on the Indian inmates. But in the camps themselves they had failed to divide the men from the basically pro-British NCOs which led to disturbances. The Hindus, for example, were happy with their Swastika symbols as they recognized in them an ancient religious emblem of their culture. The effect on the Muslims, however, was the reverse. In November there was a mutiny in one of the camps when the soldiers were told that they would have to go back and face the British forces in Libya; a year later there was another riot of this sort, occasioned once again by the fear of having to face their countrymen in action. The nascent force was doing rather better under the auspices of the Japanese who had set up an Indian National Army from those elements they had found in former British colonies which they had overrun like Singapore and Malaya. With all the insuperable problems which faced him in Germany, Bose was increasingly certain that he wished to get back to the Far East to be at their head.

At the end of the year, Trott and Bose were together in Brussels to visit General von Falkenhausen – who for some reason describes Bose as a 'Siamese' in his memoirs.[64] Meetings like these were not uncommon between Trott and Falkenhausen, who remained one of the generals most favoured by the civil plotters as a result of the wider perspectives given to him by his long service in China. Falkenhausen asked Bose about his feelings apropos the Sino-Japanese conflict. Bose, one presumes to the general's surprise, replied, 'My sympathies lie exclusively with the other side', i.e. with the Chinese.[65]

By that time everything had been settled in Berlin for Bose to be taken out to the Far East on a German submarine where he could be transferred to the Japanese and carry on his fight in more sympathetic waters. At first the Japanese had caused problems by being overly bureaucratic and telling their military attaché that no civilians were allowed to travel on or in military craft during wartime. Trott, however, managed to iron out this tangle by cabling Ambassador Ott in Tokyo: 'Subhas Chandra Bose by no means private person but Commander-in-Chief of the Indian Liberation Army.'[66]

Arrangements were made for Nambiar to take over Bose's functions and indeed the 'palatial' villa, which he occupied until it was destroyed in the course of an Allied air raid. On 16 January 1943, India's Independence Day was celebrated with a gathering of 600 people who had turned up to honour the Netaji. A few days later on 7 February, Nambiar, Werth and Keppler set out for Kiel with Bose. It was from there that Bose was to take his submarine to the Indian Ocean where he would meet up with the Japanese. Trott made his excuses; by all reports, he was so sick of the whole business he could not bring himself to be present. If stories about Bose's fondness for Trott are to be believed Trott's absence must have been a final bitter disappointment for him, to crown all the others which had occurred in nearly two years in Berlin.

The Azad Hind broadcasts continued from the Tiergarten in Berlin until intense bombing in the summer of that year forced them to shift to Hilversum in Holland. There the Indians resumed their comfortable existence in their offices in the Hotel Heide Park, while the Villa Monikenburg provided a residence for Nambiar and his friends. Never was there a transmission failure and all the religious groups – unlike the groups within the Legion – got on together. Once again Trott had an excuse to visit his friends in the Dutch Resistance without arousing suspicion from the authorities. In August 1944 the transmitter moved to its final location, the town of Helmstedt on the present East/West German borders. Werth continued in his functions long after Trott's trial and execution and was the last man in the Special India Division left in Berlin on the 25 April 1945 when he was captured by the Russians. He spent the best part of the next decade in one of their concentration camps. Bose himself was killed in a plane crash in Thailand in August 1945; at that time he was making a final bid to interest his old friends the Russians in his cause.

If Subhas Bose had not been the cause which Trott was looking for when it came to India, he had provided, and continued to provide even after his departure, further pretexts for Trott to pursue his activities against the regime, cloaking the myriad journeys he made to all parts of Europe over those two years and more in order to drum up support for the Resistance. As regards British India, it was certainly shaken by German-inspired propaganda, but its ultimate fate can not be said to have been the result of German actions or German support for Bose as an Indian Nationalist Leader – help which was sparingly and ineptly given by the chaotic ruling clique of Nazi Germany. As the Nationalist Studnitz put it, 'The way in which Bose was treated by the various German government departments confirms the correctness of Tirpitz' prophecy that we were not yet ripe to become a world power.'[67]

11
Resistance activities

Between 1933 and August 1944 there was never any moment when the German Resistance might be said to have shown a united front. It is quite impossible that such a large number of individual groups could have been aware of one another's existence. Some of the associations involved were very small indeed – like the 'Onkel Emil' group, whose aims were to aid Jews, keep them out of the camps and help them to get out of the country to safety.[1] There were any number of similar groups in the larger German cities.[2] There were Resistance cells in the universities too, notably in Munich, Hamburg and Berlin. In Munich a group called the 'Weisse Rose' began distributing leaflets around the time of the defeat at Stalingrad, and representatives of the student association travelled to Hamburg and Berlin to set up similar organisations there.[3]

Hassell noted in his diary on 22 February 1943:

> Munich is still much agitated by the discovery of a conspiracy among the students. The Party is trying to make them out as Communists. I have read the simple, splendid, deeply ethical national appeal which brought them to their death. Himmler apparently did not want any martyrs and ordered a stay of execution, but it came several hours too late. It is important for the future that such an appeal should have seen the light of day. It seems that Professor Huber, also arrested in the meanwhile, was the author. The brave Scholls died on the gallows, courageous and upright martyrs.

Like Hassell, Trott was deeply moved by the death of these young people and their philosophy teacher, and felt shame that the main opposition groups were doing so little to end the regime.[4] As the second of the Weisse Rose leaflets had said: '*Ein Ende mit Schrecken ist immer noch besser als ein Schrecken ohne Ende*' (A horrible end is still preferable to horrors without end).[5]

On a national scale, the Resistance can be packaged into half a dozen or so groupings, the most important of these being the military. Ever since his stand against the invasion of Czechoslovakia in 1938, military opposition to the regime had centred on General Beck. In 1938, Beck had assembled a number of high ranking officers and members of the General Staff who were prepared to act both then and in 1939. After Hitler's brilliant series of victories in 1940, however, they became reluctant to continue their plans. As Trott had foreseen, once the campaign had begun in earnest, it became hard to get the army to play their vital part.

Neverthelesss, the Resistance within the General Staff *did* continue after 1940 when it desperately sought a means of bringing down Hitler even though support had dwindled considerably. With the failure of the Russian campaign, which was inevitable even in December 1941, the military Resistance began to gain strength once again. In many cases, revulsion with the Nazi regime was spurred by the inadvertent sighting of atrocities committed behind the lines in Poland and Russia. For men like Axel von dem Bussche, experiences such as these were a turning point: Prussian birth had indeed inculcated a readiness to serve the state in time of war, but many Prussians were also imbued with a profound and unshakable Lutheran faith which was outraged by these acts.[6]

How much the ranks of the Resistance were swelled by soldiers profoundly shocked by the SS persecution of the Jews and the Churches is clear from the so-called 'Kaltenbrunner Berichte' – reports prepared by the Security Service (SD – Sicherheitsdienst) after the July Plot.[7] According to the interrogators, it was this which was *the principal rationale* behind the conspiracy. Count Schwerin Schwanenfeld was not the only conspirator to make this point at his trial before the People's Court, but he was quickly shouted down by Freisler.[8] Another source of how profound the effect of the massacres was, is to be found in letters written home from the front. Through his son, Ulrich von Hassell was fully aware of what was going on in the field while, like others of his circle, he had information on the concentration camps from Helmuth Moltke.[9]

Another who has left a record of his growing dissatisfaction with the conduct of the war was Colonel, later Major-General Helmuth Stieff, who played a role in the July plot. Writing to his wife after the news of the Polish atrocities of 1939, he said,

I am ashamed of being a German. This minority which sullies the name of Germany by murder, plunder and arson will prove the misfortune of the whole German nation unless we put a stop to these people soon. What has been described and proved to me [by General Blaskowitz] by the most responsible authorities on the spot is bound to arouse the avenging nemesis. Otherwise this rabble will one day do the same things to us decent people and terrorize their own nation with their pathological passions.[10]

The outrage felt by regular army officers as a result of the Polish campaign led to the removal of the SS police formations from the jurisdiction of the army in the spring of 1940. But the army also compromised their own moral integrity by allowing the executive authority for the eastern occupied territories to be handed over to the

SS. They had simply washed their hands of the problem by placing it beyond their jurisdiction. In April 1941, however, there was a fresh wave of veiled protest when an order was promulgated depriving local inhabitants of rights while German crimes against locals became virtually immune from punishment.* Writing to his wife in August from the Führer's headquarters, Stieff said,

> Every day which passes here strengthens one's dislike of this proletarian megalomaniac. Only yesterday we had another taste of his attitude in writing. It was *so* outrageous in tone that I can only say: anyone who puts up with that does not deserve any better. And the other side *must* gradually become convinced that they can go to any length if people swallow everything without a word of protest. At any rate my respect for certain people has sunk very low ... the whole thing is simply disgusting and disgraceful.[11]

The most important centre of the military conspiracy after the launching of Barbarossa in June 1941, was the headquarters of the Army Group Centre in Smolensk. The day-to-day running of the plot revolved around the person of Colonel, later Major General Henning von Tresckow, a Prussian general staff officer who combined a profound Lutheran faith and a rigid determination to eliminate the National Socialist state in the early years of which he had been something of a fellow traveller.[12] It is not hard to understand why so many of the younger Prussian officers had been in favour of Nazism at the beginning; their vocation was military, yet Weimar had been limited to an army of ten divisions (100,000 men) staffed by a mere 4,000 officers. During the twenties and early thirties, the chances of employment in the army or promotion were slim, officers remaining with the same rank for years†. With Hitler's rejection of the Versailles clauses relating to the German armed forces, the army became once again a viable career for Prussian nobles – though at the same time admitting many officers from other walks of life, who owed their advancement to Nazism and continued to believe in it to the end.

Tresckow gathered around him a staff of younger officers who could be relied upon to support his views. Among them was Fabian von Schlabrendorff, a lawyer with extensive contacts with the earlier Prussian Resistance to Hitler. He was a friend of Ewald von Kleist-

---

* *Colonel von Tresckow to Colonel von Gersdorff, 'Remember this hour. If we do not succeed in persuading the Field Marshal [Kluge] to do everything, even to exert his own influence to get these orders countermanded, Germany will have finally lost her honour, and that will be felt for hundreds of years to come. Not only Hitler will be blamed, but you and I, your wife and my wife, your children and my children.' (Zeller, op. cit., quoting letters published in the* Zeitschrift für Zeitgeschichte.)

† *Erwin Rommel took nineteen years to rise from captain to full colonel, despite his staggering record of service in World War I.*

Schmenzin, Ernst Niekisch and Nikolaus von Halem. Schlabrendorff had met Churchill and others on a mission from the Abwehr in 1939. During the war he continued to provide links with the Abwehr and with Colonel General Beck, as well as with the Resistance cell within the general staff at army headquarters at Zossen and the Paris group of plotters centred around General von Stülpnagel.

The Abwehr's headquarters on the Tirpitzufer in Berlin was a thriving Resistance centre under the benevolent eye of Admiral Canaris. Canaris was a protector of the Resistance rather than an active participant. It is quite clear that with his patronage the Abwehr was shaped into a body capable of bending the inhumanity of the regime by protecting groups which would otherwise have come to grief. Through Major General Oster it was also an *active* centre of opposition. Oster gathered together an impressive ring of diligent anti-Nazis like Dietrich Bonhoeffer, Hans von Dohnanyi, the brothers John, Hans-Bernd Gisevius and Theodor Strünck. He and his men provided not only technical support for the military opponents of the regime but, through Abwehr representatives in German legations in neutral states, carried on negotiations with the Allies.[13]

The Abwehr conspirators were essentially men of the right; nationalists disillusioned with National Socialism, who were guided by their strong patriotism to seek to remove the evil which was dishonouring Germany's name. Much the same was true of the chief civilian group of conspirators, the *Alte Herren* (old gentlemen) who gathered around the leading figures of General Beck and the former Oberbürgermeister of Leipzig, Carl Goerdeler.[14] The combination of Beck and Goerdeler was a strange marriage thrown up by the special needs of the time: Beck was a man moulded in the traditions of Clausewitz and Field Marshal Moltke, a military intellectual of the type which appears to exist only on the European Continent. Goerdeler was the conservative nationalist from local government – a man of untiring optimism and unflagging activity, who had resigned control of Leipzig Town Hall when the Nazis seized upon the opportunity presented by his absence in Scandinavia to remove the statue of Mendelssohn which had formerly stood before it.

Trott's first meeting with Ludwig Beck occurred in October 1940, when he was introduced by Münchhausen's father-in-law, Colonel General Hammerstein.[15] Beck had resigned his post in the face of what he correctly foresaw as an intentional drift on the part of the Nazi leaders towards world war. Before his resignation he had written to explain his motives, based upon his firm conviction that Hitler would destroy Germany if he persisted in his plans:

> In order to make our position clear to future historians and to preserve the reputation of the High Command I should like to enter it into the records, as Chief of the General Staff, that I have refused to approve any National Socialist

war 'adventures' whatsoever. A conclusive German victory is an impossibility.[16]

On 16 July 1938, Beck resigned his command, delivering in so doing a final admonition to the military leaders:

> We have before us to deal with the final decisions facing a nation on the brink of war. History will pass a verdict of capital crime against those generals who do not consider either their military or political expertise or their consciences. Their soldierly duty has a limit, when their knowledge, their conscience and their responsibility forbids them from carrying out an order. If they can find no justification in such a position from their advisers and their personal reservations, history and their responsibility towards their people give them the right to resign their offices. If they *all* act with resolution, then the continuation of warlike measures becomes impossible. It is their duty to protect their country from the worst, above all from decline. It demonstrates a lack of stature and recognition of responsibility if the highest ranking officers in such a time see their duties only in the narrowest interpretation of military duties without being conscious of their need to answer for the whole population. Extraordinary times call for extraordinary measures.[17]

Beck's single minded stand was noted by the Führer, who did not report Beck's resignation till after Munich, adding at the time, 'The only man I fear is Beck, one day this man might be in a position to act against me in some way.'[18]

Beck, though, was essentially disarmed by his resignation and as a civilian his hands were tied. He made his gesture before Munich, but is is notable that none of the other officers followed his example. Nor was he recalled to command, like Hammerstein or Falkenhausen, in 1939, remaining in the military wilderness throughout the years of victory. His last command was his leadership of the German Resistance up until late in 1943, though after that the younger members of the group became increasingly frustrated by the inactivity of the 'old gentlemen'. In the meetings of the opposition Beck none the less commanded a respect that the verbose Goerdeler could not, and effectively chaired a widely disparate group with all the authority of a former Chief of Staff. Schlabrendorff wrote of him:

> He was a real gentleman who united in his person kindness and unqualified authority. Admittedly, the officer of the General Staff was still very much alive in him. In this respect he was like a Michaelangelo without arms. Everything in him lusted after operational activity. Fate had denied him the exercise of this talent. Everything that the German High Command was able to achieve in the last war, everything which German generals were able to do was down to his teaching and influence. When in the summer of 1942 I faced him with Tresckow's view that, given the situation in Russia, the war was lost, he replied. 'This is no news to me. This war was lost before the first shot was fired.'[19]

Beck's thinking was Clausewitzian in the extreme: wars were fought for foreign-policy aims and only when diplomatic channels had broken down. There was no common ground between his traditional general staff thinking and the attitudes of the Nazi ideologues who saw war as a state of life conceived in the framework of some bastard neo-Darwinism where races pitch themselves against other races in a world of permanent strife.

> The ordering of the lives of different peoples is the ordinary task of politics. As in strategy, it is a fluid thing which accommodates personalities and relationships and can only achieve the possible. Politics requires a knowledge not only of your own history but a view to the world's effective forces and the prevailing situation. It moreover requires circumspection *vis-à-vis* the myriad imponderabilia which result from the fact that no people in this world lives in isolation, that God created many more races than our own and allowed them to develop without decreeing an order of rank and that no civilized people can remain set up on its own.[20]

Goerdeler and Beck collaborated on a number of memoranda during the war years which were intended to serve as the basis for a 'renewal' of German political institutions from the ground upwards. In the course of the war, their thinking became more mature, less reactionary and more inclined to accept a compromise solution with the Socialists. Goerdeler travelled endlessly during the war as he had done before it, trying to enlist support throughout the world from generals and from leaders of industry. In this he had the backing of Robert Bosch, the leading Stuttgart industrialist who had 'employed' the former mayor of Leipzig and price commissioner as a political adviser. In reality Bosch had merely given him cover for his activities. Goerdeler's experience cast him in the role of future chancellor, should Hitler be removed. Yet he was still convinced – more so than Beck – that it would be wrong to kill Hitler. There was a certain lack of realism about his character; he was an eternal optimist, formulating countless projects, yet failing to get near to the essential goal as a result of his moral scruples.

Goerdeler like Trott had an exaggerated belief in the good sense of the British which was something which was to cause him rare moments of despair.

> He based his hopes above all on the political reasonableness and experience of the English: they would not abandon the European balance of power, but rather seek to re-erect it. They would act in concert with the sole power which was still capable of doing something, Germany, in order to create a counterbalance to the Soviet Union. Certainly, they would never make peace with Hitler, but obviously with a government which incorporated the other Germany. This government must be on hand before it was too late and the political structure of Europe had been destroyed. In order to achieve this goal, Hitler must fall, if

necessary be brought down by force. The means of doing this however, remained a mystery.[21]

As it became increasingly clear to all those who were involved in negotiations with the Western Allies that the British were not prepared to deal with *any* Germans, and that they were looking for the total annihilation of German power *even* to the degree of allowing Bolshevik Russia to become the major power on the Continent, Goerdeler began to despair for the first time. He cast his mind back to his meetings with Chamberlain and others in Britain and America in 1938, when they had dismissed the German opposition as traitors, and reached for his pen.

> Influential Britons and Americans were told before this war that Hitler would unleash it and bring terrible misfortune to the world. They thought we Germans who gave this warning were men without national feeling. They did not realize that we love our Fatherland with all our heart and desire its greatness and honour, but that we knew from our suffering what course the satanic and demonic Hitler would take. In spite of our warning, Chamberlain ran after Hitler in 1938. At that time British firmness could have avoided war and exposed Hitler. We do not wish to lessen the responsibility which we Germans have to carry. But the tragedy before us was not caused only by Germans; nor have we Germans in this tragedy made the least sacrifices for our convictions. When we free ourselves, the world will learn what decent Germans have endured and suffered, and how many of them have died a death of torment for German honour and the freedom of the world.[22]

While the Goerdeler-Beck axis could count on the support of conservative nationalist elements like Ambassador von Hassell, Gisevius and intellectual soldiers like General Georg Thomas of the Economic Warfare Department, as well as to some degree, the leaders of the Protestant Churches, they could not take for granted the participation of Socialists, former trade union leaders and the bulk of the younger opponents to the regime. Along with former Prussian finance minister Johannes Popitz, the *Alte Herren* were identified with their earlier opposition to the Weimar Republic and were viewed with suspicion by former deputies like Julius Leber or Carlo Mierendorff. As the war proceeded a compromise had to be worked out which would bring together both the right and the left of the Resistance. This was where the so-called 'Kreisau Circle' came in.

The 'Kreisauer Kreis' – Kreisau Circle – was the name given by the Sicherheitsdienst after the July Plot to the collection of younger conspirators, churchmen, Socialists and trade unionists who got together for discussions about the future of a non-Nazi Germany from the spring of 1941 to the summer of 1944. The first big conference

213

took place at Kreisau at Whitsun 1941. There were to be two more sessions on the Field Marshal's estate as well as many meetings at other country houses belonging to members of the group. Principally, though, discussions took place not at Kreisau but in Berlin, either in Moltke's house in the Derflingerstrasse, in Peter Yorck's house in Berlin-Lichterfelde or at other locations such as the Trott flat in Dahlem.[23]

Writing to his chief, Bormann, on 9 January 1945, the Party's official observer at the 20 July trials, Dr Lorenzen, gave his own summary of the Kreisau Circle:

> The Kreisau Circle was a group of defeatists and opponents of National Socialism which since around 1940 had gathered around the person of the former director of the Foreign Division of the High Command, War Administration Councillor [Advocate] Helmuth Graf von Moltke on his estate of Kreisau in Lower Silesia. The group was made up of reactionary [sic – i.e. to the National Socialist revolution] federalist, religious and syndicalist elements. It met repeatedly at Kreisau, but discussions also took place in Berlin and Munich. The object of these talks was to put together a so-called collective programme to be enacted were National Socialism to come to an end. The programme foresaw that National Socialism's place as an element of order should be taken by the then surviving elements of the two Christian Churches. The executive power of the Reich would not be totally destroyed but rather extensively shifted on to about twelve newly fashioned, originally conceived, self-administering areas at the head of which would be a national administrator. The workers would be run on syndicalist lines.[24]

Both the Gestapo and later historians have exaggerated the monolithic nature of the Kreisau Circle, crediting it with a rigidity of structure and purpose which it certainly never had. The dominant influence was that of Helmuth Moltke, who took part in virtually all its councils until his arrest at the beginning of 1944, and who played host to the three Kreisau sessions proper. Various papers were written at his suggestion, while others were the result of personal initiative.[25] Some peace moves were discussed with members of the group, others were not. Kreisau has become a convenient receptacle in which to lump all those leading anti-Nazis who were not in the military and were not part of the immediate entourage of Beck, Goerdeler or Popitz.

Participation in these discussions chiefly amounted to meetings with Moltke himself. In these Peter Yorck von Wartenburg tops the league tables by a long chalk, with 141 recorded discussions. Yorck was the only one to attend all three of the Kreisau meetings. In the early years, the next most assiduous member of the circle was Horst von Einsiedel, though in the last stages, Trott overtakes him. After Trott, who ranks joint third, the table shows regular attenders to be the former Socialist deputy Mierendorff; Edouard Wätjen, who later became the Abwehr's contact man in Geneva; Adolf Reichwein, who attended two of the Kreisau sessions; Eugen Gerstenmaier; the Catholic noble and publisher of the *Weisse Blätter*, Freiherr von Guttenberg; Theodor Stelzer; Hans-Bernd von Haeften; the Jesuit Father König; Hans Peters; Bishop Preysing of Berlin; Otto von der Gablentz and Carl Dietrich von Trotha, both early collaborators of Moltke's, as was Paulus van Husen. Less regular attenders were Furtwängler, who stopped coming much after 1940; Theodor Haubach, the Socialist journalist; Fritz-Dietlof von der Schulenburg; Hans von Dohnanyi; Albrecht von Kessel; the Jesuit Fathers Rösch and Delp; Harald Poelchau, the Lutheran chaplain of the Plötzensee prison; Josias von Rantzau; the trade union leader Wilhelm Leuschner, who had been minister of the interior in Hessen; the manufacturer and historian's son, Justus Delbrück; Trott's former Berlin landlord, the Socialist industrialist Arnold von Borsig; and Julius Leber. The latter kept his distance from the organization but attended five meetings with Moltke and Trott in the latter stages of the war.

The lawyer Hans Lukaschek was an occasional participant; both General Beck and Peter Bielenberg attended on three occasions (Bielenberg was supposed to discuss the future of German industry with Moltke and Einsiedel – characteristically he got bored and ceased attending),[26] General Oster twice and Dietrich Bonhoeffer and Johannes Popitz once. Trott was present only at the third of the Kreisau meetings which took place on the estate. In 1940, while the group was as yet only half formed, he had only sporadic meetings with Moltke and his friends. From six sessions in 1940, the number of discussions doubled to twelve in 1941. The following year, when Trott was making his own peace bids through contacts in Switzerland, there were fifteen meetings. In the final year, 1943, once Leber and later Stauffenberg had begun to reinject the lost *élan* into the conspiracy, Trott was engaged in twenty-nine talks with the group. These talks could have been as simple as a half-hour discussion with Moltke on the way back from work, or as weighty as a full session taking place over several days at the houses of Moltke, Borsig or Yorck.

Implicit in the Kreisau discussions was the rejection of the national conservative aspects of thinking still advocated by some of the older group, who were seeking a return to a Wilhelmine Germany. Writing to Lionel Curtis in 1942, Moltke summed up the younger men's view of the new Europe for which they were only awaiting the elimination of Hitler to create:

For us Europe after the war is less a problem of frontiers and soldiers, of top-heavy organizations or grand plans; Europe after the war is more a question of how the picture of man can be re-established in the breasts of our fellow citizens. This is a question of religion and education, of ties of work and family, of the proper relation of responsibility and rights ... Please do not forget, that we trust that you will stand it through without flinching as we are prepared to do

215

our bit, and don't forget that for us a very bitter end is in sight when you have seen matters through. We hope that you will realize that we are ready to help you to win war and peace.[27]*

To do their bit to help the Allies win the war and the peace, Moltke and his friends believed in taking positive steps to undermine the regime through their negotiations with the other side. This role was chiefly Trott's, who was instrumental in creating Kreisau foreign policy, and also that of Moltke himself, whose work with the High Command enabled him to travel widely. While the Kreisauers did not advocate personal involvement in the *Putsch* to remove Hitler, they certainly did not reject the idea, although some of them, like Moltke himself, had their doubts about the legality of actually killing Hitler. One who had no such doubts was Eugen Gerstenmaier,† who formulated religious policy within the group.

> It has been stated that the Kreisau Circle, and especially Moltke, abandoned the idea of active resistance at the start and rejected a *coup d'etat.* This is completely erroneous. For years Moltke worked with his friends towards the one goal of overthrowing National Socialism – whether by *coup* or by engineering a military collapse. But Moltke did not belong to the military and he always said that the execution of the *coup* had to be a military matter.[28]

The Kreisau Circle set about constructing an entirely new Germany, which meant that Moltke valued very highly indeed the varied expertise of the group's members. Protestant religous experts like Gerstenmaier worked with Catholic priests like Delp, Rösch and König to elaborate ethical policy for the new state; the trade unionists were chiefly responsible for the organization of labour; the economists reviewed the structure of the economy, etc.‡ Trott and his

---

* *In the same letter Moltke vividly describes internal conditions in Germany, making it clear to his English friends just how difficult it was to maintain a conspiracy against Hitler, 'Can you imagine what it means to work as a group when you cannot use the telephone, when you are unable to post letters, when you cannot tell the names of your closest friends to your other friends for fear that one of them might be caught and might divulge the names under pressure?'* (A German of the Resistance, The Last Letters of Count Helmuth James von Moltke, *OUP, 1946*)

† *To prove his convictions on 20 July 1944, Gerstenmaier was present in the Bendlerstrasse armed with a Bible in one pocket and a revolver in the other.*

‡ *Moltke's patronage of Jesuit priests was a major plank in the prosecution's case against him before the People's Court in January 1945. As he calmly wrote to his wife after the trial: 'That I should die a martyr for Saint Ignatius Loyola is really a joke, and I am already shivering with fear at the thought of facing the fatherly wrath of Papi, who was so anti-Catholic. Some things he would approve, but that?' (Quoted in Furtwängler, op. cit., and also Balfour and Frisby, op.cit.)*

216

colleagues at the Foreign Office were obviously called upon to give their expertise when it came to foreign policy, although Moltke too had his ideas in this line, especially where organization of a future European community was concerned. Moltke also had strong views on the division of power in the post-war world which strike a strange chord today.[29]

Briefly then, on Europe, the Kreisau policy was a far-sighted desire to see a European solution which would put an end to the dangers of what Trott called 'family wars'. Europe would be reconstructed on essentially federal lines which would remove a certain number of difficulties when it came to areas like Upper Silesia. For, though Moltke was clear on the need to cede Upper Silesia to the Poles, he thought that with the powerful nation state reduced in scope, the misery caused by such a secession would be minimized. Much of this policy is to be found in Trott's paper 'Comments on the Peace Programme of the American Churches', where he postulates the need to restrict national sovereignty. Both Russia and Britain were to be excluded from this future European community as in both cases their international interests were perceived as lying outside Europe.

Trott disagreed with Moltke about Britain. Although both men retained a strong affection for the country, Moltke was less realistic in his appraisal of Britain's power after the war, believing that Britain would retain her empire and would even reassume the spiritual and political leadership of the Anglo-Saxon world. Trott believed that Britain had a role to play in Europe which was distinct from her imperial interests. Moltke's faith in the British Empire had been bolstered by his close friendship with members of Milner's Kindergarten who had fed him some of their own imperial dreams.

Moltke and Trott were also at variance over Russia. Moltke was not by nature enthusiastic about the East and maintained a thoroughly pro-Western attitude. Trott, as his paper 'Germany Between East and West' clearly showed (the paper has unfortunately been lost, but the drift of its views is apparent from the commentary of the SD men who read it at the time of Trott's interrogation), believed that Germany's position at the centre of Europe meant that the country would have to accept a *via media,* basing its foreign policy on the need to collaborate and take the best from both sides. As regards America, and again this was possibly Trott's contribution, the view was that America would revert to isolationism at the end of the war.[30]

The Far East was naturally Trott's field. It was Trott's assumption of the mantle of expertise in this line within the Foreign Office which brought him into contact with Ambassador von Hassell for the first time in May 1941. Hassell had been asked to write an article on the political situation in Europe, while Trott had been selected to do the same for East Asia. Hassell's diaries show that the relationship between the two men was fruitful over the following three years,

Hassell showing a far greater tolerance for the views of the younger Resisters than Goerdeler. It is possible that Trott endeared himself to the civilized Hassell through his corpsier connections. The corps meetings continued to be selection boards for Resistance activities. It is probable that Trott first met Fritz-Dietlof von der Schulenburg at a meeting of the Göttinger Sachsen in 1941. Münchhausen was there and remembered the men talking of finding a means to eliminate Hitler.

Given the strength of Moltke's personality and the wide gulf which separated their conceptions of foreign policy in certain areas, it is not surprising that Trott and Moltke's relations had their ups and downs. After a visit from Trott and Haeften on 15 May 1941, Moltke wrote to his wife of the 'great strain' of dealing with such people, 'as they are too aware of the routine'.[31] Haeften, however, is singled out for his willingness to follow Moltke's lead. It is worth noting that at that time Moltke still referred to Trott by his surname and not as Adam, as he did later – except, that is, when he was cross with him; in those moments he reverted to the formal style. The stumbling block that day was perhaps Moltke's lack of interest in Russia; regarding Communism and Fascism as much of a muchness, he didn't care who won.[32]

Further arguments broke out with Furtwängler over India. Furtwängler eventually conceding to Moltke that dominion status was enough. Respect for the British Empire may well have been a stumbling block with Trott too; the Milner school would have taken a dim view of German support for Subhas Bose. Furtwängler was at that time maintaining a liaison with Socialist groups around Germany, taking in the foreign workers too. With seven million foreigners in Germany there existed an untapped source of opposition to the Nazi Reich which was never exploited, though the idea must have entered many people's heads. Furtwängler was obviously happier involved in this sort of undercover work than he was pursuing the foreign policies of the Nazi regime. Trott teased him good-naturedly about his exaggerated sense of social justice, saying, 'I hope that you won't lose your Michael Kohlhaas nature while you hide behind this official mask.'[33]*

Moltke continued to be high-handed with Trott, giving him 'school exercises' to do after a lunch together in August. It was in mid October that Moltke and Trott had their first chance for an extensive exchange of views when they were staying on the Borsig's estate at Gross Behnitz. The house party lasted from 12–13 October; Moltke came alone but both Trott and Peter Yorck brought their wives. Botho von Wussow was also there with his English wife Mary. Once again Moltke and Trott argued, this time about 'the justification for thinking out how

---

* *Michael Kohlhaas, the chief protagonist (and also title) of a novella by Heinrich von Kleist. Kohlaas' sense of justice leads him to commit acts which far outweigh the wrong perpetrated against him by the Junker von Tronka.*

the state should be set up'.[34] Writing to Freya afterwards, Moltke said he thought he had won the battle, with the help of Yorck, who underpinned him throughout. With time their relationship was to become more peaceful, but for the time being it was dominated by a struggle for supremacy which Moltke was quite determined to win.

Part of the problem between Trott and Moltke might have been ironed out by some of Trott's thoughts on internal German issues at the time. For one, he had become convinced that the most acceptable figure to present to the Allies as a future German ruler was Martin Niemöller, the Dahlem pastor who had been in a concentration camp since 1937. At the same time, Hassell reports, Trott had considered the idea of some sort of restoration of a British-style constitutional monarchy, though this idea seems to have been swiftly put to bed for what were, on the whole, far-sighted reasons. Both issues he discussed with his Socialist friend Helmut Conrad, who had been quite in favour of Niemöller. Probably through Otto John (who thought Brüning a better candidate for chancellor) Trott had had a meeting with Prince Louis Ferdinand of Prussia in a *Weinstube*. Trott and he had had a few drinks and the former had expressed himself 'positively as to his [i.e. the prince's] character'.[35] Louis Ferdinand was in general the favourite among the princes – or at least among the Hohenzollerns; he had worked on the shop floor of Fords in America and was then employed by Lufthansa where he had become a friend of Otto John.[36]

The idea of a Hohenzollern restoration was that currently favoured by the older group around Beck, Goerdeler and Hassell. In time the restoration project was dropped, a measure of how much the war's progress eventually removed the possibility of a traditional solution; by 1943 even Beck and Goerdeler considered a restoration 'long time buried'.[37] Trott had obviously come to his own conclusions before November 1941 when he talked about it to Hassell. Hassell wrote:

I am always afraid we have too little contact with younger circles. This fear has now been realized, but only to reveal new and formidable difficulties. First of all I had a long talk with Trott during which he passionately contended for the avoidance, within as well as without the country, of any semblance of 'reaction', 'gentleman's club', 'militarism'. Therefore, although he, too, was a monarchist, we should under no circumstances have a monarchy now, for a monarchy would not win the support of the people and would not win confidence abroad. Converted Social Democrats, that is, Christian Social Democrats, one of whom he named (a former Reichstag representative), would never go along with us on the monarchy and would wait for the next group.

To these negative points he added the one positive thought that Niemöller should be made Chancellor of the Reich. He was, on the one hand, the strongest recognized exponent of anti-Hitlerism and, on the other hand, the most popular reformer here and the one the most likely to appeal to the Anglo-Saxon world . . .[38]

219

Trott was supported in his appeal to the *Alte Herren* by the other leading Kreisauers. Hassell discussed the issues raised by Trott with Peter Yorck, the latter giving the diplomat much the same arguments. 'Finally, at his own request, I went to see Yorck again. There I met Moltke, Trott and Guttenberg. All four, under the leadership of Trott, set to work on me furiously'.[39] Later on at the house of Popitz, the former Prussian Finance Minister, Hassell met Fritzi Schulenburg, and 'hammered away on the same theme'. Despite his opposition, Hassell still considered Schulenburg the most 'sober-minded of the five'. The *Alte Herren* were advancing the idea of the crown prince, the late Kaiser's eldest son, and a man much more tainted with the stain of Nationalism or even Nazism than Louis Ferdinand. As usual Goerdeler high-handedly dismissed the younger men's opinions and reservations on the subject; he was, Hassell noted, 'almost completely unfavourable . . . to the ideas of these young men, who, on their part, disapprove of him'.[40]

A few days later Hassell tried once again to find common cause with the Kreisauers.

> I am trying to find a connecting link with the younger men by arguing as follows: the premise 'no reaction, but attempt to get popular support' was correct. Therefore it is most earnestly to be desired that we get, as head of government, a man whose name will be considered both as a deliverance and as a programme. It is important too, in the interests of foreign policy, if only to a limited degree. The latter qualification is necessary because the national character of this change, rising out of the peculiar will and needs of our people, can be maintained only if we do not look over our shoulder at other countries. Also because the Christian pacifist circles among the Anglo-Saxon peoples, on whom Trott counts most heavily, are entirely useless as a dependable political factor.
>
> In general I am against Trott's theoretical and illusionary outlook. Unfortunately such a personality as we look for is not there. I am convinced that the man Trott proposed has some unsuitable characteristics. He is somewhat unbending, non-political and not a good strategist. Aside from all this, I think that, after the first effect had worn off, he would not be a successful symbol. On the contrary, he might even create opposition.[41]

Trott had one more go at pushing through the Niemöller idea when he suggested to Hassell that the latter might choose to change his mind if Field Marshal Brauchitsch were to agree.[42] Brauchitsch had a largely unconvincing reputation as an opponent of Hitler, and after being handsomely bribed by him he resisted all attempts to link his name with the plotters'.[43] Brauchitsch was Haeften's uncle, and Trott perhaps saw a way to influence him through his colleague at the IA. Hassel had fewer illusions about Brauchitsch than Trott, having bitter memories of trying to win him over in 1938 and 1939. Hassell countered Trott, 'by asking whether he, Trott, wanted to influence

Brauchitsch in this sense'. The issue was laid to rest by the dismissal of the Field-Marshal as Commander-in-Chief of the armed forces on 19 December as a result of his failing to win a blitzkrieg against Russia. Hitler made himself Commander-in-Chief, once again humiliating the officer corps and weakening their ability to resist.

At the time of Brauchitsch's dismissal, Trott was in Switzerland. On 20 December, he wrote his penultimate letter to Diana Hopkinson in England, from the house of Jenny Thurneysen – a friend of Peter and Christabel Bielenberg – in Basle.

> Recently there have been several indications that you over in your country tend more and more to consider us as being already under the Teuton fold [*sic*] or identified with their aims. Actually this is less and less the case in 'German' Switzerland and you and your friends must *insist* on this distinction. Personally I have no doubt that you still do.[44]*

At the beginning of the following year, 1942, Adam von Trott became a close friend of the half-German, half-American journalist Margret Boveri.[45] Margret Boveri had been based in New York until the outbreak of war when she had been interned as an enemy alien. While she awaited deportation, she met Julie Braun-Vogelstein, who was then under grave suspicion as a result of her close contacts with the 'master spy' Trott. Mrs Braun-Vogelstein had spoken to Miss Boveri about her German friend. Margret Boveri and Trott had a further contact in common in Albrecht von Bernstorff and it was he who introduced them to one another when the journalist got back to Germany. With Christabel Bielenberg, Trott especially valued Margret Boveri for her 'Anglo-Saxon way of thinking', a quality hard to come by in Germany during the war.

Margret Boveri found Trott and his circle a breath of fresh air after her contacts with some of the older Resisters, notably Hassell, whom she characterized as being obsessed with the question of whether Hitler would acknowledge him in public or not, long after he joined the fight against the regime. In the younger men she found nothing of this; from the first Trott made it clear to her that he did not believe in the possibility of German victory, while the Hassell-elements were still compromised by their desire to see a reversal of 1918 – of which Hassell still retained bitter memories as a badly wounded subaltern.[46] The Resistance divided up at that time, and later, between those who had grown up before 1914 and those who had only known post-Wilhelmine Germany. A further split was noticeable between the activists and the pacifists. Trott was with the former, while Moltke definitely had leanings in the other direction.

---

* *Trott's last letter to Diana Hopkinson is sent from the same address on 24 March 1942. 'We think and talk of you so often and hope, that is, in spite of all – there remains at heart a realm of peace in which, one day, we may meet again.'*

Another reservation which Margret Boveri had about the older men was their tendency to indiscretion, which was certainly a tendency shared by Hassell and Goerdeler.

The younger men were never guilty of such lapses. I knew Adam von Trott zu Solz well, and we often had political conversations without my ever suspecting for a moment that he was an active leader in a revolutionary plot. I recall once remarking that no conspiracy could ever be a success in Germany, *because* conspirators could not hold their tongues: Trott just laughed.[47]

It is a measure of the truth of Margret Boveri's statement that none of the younger men connected with Kreisau gave themselves away to the Gestapo until Moltke himself was arrested simply for tipping off Consul Kiep. Later Reichwein and Leber were arrested as a result of their meeting with the Saefkow/Jacob group in July 1944 (when the third man present turned out to be a police spy). The incarceration of the others happened solely as a result of the failure of the July plot. Margret Boveri found the older men both 'spooky' and 'ephemeral' while her visits to Trott in 1942 'were of a very different kind. Trott spoke of the tasks facing a new Germany – the re-establishment of contact with a Nazified German youth,* the development of a social programme which would not be a return to the bureaucratic sterility of the Weimar Social Democracy.' Trott's mind also went back to his failure to win the trust of his English friends, something which caused him untold bitterness at the time.

I suspect that some of my English friends are all too prone to identify a European illness solely with Germany. They seem to make their friendship with me dependent on the degree to which I accidentally fit into their English way of life. I consider their judgement to be false and unfair. I want to have nothing to do with that sort of acceptance, for it is sterile and irresponsible, though I do not deny that I see good reasons for their attitude. Yet it is precisely at this time in this our terrible dilemma that friendship among men of different nations, indeed with those at war with each other could, I think, have been most useful.[48]

Even during the war Trott was obsessed with the need to maintain mutual trust and respect between people and nations in order to prevent future wars from occurring.

Trott put his theory into practice when, armed with an introduction from Visser't Hooft, he presented himself to members of the Dutch underground. In the late spring of 1942 he came to the house of Professor Dr C.L. Patijn in the Hague where he met Dr van Royen, Professor Baron F.M. van Asbeck and his old friend from the Liverpool conference Dr Jur. G.J. Scholten.[49] Patijn and Asbeck he had met before

---

* *It may have been this interest which led Trott later in the war to have lunch with Artur Axman, the Hitler Youth leader.*

at the beginning of the previous December, when he had employed a pretext of needing to speak to them about Far Eastern affairs in order to win their confidence.[50] The specific issue was that of the Japanese control of Dutch Java and the Dutch prisoners interned there. Trott told the group he was working for the Resistance but named no names, though once in 1943 he was accompanied on his visits to The Hague by Moltke. Patijn wrote later of this meeting.

> That evening Herr von Trott needed to make little effort to win our trust. The introduction from Visser't Hooft and the style of his person – calm, serious, at the same time completely businesslike – his judgement of the German regime and position which was completely lacking in illusion. It was clear that one had here a reality which enshrined qualities which rendered our support worthwhile.[51]

Patijn adds, 'It was the function of Herr von Trott to seek help and support abroad for a possible German revolution.' As Trott left, he promised to do his best to have some Dutch prisoners released, as a gage of friendship.

The beginning of the year was still much occupied with work for Bose and the Indian cause. Trott was able, however, to get one or two things done as a result of the power conferred on him by his office. One of these was to engineer the liberation of a number of Jews from concentration camps, (including a Frau Rosa Spira) using the case of a Viennese Jew called Eidlitz as a pretext. Eidlitz had been interned by the British in India as a German national. As he had good contacts with many leading Indians, Trott was able to bring pressure to bear on the SS to have his family released from camps within the Reich and Eastern territories. In March he quarrelled with Bose and the department received a report on the trouble Bose was causing him. The Indian was sulking in Gastein. Trott's falling out with Bose may have been as a direct consequence of the scuttling of the Cripps Mission which was taking place at the time. On 14 March he wrote to Ribbentrop on his special train, '. . . he [Bose] does not think it propitious to provide further stimulus [for revolt] by means of an open letter to Cripps sent out on the transmitter. That it would be the tactics of an uncompromising nationalist [here the words 'these British compromise proposals' have been crossed out] to disregard the possibilities introduced by the person of Cripps.'[52] The letter was, however, broadcast on Keppler's orders during Trott's absence from Berlin at the end of March. It is intriguing to speculate whether Trott's report was written with Bose's connivance, or if Trott had merely sought to do something positive to rescue the beleaguered Cripps Mission.[53]

In Berlin, the usual problems were bubbling up between the *Alte Herren* and the younger conspirators, and within the ranks of older men themselves. That Popitz would not speak to Goerdeler was well

223

known but now he had adopted the same stance towards General Oster. Beck had been chosen as the leader of the Resistance in an effort to find a compromise which suited all parties; in the meantime Hassell was chasing his tail in an attempt to placate the younger men and reconcile the differences between Popitz and the rest. Hassell's efforts were dogged by a growing distrust occasioned by his indiscretions. He had come under the suspicion of the Gestapo and was endangering the whole project as a result. A bitter blow was dealt by Weizsäcker, who asked Hassell to 'spare him the embarrassment' of his presence. Hassell noted in his diary on 29 April that as he left Weizsäcker's presence the latter had said, 'Now *aufwiedersehen*, but please not too soon.'[54] During Weizsäcker's trial, his spurning of Hassell was used in evidence against him, though with greater hindsight it seems that 'Der Staats' was merely being cautious with an eye to the entire structure of the resistance which could have been destroyed had Hassell continued to enjoy such freedom of movement.

Weizsäcker continued to warn likely subordinates of the danger of having too great a commerce with Hassell, as in the case of Gottfried Nostitz, who had played an early role in the conspiracy as part of the group around the brothers Kordt. On 1 May Trott called on Hassell, who wrote in his diary:

> His chief, Weizsäcker, had sent for two of his subordinates to warn them about me ... I was being watched because I criticized the regime, said Hitler must be removed and such things. I met Trott again a little later and he told me his chief had subsequently given an order that in no event was I to be told of this. Trott also said that Papen, upon his departure from HQ, had heard how Hitler had inveighed against the diplomats and had pointed to me and my wife as particularly impossible types.[55]

Work for Bose and the Indian Nationalist cause, and a fresh outbreak of maxillary sinusitis, forcing him to take a holiday in Switzerland, kept Trott away from the second of the Gross Behnitz meetings of the Kreisauers which took place from 13–16 March. Moltke's difficulties on this occasion were rather more with Dietrich Bonhoeffer, who vexed the serious Moltke with his sense of humour and his contrary conviction that Hitler should be killed. From 22–25 May there was the first of the conferences at Kreisau proper with the guests staying at the 'big house' while Moltke and his family occupied their usual home in the Berghaus on the estate. Again Trott was absent from this session at which the host described his role as being 'like a foreman in a gang of labourers'. Although Moltke and Trott had got together on average once a month over the winter months, they did not meet between 7 April and 17 June 1942.[56]

Trott's absence from the councils of the Kreisau group was

224

occasioned by another important piece of business, namely the first of his major attempts to get the Allies to agree to a positive attitude towards the German opposition by means of proposals transmitted via Geneva and Stockholm. As Gerstenmaier tells us in his memoirs, the idea of making new representations to the Western Allies was first broached within the IA in the winter of 1941/2.

> Hans von Haeften and Adam von Trott became convinced that the tempestuous advance would come to grief in the Russian winter, and that therewith the painful second half of the war would begin. Haeften in particular construed from Hitler's character the prediction that the second half would end in a scorched-earth policy. In contrast to the friendly expectations which Helmuth von Moltke entertained in respect of relations with England, Adam von Trott made out gloomily that in his view, the Western – Anglo-American – influence would do little to temper the victorious Soviets. We believed that it was therefore now, while we were still at the high-point of German strength, that it was the best moment to approach the British government. After a brief analysis of the situation and of expected developments, the political picture would be sketched out, showing that the German Resistance to Hitler was united at that time. The practical aim of the whole affair was to maintain political dialogue with London, in order to further an attempted coup on behalf of the critical German military.
>
> During discussions the three of us were wholly of one accord. I was asked to make up a draft. Adam von Trott would then prepare an English version. For several evenings we sat together over the proposals in my home at 12 Goethestrasse until we had agreed on every point. A little while later Hans Schönfeld took it away with him to Geneva, but before handing it over to Visser't Hooft he gave it to our friends at the German Consulate in Geneva, Albrecht von Kessel and Gottfried von Nostitz, so that they too could have a look at it.[57]

It was at that point that Kessel and Nostitz made their own adaptations to the draft. Gerstenmaier makes it clear that he never set eyes on the finished proposals.[58]

Visser't Hooft, the European Secretary of the YMCA and the General Secretary of the World Council of Churches, arrived in London at the beginning of May. The Foreign Office reported that he held conversations with Dr van Kleffens and Ivone Kirkpatrick and other people and that 'he brought with him a memorandum alleged to have been composed by one Herr von Trott.'[59] The others must have included David Astor and Wilfrid Israel as the latter made a special appeal to Sir Stafford Cripps at this time to recognize the German opposition. A copy was shown to A.D. Lindsay at Balliol;[60] other copies were intended for Sir Alfred Zimmern, the Professor of International Relations at Oxford, and Arnold Toynbee. The main thrust of Trott's mission, however, was to Cripps himself, who was now a member of the War Cabinet.

British policy towards Germany and the idea of a negotiated peace had changed since the end of the 'phoney war'. The new government of Churchill had put away the policies of Chamberlain and Halifax, citing the Venlo Incident of November 1939 in justification. In response to some peace feelers from Berne, received at the end of December 1940, Churchill had written to his Foreign Minister, Anthony Eden, 'I presume you are keeping an eye on all this. Your predecessor was entirely misled in December [sic] 1939. Our attitude towards all such enquiries should be absolute silence.'[61] The isolated incident of Venlo was not enough to justify the abandonment of all idea of a negotiated peace. Churchill was making a stand, outlining his intention to fight to the last ditch after the humiliation of Dunkirk; the Prime Minister was making it plain that he was fighting a war to destroy Germany.

On 10 September 1941, following the Russian entry into the war, Eden sent Churchill a summary of German peace proposals, including one from Goerdeler who claimed the support of Generals Halder and Blaskowitz. The tone of the request for permission to deal with these overtures was supercilious in the extreme. Eden knew his man; on the same day he received the following reply: 'I am sure we should not depart from our policy of absolute silence. Nothing would be more disturbing to our friends in the United States or more dangerous to our new ally, Russia, than the suggestion that we were entertaining such ideas. I am absolutely opposed to the slightest contact.'[62] Eden's reply gives voice to his evident feelings of happiness at the Prime Minister's decision: 'I do agree and am in fact relieved at your decision. The case in favour was, I thought, worth a mention.'[63] Churchill minuted on Eden's reply, 'Please keep.'[64] The Prime Minister did not wish his Foreign Secretary to forget that this was to be his policy for the rest of the war. As Richard Lamb has written, Churchill 'bears a heavy responsibility for refusing to encourage the anti-Nazi German patriots who might have been able to bring the war to an end.'[65]

Visser't Hooft had told Trott in Switzerland, before he left for London, that Bishop Bell of Chichester would soon be making a trip to Sweden. The visit was to be part of an Allied scheme to better Anglo-Swedish relations in the face of German propaganda. Trott acted with the utmost speed, despatching Hans Schönfeld to Stockholm with a copy of the memo.

Bell was the right man, as Trott knew from Gerstenmaier. As early as 1934 Bell had spoken out against Nazi attempts to Aryanize the Church, and over the next few years through his friends in the German ecumenical movement he had kept in close touch with developments in the persecution of the Churches in Germany. From the beginning of the war Bell had made his views plain, that it was the duty of the British to work for a just peace, announcing to the House of Lords on 13 December 1939, 'I am not a pacifist, nor am I one of those who would ask that peace should be made at any price.'[66]

At the beginning of 1940, Lord Noel-Buxton pressed Bell for

clarification of his views as they were upsetting the hawks in the House. Bell replied, '. . . I believe that the Evangelicals and Catholics in Germany are terribly handicapped and puzzled by the absence of a constructive and positive plan coming from the Allies.'[67] He made it clear that for there to be any justice to the conflict there was a necessity for war aims to be made clear, something that the British were very reluctant to do. 'Germany and National Socialism are *not* the same thing,' he wrote in *Christianity and World Order*. 'The West can never make terms with National Socialist ideology. But the West can make terms with Germany.'[68]

Bell's Swedish visit was part of a package designed to appeal to that sober race; his arrival was intended to coincide with that of T.S. Eliot and the art historian Kenneth Clark. On 26 May, he was astonished to meet Hans Schönfeld in the house of the Swedish Pastor Nils Ehrenström. It was at this point that Schönfeld filled him in on the state of the German Resistance and explained to the bishop the aims of the conspirators. The terms given by Schönfeld were those of the Trott-Gerstenmaier-Haeften memorandum: a restoration of the rule of law, of responsible self-government in a federal administration, a Socialist constitution and the close co-operation of European nations – an essentially Kreisauer programme, even if not directly Kreisau-inspired, and a clear response to Hitler's latest speech of 26 April when he had declared himself to be above all laws.

Bell reported Schönfeld's approach and his idea of a possible Himmlerian interlude to the British minister in Stockholm, Victor Mallet. On 31 May he travelled to Sigtuna,

> a small town with a famous residential adult education centre, at some distance from Stockholm. There an extraordinary thing happened. A second German pastor walked straight in from Berlin to see me. It was Pastor Dietrich Bonhoeffer.
>
> I had known him very well since 1933. He was an uncompromising anti-Nazi, one of the initiators of the opposition who enjoyed the entire trust of the leaders of the Confessing Church. While Bonhoeffer and I were alone, I asked him in the strictest confidence whether he would give me the names of the most important conspirators. He did so immediately. He told me that the ranks of the conspiracy contained: Colonel General Beck who had been Chief of the General Staff up until the time of the Austrian crisis of 1938, enjoyed the full confidence of the Wehrmacht and was a conservative Christian with contacts in the trade union movement leadership; Colonel General von Hammerstein, the Head of the Armed Forces when Hitler came to power and a convinced Christian; Carl Goerdeler, the former Oberbürgermeister of Leipzig and one-time Reich commissioner for price control, highly respected among the civil service and civilian leaders; Wilhelm Leuschner, president of the United Trade Unions before they were abolished; and Jakob Kaiser, a Catholic trade union leader.
>
> The leaders were Beck and Goerdeler. In Bonhoeffer's opinion, a govern-ment under their leadership could be relied upon. An organization existed

where the opposition was represented in every ministry and to which officers in all the big towns belonged; in all the home-front commands there were generals or officers near in rank who were part of the group. He mentioned von Kluge and von Witzleben.

While he presented me with these facts, I could see that he was extremely unhappy that things had taken this direction and that such a move should have been necessary.[69]

Bonhoeffer's arrival on a mission from the Abwehr was no coincidence; Bonhoeffer had been to Geneva to see Visser't Hooft only to discover that the latter had gone to London to deliver the Trott-Haeften-Gerstenmaier memorandum. From Visser't Hooft's wife, Bonhoeffer had learned that Bell was to visit Stockholm. Bonhoeffer cur short his visit to Geneva and, stopping in Berlin to acquire a courier's passport from the Auswärtige Amt, flew on to Stockholm. Bonhoeffer seems to have been wholly aware of Schonfeld's moves on Trott's behalf, even if Schonfeld knew nothing of Bonhoeffer's mission, hence Bonhoeffer's recommendation of Trott as the go-between for negotiations between the two sides.[70]

Bell and Bonhoeffer had another meeting on 1 June at which Bell summed up Schacht as a 'seismograph of contemporary events'.[71] When the bishop returned to London, filled with optimism as a result of his talks with Schönfeld and Bonhoeffer, Trott's memorandum had been circulating in high places for the best part of a month. The seven points of this programme were conditional on the success of a *coup d'etat* which was to be an *internal affair*. The programme would mean a return to the European tradition of government, the condemnation of National Socialism and the restoration of the rule of law and civic rights. 'Anti-Semitism would likewise be condemned.' The German armies in the west and north of Europe would return to the old German frontiers. Austria's fate would be decided by plebiscite. The group would not advocate the withdrawal of German armies from Russia until the Western Allies were able to provide certain guarantees (this was occasioned by the fear of what the Russians might do). Conditions in the Baltic 'seemed too chaotic to allow Germany to withdraw forthwith. Relations with Japan would be severed. It was hoped that a European Federation could then be established, Germany being prepared to renounce some considerable part of her sovereign rights to the federation.'[72] The proposals which Bell took to the Foreign Office on 30 June were slightly different as they contained an amalgam of Schönfeld (Trott-Gerstenmaier-Haeften) and Bonhoeffer (whose programme was that of the Abwehr).

The Genevan programme warned the West of the consequences of pursuing the war, which would occasion destruction on such a huge scale that it would reduce even the victors to great poverty. It appealed to the solidarity of the civilized world to heed the German opposition.

The authors were also careful to warn the British of the dangers a Russian victory would bring about for Western democracy. This last point may well have been as a result of Canaris' successful decoding of the American signals from Switzerland to Washington. Dulles, the OSS man, was pathologically worried by the implications of a Communist victory and the Russian bogey was thought to be a useful way of gaining his support.

Sir Stafford Cripps showed a 'sincere interest' in the memorandum, and promised to show it to the Prime Minister. He also expressed a friendly interest in 'the author'.[73] He fixed a meeting a week later with Visser't Hooft and in the meantime, passed the paper to Churchill. The Prime Minister, caught off guard, minuted 'very encouraging'.[74] Toynbee handed on his copy to Professor Tom Marshall at Balliol* who asked Richard Crossman to submit a report on Trott for the use of the Foreign Office in this connection. Crossman submitted the following facetious and astonishingly irresponsible trivialization of his former friend on 27 May 1942.

I knew Adam von Trott throughout his period at Oxford, a difficult period of transition from democratic to Nazi Germany. A tall, extremely handsome young man, he was probably the most successful German Rhodes Scholar in achieving popularity both among dons and undergraduates; incidentally he had a great way with women and was able to discard his worshippers whenever convenient. He always claimed to be a Hegelian Socialist which meant, in fact, that he had vague Socialist ideals but came from too good a family to link them with the working-class movement in anything but theory. He took his philosophy very seriously indeed; of the quality of that philosophy one can best judge when one remembers that he did not find the Master of Balliol a confused thinker.† Indeed I think that the close friendship of the Master of Balliol is due to the fact that in the realm of philosophy each is as high minded as he is woolly. Adam always found me slightly too earthy in my outlook on politics and I always found him so Hegelian that almost any action could be given its dialectical justification however slippery it might have been. In brief, I did not trust him very far and he did not trust me.

In either 1936 or 1937 my wife and I during a tour of Germany stayed at Kassel where Adam was supposed to be training as a lawyer. We saw him every day, mostly in the evenings, in a small bar where he spent his time dicing. He was extremely unhappy and torn in mind, and my feelings were even more strongly confirmed that in any serious political conflict Adam's high-minded idealism would somehow twist to avoid the really unpleasant decision to work for a revolution in Germany.

---

* Lindsay, the Master of Balliol's reaction to the paper was to tell Visser't Hooft that it would be indecent to drive a wedge between the Allies as Hess had just landed in England with a crude attempt of this kind. (Visser't Hooft in Encounter, 1969).

† In the light of the statement referred to in the foregoing footnote, it is interesting to read Crossman's assessment of Lindsay's thinking.

The private paper which Visser't Hooft brought from Adam for the personal perusal of Cripps, Temple [the Archbishop of Canterbury] and Lindsay, is an almost perfect specimen of Adam's thought, ingenuous in its politics and unaware of its intellectual and political dishonesty. On the other hand it probably very truthfully represents a section of the German diplomatic service, army and church inside Germany whose line of thought is reflected outside by such men as Rauschning,* but there would be very little difference in practice between the actions recommended by each.

I believe therefore that the group Adam represents really does exist and that it is of some importance for our political warfare and it should be misdirected by us in ways useful to HMG. Adam von Trott is not fully aware of his ingenuousness in politics, can claim a really extensive knowledge of England, and may therefore be able to persuade harder headed men than himself to share his illusions.[75]

Crossman's paper was extremely patronizing and shorn up to a monstrous degree by intellectual smugness. The high-handed condemnation of his friend's intellectual processes smacks of senior-common-room bitchiness and no more, but in the light of the fact that Crossman actually affirms his belief in the existence of Trott's group, such a cheap jibe is particularly shocking in an official paper. What was even more extraordinary is that the Foreign Office chose to take Crossman's word about Trott rather than that of any of his other friends, even that of Cripps, who was a member of the War Cabinet.

By this stage, the memorandum was doing the rounds of the Foreign Office, where it was minuted by the more important heads of department. Cripps, anxious to know what its effect had been, made enquiries. On 6 June, Geoffrey Harrison pooh-poohed the idea of an opposition in Germany, at the same time echoing the 'positive' aspects of Crossman's paper.[76] A week later he circulated a new minute on the programme in which he suggested that the circulation of such a document was a danger to Allied morale in view of the number of copies which had been made and the likelihood of its having an effect on 'influential people'. The note ends,

---

Hermann Rauschning, a former high-ranking Danzig Nazi who had been close to Hitler in the early years of National Socialism but who had turned against him for ethical reasons in the mid-thirties. He emigrated first to Paris and later to the United States where he spent the war gathering around him a group of important emigrés. His books, Die Revolution des Nihilismus (Zurich 1938: translated into English as Germany's Revolution of Destruction, London 1939), and Hitler Speaks (London December 1939), had a profound effect on English thinking on Nazism. It should be remembered that the date of publication of both books in Britain corresponded with the first unabridged edition of Mein Kampf. Many of the earlier histories of Nazism were echoes of Rauschning's work, even after the accuracy of much of Hitler Speaks began to be questioned. It should be unnecessary to add that to compare Trott to Rauschning was not only unkind but unworthy of Crossman.

230

I understand that Sir S. Cripps suggested that Miss Wiskeyman [*sic* – Miss Elisabeth Wiskemann, who was based in Switzerland]* should be told to 'cool off' Adam von Trott on the grounds that he is too valuable. It seems to me regrettable that it should be known that Herr von Trott is in contact at all with Miss Wiskeyman and I am doubtful about asking her to 'cool him off'. In fact I do not think it is in our interest to do so since his value to us as a 'martyr' is likely to exceed his value to us in post-war Germany.[77]

A.L Rowse's friend Roger Makins was the next to take up the cudgels against Trott and his well-wishers. Makins made a search of the files to find out the gist of Trott's conversations with the discredited former Foreign Secretary Halifax, but found nothing. Again sentences in his memorandum echo Crossman. He finishes the paper by suggesting that difficulties be made by passport control for Visser't Hooft and others bringing in reports of this sort. By this stage the Foreign Office had received the first news of Bishop Bell's meetings with Schönfeld and Bonhoeffer and therewith further evidence of the existence of a conspiracy, Bell having visited Geoffrey Warner at the beginning of June. Of all the parties interested, only Tom Marshall in Oxford appeared to see potential in the information from Visser't Hooft and Bell. 'Religious opposition has been growing in Germany,' he wrote. 'Though the details are unreliable, the document [i.e. Trott's] provides strong evidence that church circles are prepared to collaborate in some way in the initial revolution ... These people it is alleged have been actively planning the overthrow of Hitlerism by assassination.'[78]

Pressed by Cripps for an answer on the Trott memorandum, Eden consulted his department who were able to present him with the Crossman paper. He wrote back to Cripps on 18 June:

My dear Stafford,

You spoke to me a few days ago about a memorandum said to be written by Freiherr Adam von Trott, which M. Visser't Hooft recently brought over to this country. You asked me what we knew of von Trott and what our attitude was towards M. Visser't Hooft and the document he brought with him.

As regards M. Visser't Hooft, he is, as you know, both European Secretary of the YMCA and also one of the joint Secretaries of the World Council of Churches in Geneva. To the best of our belief he is a man above reproach or suspicion.

The memorandum is an interesting document, and we believe it is quite likely there are a number of people in Germany who would endorse it. We have, however, no evidence so far that they form an organized group, and there is

---

* *Trott had already seen Elizabeth Wiskemann, whom he took the trouble to look up whenever he came to Switzerland, where she was working for the British Secret Service. Miss Wiskemann later described Trott as 'a bewilderingly brilliant creature, infinitely German in the intellectual complexity in which he loved to indulge'.* (The Europe I Saw, *London 1968*)

always the possibility that in due course they may be used by more hard-headed individuals, e.g. as a cover for peace overtures. We do not ourselves attach much importance as yet to these people, nor do we propose to respond to any overtures from them. *Our view is that until they come out into the open and give some visible sign of their intention to assist in the overthrow of the Nazi regime, they can be of little use to us or to Germany* [author's italics].

Baron von Trott [*sic*], who was a Rhodes Scholar at Oxford in the late nineteen twenties [*sic*], is a curious mixture of high-minded idealism and political dishonesty. Here is a short summary of an appreciation by a contemporary [an extract from Crossman's paper follows]. Adam von Trott is in fact not untypical of a number of young Germans in the German ministry of Foreign Affairs who, profoundly anti-Nazi in upbringing and outlook, have never quite been able to bring themselves to pay the price of their convictions and *resign* from the service of the Nazi regime. Von Trott has an extensive knowledge of England. He was here just before the war broke out and met Edward Halifax among others.

Yours ever,
Anthony.[79]

Cripps replied in an acid tone:

My dear Anthony,

Thanks for your letter of June 18. I know both these men quite well, and I think I probably know von Trott a good deal better than your informant since he has spent long periods staying in our house in the past. It is a complete failure to understand either him or what he stands for that dubs him politically dishonest.

As a matter of fact I spent a long evening with him in July '39 when we were both clear that the war was going to break out before the autumn and discussed at great length his attitude towards the Nazi regime. I have also met a very great many of his friends in different walks of life and he has since the Hitler regime came to power maintained a close contact with the working-class movement very much to his own danger.

He felt strongly that it was his duty as a German, in spite of the imminent personal risks, to go back to Germany and remain there while the war was on although he was bitterly antagonistic to the Nazi regime and has always refused to become a member of the Party [*sic*].

Any such superficial judgement as that indicated in your letter would lead to a grave misunderstanding as regards the outlook of himself and his friends. *It is not a question of his bringing himself to pay the price of his convictions by resigning from the service of the Nazi regime, which would have been a very simple solution, like that of many emigrés. He paid the far higher price in risk in refusing to join the Nazi regime but going back to Germany to fight for the things which he believed to be right* [author's italics].

I only write you these particulars that you may have better information as regards his personality.

Yours,
Stafford.[80]

Eden did not heed the rankled Lord President of the Council, whose criticisms offended his considerable vanity. The letter was passed on to his department but the matter was dead from that moment onwards. It may be that Eden had other reasons for paying no attention to the memorandum and that his judgement was influenced by a large intelligence dossier on Trott. While the SIS files for the period remain firmly closed it is impossible to say. On the other hand the FBI report on Trott runs to some *900 pages*,[81] and we also know that British Intelligence liaised with the American service. Given the contents of his American file it is no surprise that the Foreign Office should tell the SOE in September that Trott was 'an extraordinarily suspicious character'.[82]

By late June Bishop Bell's report was before the Foreign Office and Eden was once again faced with a certain pressure on his rigid observation of the rule of 'absolute silence'. If he had found criticisms from fellow members of the Cabinet hard enough to take, he was certainly not going to have much truck with this turbulent priest. Added to whatever he had in his 'Pandora's box' on Trott there was a growing confusion as to the identity of the various agencies suing for peace at the time, which led the Foreign Office to believe that both Schönfeld and Bonhoeffer (who had told Bell that he was praying for German defeat) were being manipulated by the Nazis for their own ends. Similar moves for negotiations had been put forward in Spain and Turkey (in the first case it was Otto John who met the Allied representatives). Some at least of these moves came from Ribbentrop, while the SS was putting out feelers through Portugal.[83] In London it was thought that this was a Nazi-inspired move to split the Allies in response to Eden's speech of 8 May in which he had appealed to the German opposition to come forward. Given the basic lack of motivation to have dealings with the Germans and the prevailing wind in British administration at a time when people still looked up to Vansittart,* it is hardly surprising that no one was prepared to take any notice. As one recent German historian has put it, it was 'impossible in the wide-ranging palette of peace offers through agents of the Abwehr, SS men, Church leaders, diplomats and members of the Resistance, to tell the difference between the official and the unofficial'.[84]

Eden saw Bell at the end of June. In the period which intervened between Bell's return and the meeting with the Foreign Secretary, Bell had been to see Cripps, who was enthusiastic about the Trott memorandum and about Trott himself. Eden was cool. He listened to the Bishop and read the Schönfeld memorandum, but later wrote to him telling him that no further action would be taken. On 25 July, Bell wrote a fiery reply to the minister:

---

* *Lord Vansittart was currently regaling radio audiences with 'Germans Past and Present', an account of the barbarities of the German people from Tacitus to Hitler.*

If you would at some stage make it plain that the infliction of stern retribution is not intended for those in Germany who are against the German government, who repudiate the Nazi system and are filled with shame by the Nazi crimes, it would, I am sure, have a powerful and encouraging effect on the spirit of the opposition . . . I do not believe that Lord Vansittart's policy is the policy of the British government but as long as the British government fails to repudiate it, or make it clear that those who are opposed to Hitler and Himmler will receive better treatment at our hands than Hitler, Himmler and their accomplices, it is not unnatural that the opposition in Germany should believe that the Vansittart policy holds the field.* Mr Churchill said in his first speech as Prime Minister in the House of Commons on 13 May 1940 that our policy was 'to wage war against a monstrous tyranny never surpassed in the dark and lamentable catalogue of human crime', and that our aim was 'victory at all costs'. If there are men in Germany also ready to wage war against the monstrous tyranny of the Nazis from within, is it right to discourage or ignore them?

On 4 August, Eden stated that there was little proof of the existence of the German opposition. The Bishop countered on 17 August saying that the German Resistance differed from the others in Europe in that it had received no promise of liberation.[85]

Soon after Visser't Hooft returned to Geneva, Trott called on him to learn the results of the proposals. When the Dutchman told him of his reception in London, Trott was bitterly disappointed, 'I have not forgotten,' wrote Visser't Hooft later, 'that summer night in my garden in Geneva when I was trying to find words to encourage Adam who was near despair.'[86] It was from this moment that Trott began seriously to doubt the capacity of the English to seek an equitable settlement to the war, even though in his heart he continued to hope against hope that they would send some positive signal to the German opposition. Moltke, on the other hand, was more sanguine and even less prepared to see the British in a bad light than Trott. When he met the latter on 27 June he declared the results of the mission so far to be 'not so bad'.[87] Moltke himself had a better press all round in England where he was almost as well known as Trott, but in the end he got no better results from his attempts to interest the Allies than Trott.

It was possibly on a visit to Switzerland in 1942 that Trott had a meeting with the Chinese revolutionary Lin-Tsiu-Sen in Berne. The Chinaman recalled in an interview with Hsi-Huey Liang, 'I told him the German opposition was much too passive. Revolutionaries must keep

---

* Goebbels wrote in his diary on 30 March 1945, 'Vansittart has roundly declared that as regards war criminals it is now only a question of the place of the gallows and the length of the rope. This crazy lunatic is always allowed to shoot his mouth off in England without any sign of any reasonable man calling him to order.'

[the] initiative and strike at the enemy, even when it means self-sacrifice. If you can't kill Hitler, then kill Göring. If you can't kill Göring, kill Ribbentrop. If you can't kill Ribbentrop, kill any general in the street. But Trott said, "Germans don't kill their leaders." '88

Trott was in Switzerland three times that year, making his last visit in October and November. The illegal nature of his work meant that he put himself in constant danger; as he told his wife when the latter expressed concern for his safety, 'Yes, it is certainly true, with every trip I place my head in the noose.'89

On his return from Switzerland in July, Trott threw himself into the Kreisau group with more enthusiasm than he had shown in the past. Up till then, Moltke had doubted his ability to take the full package offered by the group. Even after July, Trott kept one foot free for manoeuvring in other Resistance groups which maintained a more positive attitude to the basic need to remove the man and the regime as quickly as possible. The Kreisauers continued to build up their plans for a non-Nazi Germany which would come to the fore after Hitler's defeat. Of the Jesuit Kreisauers Trott maintained a warm relationship with Father Rösch, seeking him out in Munich, and Frau von Trott recalls a visit of Father Delp to their flat in Dahlem. According to Dr Lorenzen, it became clear at Delp's trial that their discussions hinged on the need to formulate a German response to the Atlantic Charter.

At the end of the month Herman Maass gave a long (and very dull) discourse on the subject of trade union organization which gives something of the tenor of Kreisau meetings (in Berlin) at the time. Apart from one or two enthusiastic or polite people, Moltke tells us,

the rest of us slept through long stretches of the lecture, Peter [Yorck] and I shamelessly while Friedrich [Mierendorff]'s cigar kept dropping out of his mouth, at which he woke up, looked at me, smiled, put it back in his mouth and went to sleep again. But these ninety minutes made us realize that there was a man talking who really had something to say about the position of the workers. And the ninety minutes included high-points where we all listened with fascination, while several pearls were concealed among the banalities.90

Through Trott, the former Socialist student leader Curt Bley had found a niche in the IA.91 In August 1942, however, an incident occurred which rocked Berlin and disturbed opponents of the regime, as the Gestapo swooped down on a large number of highly placed civil servants. These men and women formed part of the so-called 'Rote Kapelle' – or 'red orchestra' as it was dubbed by Admiral Canaris – whose organization the Abwehr was responsible for uncovering. The group was Communist in direction, betraying secrets directly to the Russians, although many of its members were 'fellow travellers' who looked upon the Soviet Union as a salvation from Hitler, without setting much store by ideological issues. The leader was Harro Schulze-Boysen,* a well-connected official in the Air Ministry whose wife, Libertas Haas-Heye, was descended from the aristocratic Eulenburgs.

By 1942, there were 100 or so transmitters betraying secrets to the Russians. In August the Gestapo were able to put their hands on forty-six members of the group, all of whom were later hanged or guillotined at Plötzensee Prison in Berlin. Bley had substantial contacts with Socialists and sympathetic industrialists like Dr Walther Bayer.[92] He might easily have incriminated men like Leuschner or Hermann Kaiser, the trade union leader, or Otto John, with whom he had been linked through Trott. Both Bley and Trott were questioned by the Gestapo about their connections with one of the group, Ernst Harnack. Bley sagely volunteered for the Wehrmacht to get himself out of the way of further embarrassing questions. Trott tried, unsuccessfully, to get him into the Indian Legion.

From 18–28 September 1942,[93] Trott made his first visit to Sweden. Moltke was to visit the capital, Stockholm, the following month. Even more than Switzerland Sweden was becoming the most important centre of negotiations between the two sides, not just for the Resistance organizations but later for Ribbentrop's men and the SS. As the Gestapo interrogators noted after the failure of the July plot in 1944, 'Despite the Abwehr's links with Switzerland and Spain the interrogation of Dr Strünck once again takes us back to Sweden. Sweden was the principal focus for information gathering and transmission in all the efforts of the plotters' clique, not only in dealings with the West but also, perhaps, with the East . . .'[94] The purpose of Trott's journey was once again to enter into a dialogue with the British and to open up a channel for transmitting information to the Allies on the state of readiness of the German Resistance, while emphasizing the danger of 'European Bolshevization' through Russian victory.[95]

Trott made his intentions clear in a letter to Harry Johansson at Sigtuna, written on 26 September. 'I feel that you have fully understood that we do *not* intend to plead for support or even

---

* *After the war some of Schulze-Boysen's poems were found in the wreckage of the Gestapo headarters in Prinz Albrechtstrasse. Particularly touching are the last lines of 'Rechenschaft' or 'Reckoning': Die letzten Argumente/Sind Strang und Fallbeil nicht./Und uns're heut'gen Richter/Sind nicht das Weltgericht. (Neither noose nor guillotine is the ultimate argument, and those who judge us today do not deliver the verdict of history. Rudolf Pechel, Deutscher Widerstand, Zurich 1947.) I have slightly corrected the verse quoted in Pechel according to the manuscript displayed at the Gedenkstätte Deutscher Widerstand, the permanent exhibition of the German Resistance in the Stauffenbergstrasse (former Bendlerstrasse) in Berlin. The rooms are those in which the* dénouement *of the conspiracy took place and which miraculously escaped the Allied bombing.*

encouragement from friends – the other side – but that we wish to repose our faith in the necessity of some movement springing from like-thinking minds in the world of Christian Europe to make salvation possible.' Trott's constant harping on Bolshevism as a means to win round the Western Allies was unwise; even if it had some effect on rabid anti-Communists like Allen Dulles it was not the policy to cut any ice with the British. They were still in the honeymoon period of their relationship with their new ally and were to remain committed until Yalta finally began to open their eyes. As Peter Hoffmann has written,

It is fair to ask if the many misunderstandings Trott encountered were not at least partly caused by his tendency to reason and argue on very varied levels. It was certainly pointless to deal with Britain on any level other than that of practical politics; and the suggestion of a possible Bolshevization of Germany from within, or of a solidarity movement for the salvation of Europe, were obviously not on this level. Had Trott forgotten that Britain wanted no part in the Holy Alliance of 1815, and that the danger of the Bolshevization of Germany in 1919, when this was a much more unknown and horrifying quantity, had caused Britain to do her utmost to modify the Treaty of Versailles in order to make it more acceptable to the German people? At this point Britain was inevitably more anxious to keep the anti-Nazi coalition going and to win the war. The Bolshevization of Germany would depend on the will of the occupation powers much more than on the wishes of the German people, and Trott's suggestions looked suspiciously like an attempt to split the coalition. Moreover, a certain amount of contradiction in Trott's statements could not be overlooked, and it was not at all clear whether Trott was speaking for a group able or willing to overthrow Hitler, or for a group that expressedly did not wish to do so.[96]

At the IA, Trott was having increasing difficulty with his boss in the shape of SS Major General Stahlecker who had brought a chill air to the otherwise friendly offices, with his 'high boots, swinging a whip, a German shepherd at his side'.[97] Trott put his foot down when the SS officer tried to use his bully-boy tactics on him, removing his coat, crossing his arms and putting his feet up on the desk until Stahlecker adopted a more reasonable attitude.[98] Stahlecker was a sinister character, who had operated one of the most bloody Einsatzgruppen in the East and had been responsible for the deaths of tens of thousands of Jews and others. He was finally killed when his jeep was blown up by a mine in 1942 in the course of a partisan ambush in Estonia.

With Keppler, Trott's relations remained civil. Clarita von Trott recalls Keppler's coming to dinner once and the enormous efforts her husband made to put him at ease, going so far as to lay his hands on a portrait of the Führer and hang it on the wall of the dining room before their guest's arrival.* To Furtwängler, Trott summed Keppler up as a

---

* Trott's former Nibelungenbund friend Otto-Hans Winterer was once asked by a high-ranking Nazi why there was no portrait of Hitler in his Luftwaffe quarters. Winterer quickly replied that there was no need because 'he carried the portrait of the Führer in his heart'. (Otto John)[100]

man having the 'cunning of a peasant crossed with a eudaemonistic belief in the Führer'.[99] Trott was wont to stress the human side of the veteran Nazi and his devotion to his old mother. As Clarita von Trott points out, his desire to see a positive side to people like Keppler was connected to their ultimate usefulness to the cause of the German Resistance.

Through his propaganda work and the attempts to counter Allied attacks on Germany in neutral countries, Trott came into contact with Professor Gerhard Ritter. He may have met Ritter as early as April 1939 when he and Geoffrey Wilson paid a visit to Freiburg University where Ritter taught history. In the autumn of 1942, Dietrich Bonhoeffer had been to Freiburg where he had found a Resistance cell in operation. As a result of Bonhoeffer's visit contacts were cemented with Goerdeler and others in Berlin. After 20 July 1944 the Freiburg group was rounded up and would no doubt have been executed in due course had the Russians not taken Berlin in April 1945.

Trott was anxious to counter the Allied notion of German militarism and asked Ritter if he could not refute their arguments by making a convincing study of the whole question. To this end he made available to Ritter the facilities of the IA as well as Allied propaganda of all sorts. Later, through Trott, Ritter successfully applied for permission to visit Turkey in order to lecture on the subject of militarism and Germany. The Allies continued to misrepresent German history and showed every sign of believing their own propaganda. To this day it seems extraordinary that so much of Allied propaganda was directed against the 'Prussians' and 'militarism' as if these were the central tenets of National Socialism. Even German *emigrés* happy to be in England reacted impatiently to this uncomprehending approach to German history. Trott's friend Gerhard Leibholz, who had married Sabine Bonhoeffer and was living in Oxford, wrote on 15 July 1942:

> Concerning the thesis that there is a necessity to crush 'Prussianism', the following facts should be of interest. The leading National Socialists and ideologues are not Prussians (Hitler, Hess, Darré, the Baltic author Rosenberg, the Frenchman Gobineau, the Englishman Chamberlain). The National Socialist movement originated in Austria and South Germany and absolutely not in Prussia. What's more, the Confessing Church derives its strongest support from the old Prussian provinces. Finally, the most Prussian social elements were those which approved of the bond between throne and altar. Only those who would not see this bond as a representation of Christian life, would contend that the strength which is even today present within the armed forces is in many ways based on close contacts with the Catholic and Confessing Churches and maintains its opposition to the regime.[101]

238

If the German opposition had failed to grasp the attitude of the Western Allies in the course of 1942, 'unconditional surrender' and the accords of the Casablanca Conference between the British and the Americans should have spelled it out to them: there were to be no negotiations and no early end to the war. Germany was to be crushed, ostensibly in order to prevent any repetitions of the 'stab-in-the-back' lie which circulated in Germany after the First World War. The idea was Roosevelt's, specifically made to appeal to Churchill with its reminder of the American Civil War. Originally this Draconian formula was intended only to include Germany and Japan, but Eden stamped his foot in London, and the effect was felt in Italy too. Eden was particularly anti-Italian after what he considered to be a humiliation he had received on a visit to that country. The disastrous consequences of that decision and the 'Morgenthau Plan' are plain from the pages of Goebbels, who capitalized on the Allied stance to strengthen the resolve of German morale.

Marion, Countess Dönhoff remembers the effect that the Allied announcement had on the German opposition.

I was with Peter Yorck in Berlin in January 1943, the day on which the Allies announced unconditional surrender as the condition for the capitulation. When we heard this news on the radio we said with one breath: 'Now it's all up with us.' For unconditional surrender meant that Nazis and anti-Nazis would combine to do their utmost to prevent just this. For the opposition the great difficulty had been the right timing. As long as Hitler was victorious on all battlefields, any attempt to eliminate him would have created a new stab-in-the-back legend. One had, therefore, to wait until the tide turned. But no one could risk waiting until the Allies had no more interest in negotiations with the Resistance because they were anyway within a short distance of victory. This was why it was important to make a distinction between Nazis and Germans.[102]

Nor was it long before Hitler's luck came to an end and the war began to turn in favour of the Allies. In February Field Marshall Paulus surrendered what was left of his army at Stalingrad. He had already lost a quarter of a million men. Ordered by Hitler not to retreat, he chose to hoist the white flag. Of the 90,000 men who went into captivity with him, only around 5,000 made it back to Germany after the war. Since November 1942, the British had been mopping up the remnants of Field Marshal Rommel's Afrika Korps after the decisive Battle of El Alamein the month before. Following Stalingrad, the West developed a new attitude to the Russian Alliance and a respect for all things Russian which made any German attempt at a separate peace with one or other of the Allies unlikely to succeed.

Trott was as aware as anyone that the decision of Casablanca effectively removed any surviving distinction between good and bad Germans, although, as Margret Boveri pointed out, 'he never stopped hoping emotionally that he might be wrong about that'.[103] On the other hand there was one positive side to Stalingrad; dead wood was cut away from the military commands making way for younger men who had learned something from the Nazis, not least in terms of organization; 1943 marked a new phase for the German Resistance *not* because defeat brought the military over to the opposition – although there was without doubt an element of that – but because the opponents were now in the position to take over important posts from those discredited by the defeat. One of these was Claus Stauffenberg, who had been severely wounded in North Africa, losing an eye, one hand and most of the fingers of the remaining one. It was after 1943, too that positive-thinking Socialists decided to co-operate with the forward-thinking elements of the Resistance; 'Count Stauffenberg and the Socialist Julius Leber were entirely agreed that they were not going to stage a "revolution of the senile".[104]

In this unpropitious atmosphere of Allied triumph, yet two weeks before Casablanca was announced, Trott paid another visit to Geneva. Visser't Hooft had written to Allen Dulles to make the position clear and asking him if he was prepared to talk if the opposition succeeded in bringing off the *coup*. If not anti-Western feeling would prevail. When he met Visser't Hooft, Trott was in a mood of deepest melancholy and pessimism. Disappointment had a way of affecting his way of thinking, the Dutchman noted, lending a strong emotional element to his analysis. 'It no longer makes any sense to continue the conversations with the Western powers,' he told him.[105] He disliked the haughty attitude taken by Anglo-American propaganda towards the German opposition which refused to recognize that the Germans, like the French and the Dutch, were living in an occupied country. Despite the enormous risks they were taking all they received were 'pharisaic attitudes'. Trott told Visser't Hooft that many Germans were turning towards the East. The Dutchman transmitted the essentials of this conversation with Trott to Allen Dulles, the OSS resident in Switzerland. He did not know that Trott possessed another means of communicating with the American – through the Swiss-German Gero von Schultze-Gaevernitz.

Dulles was well aware of Trott and his mission, 'For reasons of security I never met him personally. He made only two trips to Switzerland in the latter years of the war, and had to be extremely cautious. But on both occasions I was able to get a statement of his views.'[106] Trott was also in the habit, Dulles informs us, of bringing a message for 'some Allied representative'.[107] Dulles, for his part, was quite sympathetic to Trott and the German Resisters in general as he was aware of the menace of Communism. Trott's talk of a new Eastern drift, however, alarmed him, especially when it had been blown out of all proportions by the right-wing Gisevius, the Abwehr's permanent representative in Switzerland. The latter wrote in his early study of the German Resistance:

> As early as January 1943, Trott zu Solz, when visiting Geneva, had made a statement to the effect that this social-revolutionary turn towards the East on the part of the opposition had already been completed [*sic*]. His remarks were intended for the ears of the British. For my part, I always feared that such commentary would simply intensify the determination of the Allies to let this German crater burn itself out thoroughly.[108]

Gisevius had allied himself too closely with the Goerdeler group. Writing with hindsight he was exceptionally hard on the left-wing conspirators who came to the fore in 1943 and eventually took over the machinery of the Resistance.

In the message he transmitted to Dulles, Trott dwelt on the old theme of the possible fraternization between the Germans and the Russians. Trott compared their situations: both had broken with bourgeois systems of government, both had suffered deeply, both desired a radical solution. Trott also contended (a slightly less credible argument) that 'both are in the process of returning to the spiritual (but not the ecclesiastical) traditions of Christianity'.[109] Trott foresaw a revolutionary situation developing on both sides.

> Fraternization between Germans and imported foreign workers is also an important element. Hitler has been forced to play up to the labouring classes and has given them an increasingly strong position; the bourgeoisie and intellectuals and generals are of less and less importance. Hitler will fall and the brotherhood of the oppressed is the basis on which a completely new Europe will be built.[110]

Trott asked Dulles whether it was not the moment to make a separate peace in the West. As Dulles told Gisevius, this was plainly unrealistic. Dulles' negative response came two weeks before the announcement at Casablanca. To all such moves on the part of the Germans, Roosevelt sought advice from Bowra's friend Felix Frankfurter, with the result that he cast aside the memoranda of Trott and Moltke with a contemptuous reference to 'these East 'German Junkers'.[111]

Trott's representations in Geneva came within the framework of an upsurge in Resistance activity abroad, particularly on the part of the Abwehr. This culminated in the summer of 1943 with the dramatic meeting of the three secret-service chiefs – Menzies, Donovan and Canaris.[112] Through Moltke Trott's group would have been well aware of the developments of negotiations which took place chiefly through the Abwehr under Leverkühn in Istanbul. In January 1943, Leverkühn had arranged a meeting between Canaris and George Earle, the OSS representative in Istanbul,

> to seek out an accommodation between Hitler's German opponents and the Western Allies . . . its purpose being to shorten the war and concentrate all available forces on the threat from Russia. He argued that the only terrible alternative was the unconditional surrender formula, which would enable Hitler to call forth the most fanatical war effort in German history and prolong the conflict for an indefinite period.[113]

In June, Canaris sent Moltke to Istanbul to propose that an officer of the German General Staff be sent to England to negotiate. The meeting between the chiefs of intelligence later that year was one of the oddest occurrences in recent history. 'It must have been a remarkable occasion,' writes Heinz Höhne, 'this clandestine encounter between the three men who controlled the most powerful espionage networks in the contemporary world.'[114] Once again, however, Canaris presented the classic *Westlösung* – the 'Western solution' – that Hitler should be killed or handed over to the Allies, while the Germans would make peace in the West but continue the fight in the East. Allied fears of one another, especially the terror that either side might desert to leave the others to fight on alone, made them hold on firmly to the formula of unconditional surrender. Roosevelt called Donovan to heel and Menzies for the British 'minimized' the significance of the meeting.[115]

Directly after Trott's return from Geneva a joint meeting was convoked on 8 January 1943, of the younger Resisters and the *Alte Herren*; the meeting took place at Peter Yorck's terraced house in Lichterfelde. The younger group were more united than ever. In November Moltke had found Trott 'stubborn' – presumably in not agreeing with him – but Gerstenmaier had proved a calming influence on Trott and the trio had had a three-hour discussion. 'He is astonishingly intelligent, but immensely tense with it. It is always rather comical,' Moltke wrote to his wife. 'Besides, he has an inferiority complex towards me, which leads to his adopting ever more aggressive attitudes and opinions. That is always very funny . . .'[116] Later that month they presented a united front to Hassell, who was himself growing dissatisfied with 'the group around Weizsäcker'. Hassell had 'a very satisfactory exchange of ideas' with Yorck, Haeften, Schulenburg and Trott.[117]

The January joint meeting was not satisfactory, and served to show just how little the Kreisauers had in common with the old national conservatives around Goerdeler. According to Moltke,

Trott spoke on foreign policy [he wrote to his wife]. Yorck on our idea of the state reform and Moltke on the situation of the Resistance. A really controversial discussion did not come of it, despite the fact that ideas went certainly further than those of 'their excellencies'. Goerdeler addressed us like a candidate for the Chancellorship who was speaking to the representatives of a small party whom he was obliged to win over in order to lead a coalition government.[118]

Gerstenmaier's account gives a better indication of Moltke's role in these abortive discussions:

When we began to outline our economic, social and political ideas, Goerdeler dismissed us with so much pedagogical wisdom and fatherly forbearance that even Fritzi Schulenburg found it unpleasant. Moltke's silence bordered on disdain, a disdain above all directed at Trott and myself, who had taken so much trouble to set up the meeting.

Finally it was all too much for me. I said that the Herr Oberbürgermeister might deign to comprehend that our social and political ideas were not meant to be seen in the light of patriarchal condescension with a view to some future German state. We wanted to create new offices and laws which would serve every German citizen. The first reaction was one of silence, embarrassed silence. I thought now someone else would stand up and speak, but no, Goerdeler spoke again. It was almost half past eleven, which was late in those days when early-warning sirens destroyed our sleep. Goerdeler spoke with self-control and in the end with precision and firmness. To be just he was being accommodating. In the middle of his discourse, Moltke said to himself, half out loud, 'Kerensky.' I am not at all certain whether Goerdeler heard or took in the offending remark. But the other seated members of our circle heard it. When Goerdeler had said his piece, Moltke looked set to return to a deliberately polite tone. This he did, expressing his sorrow that the discussion ought really to have begun, but that it was now already too late. The last question was addressed to Beck. When was the decisive moment to happen? All eyes were fixed on his tranquil, peaceful countenance with its cerebral features. He could give us no answer, he had first to see what could actually be done and how strong the available forces were.

It was a disappointing meeting for both sides. The pea soup which we then consumed in the best manner possible had, in my experience, tasted better. In a somewhat embarrassed way the four of us sat together, detached from the rest; Moltke, Yorck, Trott and myself. The disaster seemed unavoidable.[119]

Whether Goerdeler did receive Moltke's Kerensky dart or not, the latter was pleased with himself for having fired it. 'It quite obviously went home well – and with it the affair ended – dramatically, and, I'm glad to say, not flabbily.'[120]

Unconditional surrender had not been unconditionally accepted in Britain. That great voice in the wilderness, Bishop George Bell of

243

Chichester, was not slow to react. Speaking out against Lord Vansittart in the House of Lords on 11 February, 1943, he said,

> The noble lord has now threatened all Germany with destruction. To do anything of that kind is to hound the bestial Germans to more bestialities and to play the very game that Goebbels wants the Allies to play, by uniting the anti-Nazis and the non-Nazis with the Nazis under the lash of despair. The war has never been popular in Germany. It is hated now.[121]

Bell had taken as his starting point the speech which Stalin had made on 6 November 1942, in which the Russian leader had said, 'It would be ridiculous to identify Hitler's clique with the German people and the German state'. This speech has been echoed by Lord Simon in the House of Lords on 10 March 1943, 'I now say in plain terms, on behalf of His Majesty's Government, that we agree with Premier Stalin, first that the Hitlerite state should be destroyed, and, secondly, that the whole German people is not (as Dr Goebbels has been trying to persuade them) thereby doomed to destruction.[122]

Simon's statement was in response to a motion tabled by Bell asking whether the British shared Stalin's views. Bell thought that the government should, 'declare as plainly that we take a very different view of the other Germans who loathe the Nazi regime and repudiate the lust for world dominion, and that we appeal to them to join us from within Germany in overthrowing Hitler and all his gang'. Bell also pointed out the presence of seven million foreign workers in Germany for whom no one had found a use in fomenting internal discord. Bell finished his speech with a call for sanity in dealing with Germany,

> . . . we should, I believe, declare in unequivocal terms that a Germany that has overthrown Hitler and all he stands for, a Germany which repudiates all desire for military domination and renounces Hitler's crimes and anti-Jewish laws and Hitler's gains, that such a Germany can be saved and will be welcomed to a proper place in the family of nations.*[123]

After Bell's speech, Richard Crossman, then working for the Political Intelligence Department of the Foreign Office, congratulated him, noting that German propaganda had been silent in response.

Given the different stance which Stalin was maintaining towards Germany, a number of Resisters, including Trott, were interested in

---

* *Many believed at the time that Bell's attitude to the government was responsible for his being passed over for the Archbishopric of Canterbury after Temple's death in October 1944. Bell is presumably the model for the bishops in Noël Coward's wartime song, 'Don't Let's Be Beastly to the Germans', which contains the line 'we can send them [i.e. the Germans] out some bishops on a form of lease and lend'.*

seeing whether there was more to offer from Russia now that the West had closed the door. Stalin's attitude was based on his distrust of the Western Allies and his belief that he was, for a large part, fighting the war on his own. German armies were still 1,000 miles into Russian territory and the Russian soldiers and civilians were suffering appalling losses. One of the generals who was most successful in the Russian campaign was Manstein, and the Resisters were keen to bring him in on the plot. They had no success, however, and Trott was able to tell other Göttinger Sachsen of the failure to bring him round at a *Corpsabend* at Easter. Manstein was sacked by Hitler in October for failing to achieve a breakthrough in the Battle of the Kursk Salient.

In March there appears to have been a breakthrough in the Kreisau talks. The agreement was on foreign policy, which was to a large extent accepted as Trott's domain. Trott frequently despaired, causing Moltke to observe, 'Adam, who was excessively confident the last time I saw him, is now excessively worried again. All these changes of mood seem to me so uneconomical, it must take a lot out of one to join in them.'[124] In his very anti-left-wing way, Gisevius gives an idea of the current drift of thought which is not evident from Moltke's letters. In April, Gisevius was 'frankly shocked to find out how radically this diplomat, whose fundamental attitude had been a 'Western' one, had made the choice for the East – or rather had completed psychologically his rejection of the West.'[125]

From 12–14 June 1943, over the Whitsun holiday, Trott attended the third and last meeting at Kreisau proper. Also there were Peter Yorck and his wife Marion, Father Delp, Gerstenmaier, Reichwein, Haubach and Husen. The discussions were governed by Utopian Socialism with various decisions being taken as to the future constitution of Germany. Again the Kreisauers stressed the need to break Germany down into units and to remove the great monolith of Prussia which made up a third of the Reich, with its territories in the east and west. Some strange-sounding ideas were aired, such as the provision of extra votes for every child in the family – to be granted to the father (something which might have encouraged aspiring despots to breed large families!) 'No doubt practice would have looked very different from theory,' says a modern German historian compassionately.[126] Trott once again contributed his wisdom to foreign policy – though he appears also to have worked on plans for an Anglo-Saxon-style university system – and a couple of papers recently brought to light bear his stamp. These are 'Pacification of Europe', which treats the nature of East and West and dwells on East Asian interests, and 'The European Constitutional Problem'.[127]

From 17 June to 3 July 1943, Trott was in Turkey once again. The aim was once again to establish contact with the Allies, but only in Lord Elton's letter to Allen and in his discussions with Snowden (see below, p. 248) is there any indication that talks took place.[128] Later

Moltke, with the support of the Abwehr achieved a little more by talking to the Americans. The background to Trott's trip lies in an otherwise unexplained note in his record of service. On 6 June, Franz von Papen had *requested* Trott's transfer to the German Embassy in Ankara. Papen's application had been turned down by Keppler on the basis that Trott was indispensable in the Indian Department; however, he had allowed Trott permission to visit Papen in the Turkish capital. Trott, Wolfram Eberhard reported, had had discussions with Papen on the German opposition and had let slip the name of Weizsäcker. Weizsäcker and Papen were fellow-Swabians, and retained the closeness of purpose associated with people from that part of Germany. It is not known what sort of success Trott had with Papen, but it is clear the Ambassador did not leak the story of their discussions back to Berlin. According to Trott's widow, Trott wanted to speak to Papen about Nikolaus von Halem, hoping that the ambassador would use his influence on Hitler in order to obtain the businessman's release. Trott had probably promised his brother Werner that he would speak to Papen about Halem.

Trott's former Chinese teacher, Eberhard, had been living in Turkey ever since he had left Trott in China. He found his old friend 'very harassed and tense; he seemed to know what fate had in store for him'. A letter to his wife Clarita shows Trott in a reflective mood:

> How often it has troubled me that you have not been with me to share in this return to Asia. From the moment I recognized the mosques on the moonlit Bosphorus, when I saw again the people, pictures and landscapes, experienced the noises and smells, I knew once more how much my life in China had fulfilled and transformed me.[129]

On his arrival at the station in Istanbul on 17 June Trott was met by Erich Vermehren, then a junior member of Paul Leverkühn's Abwehr team in Turkey. During the course of his stay Trott had at least one meeting with his former Berlin pupil-master, possibly he wished to talk to him about the chance of interceding with the Americans in Istanbul. Another possibility was that Trott had excused his journey by telling the Berlin authorities that he needed to get in touch with the ex-Grand Mufti of Jerusalem, Muhammed el-Huseini, in whom not only the Abwehr, but also the Indian Department of the AA had an interest.

Vermehren was the son of a Lübeck lawyer who was an old friend and colleague of Leverkühn's. Vermehren *père* succeeded in convincing Leverkühn that he could use the help of a legal junior in a complicated case involving the ownership of a fleet of Danube river barges. Leverkühn managed to have Vermehren transferred to Istanbul by coopting him into the Abwehr with the rank of corporal.

Trott knew young Vermehren well. He had met him in 1937 when Vermehren had been shortlisted for a Rhodes scholarship. When he was awarded the scholarship the following year, Trott advised him to opt for his own college, Balliol. As Vermehren had already been noted for his negative attitude to National Socialism the Nazi authorities impounded his passport, deeming the holder to be 'unfit to represent the youth of the Third Reich at Oxford'. In 1941 he married Elizabeth, Countess Plettenberg, a relative not only of the anti-Nazi Bishop of Munster, Count Galen but also of former Chancellor von Papen, the Ambassador to Turkey. She was a devout Catholic several years her husband's senior. At the time of the marriage he converted to Catholicism. The Vermehrens' strong moral revulsion to Nazism was later to have controversial results in the twilight months of the Nazi regime.[130]

On his return to Berlin, Trott continued to pursue a busy round of meetings in which he seems to have been second only to Helmuth Moltke in unflagging energy. On 17 July he was with Hassell, Langbehn and Popitz. The old theme was aired of which of the generals might be relied on to bring off the *Putsch*. During the course of the meeting, it became 'evident that at least one of the generals now appears to think it urgent to avoid complete descent into the abyss. This man, Stülpnagel,* had sent Grumme to Popitz because he didn't altogether trust Goerdeler's efforts.'[131] On 19 July he was with Moltke, and Peter and Marion Yorck for a meeting which seems to have gone off without a qualm for once. With Hassell and Popitz, on 4 August, Trott once again tried to build a bridge between the two generations of the opposition. Hassell, however, was put off by the mention of the word 'Socialism', which the ex-ambassador called 'another cuckoo's egg that Nazism laid in the German nest'.[132]

In early August Trott travelled to Brussels to see Falkenhausen. In all probability Trott was sent to get the general's assurance that he would act in the event of the plot being brought off in Berlin. Whether the general agreed or not, Moltke considered the trip an 'astonishing success'.[133] Falkenhausen played host to a large number of opponents of the regime who came to stay with him at his residence at Seneffe. Hassell, Jessen and Popitz were the emissaries from the older men, while Trott and Moltke came from Kreisau to discuss their plans. On his last visit, in the summer of 1943, Moltke told Falkenhausen that he thought 'the German people must touch the bottom of the abyss before they will be able to pick themselves up again'.[134]

That same month, as part of his work for Bose, Trott met an old friend in a prisoner-of-war camp in Berlin. This was R.W. Snowden,

---

* *Karl Heinrich von Stülpnagel (1886–1944), Military Governor of France from February 1942. Stülpnagel had made no secret of his antipathy towards the Nazi leaders. On 20 July 1944 he put through the Walküre orders, imprisoning the SS and the Gestapo. Ordered to face the court in Germany he tried to commit suicide but succeeded only in blinding himself. He was hanged in August.*

who had been up at Magdelen College from 1929–32. Writing after his release in 1945, Snowden told Allen at Rhodes House that 'I was fortunate to catch sight of him and have a longish conversation'. Trott told Snowden that he had just returned from Ankara, 'where he had seen a number of his old English friends . . . He [Trott] was wearing the *Parteiabzeichen* and expressed approval of the Führer.' Allen sent the letter to Lindsay at Balliol. Lindsay replied, 'At the time that Snowden met him, though he may have expressed approval for the Führer, he was already conspiring against Hitler, because the message to me about it came earlier in that year' (*sic* – Lindsay presumably means the year before).[135]

Despite the adulation of the Allied Leaders of Britain and the United States, Stalin was not as keen on the idea of a *guerre à l'outrance* as they were. In the spring and summer of 1943 he put himself in readiness to negotiate with the Germans. Trott and his friends doubtless picked up the story in the corridors of the Wilhelmstrasse. Even if peace could not be organized to Stalin's satisfaction, the effect in the Western Allied camps would be enough to speed up invasion plans for France.

> If the peace probes were to have success, then Stalin could still conclude the war which was so damaging to Russia before she was completely exhausted and confronted by an America hardly affected by the war. Further, remembering the German-Soviet understanding from 1939–41, Stalin seemed to be hoping to gain more easily from Hitler than from the Allies the territories which for a long time had been the envisaged aims of Russian policy . . .[136]

A negotiated peace with Russia was the dream also of Ribbentrop (Hitler's 'second Bismarck'), who saw the conclusion of the accord with Molotov in 1939 as his finest hour. But when Ribbentrop broached the subject at the end of 1941, Hitler hear nothing of it. When the new initiative came from Russia in 1943, Hitler once again spurned it, although the terms would have repeated the ultra-generous concessions of the Brest-Litovsk Treaty of 1917. 'Both von Ribbentrop and Goebbels had to hold back.'[137]

With rumours like these floating in the air, it was only natural for the Resistance to keep an open mind about the possibility of receiving help from Russia, although, as the Gestapo reports show, very few of the group, apart from Reichwein, ever seriously entertained the idea of any good coming out of it. With Trott's conception of Germany as a halfway-house between the West and the East, it was natural that he should want good relations with both sides, but he was by preference a Westerner, by virtue of his background and education. When the subject of Russia was raised, Trott would refer the interlocutor to his strange brother Werner, the former Communist of the family.

Gerhard Ritter, who knew Trott, vehemently rejects Gisevius' view that he had gone over to the 'Eastern solution'. Trott had, at the end of 1943, moved closer to Julius Leber, 'an old Socialist bitterly hostile to Communism'. Leber was later to have equal confidence in Stauffenberg, thereby forming with the Socialists, Leuschner and Mierendorff, a separate group of Resisters untainted by the national conservatism of the *Alte Herren*, yet vowed to action in a way that the Kreisau circle was not.

> Trott had offered himself as a transmitter of their views to Washington and London; that is, made it possible for the Socialists to pursue a political action of their own, apart from Beck and Goerdeler. Such action, however, was not directed towards stealing a march on the middle-class groups, but to ensure the participation of the Socialists in the future government to which they were entitled. Trott did not say that the opposition would file into the Russian stream. If, in this sense, he played East against West, it was not because of a preference for the East but a tactical manoeuvre whose usefulness and even necessity Hassell himself recognized.[138]

From 27 October to 3 November 1943, Trott was in Stockholm. On 30 October he had a long talk with the editor of the *Svenska Dagbladet*, Ivar Andersson, who made a note of the conversation in his diary. Trott told Andersson some of the things he had communicated to Dulles, but in Stockholm he was more clearly acting in Western interests. The present agitation against the United Kingdom in Germany, he told him, could be easily redirected, there was a strong drift towards Communism, especially in Saxony. He had high hopes, however, for 'Christian Socialism' in a future German administration. At present there were two courses of action. One was Moltke's policy of wait and see. The other was to 'effect a change'; here Trott's friends in the army came in. He also mentioned the police. (Helldorf, the police commander of Berlin, and Trott were now known to one another through Missie Vassiltchikov and Gottfried von Bismarck.)[139] 'Even within the SS there are groups which are not loyal to the regime.' Trott wanted the Western Allies to advise him what to do next.[140]

Andersson told Trott that a change in the regime would make the Allies more inclined to make peace. Trott replied that the Resistance 'would need help more or less immediately after [the *coup*] in order to stave off civil war'. Trott wanted to know what the chances were of this succeeding. Andersson was sceptical, he did not see an attack in the west as likely. Then, replied Trott, the Moltke solution would have to remain; otherwise, 'Russia will win the game.' Andersson wanted to know whether Trott thought a new German victory in Russia would restore confidence in the regime.

I think that public opinion in Germany is such that nothing can save the prestige of the regime. It is now sustained exclusively by terror. The actions of the police and of the Gestapo have become considerably tougher during the last few months. Herr Himmler and Herr Hitler are in the same boat. I do not believe the rumour that Herr Himmler is planning to depose Herr Hitler and seize power himself *Neither do I believe in the possibility of a separate peace with Russia, and do not agree with those who think that M. Stalin would give us peace on easier terms than the western powers* [author's italics].[141]

The fruit of this talk with Andersson was a meeting with the Swedish Foreign Minister, Mr Günther. Günther formed a 'very favourable impression of him' and gave Trott 'a very favourable piece of information'. Before he left Stockholm, Trott visited his acquaintance Inga Kempe. She was the sister-in-law of Heinz von Bodelschwingh with whom Trott had been at Munich University. Mrs Kempe had no idea as to why Trott was in Sweden and inadvertently mentioned some friends at the British legation. 'Suddenly Adam asked me if I could help him to get in touch with somebody there.' Finally Mrs Kempe was able to arrange a meeting with two political intelligence officers, the art historian Roger Hinks and James Knapp-Fisher, who in peacetime worked for the publishers Sidgwick and Jackson.[142]

Hinks had to get permission to meet a German and this he obtained from the minister, Mallet, or from the head of the 'press department', Peter Tennant. 'I met one of the most charming, honest and decent men I have ever had the pleasure of meeting,' Hinks later wrote to Christopher Sykes. Hinks invited Trott back to the flat he shared with Knapp-Fisher. As chance would have it, Harold Nicolson had arrived unexpectedly in Stockholm. Trott knew Nicolson, and was obliged to hide in a doorway until he left. Then he and Hinks spoke together till 4 a.m. during which time Trott revealed the details of Walküre. In exchange he wanted a modification of unconditional surrender and some end to the indiscriminate bombing of civilian targets in Germany once the *coup* had taken place. Trott was not deeply impressed with the two British agents, and suspected the clumsy arrangements for the meeting would lead to its being relayed to the SD (the SS security service). As Mrs Kempe put it, 'None of them was capable enough to manage a thing of the first importance it turned out to be.'[143] The American minister, Johnson, was told of the meeting and details were sent to Washington.

The Walküre orders were the elaborate plans for a *coup d'état*, worked out through the length and breadth of the German Resistance, which aimed at replacing Hitler and his men with a civilian government pledged to ending the war. The orders were long in the making, as complicated directions had to be drawn up which would be heeded by every separate German command structure. Essentially the Home Army – in which General Olbricht was the second-in-command – would issue Walküre, stating that Hitler had been killed as a result of a power struggle within the SS and the Party. To avoid civil war, the army command had instructions to imprison the local SS and the higher Party Officers. In the meantime, the military under General Beck and Witzleben would appoint a civil government and dispatch emissaries to negotiate terms with the allies.

In London, Mallet reported what Trott had said about the Communists and the bombing, noting his remark that the Russian defeats were 'easier to bear than the indiscriminate murder from air raids from the West'. The stress was again on whether the West could guarantee winning the peace as well as the war. The memo did not climb very high in the Foreign Office hierarchy this time. Geoffrey Harrison minuted, 'This sounds like our old friend von Trott. Note the skill with which he propagates the Communist bogey and generally mixes up fact and propaganda.'[144]

On his return to Berlin, Trott ran into Peter Kleist, one of Ribbentrop's collaborators in the AA. In an astonishing conversation they exchanged views on their separate dealings in Stockholm.

> The few men with whom I discussed my experiences after I returned to Germany urged me to go on with what I was doing. Herr von Trott of the Foreign Office, whom I had already met in Stockholm, told me he had had a wide variety of talks with a number of Swedes and German emigrants. A whole host of well-meant but absurd suggestions had been made to him, but nobody had shown him a way over to the other side into the enemy camp, 'so we must follow up every opportunity that presents itself no matter how doubtful it may seem.'[145]

Although Ribbentrop's emissary says that he was working in a private capacity at the time, he calmly exchanges experiences of undercover work with the representatives of the Resistance. It becomes even more sinister when one learns that Kleist had (a presumably honorary) rank of Obersturmbannführer (lieutenant colonel) in the SS. Kleist is confused about dates, and one is tempted to believe that he made it up, especially as what he says about Trott relates to the Eastern solution, that is, negotiations with Russia which were so dear to his master. Perhaps Trott was aware of Ribbentrop's démarche, and felt safe admitting that he too had sought contacts with the Russians. Kleist's goal was to have a meeting with Madame Kollontay, the Soviet Ambassador to Sweden, through his contact in Sweden, Edgar Klauss. Later, with the support of Leber and Stauffenberg, Trott too was to come close to arranging a meeting with Madame Kollontay, but at the last moment thought it too risky.*

---

* As Kleist put it, the 'idea of getting in touch with Madame Kollontay was not unattractive. She was the daughter of an aide-de-camp to the Czar and had gone to the barricades in the Soviet Revolution in 1917 as the wife of a Communist sailor_ she wrote books about free love and was one of Lenin's closest collaborators.' (Kleist, A European Tragedy, Isle of Man 1945.)

In November 1943, Trott's 'Observations on the Peace Programme of the American Churches' were presented at the Ecumenical Council in Geneva. Trott may have deposited the paper in Geneva when he had last been there in September. On the other hand, Schönfeld may have taken the paper in to the meeting. Schönfeld told Clarita von Trott after the war that it was her husband's work.[146] The main points were these: that internal German federal organs would be based on the rule of law not force; that a measure of cultural autonomy and equality would be ensured for all peoples and racial groups; that the inadequacy of the nation state as the ultimate international authority was recognized; that there was a need to limit national sovereignty without which there was no solution to the problems of Central and Eastern Europe. The memorandum stated, 'Without some restriction of national sovereignty, moreover, effective limitation of armaments and prevention of recurrent misuse of armed force are not possible.'[147]

The memorandum is sceptical on the subject of instant disarmament as a punishment for aggressor states viewing it as bound to create second-class nations. 'International co-operation, burdened from the outset with the mistrust of entire peoples, cannot be lasting.' In the long term peace cannot solely be maintained by the use of an international police force or the reduction of arms. The world must instead enjoy, 'continuous practical and constructive cooperation between nations'.[148]

Trott had yet more discussions in Switzerland in December, this time meeting Robert Elliot of the Student Christian Movement. Again a report was filed at the Foreign Office, stating that after the *coup* a provisional government would return all German-occupied territory in the East and end the persecution of the Jews. The withdrawal did not, however, mention the Sudetenland or the Corridor; once again Trott had said that the Versailles frontiers must not be reimposed. In the Foreign Office it was minuted that Halder was a member of Trott's group and that Halder and Weizsäcker's proposals coincided with Hitler's and Ribbentrop's and therefore 'the open and clandestine trends of peace proposals have temporarily merged'.[149] It was the sort of situation to which amicable conversations between a Kleist and a Trott were bound to lead. Even if the Allies *were* prepared to consider a move for peace it cannot have been at all easy to have known just to whom they were talking. The territorial demands, after all, were so often the same.*

---

* *To a very great degree the identity of demands was due to the Generals involved in the plot who did not believe that the German people would 'buy' loss of territory.*

Missie Vassiltchikov recorded in her diary on 23 November 1943: 'Last night the greater part of central Berlin was destroyed.'[150] Studnitz, the press attaché, adopted the sort of detached attitude to the destruction which enabled the Berliners to endure their blitz much as the cockneys of London had shrugged off their own (except that the cockneys had not received quite the same treatment as the Berliners). Writing on 30 November, Studnitz noted, 'The British press has been exultant. Air Marshal Harris has stated that 12,000 tons of bombs have already been dropped on Berlin; he says, a total of 60,000 tons will be required. So I suppose we have another 48,000 tons coming to us!'[151]

Ursula von Kardorff went out into the Kurfürstendamm on 24 November, after another night of terrible bombing. Fashionable Berlin had been wiped out with the rest:

> The Gedächtniskirche was like a blazing torch, and for the first time in history it looked almost romantic. The whole square seemed to be in flames. The Romantisches Café, which lost its soul long ago when the Nazis robbed it of its old bohemian atmosphere, was also on fire. The zoo was badly hit too. Many of the animals were killed and others escaped. It is odd to feel that a tiger might bob up at any moment.[152]

One did apparently. 'An escaped tiger made its way into the ruins of the Café Josty, gobbled up a piece of *Bienenstich* pastry it found there – and promptly died. Some wag, who drew uncomplimentary conclusions regarding the quality of Josty's cake-making, was sued for libel by the *conditerei*'s owner.[153]

The bombing had destroyed the offices of the Informationsabteilung. Missie Vassiltchikov wandered over on the same day as the bombing of the zoo.

> The ex-Polish Consulate on the corner, where Tatiana, Luisa Welcek and I had all worked together for a long time, was burning brightly, but the embassy building next door seemed undamaged. I took a flying leap past the former and dived into the latter's entrance, where a sorry little bunch of people had collected. Seated on the stairs were Adam Trott and Leiphold, both with sooty faces. They had been there all night as the raid had caught them still at work. As nothing seemed to be happening we agreed to meet there again the following morning at eleven.[154]

Allied raids on Berlin destroyed approximately nineteen buildings out of twenty, transforming the centre into a vast desert. After the raids of November 1943 parts of the ministries were transferred to other locations in the Reich, Missie and her department going to Krummhübel in the Sudeten Mountains.[155] One house which was destroyed was the Derflingerstrasse, home of Helmuth Moltke who was thereafter obliged to reside with Peter Yorck and Eugen Gerstenmaier in Lichterfelde. Two weeks before, Trott had contacted

Moltke from Sweden. Moltke noted at the time that the activities of Leber, whom he distrusted, 'were getting out of hand'.[156] Goerdeler too, seemed optimistic as a result of Swedish reports (when was he not?). To Hassell, whom he had met at the station, he 'maintained that Churchill had made an authentic statement . . . to the effect that he could make no binding arrangements before the government was overthrown in Germany. But if the revolt should succeed and should prove itself possessed of sufficient authority, he believed that a practicable way would be found.'[157] Goerdeler had presumably had this news from his friends the Swedish banker brothers Wallenberg.

Moltke was increasingly critical of Leber, which must have led to conflicts with Trott. To his wife Trott had said on one of her visits to Berlin from Imshausen, 'Such a pity I can't let you meet "den Leber". He is away at the present.'[158]* In the months leading up to 20 July, their close working relationship was only matched by that sustained by Trott and Stauffenberg, of whom Moltke also disapproved – presumably because both the Socialist and the general staff officer put the emphasis on the physical elimination of the man rather than on endless plans for the future of a non-Nazi Germany.

Moltke's attitude towards Leber underwent a change at the end of the year, after Carlo Mierendorff was tragically killed during an Allied air-raid on Leipzig. On 2 January 1944, Moltke wrote to his wife, 'Adam came to Peter [Yorck] at 12 and Julius [Leber] joined us and we have talked to now – 6.30. He is a convincingly good man who, now that Carlo has gone, at any rate keeps a firm grip on the purely practical and attaches a good deal less importance to things of the mind than I do.'[159] On 9 January 1944, Moltke had still not fully come round to Leber.

> At 10 I cycled to Julius and stayed with him till 1. It was useful and on the whole a satisfying morning. But I must make a fresh effort to get this man to think as we do. He is a far coarser man than Carlo and much less congenial to me. So the balance that we need for stability won't come automatically. But all the same I am very hopeful.[160]

The Kreisauers were shifting their support to an entirely new body of men to lead a new government, with Leuschner at the head and Leber as Minister of the Interior. The inactivity of the older men had driven Trott and his friends to despair. Personal relations with Hassell remained good, as he was one of the more positive elements among the *Alte Herren*. Goerdeler thought it wrong to kill Hitler but Hassell

---

* *When possible women and children had been evacuated from Berlin. Clarita's visits were made difficult by the distance from Imshausen to the capital, and by the birth and feeding of their two daughters.*

was of the other opinion.[161] On 27 December, Hassell noted a conversation with Trott just before Christmas when the latter had filled him in on some of the more recent developments abroad,

I spoke with Trott, shortly before my departure from Berlin [in the same way as with Schwerin]. He judges the situation much as I do. On his official trips he has the opportunity, as have few others, to look at things from the outside, and even to make contact with Englishmen. His English acquaintances were greatly concerned about Russia and deeply interested in developments here. They were, however, suspicious lest a change should turn out to be only a cloak, hiding a continuation of militaristic Nazi methods under another label.[162]

In the meantime, 1943 had seen a growing weakening of the ranks of the Resistance through the arrest of its members. In April 1943, Hans von Dohnanyi, Dietrich Bonhoeffer and Josef 'Ochsensepp' Müller were arrested and General Oster suspended from duty, moving to retirement in Leipzig. The pretext involved illegal currency deals but the SD were on to the existence of a plot against Hitler and suspected that it was to be found in Abwehr. In September that year, the Bielenbergs' Dahlem neighbour, Carl Langbehn, was taken into custody. Trott had enjoyed long talks with Langbehn, who had previously run rings round the SS by dint of his personal relationship with Himmler. Himmler and Langbehn had daughters the same age and the two men had met after a children's party. The Reichsführer SS had asked the lawyer if he would consent to do the conveyancing on a house for him. In return Langbehn was issued with a paper informing all concerned that he was acting on the authority of Himmler and this he used to have people released from concentration camps.*

Through his contacts with the SS, Carl Langbehn discovered that there was a cell of opposition – chiefly of Communists – at the very centre of Himmler's 'new German élite'. He told Hassell that 'two souls dwelled in each breast [of the SS] in strange combination; one a barbaric Party soul, the other a misunderstood, aristocratic soul.'

Langbehn thought that it might be possible to use Himmler against Hitler by convincing him that the war was lost and that he should do his best to make peace. To this end both he and ex-minister Popitz had interviews with him. Himmler was tempted but clearly not enough. In

---

* Later Langbehn paid dearly for making a fool of the SS. Peter Bielenberg remembers waiting to be interrogated by the SS torturer Leo Lange when Langbehn was brought out from the room. He was wrapped in a blanket. He had been so badly beaten he was virtually unrecognizable. (Conversation with Christabel Bielenberg, April 1988.)

In Ravensbrück a similar treatment awaited Popitz. Lagi Ballestrem remembered hearing Lange's arrival in his cell which was under hers. Lange would announce, 'Well minister, you old pig,' before subjecting Popitz to appalling brutalities. (Countess Ballestrem in We Survived, Boehm 1966.)

September the German security services cracked an Allied coded transmission from Switzerland which showed that Langbehn had been having talks with the enemy. Himmler had Langbehn arrested and put into 'protective custody'. According to Schellenberg, Langbehn's trips to Switzerland had taken place with the blessing of the SS, but presumably news had got out to the Party organization and Himmler had to do something to save his own neck. Hassell noted,

> The case of Langbehn is particularly disastrous to our plans for bringing about a change in Germany. Langbehn who still enjoys the hospitality of his 'friend' Himmler [in a concentration camp] is being severely questioned, especially as to why he brought Popitz to Himmler. An attempt is thus being made to establish some connection between what they had thought they had learned about Langbehn's business in Switzerland and the Popitz-Himmler talk. They are trying to interpret this talk as if Popitz and Langbehn had been attempting to entice Himmler to follow this line. This is why questions are continually being asked about men who might be [at the] back of Popitz, especially generals. This is a bad situation, first of all for Langbehn, because Himmler, for his own protection, won't let him out as long as the Party suspects him. It will also be bad for Popitz, who may yet be cross-examined, and finally for everybody who is working on the scheme.[163]

The next wave of arrests came with the exposing of the Solf Circle through the infiltration of the group by the Gestapo V-Mann, Dr Reckzeh of the Charité Hospital. Reckzeh had wormed his way into the trust of an anti-Nazi headmistress called Elizabeth von Thadden, and had got her to agree to his meeting people in opposition circles. Fraulein von Thadden took Reckzeh to the house of Frau Hannah Solf, the widow of the last Imperial German Foreign Minister, in Berlin-Zehlendorf. Reckzeh passed for a Swiss and had a letter from ex-Chancellor Wirth. Reckzeh's operator, SS-Stürmbannführer Kriminalrat Leo Lange (the chief torturer of those involved in the July Plot) had conceived a plan whereby he would lure Wirth into Germany.

The Solf Circle was a group composed mostly of former diplomats who had left the Auswärtige Amt at the accession of Hitler. Over tea with Ambassador Solf's widow, they gave vent to their hatred for the present regime, but hatched no constructive plans. Frau Solf's daughter Lagi had married the industrialist Herbert Ballestrem. Lagi Ballestrem wrote after the war that her mother's house was

> a sort of political oasis where our friends and other like-minded people could speak freely, vent their disgust and despair, receive information and take counsel. We listened eagerly to foreign radio stations; foreign diplomats visited us and we made them realize that the reports they heard about concentration camps were not mere horror stories, as the Nazis would have it, but a small portion of the bitter truth.

Lange intended to get letters from the Solf Circle which Wirth would assume made it safe for him to cross the border. Wirth had asked Reckzeh to negotiate with General Halder on his behalf, to find out how much he was prepared to work once more with the opposition. Halder saw the Gestapo agent and fell into the trap ensuring his arrest after the July Plot by telling Reckzeh that he would be obviously 'at their disposal when the time came to save Germany from chaos . . .' and he could 'transmit that to Dr Wirth'.[164]

After Reckzeh's visit to the tea-party at the Solfs', Lange decided to have the telephones of all those present tapped. This required the consent of Göring's Research Office in the Air Ministry. Reckzeh's behaviour in Switzerland among the German *emigré* community was beginning to arouse the suspicion of the Swiss police, and the Gestapo began to fear that he would be arrested. They decided therefore to move in on the Solf Circle. Before this could take place, however, a member of Göring's staff, an ex-naval officer called Plass, informed his old comrade in arms, Canaris. Canaris told a subordinate, Gehre, who told Moltke. Moltke then called Otto Kiep to warn him. Presumably nobody had informed Moltke that the telephones were being tapped, and he thereby incriminated himself.

The whole group, including Moltke, was arrested on 19 January 1944. The women taken were Fraulein von Thadden, Frau Solf and Frau Solf's daughter, Countess Ballestrem; the men were Hilger van Scherpenberg (Schacht's son-in-law), Councillor Künzer of the Foreign Office, Otto Kiep and Trott's old friend Albrecht von Bernstorff. Had Reckzeh been able to get further in his work the arrests would have been more comprehensive; even Trott had the Solf telephone number in his address book and it was clear that he was aware of the existence of this circle. Fraulein von Thadden and Moltke's friend Kiep were beheaded. After July the others, apart from Frau Solf and her daughter, were to suffer similar treatment.* Frau Solf escaped as a result, it is said, of Japanese intervention (her husband had been well-respected ambassador to Japan). Moltke's arrest had the greatest effect of all when it came to the Kreisauers, he was the element to which everything cohered, maintaining the basically pacifist organization strictly by his own standards. After his arrest, the Resistance went over to the attack.

---

* Elizabeth Wiskemann, who had last seen Bernstorff in 1943, learned of her old friend's execution after the war. '. . . I met someone who was transferred from one prison to another in the same police van with him in the middle of April 1945; he was then gaily planning which bottles in his cellar he would drink to the destruction of Hitler!' (The Europe I Saw, London 1968)

257

12
1944

In the autumn of 1943, the German Resistance movement underwent a change of direction. The German defeat at Stalingrad had led to a redistribution of commands within the army. Before the end of the year a radically different cadre was in control. Many of these were National Socialists, but by no means all. Some like Count Stauffenberg had scaled the ladder to a Berlin posting, which had always been vital to the Resisters' plans. The inactivity of Beck and Goerdeler was gradually discrediting them among the younger, more radical opponents to the regime. In the fifth year of the war they were no closer to bringing off the *coup*. Goerdeler himself had moral scruples about assassination.

Another factor in the realignment of the Resistance was the incarceration of Helmuth Moltke. Moltke had injected his stupendous dynamism into the movement, but while he was at large his own, pacifistic, ideology had held sway. After January 1944, many of his closest collaborators, even to some degree Peter Yorck,[1] began to demand the more radical approach, which involved killing Hitler. The most important factor of all, however, was the new impetus generated by Julius Leber and Claus Stauffenberg.

Although Trott had been close to Leber since 1940, their collaboration took on a new meaning after the summer of 1943. Trott once again broadened his position, multi-faceted as it already was, within the opposition. Leber had kept his distance from Kreisau, having a distrust for their 'planning euphoria'[2] and learning of their deliberations second-hand from former Socialist deputy friends like Carlo Mierendorff or Wilhelm Leuschner.[3] Leber wanted action and saw in Trott one who could get something done through his contacts in neutral countries. From the summer of 1943, Trott never travelled without talking his trip over with Leber first.[4]

Trott had always made his strongest ties with women. It was the war to a great degree which made him conscious of the benefits of male society. In Claus Stauffenberg, many people have seen the close friend till then absent from Trott's life, 'the human fulfilment of his existence' as Werner Trott put it.[5] To Missie Vassiltchikov Trott confessed that Stauffenberg had been his 'closest friend'. Until the aftermath of 20 July she had never heard Trott even mention his name.

After 20 July it was Kaltenbrunner's men in the SD who were most interested in finding out how much Trott and Staufffenberg had worked together in those last months. They came to the conclusion that the two had been introduced by Stauffenberg's brother Berthold in 1938 or 1939. Berthold had worked before the war at the Kaiser-Wilhelm Institute for International Law in Berlin. Trott had used the Institute as a base in the winter of 1936–7 and once again after his return from the Far East, when he had given talks on international law and Asia. There is no reason to distrust the Gestapo's report; it probably came directly from Berthold Stauffenberg's interrogation.

Trott's friendship with Stauffenberg dated from the soldier's posting to Berlin in the late summer of 1943. Gerstenmaier recalled seeing Stauffenberg at a Kreisau meeting in August of that year, prior to his posting to the Home Army. He almost certainly owed his introduction to the group to his brother Berthold or to Peter Yorck. In the spring of 1943, witnesses remembered Stauffenberg visiting Trott at the Auswärtige Amt and the two greeting one another like old friends. A further link came from Stauffenberg's adjutant, Werner Haeften, the brother of Hans-Bernd. Trott none the less shrouded the friendship in mystery, and his widow does not recall ever hearing Stauffenberg's name spoken in her presence.

Moltke had met Stauffenberg through Peter Yorck. Yorck was, through this mother, a cousin of Stauffenberg's, both of them were descended from the great General Gneisenau, one of the heroes of the German War of Liberation. Moltke was worried about the effect of Stauffenberg and Trott working together and had told Trott, 'I won't let you meet Stauffenberg'[6]. Moltke failed to effect the ban, and it was Trott, according to Otto John, who brought Stauffenberg and Leber together and cemented the union which created the new, revolutionary *élan* of the Resistance at the end of 1943.

Stauffenberg was born two years earlier than Trott. He was the third son of an old, noble Catholic family from Bamberg.[7] Despite a similar academic ability to his elder brothers, Alexander and Berthold, Stauffenberg early on resolved to make his career in the army. When he was a young subaltern, he and his brothers formed part of the circle of the elderly, charismatic poet Stefan George. George's poetry, calling for a national revival as it did, might well have been construed as something which much in common with the National Socialist movement, but George himself took a dim view of the Nazi revolution, fleeing to Switzerland at their accession and dying there a few months later. Like his brothers, Stauffenberg retained his fondness for George's poetry until his death and was able to cite large tracts by heart.*

---

* *Poetry was a considerable passion of the Stauffenberg brothers; on Claus Stauffenberg's last night on earth, he sat up with his brother Berthold in order to*

259

As a brilliant young cavalry officer Stauffenberg went on to study at the Military Academy in Berlin, which allowed him to enter the General Staff, the intellectual elite of the German army. Like others of his background, he was not overly sanguine about the Weimar Republic, and was of the right politically. After the war, many people came forward to say that he was in sympathy with the Nazis; most of these stories have since been proved to be scurrilous. The government which assumed control in January 1933 *was* a National Socialist/Conservative coalition, and it was possible to be a conservative without being a Nazi.

It has also to be stressed that the expansion of the armed forces which resulted from Hitler's tearing up of the Versailles Treaty provided the sort of career opportunities which had been lacking for upper-class men under the Weimar Republic, and most of them could be expected to appreciate what rearmament and conscription meant to them personally. Still, at the time of Munich, Stauffenberg was genuinely shocked to realize that the Führer was hell-bent on war, commenting 'Der Narr macht Krieg' (the fool is leading us to war). He was not involved in the 'Generals' Plot' of that year and when the war started he saw action as a staff officer in the victorious campaigns which marked the early years of the war. After serving in Russia, he was transferred to North Africa. It was there that he was severely wounded and flown back to Germany to recover.

Given the extent of Stauffenberg's injuries and his undisputed talent as a staff officer, moves were made to have him attached to Army Headquarters at the Bendlerstrasse in Berlin. His uncle, Baron Üxküll, had already informed Stauffenberg of the plot against Hitler which focused on the Smolensk HQ of the Army Group Centre and the figure of Major General Tresckow. In all probability he had spoken of the conspiracy to Tresckow and his officers during the time he was serving in Russia. One of the plotters who saw Stauffenberg's potential within the military conspiracy was General Olbricht the Deputy Commander of the Home Army. In October Stauffenberg became Chief of Staff to Olbricht, and finally, in June 1944, Chief of Staff to General Fromm, the Commander-in-Chief of the Home Army. It was in that latter position that he aimed to put into practice the lines from his favourite Stefan George poem, 'The Antichrist': 'When once this race has cleansed itself of shame/and flung from its neck the tyrant's chains . . .'[8]

Once he was installed in Berlin in October 1943 there was little question that from the military point of view it was Stauffenberg who was the man to bring off the *coup*. Leber suddenly changed his course:

review the latest verses sent to them by their brother Alexander. (See Christian Müller, 'July 19th 1944', in July 20 1944, Germans Against Hitler, An Anthology, ed. Hans Adolf Jacobsen, Bonn 1969.)

'The turning point for closer co-operation was brought about by his meeting with Stauffenberg. Between the two personalities instantly sprang up an intimate human rapport.' Between the two of them stood Trott and Fritzi Schulenburg, the latter having known Stauffenberg since 1927, when both men were at the School of War in Potsdam.[9] The four of them were to form a new nucleus in the conspiracy against Hitler.

Ursula von Kardorff, an old friend of Werner Haeften ('a kind of Siegfried with a sense of humour') was introduced to her friend's commanding officer on 14 February 1944:

> He is an unusually attractive man, tall with thick dark hair and a black patch over one eye which detracts in no way from his good looks. He is very masculine, but with a touch of South German polish, a mixture which one does not often find in Prussia. He has lost an arm [sic] and three fingers from his remaining hand. I sat next to him and had to cut up his meat for him. We talked about Jean Paul, whom he advised me to read, and about music. Before he was wounded he apparently played the 'cello very well.
>
> As we were strolling through the park [at Neuhardenberg, the Hardenberg seat], Fritzi [Schulenburg] said to me, 'Stauffenberg is the best horse we have in the stable.'[10]

Soldiers were also fascinated by this charismatic officer. Lieutenant Urban Thiersch, whom Staffenberg recruited into the conspiracy, had this to say:

> I was fascinated by his appearance: the fine proportions between his powerful head and body; he was wearing riding breeches with a red stripe and a lightweight white tunic. His complexion was fresh and healthy, his sound eyes flashed unimpaired, as if kindled by some fire within, and independent, it seemed, of whatever cheerful or serious emotions his face registered. The other half of his face, with the black patch covering the eye, appeared less active, yet it had peculiar power because of the bold features, the shape of the head and the imprint of his experience. And looking at him from that angle only this part of the face gave Stauffenberg something remote, something monumental.
>
> The telephone conversation completed, he turned to me again: 'Let's get straight to the point,' he said. 'I am committing high treason with every means at my command.'[11]

The imprisonment of Helmuth Moltke completely altered the nature of the Kreisau group. From the beginning of February, the elements who remained in touch with the conspiracy were brought together by Trott, meeting either in his house in Dahlem or in the Foreign Office itself, as often as not in the outer office of State Secretary Keppler who was absent for large parts of the time at the court of the Führer in Rastenberg.[12] The irony of using Keppler's office for illegal meetings was not lost on Trott; as Furtwängler recorded,

The preparations for the July Plot were discussed in Keppler's offices in the Wilhemstrasse. Colonel Stauffenberg, Counsellor von Hentig, Legationsrat Melchers – the whole underground group of the Foreign Office and gentlemen from the Wehrmacht were received there. When I commented on how grotesque it was that we were carrying on these treasonable conversations next door to the chair of the friend and most faithful follower of the Führer, he [Trott] said 'You nest best in the pocket of a scarecrow,' and laughed.[13]

Without Moltke, Trott succeeded in realigning the Kreisau group behind Stauffenberg and Leber. Moltke was not so badly treated for the time being. There was no particular evidence against him until the July Plot gave the pretext for a massive purge of all opposing elements in Germany. He was in custody at Ravensbrück concentration camp where Freya Moltke and other relations and friends came to see him. One day they permitted him to walk with his wife as far as the local inn. He was allowed his books and even Hansard! Moltke's guards took him to his meetings in a car with a tea-pot so they could make tea. Freya commented, 'Really these are quite nice people!' 'Except that they tear off fingernails,' was Moltke's more far-sighted reply. For the time being the Field Marshal's great nephew had been granted special treatment which prevented his SS guards from torturing him. Count Gottfried Bismarck, who was arrested after 20 July, provided another instance of the Gestapo holding back in the cases of famous names. Bismarck was acquitted, one of the few to get away scot free. As Studnitz commented at the time, 'At least we are spared the spectacle of the Third Reich executing the grandson of the Iron Chancellor.'[14]

Trott had spent the New Year at one of Peter Yorck's estates at Kauern, shooting. Normally he would have rejoiced at the opportunity to get out into the woods but this time he seems to have returned to Berlin with flu and a bad back. His infirmity did not prevent him from entertaining, now that he had his Emma, his housekeeper. Emma's appearance in the Trott family can truly be said to have been a small factor in the transformation of the Resistance movement, as from the time of her engagement Trott was able to entertain his fellow conspirators to meals – meals apparently cooked with consummate skill.*

The changes wrought by Emma are clear from Trott's letters to his wife. On 5 January he gave a dinner for Peter and Marion Yorck, Eugen Gerstenmaier and Hans Haeften. After the meal Hans Haeften resumed a letter he had begun before dinner to his wife Barbara, 'I've

---

* '... The meals were nicely done though very frugal. One was content with very little those days. Werth's ... Indian money and trunks certainly did not get into our household. I kept nourishing Adam with part of the food tickets I got because I was always busy expecting or feeding a baby.' (Clarita von Trott, notes for the author, 1989.)

just come back from Adam's. It was very nice and the food was great. He's got a new, and very good girl. Marion wants to give me carrots.'[15] On the same day Trott received a final greeting from David Astor, which filtered through from the Red Cross.

On 19 January, *Pravda* published news of German peace negotiations being conducted through the British Embassy in Madrid. Studnitz reveals that the Russian paper had said that Ribbentrop was behind the talks, but in all likelihood this was yet another approach on the part of Otto John. 'London and Washington are making strenuous endeavours to clear themselves of this Russian accusation.' Studnitz tended to the opinion that the Russians have made up the story about Ribbentrop and his secret talks.

> If our own people had any comprehension whatsover of the war of nerves, their logical course would have been to refuse to deny or to confirm the statement. In this way they would perhaps have increased the confusion in the Allied camp and might even have roused suspicions in the minds of the Russian inventors of this newspaper story. It would be hard to imagine a more favourable opportunity of bedevilling relations between England, Russia and America. Instead we have issued an indignant denial![16]

Studnitz' complacency about the non-existence of these talks was not shared by Ulrich von Hassell.

> Indication of the situation is the stink-bomb *Pravda* has thrown at the Anglo-Americans in the form of the news report that Ribbentrop has negotiated with Hoare in Spain. The result in Germany is heightened suspicion on the part of the rulers, who assume that it was not Ribbentrop who was making contact with the Allies, but other groups, Schwerin says that they suspect some younger group in the Foreign Office.[17]

It might well have been a move on the part of the SS. Trott's new chief, Dr Six, was at that very time on a mission to Spain and Portugal. Another possibility was that someone in the British Embassy in Madrid was trying to prevent the Western Allies from being tempted to make a separate peace.

Already, in January 1944, Trott was active as Stauffenberg's foreign-policy adviser. Part of his work was to prepare a memorandum for Stauffenberg's use in weighing up the foreign political options for a non-Nazi Germany. The memorandum was to be entitled '*Deutschland zwischen West und Ost*' (Germany Between East and West). This document was later found by the Gestapo in the house of Count Schwerin Schwanenfeld, and so impressed them that they presented a copy to the Foreign Office. This – like all the others which had been hidden – was lost in the aftermath of the war.[18] Apart from drawing up papers for his guidance and giving him and Leber the gleanings of his foreign travel, Trott carefully sifted through the incoming telegrams at the Foreign Office in order to be abreast of all the developments taking place in the various German embassies abroad. In January 1944, Stauffenberg told John, whose particular role was to contact the Allies on the Iberian Peninsula,

> Let me play the devil's advocate for once ... Trott has told me that he has read a telegram from our embassy in Ankara. It reports on a conversation between an assistant to the Soviet military attaché and a Turkish general. In this conversation the Russian complained that the English and Americans were not going to stage an invasion this year either, and yet again the Russians would have to bear the brunt of the war against Germany.[19]

As Stauffenberg correctly surmised, the Russians were still not averse to German peace feelers.

Despite an illness which wracked him all through January, Trott was out and about. On 15 January he lunched at the Gersdorff's villa, one of the few buildings left standing on the edge of the Tiergarten, where Freiherr Heinz von Gersdorff and his wife Maria operated something of a Resistance salon up until 20 July 1944. The next day was a Sunday. Trott worked on the question of the future of Poland for his paper and read Bruce Lockhart's memoirs. In the evening Paul Metternich, Peter Bielenberg and Missie Vassiltchikov turned up at the house. 'As it was already six by the time I got there, we combined tea with cocktails and then soup.' Missie was moving to Krummhübel with her department. Trott telephoned Count von der Schulenburg,[20] the former Ambassador to Moscow who had engineered the Molotov-Ribbentrop Pact, in order to find her decent accommodation. Schulenburg, a cousin of Fritz-Dietlof, was on the fringes of the conspiracy. He was believed to be a suitable emissary to the Russians when the time came to sue for peace.

Trott continued to entertain friends and conspirators in his Dahlem home. On 18 January his cousin Waltraud 'Teddy' von Götz was there with Count Berg, an army officer to whom a large part had been assigned in the Walküre planning, and who was to offer Trott yet another means of escape when the time came. On the 25th it was the turn of Haeften, John, Curt Bley, Eugen Gerstenmaier and Peter Yorck. This was a proper discussion on the theme of the use which could be made of the *Gastarbeiter*[21] (the foreign workers who had been drafted into Germany to work and whose numbers had risen to over twelve million). The verdict of the group was that they could be made to revolt. Certainly it was true that there were periodic outbursts of violence among the foreigners, often directed at their German overseers. This was especially true among the more politically organized Poles and Ukranians.*

---

* *Many of the French were to play a part in saving Germans from the arbitrary violence of the Russians in 1945, when the latter swarmed over Eastern Germany.*

By 29 January Trott was so ill that he was unable to put on his own socks, but in his letter laughs it off with 'enough of Lazarus'.[22] On the 31 January there were further heavy raids on the city. His health was still dicey and Emma was complaining that the doctor was not doing enough to cure him. Haeften had been bombed out of his newly repaired house in the latest Allied raid and there was some question of his coming to live with Trott. In the end Haeften thought that this would represent too much of an inconvenience and decided to go elsewhere. In the same letter Trott alludes to the fact that things had begun to move again. He had to make another trip to Geneva.

Veiled references to the work with Stauffenberg are present in the letters to Clarita of 31 January and 23 February. Stauffenberg's determination to act was causing the whole movement to accelerate. There is some evidence that they had been together at the end of February when Trott had written to Clarita that he was 'working hard and hoping for results'. A relapse into illness at the beginning of March postponed a trip to Switzerland for which he had been working for some time. It was not till the middle of March that he found himself well enough to travel, and then it was not Switzerland, but Sweden which called.

Trott must have found it a relief to leave Germany, as he had written to his mother on 10 February, 'Berlin has once again experienced some apocalyptic moments – especially at the end of last month and the beginning of this. The people are astonishingly composed and long suffering, seldom does one hear complaints, which is somehow distressing in itself . . .'[23] On the night of 3 February, the office in the Woyrschstrasse had been bombed out and Trott had telephoned Missie to get her up to Berlin to see to things. When she got to Berlin the next day she found both Trott and Alexander Werth in the office, working. Werth's house had been bombed too. 'He has been billeted with our top boss, Dr Six, and though we all loathe and despise the latter, so long as Alex has a foot in that door he can occasionally use his influence to good purpose. As a result things are not quite as unpleasant as they used to be.'[24]

Werth had made a considerable sacrifice in going to lodge with Six, a former university teacher who had thrown in his lot with the Nazis in a shameless manner. Six was also interested in peace, the sort of peace which was likely to save his skin. Trott and his friends had put pressure on Werth to move into his house for the sake of monitoring his reactions to their activities and finding out just how much he knew about their work, given his own journeys in behalf of Himmler and Schellenberg. Six appears to have respected Trott's intelligence and efficiency which led him to admire him and later to regret that circumstances made it impossible to save him after 20 July. Trott did not like Six; he told Furtwängler one day, 'Franz Josef, I'm having a hard time – the fellow reminds me of a badly shaved police dog.'[25]

Trott's visit to Sweden was prompted by an urgent call from Roger Hinks which was relayed through his Stockholm friend Inga Kempe. Hinks told her that 'Adam was the only person with whom the Allied [*sic*] wanted to deal in a matter of great importance; there would be no use sending someone else'.[26] It took Trott ten days to get permission for the trip which once again put him in the greatest danger. When he arrived there had been a clamp-down on British contacts with the enemy and all those who had applied to speak to Trott were told that their conversations could no longer go ahead. Instead Inga Kempe was instructed to take down Trott's views and to relay them to the British delegation afterwards.

> It became soon evident that behind the urgency of the matter of Adam's coming to Stockholm was the Allied plan to start the heavy bombing of particularly the heavy industries in West Germany. But before they undertook this they wanted to know the strength and power of the German underground and, depending on the answer, how much they could do to help the Allied [*sic*] to a speedy end of the war by their participating from the inside – and [how much] could thus the bombing, in itself undesirable for the Allied side, be avoided.[27]

Trott's conversation with Inga Kempe was forwarded by Mallet to the Foreign Office in London. In it Trott dwells on the effect of the bombing, saying that the daylight bombing was excusable, but the British night raids with the concomitant destruction of German cities 'did the British cause great harm.' The average German was saying, 'the British are as bad as the Nazis; there is as little to be hoped for from the English as from the Russians'* Once again he stressed the need for the Allies to make their war aims crystal clear, repeating them over and over again on the radio so as to clear up any doubts engendered by Goebbels' propaganda. He was himself prepared to name the generals involved *if* he could be given the war aims to transmit to his men. He recognized the need for an occupation of the country, but felt that the complete suppression of the German military tradition would be likely to cause an unhelpful resentment on the part of the people. Trott also told Inga Kempe that the generals had already discussed the idea of letting the Allies through in the West.

Trott's pretext for coming to Stockholm concerned his health – in this case a liver complaint – about which he consulted a Stockholm specialist.[28] He took over Inga Kempe's small flat for an office during that time. On the 14th and the 18th he called on Ivar Andersson again. The editor of the *Svenska Dagbladet* arranged for Trott to have a talk

---

* *When the Russians arrived in Berlin in April 1945, the women joked, 'Better an Ivan on the belly than an Ami on the head' (i.e., it was preferable to be raped by a Russian than killed by an American bomb).*

with Sverker Åström, a former attaché at the Swedish consulate in Moscow. Naturally the talks this time hinged on Russia. After the shoddy treatment he had received from the British, Trott was evidently trying to recoup something from this dangerous Swedish mission. He asked Åström whether the Russians would accept another German regime which had the support of the generals. The Swedish diplomat told Trott that this was in his opinion the case. Andersson concurred, 'I considered myself capable of answering this question in the affirmative', on the basis of information from Mr Assarsson.* Trott asked Andersson whether it was possible to meet Mr Assarsson, but Andersson advised him against it, arranging a meeting with the Foreign Secretary, Günther, instead. He also had an appointment to see the Nobel prize winner Senator Gunnar Myrdal and his wife the next day. (Trott had met Myrdal through the British Council in 1939, possibly in America).

> His main problem was now [noted Anderson] how could he let the English know that the greatest menace thereafter would be the continued aircraft bombing operations against Germany, even after a change in regime? This would mean to the German people that England was not fighting the war against Hitler but against Germany as such, and that the object was to destroy Germany completely.

Trott made it clear that he had the support of Julius Leber, 'one of the foremost Social Democrats and trade union leaders who had now been freed after a long imprisonment in a concentration camp'. Andersson thought on balance that the Anglo-Americans would be kind towards a non-Nazi regime and would discontinue the bombing.[29]

A few days after Trott's departure from Sweden, the American secret service received a report that the Wehrmacht had now established a direct link to the Russians in Stockholm.

That spring and summer, Clarita von Trott was confined to Imshausen with her two young daughters and was unable to join her husband in Berlin. For the sake of camouflaging the more interesting contents of his letters to his wife, Trott had elaborated another of his codes to fox the Gestapo censors. His immediate circle was described as parts of the body: Moltke was the head, Yorck, the shoulder, Haeften, the heart, and Gerstenmaier (one wonders whether this had some more earthy significance?), the belly. Using his code he wrote at the beginning of March to explain the fact that Moltke was still under arrest: 'As far as the head is concerned it is no better; the shoulder is in pain as a result and seems weakened by the experience. That I am

---

* *Per Wilhelm Gustaf Assarsson, from 1940 Ambassador to Moscow.*

perhaps in the grips of this too stems from other more fitting and sensitive reasons.'[30]

Just prior to flying to Sweden, Trott had had talks with Johannes Popitz, the monarchist minister. Popitz' relations with Goerdeler and Beck had collapsed, and his attempts to use Himmler against Hitler had made him something of a pariah in opposition circles. Trott still maintained relations with this highly cultivated and erudite man. On his return Trott told his wife that the trip had been, 'interesting and extremely fertile from an "official" point of view.'[31]

At the beginning of March Trott had a harrassing time as a result of the activities of his young friend Vermehren, which resulted in his being interrogated several times by the Gestapo. In December 1943 Vermehern had been in Berlin on leave from his post in Istanbul and had been to see Trott with a request: he wanted to find a way whereby his wife could join him in Turkey, but knew that this was not permitted under the terms of his Abwehr appointment, Trott discussed the matter with Freiherr Marschall von Bieberstein of the Personnel Department of the Foreign Office, and eventually she was assigned a courier's passport. With one or two technical hiccups, she thus succeeded in joining her husband in Istanbul.

Vermehren had not told Trott the reason why he wanted his wife with him in Turkey: three days after her arrival he contacted Major Nicolas Elliott of the British Secret Service (SIS) and the couple arranged to defect. Elliott got them out through Smyrna, cleverly disguising their flight as a 'Night and Fog' operation. It was not until mid-February that the German authorities became aware of their defection. It was at that point that Trott was questioned by the Gestapo about his involvement with Vermehren. Leverkühn too was roughly handled, and the families of both Vermehren and his wife were thrown into concentration camps until the end of the war.

The defection of the Vermehrens as well as another pair of Abwehr agents stationed in Turkey came at a time when the Abwehr's activities were under suspicion from Hitler and the SD (SS Security Service) of Kaltenbrunner. Ultimately they provided at least one pretext for scrapping the Abwehr and for the absorption of the majority of its functions by the SD. On 3 March, Radio Cairo broadcast a statement purporting to be by Vermehren. Later the Times too published an article on the affair entitled 'A German and his Conscience'. At a time when Trott was heavily involved in negotiations in Sweden and Switzerland, shocks like these must have been hard to bear.[32]

On 26 March, another Allied raid on Berlin claimed the life of his devoted secretary, Hilde Walther, 'a humble and rather unprepossessing creature whom Trott described as "under-privileged" '. None the less he was always very kind to her. After the raid she was trapped with her mother in the cellar of her apartment block, and Trott worked night and day in an attempt to free her. Later he told Furtwängler that it 'froze his soul to think of her dying there in that hole after her awful life'. Her death had a profound effect on him.[33]*

Trott exercised considerable discretion when it came to his meetings with Stauffenberg. After the war Clarita von Trott sifted through her husband's last letters and was able to come up with the occasional oblique reference to Stauffenberg, who, thanks, to Emma, was entertained at their Dahlem home. The first reference to Stauffenberg in this correspondence was to a 'most gifted and competent young officer',[34] for whom Emma was preparing dinner that Easter. In the same letter, Trott refers to the coming 'last test', and to a 'transformation'.[35]

At the end of March, Trott had an argument in his house with the irrepressible Loremarie Schönberg, Missie Vassiltchikov's gossipy friend, who was lusting to play some part in the conspiracy and as a result endangering the whole affair with her reckless behaviour. After the plot had failed she buried part of the unused explosive in the garden of Gottfried Bismarck's Potsdam residence – an act which she carried off with great speed and fortitude. From that moment, she became something of a celebrity in upper-class, anti-Nazi circles. Lalli Horstmann, the half-Jewish wife of the diplomat friend of Harold Nicolson, Freddy Horstmann, remembered seeing her at the wedding of Baron Lotow in January 1945,

One of those present [at the wedding] was an attractive Austrian girl, a Princess S—, who had been a friend of the conspirators, yet was not implicated and after its failure had obtained permission to visit the prisoners. Two of her brothers had disappeared after the capture of Stalingrad. It was persistently rumoured that the Russians had permitted German prisoners to write to their families through Turkey and Switzerland. Hitler had ordered the letters to be held back, for he feared that at this hopeless stage of the war, evidence of Russian kindness towards prisoners would act as an incentive to German soldiers to desert. The girl obtained an appointment with one of the generals [Olbricht], and implored him to have the mail looked through to see if it contained news of her brothers. When the general admitted the existence of the letters and told her they had been destroyed unread, she lost her head and expressed her contempt for his refusal to help in the killing of a leader who had brought nothing but disaster. The general was secretly an active member of the conspiracy, so this violent attack was a shocking blow to him and he could not guess whether the girl were indiscreet or if she were trying to compromise him, to endanger the success of the plot. As soon as she left him he got in touch with the other conspirators and they decided that it was necessary to have her done away with immediately. But luckily, two of those whom the general consulted were acquainted with her and, by vouching for her, succeeded in saving her life.[36]

---

* Trott's acts of selflessness towards humble people were not rare. Furtwängler recalls another occasion when he dropped everything to prevent an old Communist porter from being sacked.

At the end of March, Trott made another trip to Switzerland, staying with Gogo Nostitz in Geneva. Unbeknown to him there had been a faintly positive reaction to his last Swedish journey in the Foreign Office in London. Most of it is fairly begrudging, but on the point of a declaration of peace terms there was a glimmer of enthusiasm among the civil servants. Geoffrey Harrison still believed that Trott was a conscious or unconscious agent of the German secret service. Frank Roberts makes the curious remark that Trott had not 'cut much ice' with the clearly devoted Inga Kempe. Cadogan was the most positive when it came to the declaration, admitting he still 'hankered after it'. The memorandum was finally minuted by Eden with a 'This can certainly be examined afresh.'[37]

In Geneva he contacted Dulles through Gaevernitz. In his communications with Dulles, Trott once again pursued the Communist menace theory, knowing that it would sink in with America's OSS representative in Switzerland. Dulles reported to Donovan,

> The principal motive for their action is the ardent desire to prevent Central Europe from coming ideologically and factually under the control of Russia. They are convinced that in such an event, Christian culture and democracy and all that goes with it would disappear in Europe and that the present dictatorship of the Nazis would be exchanged for a new dictatorship. The group points out most emphatically that the dangers of such developments should by no means be underrated, especially in view of the completely proletarianized millions now populating Central Europe. The group also says that if the surrender is to be negotiated primarily with Moscow, a different set of men, not 'Breakers' [Dulles' name for the German Resistance], would do the negotiating. After the overthrow of the Nazis, the German generals now in command on the Western Front, especially Falkenhausen and Rundstedt, would be prepared to surrender and to facilitate the landing of Allied troops. Likewise arrangements could be made for receiving Allied parachute troops in key points of Germany.[38]

In a long talk with Gaevernitz, Trott outlined the views of himself and Leber as to what appear to be genuine fears of a Communist takeover:

> There exists in Germany a Communist Central Committee which directs and co-ordinates Communist activities in Germany. This committee has contacts with the Free Germany Committee in Moscow* and receives support from the

---

* *The Free Germany Committee was set up in the wake of Stalingrad by Communist exiles, Walter Ulbricht (later the East-German leader) and the poet Erich Weinert. At first only a number of low-ranking officers consented to sit on the committee which drew up plans for a post-war Germany with a strongly pro-Communist bias. After the routing of Army Group Centre in the summer of 1944, the mood changed among the officers and a number of the fifty generals who were captured lent their support, chiefly General Seydlitz.*

Russian government. Its power is greatly enhanced by the presence of millions of Russian prisoners of war and labourers in Germany, many of whom have been secretly organized and have come under the direction of Moscow. Their activities are helped by the shortage of German guards.*

Constructive ideas and plans for the rebuilding of post-war Germany constantly come from Russia. These ideas and plans are disseminated by the Communists among the German masses chiefly by means of well-organized whispering campaigns.

Compared to the above, democratic countries offer nothing concerning the future of Central Europe. Socialist leaders in Germany emphasize the importance of filling this vacuum as quickly as possible if the ever increasing Communist influence is to be counteracted. The drift to the extreme left has assumed stupendous proportions and steadily gains momentum. If it is permitted to continue, German labour leaders fear that in spite of military victory the democracies may lose the peace and the present dictatorship in Central Europe will be exchanged for a new one.

To win the German working classes for a moderate and orderly policy of reconstruction the following suggestions are being advanced by German labour leaders:

1) A series of encouraging statements by the democracies addressed to German labour. These statements should emphasize the participation of Socialist leaders in any future German government and the collaboration of German labour in the rebuilding of Germany will be welcomed.

2) A statement to the effect that German labour will be permitted and encouraged to organize the German labour movement according to its own wishes without interference from capitalist groups of the West with anti-labour tendencies.

3) A fundamental statement on the future of self government in Germany that includes some indication of how much independence the democracies intend to allow to a German administration. It is recommended that a special emphasis be placed on the question of regional and local self government.

4) An announcement to the effect that the democracies do not intend to follow Hitler's methods and create a puppet government in Germany composed of German Quislings to represent Allied interests and to rule over the German people.

5) A message of encouragement from the American government to be passed on confidentially to the Socialist leaders in Germany.

6) Though dropping leaflets over Germany had little effect in the heyday of German victories, the German mentality is now susceptible to leaflet propaganda. To be effective, leaflet raids should be separated from bombing raids (!). Leaflets should be dropped in such large quantities that the Gestapo cannot quickly remove them. Leaflets should be edited in co-operation with the German Resistance movement so that they are in harmony with the steadily changing pyschological trends in Germany.

7) The close contact between the German Communists and Russia should

---

* As the war continued guards used in forced labour and the concentration camps were no longer for the major part German. Russians – often Ukrainians and Russian Balts – were used, as were Hungarians and Romanians. The Romanians had the reputation for being the cruellest.

be balanced by an equally active contact between the German Socialist labour movement and progressive forces in the West. An active exchange of ideas should be inaugurated.

8) The bombings of large populated areas are rapidly completing the proletarianization of Central Europe. Labour leaders therefore suggest the bombings be concentrated as much as possible on military and industrial targets.[39]

Dulles was convinced that the 'breakers' were sincere and transmitted their views (Trott's and Gisevius') to Washington. Clearly Gisevius' proposals had included the names of a number of unlikely generals like the Chief of Staff Zietzler. The British Embassy in Washington reported back to the Foreign Office who counselled the Americans to steer clear of any dealings with the group. In Richard Lamb's sifting through the papers in the Foreign Office he located the memo with the annotations made by the London officials: 'This looks very bogus', 'Very bogus and old friends', 'Uncle Tom Cobbley and all'. Yet the paper contained the names of Goerdeler, Leuschner, Oster and Beck, all of which the Foreign Office had heard before and which they had no reason to doubt were central to the conspiracy.[40] A similar message from Gisevius in May brought a similarly short-sighted lack of reaction.

On 1 April Trott was back in Berlin, giving dinner to Peter Bielenberg, Herbert Blankenhorn and a soldier friend of Heinrich Trott's (who had doubtless arrived on Trott's doorstep, much as soldiers often do, in order to find a bed for the night). Herbert Blankenhorn was a Rhenish Foreign Office official with whom Trott had become particularly close in recent months. At the end of January he had had a long discussion with Missie Vassiltchikov in which he had set out his ideas for German constitutional reform after the collapse. Missie found him, 'extremely quick minded'.[41] After dinner, Trott and Blankenhorn went for a moonlit stroll in the nearby Grunewald; later that night Trott wrote to Clarita that Blankenhorn was 'besides Haeften the most capable and sympathetic of the younger colleagues I have found in the office. Sadly he is permanently in Krummhübel.'[42]*

The next day, seizing the opportunity presented by another moonlit night, Trott had a long walk in the woods with the monarchist Otto John. The conversation developed 'to his [i.e. Trott's] advantage'.[43]

On 14 April Trott was once again in Switzerland, where he saw Elizabeth Wiskemann for the last time, 'He looked a shadow of his

---

* *Like many of the Foreign Office men who were on the fringes of the plot, Blankenhorn was not arrested after 20 July. After the war he had the chance to put his constitutional ideas into practice as one of Chancellor Adenauer's closest advisers.*

former self, grey and haggard. He was obsessed with the effects of the air-raids on Berlin and other German towns, and he brought me photographs of rows of corpses, many those of children. It was a fearful evening, impossible to sleep that night. I had to say, 'Adam, this human misery is horrible, but there is no message I could send that would affect the directives given to the RAF; I have nothing whatever to do with the fighting forces directly or indirectly. If I were to say what I think, that this kind of bombing is bad policy as well as cruel, it would make no difference . . .' He was like a broken man and said he expected to be arrested soon after his return to Germany. The usual exchange followed: – 'Must you go back?' 'Yes, I absolutely must'. After he had left he telephoned me once more . . . I forget what he had to say, but I told him that he had left his gloves behind, a very fine pair. He said, 'Keep them as a gage.' For his safety, he meant – I think I had the sense not to say any more.'[44]

That spring was also the last time that Christabel Bielenberg saw Trott. Arriving unannounced at Trott's flat, she met the redoubtable Emma who told her that Trott had gone for a walk but would be back presently. Left to her own devices she had looked at the music he was playing — the Mozart *Requiem* — and the book he was reading — *The Last Enemy* by Richard Hillary — the work of a Battle of Britain pilot which had impressed Trott by its frankness. Emma came to give them lunch; Trott put his arm round the housekeeper and said, 'Emma is a marvel, I just don't know how she manages to give me such meals. I have a strong suspicion she is clearing the district of dogs. I get meat galore.'

It was an opportunity for Trott to look back on the years since his return from China, the testing years of the war and his part in the Resistance.

I don't regret for a single moment that I came back. This is my home Chris, this is where I have my roots, and I am firmly convinced that any German who wants to help in the reconstruction of a post-war Europe must have experienced – personally, intimately – what has gone on in this country. What made a man a Nazi, what makes men sit tight and do nothing, what it has meant to be in opposition, to oppose, always to oppose. The bust-up hopes, the heroism – and there has been heroism, seemingly useless heroism – and then the shame. There are things which will need all our strength to unravel – to try and make intelligible after this war is over. Those who left Germany, and may come back afterwards, will be uprooted strangers speaking a different language, and whatever advice they may have to offer will hardly lure any old dog out from behind the stove.

I can't believe that they want to create a vacuum here in the centre of Europe – a vacuum fills, and if this bombing goes on, it will fill from the East. Even Stalin realizes that when the Nazis are gone he will have to deal with the German people – even he is making overtures. But the Allies – unconditional surrender, unconditional surrender, like a broken gramophone record. We have to face it, I have to face it, that is the only echo which has come back from across our borders from the West. And yet I know there are people out there who must realize that the Nazis and all they stand for are as much our enemies as theirs.

His mind turned to his secretary and her mother killed under the rubble of the bombing raid: 'We couldn't get near enough for the heat'. Then the conversation went on to deal with the looming Allied invasion of Europe and the imminence of talks in Berlin on the future of Germany.

> But perhaps you won't have to wait that long, Chris, not even for the landing, I mean. I don't think I will be able to go abroad again. The last time I was in Sweden – well, it has become increasingly difficult and dangerous, I guess. I don't know if I have done more to try and persuade outsiders that there is another Germany, but one way or another I feel that chapter is now closed. I wish I could tell you more, but it's no use burdening you – you'll hear soon enough. We've not been idle, in fact the last few weeks, in spite of all, have been positive ones – exciting, in fact. From now on this is a German affair. We must rid ourselves of this regime by ourselves, and believe me if you believe nothing else, it will be done, it will and must be done before the Allies have to do it for us.[45]

The last Swedish trip had been risky, and the Allies were not biting at the bait. The Resisters did not want Allied help in order to overthrow the government, but to win over the confidence of the German people and to give the non-Nazi government a legitimacy once it had come to power through the *coup d'etat.*

Documents are scanty for Trott's movements that spring, although Missie Vassiltchikov saw him on her trips from the Sudeten Mountains, where her office had been transferred. A series of bombing raids in Berlin had eliminated the offices of the Informationsabteilung and their replacements and Trott, Werth and Richter were now holed up in the Karlsbader Hotel. The night before Missie's meeting with him on 2 May, Trott had another *diner à deux* with Stauffenberg in his Dahlem flat. Trott had written to his wife beforehand, 'Emma is busy in the kitchen preparing dinner for myself and a good friend.'[46] Missie saw him the following evening; she was more and more stunned by Trott, and the lofty intellectual plane he inhabited, 'He is a man completely out of the ordinary. All his thoughts and efforts focus on things and values of a higher order, to which neither the mood of this country, nor that of the Allies seems attuned. He belongs to a more civilized world – something, alas, neither side does.'[47]

Two days later Missie found Trott in a pensive mood. On her way to Gottfried Bismarck's house in Potsdam she stopped off to see him in Dahlem and they 'went for a long walk in the Grunewald. It rains in showers but still it is spring and although cold, there are flowers and shrubs in bloom everywhere. Adam told me of his first love and his life in England and China. There is always another angle to him.'[48]

274

On 9 May, the night before her leave ended and she was required to return to Krummhübel, Missie dined with Trott. 'Later, a young friend of his, Werner von Haeften (a brother of the personnel chief, who is on the staff of the Replacement Army here), dropped in and they had a long talk in another room.'[49] Werner Haeften, Stauffenberg's adjutant, was bringing Trott the latest moves in the military conspiracy, direct from his commanding officer. On 25 May, Margret Boveri found him reading Churchill's speech of the day before – 'He had been trying to read between the lines.'[50]

Shortly before Whitsun 1944, he was joined by his friend Albrecht ('Teddy') von Kessel. Kessel was based at the German Embassy in Italy which, since the Italian invasion, was located on Lake Garda. Kessel proposed that the two of them go off for a few days to Venice. It was to be Trott's first and last visit and the last experience of beauty and contentment in his short life.[51]

On the way Trott asked whether it 'was appropriate to push through a solution or whether one should await the military developments of the next few weeks'. He had been frankly discouraged by his latest experiences in Sweden. Kessel, in his turn, told Trott of his decision to retreat into the embassy in the Vatican, adding, 'In Berlin our circle is big enough. . . .'

Kessel and Trott spent four days in Venice. That Trott should have cleared these days with his office, was 'a real stroke of luck'. Despite the absence of bomb damage, the war had taken its toll of the city. All the museums were closed and the churches walled up. None the less, 'in this atmosphere the war was impossible to believe in'. At the sight of Venice, 'Trott's inner resistance quickly melted. Never before had I seen him so relaxed and happy. It had the effect of fulfilling him, so that people in the alleys would stop and stare after him as he went by.'

One day they took a gondola together, Trott stretching out his long form in the boat

> while it slid over the canals like a slender beast of prey, shooting round the corners at the call of the gondolier. In all the fifteen years of our friendship we had never been so close, at my side he recognized the beauty of life and it gave me a childish pleasure that I had myself constructed this city as a gift to him and indeed to all my friends, for whom he was the emissary.

Trott and Kessel returned to Lake Garda and the embassy there and from Garda travelled on to Verona. Once again, perhaps a little inspired by the 'beauty of life' he had witnessed in Venice, Trott thought about going over to the other side. It was only a fleeting thought. Putting his hand over the barrier in Verona Station, he said goodbye to his friend Kessel. 'At least we know that one of us is safe.'[52]

Whit Sunday fell on 28 May and Trott took the opportunity of the holiday to visit his wife and family at Imshausen. It was the last time he saw his home, his mother and his two small daughters. Together with Clarita he walked in the woods that he loved, taking in image upon image to keep with him after his return to Berlin, 'His facial expression lost its disharmony and the beauty of his features was striking.' Clarita thought he looked like a young soldier who would soon be claimed by the war.

On 16 June Trott said an unconscious farewell to Clarita. After returning from Italy Trott and his wife had spent the best part of a week together, beginning with a weekend at Gross Behnitz, the Borsig estate, and followed by a couple of days in Berlin. Trott was to meet a Swiss friend, Philippe Mottu, and his wife in Stuttgart on the 15th.

Mottu had been attached to the Swiss General Staff at the beginning of the war and later to the Foreign Ministry. In 1940 he had met Herbert Blankenhorn in Berne, who told him that Germany would lose the war.[53] Mottu, who was involved with the Oxford Movement of Moral Rearmament, met Trott through Schönfeld and the World Council of Churches in Geneva. In the course of 1942, Trott invited him to come to Berlin for discussions with various Kreisauers. Mottu was particularly impressed by Hans-Bernd von Haeften, who was going through a moral quandary at the time as to whether the taking of Hitler's life could ever be justified.

In 1944, Mottu had received a letter from Frank Buchman, the leader of the Oxford Movement, inviting him to come to the United States. He received permission from the Foreign Minister to go and he was further encouraged by Trott when he visited Switzerland that Easter. The problem was travelling from Switzerland which was wholly cut off from the outside world by the German conquest of Europe. Trott however, promised to find Mottu a way through to Portugal.

At the beginning of June,

by an indirect route, I received instructions to go to Stuttgart to meet von Trott. When we arrived at Stuttgart Airport, on a Swissair plane, von Trott was not at the rendezvous. After a two-hour wait we decided to go into town. Step by step, we were guided by providence to where I found my friend. He had been followed by the Gestapo and had had to take all kinds of precautions. Next day, in the home of a German industrialist who was also part of the Resistance, we had a conference with Adam von Trott, Eugen Gerstenmaier, the industrialist Knoll [of the furniture firm] and others.*

As the *putsch* was about to take place, Trott and his friends had

---

* *The others included Schönfeld, and the son of the Swiss theologian, Brunner.*

drawn up a list of the provisional government to be taken to America by the Mottus and transmitted to Washington. The Trotts came to see them off the following day on their bumpy ride across France to Portugal. The *coup* caught up with the Mottus in Chicago on 20 July. They were astonished to see how little importance was attributed to this move to shorten the war in the American press.

On 6 June the long-promised attack in the West took place in Normandy. The lack of a convincing second front in Europe had been the real bone of contention between the Russians and the Anglo-Americans. From now on, the Resisters could look forward to better relations between the Allies. These lasted until the Allies began to quarrel over the spoils of war after Yalta; by that stage the German Resistance would be dead, and with it virtually everyone who had been involved in it.

The Normandy landings further accelerated moves to rid Germany of Hitler. As Trott had told Christabel Bielenberg, this was to be a German affair – the Germans had to do it themselves. From the headquarters of Army Group Centre, Tresckow summed up the mood in a letter to Goerdeler transmitted through Count Lehndorff, 'The attempt must succeed, *coûte que coûte*. If it fails, we must act in Berlin. It is now no longer a question of practical results, but of showing to the world and to history that the Resistance movement risked the last throw. Nothing else matters now.'[54]

Only a few days later, on 18 June, Trott had discussions with Stauffenberg and Colonel Hansen who had replaced Canaris as head of a much diminished military intelligence.[55] The German secret service had received a cataclysmic shake-up in the previous months, to some extent triggered off by Trott's friend Vermehren. Canaris was sacked in February, with suspicion growing about his contacts with various groups opposed to the regime. After the Vermehren case and a hefty report from Ribbentrop, the Abwehr had been absorbed into the SD, though Hansen had been able to carry on his duties in Military Intelligence. Later on in June all offices were assumed by Kaltenbrunner's men.*

As the Gestapo later reported on that 18 June meeting between Trott, Stauffenberg and Hansen, the Abwehr chief and Trott 'already knew one another from work'.[56] It was Stauffenberg who brought Hansen to Trott's flat, presumably in order to talk over Trott's next Swedish journey. The two visitors had arrived for tea and stayed on for

---

* *When Vermehren got to London, he saw Ivone Kirkpatrick of the Foreign Office, and spoke of the opposition. The report mentioned Trott as the source of his knowledge. The document is vague as to the heads of the military opposition and though it cites Oster, does not appear to be particularly well informed on the Resistance cell of the Abwehr. Vermehren recommended that British Intelligence get in touch with Trott.*

dinner. Trott was well pleased with the conclusions arising out of this meeting. 'It could only have been improved by your being there,' he wrote to his wife in Imshausen. After his guests had left him, 'I walked silently out to our lake under a grey clouded summer night's sky thinking over the discussion and yours and my existence together with grateful hope.'[57]

The morning after this meeting, 19 June, Trott set out on his final visit to Sweden. Before he left he also had a meeting with Leber during which the Social Democrat asked him emphatically not to try to force a split between the Allied camps. The sole chance lay in their attitude after the *Putsch*, when an appeal would be made by a government formed by the Resistance groups under an open truce. There was no alternative, said Leber, to capitulation; it was irresponsible to deliver up the German people to further misery stemming from this mindless war. . . .'[58]

One of the first people Trott went to see after checking in with his faithful Mrs Kempe, was the Socialist exile and future German Chancellor Willy Brandt.[59] Brandt was from Lübeck, where as a young Socialist he had sat at the feet of Leber. In 1933 he had emigrated to Norway where he had taken up Norwegian citizenship and worked as a journalist. When Norway was invaded by the Germans in the spring of 1940, Brandt sought asylum in Sweden. He maintained links with the German Resistance through the Kreisauer, Theodor Stelzer, who was serving as an officer in the army in Norway.

Brandt knew nothing of Trott. As a journalist he worked at home in the Hammerbyhöjden. On the morning of 19 June a Swedish clergyman rang him to ask him if he would agree to meet an acquaintance of his. A little while later the pastor from Sigtuna, almost certainly Johansson, arrived at his door with Trott and then left the two Germans together, 'The tall, bald, self-assured man in his mid thirties stepped forward and said, "I bring greetings from Julius Leber, please trust me." '

They had a short discussion that day, and another a couple of days later. Trott told him something of his background, and of the influence the *Neue Blätter für den Sozialismus* had had on this mercurial man.' Trott filled Brandt in on developments in the Resistance with news of Goerdeler, Moltke and Stauffenberg. Brandt had no idea that the attempt was so imminent. Leber, Trott said, was prepared to participate in a Goerdeler-led government as the minister of the interior, but it was Stauffenberg who rejected the idea of a transitional government, thinking that the progressive regime should be put into office immediately after the *coup*. Trott told him that they had decided to give him the office of state secretary – or under secretary of state in the Auswärtige Amt.

Trott asked Brandt whether he would consent to serve in such a government. 'Another thing he asked me, and that was more difficult to answer, was whether I would be able to help him set up a meeting with Consul [sic] Alexandra Kollontay to establish what the Soviet position would be after the revolt.' Brandt had met the seventy-two-year-old Soviet ambassadress Madame Kollontay once, and thought this was possible, despite her statements to the British press that she would never enter into talks with a German.

The following day, on 22 June, Trott called again on Brandt. He asked the journalist *not* to go ahead with the attempt to arrange the meeting with Madame Kollontay. He had heard from one of his friends in the German Consulate that the 'Soviets in Stockholm were "leaking" and that through this he and his friends might be exposed'. Again there was a friendly talk between the two men, Brandt showed Trott the sketches for a Socialist foreign-policy document he was working on. Trott read them with interest.

Part of Trott's job as assigned to him by Stauffenberg, was to locate some literature produced by the Free Germany Committee in Moscow to see whether it was possible to work with this group in the event of a *coup*.[60] Stauffenberg had expressed considerable reservations, adding that he 'didn't think much of declarations issued from behind barbed wire'.[61] At exactly the same time, Peter Kleist, this time possibly with Hitler's permission, was looking to see if some accommodation could be arrived at with the Russians.[62]

Trott was also seeking guarantees from both sides, in the event of the plot succeeding, that they would deal with the new government and cease the indiscriminate bombing of German cities. It was at precisely this moment on 22 June that Leber and Reichwein finally consented to meet representatives of German Communism in Berlin with disastrous results. The German Communists of the Saefkow-Jacob group had accepted the need for a popular front against fascism. Many of the German Communists in exile in Sweden had not, and Madame Kollontay herself dismissed them as 'old-fashioned Marxist-Leninists' or worse, 'Trotskyists'.

Trott had also sought to get to the Soviet ambassadress through his friend Senator Gunnar Myrdal. It was Myrdal who arranged the meeting which Trott had with John Scott of *Life* magazine, the OSS representative in Stockholm. Scott certainly believed that Trott had seen Madame Kollontay, and it was his version which was accepted by Dulles.[63] Trott's visit was intended to prepare her for an eventual meeting with the former German ambassador to Moscow, Graf von der Schulenburg, accompanied by the ex-military attaché General Köstring. Trott's conversation with the conductor Leo Borchard on 10 July was, however, probably a further indication of the fact that *he had not* made that preliminary contact with the Russian woman, and that someone else would therefore have to go to Stockholm to prepare the ground.

Trott left Sweden on 28 June and as he was present at a meeting at the Austwärtige Amt on the 29th. His movements in Stockholm had been monitored by the SS and Party officer Peter Kleist and his contact man Edgar Klauss. Later they took a similar interest in the meetings arranged by Alexander Werth who had travelled to Stockholm at the beginning of July in the company of Dr Six. Kleist was probably reporting to Walter Schellenberg who was interested in any peace moves which were likely to ensure a better treatment for the SS and Himmler. How much they knew of Trott's contacts cannot be certain, but after 20 July Horst Mahnke, the SS man in the Auswärtige Amt, revealed that Trott's reports on his trips had been read by Dr Six. We do not know what these documents contained. We do know, however, that they were not forwarded to the Party Office and Bormann.

On 21st, Trott met another British secret service man, David MacEwan. Contact again was through Inga Kempe and the interview took place in her flat. MacEwan was a friend of the tennis star Gottfried von Cramm, whom Trott knew too from Berlin social circles. MacEwan, however, was not meeting Trott for the sake of talks on Allied guarantees, but looking for intelligence on the state of German morale. Trott handed the British agent a memorandum, which was the last thing he was looking for. Trott was distinctly reticent about giving him information

> which would . . . be used against the very thing he was working for. The Allies, on their side were not willing to promise anything until they had found out exactly the importance of the Resistance. Who were their leaders, how much of the army could be trusted to revolt and – most important – did the former, or what was left of the former, labour movements participate? [64]

Trott once again despaired of anything coming from the British side. He answered MacEwan that he would say all that he wanted, and would reveal the answers to some of his questions only if he could have some modification of the unconditional surrender stance. He also told Mrs Kempe that he considered the Russians 'doubtful associates for the future'.

The British were still asking themselves whether or not these moves were being made by the German secret service and whether any real German Resistance existed. Harrison noted in a memo of 8 June:

> There are undoubtedly in Germany a considerable number of individuals in all spheres of life who are genuinely anti-Nazi. There is, however, insufficient evidence to justify the assumption that these individuals are linked together in any kind of subversive organization. The balance of evidence suggests, on the contrary, no organized oppositional group exists in Germany. Furthermore even if one or two small groups do exist, it seems clear that, in the absence of widespread popular support, of which there is not the faintest sign, they would be powerless to render us any service at the present stage. The indications are

that these individuals are in fact less concerned with active steps in eliminating the Nazis than in stepping into the Nazis' shoes when the Nazis have been eliminated.[65]

Harrison and the Foreign Office had no wish to believe in large-scale Resistance activity in Germany. The report gives leave for some sort of negotiation being struck up between 'commanders in the field'.

On 26 June Trott had his talk with John Scott, hoping that the Americans would prove more receptive than the British. Scott's report[66] was scrupulously forwarded to the British from Washington. To Scott, Trott told of the existence of a Free German Committee inside Germany which had been landed by parachute by Russian plane. Trott's group had no objection to the idea of talking to this committee as they wished to maintain equal contacts with East and West; however, they had since learned that the Committee had been infiltrated by the Gestapo and had decided to keep clear for the time being.

In the course of the meeting with Scott, Trott expressed disbelief at the idea of continued good relations between the Allied camps after the war. He mentioned the fact that he would have to return to Germany and could not stay on in Sweden because of his wife and children. Morale in Germany was good because the Allies offered the German people no other policy than to go on and fight to the last. With this statement he added that 'unconditional surrender . . . plays perfectly into the hands of Goebbels. The Russians have been cleverer with their Free Germany movement, and this has been a factor in the increase in pro-Russian sentiment in Germany.' Despite Myrdal's assurances as to Trott's anti-Nazi activities since 1939 and his contacts with high-ranking Swedish churchmen, Scott told his consul, Johnson that he thought Trott was 'possibly a Nazi propagandist'.

Distrust, short-sightedness, constant up-hill efforts with incredulous people was taking a further toll on Trott's fragile physique. On one of his last nights in Stockholm, he looked so ill that Inga Kempe told him to go back to his hotel and sleep.

He looked at me and said: 'Why should I need sleep when there is so much to do? – and besides, old people do not need so much sleep.' Whereupon, I logically answered: 'But you are only thirty-five [*sic* – Trott was thirty-five on 9 August]. 'No,' said Adam, 'I am at least sixty and I will never be younger. I think I have done what I am supposed to do in my life, whatever was asked of me to do, and I am ready to die, but still there are a few things to do.' The day before he left, he told me that he had been asked by the British and the Americans not to go back to Germany, because at that moment he could do more good outside his country than inside. Then he shook his head and said: 'Perhaps I could, but that is no more the question for me. I have done what I could for my country, but I also have a duty towards those who are dedicated to the same cause as I,

I must share with them, whatever comes. And – there is Clarita and the children.'
– these were his final words.[67]

On 29 June Trott attended a meeting at the IA in Berlin chaired by Dr Six.[68] Missie Vassiltchikov was there, sitting between Trott and Werth at the table,

Adam kept shoving *streng geheim* [top-secret] papers to me under the table – mostly news items from abroad. We kept up a whispered conversation *à trois* and smoked while the men were shouted at in turns. This morning Six was in a rotten mood and poor Judgie Richter at his right had a hard time calming the troubled waters. In between outbursts, Adam made sarcastic remarks which were swallowed by all present. I like the way he contradicts Six. Later, he folded his arms and went to sleep.[69]*

Over the following few days, Trott made his final journey abroad, this time to German-occupied Holland. There on the pretext of Free Indian business he convened a meeting with Van Royen, a Dutchman called Reinink and Patijn in the office of Herr von Goersche in The Hague. Patijn described Trott as 'impartial and detached'. He told the Dutchmen in detail about the Walküre preparations and the progress of the conspiracy and added that he thought it had a twenty-five-percent chance of success. To their repeated questions as to why Trott was telling them this, he replied, 'that in the event of a favourable outcome of the *coup*, they would be in a position to supply their government (in exile) with information that our group, which would surrender immediately, was an acceptable negotiating partner for the Allies'.[70]

The air raids on Berlin continued to be heavy. At the end of 1944, Lalli Horstmann remembered the last time she had seen Trott and possibly Haeften in the shelter under the Adlon Hotel at the beginning of July.

He had just returned from Switzerland [*sic*] where, with the connivance of his fellow conspirators, he had tried to ascertain what the American and British attitudes would be in the event of the overthrow of National Socialism. But he had found it hopeless because of the rigid formula of unconditional surrender; he had decided that the only course was to negotiate with Russia. His friend, a fair young East Prussian landowner, had contradicted him vehemently: 'No good can come out of an arrangement with the Soviets; it would only bring a

---

* *Of Six: 'Adam Trott hates him with a cold hatred and tells me that however amiable he may try to be, we must never forget what he represents. Six, for his part, seems grudgingly to realize what an extraordinary man Adam is and to be somehow fascinated by him and even to fear him. For Adam is perhaps the only man left in his entourage who is never afraid to speak up. He treats Six with infinite condescension and, curiously, the other takes it.' (Missie Vassiltchikov, Diaries)*

new totalitarian influence', he said. 'Besides it's too late. Peace with Russia was obtainable only before the fall of Stalingrad . . . .'

The dark man changed the subject to discuss Huxley's *Grey Eminence*. Like Huxley, he believed that men must lose themselves so deeply in their convictions as to be willing to die for them. 'We will live to see martyrs in this world again. There will have to be a long line of believers to lead us through the darkness of tyranny to future freedom. There is an important, an essential distinction between martyrs and victims,' he urged. 'The latter are passive, they appeal to pity, must be defended and avenged. The others are fighters; they consciously risk failure and death in their determination to rebel.' Shortly afterwards we heard of their courage under torture and their deaths and we were moved all the more by the memory of the words by which the two men had hinted at their destiny.[71]

On 3 July, Gogo von Nostitz, the German consul in Geneva, arrived in Berlin for a few days.[72] On the same day he dropped in to see Trott who was, as usual, occupying Keppler's room in the Wilhemstrasse. Nostitz reflected on the good use Trott made of having two offices at the same time 'in different buildings and in different parts of the city, giving him the advantage of having a car at his disposal as well as that of being untraceable at any given time' – an enormous plus point when it came to his illegal work. Nostitz thought Keppler 'a queer fish . . . . one of the oldest party members, a personal friend of the Führer's – inasmuch as the latter had personal friends! – and an SS Obergruppenführer [general]. In his private life he was unpretentious, doctrinaire, a fantasist and an indescribable scatterbrain without the slightest mind for political reality, and withall a limitless credulity when it came to his Führer.'

It was a very hot day in Berlin. Nostitz found Trott suffering from depression and a severe toothache, laid out on 'Herr Staatssekretärs' sofa, but was none the less received with an amicable 'Hallo, Gogo.' In the course of their talk that morning various people came and went, among them Werner Haeften, keeping Trott posted on Stauffenberg's latest plans, and Keppler himself, who was just about to shoot off to whatever front on which his presence was required at the side of his Führer. On the next day, 4 July, Nostitz sought Trott out in his other office, that of Councillor Six in the former Polish Embassy in the Kurfürstenstrasse, 'Ribbentrop's propaganda factory'. Nostitz did not have much time for the IA – an expensive institution established only for the sake of Ribbentrop's jealously when it came to his arch rival Goebbels, staffed by hundreds of unqualified people, and stuffed to the brink with ludicrous books and photographs. 'In this atmosphere of total hot air Adam von Trott had, with one or two interruptions, worked and endured for four and a half years'.

Nostitz ran into Trott's few friends in the section – Rantzau (now posted to Budapest whence he sent Missie Vassilitchikov hams), Haeften and Werth. The latter had, with 'a true spirit of sacrifice' allowed himself to become a buffer between Trott and Six' by going to live in his house, 'in order to keep an eye on him and to influence him in Trott's way of thinking'. Werth had just returned from Stockholm, where he had gone in another attempt to contact the Allies on Trott's behalf. He had found that the only way in which he could rid himself of Six, who came with him, was to get him so drunk that he passed out. This way he could use the early mornings for his visits to the Allies while Six suffered in bed.

On Tuesdays Trott's office was in a corner room on the first floor of the building overlooking a verdant garden filled with old trees. They went off to lunch with the Gersdorffs. Around a table for five there were ten people assembled for the meal:

A remarkable mixture of people you found there that day: there was a young Russian woman, a former celebrated beauty of pre-war Berlin society [Missie Vassiltchikov, who was on her way back to Krummhübel] [73] and now a secretary at the AA; the still somehow 'believing' sister-in-law, Gisella Schulenburg, whose husband, a parachutist and Knight's Cross holder was shortly to fall in Normandy, while his brother, Fritzi Schulenburg was hanged at the same time in connection with 20 July; the rather gangling son of the ex-ambassador Solf in the uniform of one of the Cossack regiments we have created, rather obviously narrating that his people did not indulge in the officially granted privilege of rape, murder and plunder, and that his mother, who has been in prison for weeks, will not now be condemned to death by the People's Court; and others . . .

Trott, Nostitz observed, seemed relaxed in this world, and had long conversations with everyone.

On 5 July, Nostitz went to stay with Trott at his flat in Dahlem. Trott, he noticed, had problems getting his body into his little car. The west end of Berlin was unrecognizable after the destruction by Allied planes. 'The "Ku'damm" had been almost mysteriously cleared and its tarmac shone and glistened in the hot sun.' The Rheinbabenallee, where Trott lived, was untouched by bombs and Trott's life at home had been rendered milder by the cares of the 'pearl Emma', whom Trott treated like a grandmother.

Peter Yorck and Hans Haeften, both of whom Nostitz had known for years, came to dinner. On that hazy July evening Trott told Nostitz about the plot, mentioning Stauffenberg and the names of one or two generals, and asking Nostitz for his help when the time came. Yorck and Haeften asked Nostitz about the political and ethical justification of assassination. Nostitz, however, was utterly convinced it was for the best. In his opinion *only* the killing of World Enemy Number One could alter the international situation and rescue Germany as the heart of Europe. Given the Swiss-based Gisevius' later indictment of the plotters' religious scruples, it was possibly Nostitz who reported this conversation to him.

It was at that point in the conversation that Gerstenmaier dropped in to break an alarming piece of news: Leber and Reichwein had been arrested twenty-four hours before.

Leber and Reichwein had been holding talks with Anton Saefkow and Franz Jacob, two popular Communist leaders who had adopted the Soviet policy of collaborating with the bourgeoisie in the fight against Hitler. The two of them controlled the largest network to exist since the winding up of the Uhrig Group operating in the Osram works. Their co-operation, the plotters thought, was necessary in order to achieve a broader base to the conspiracy. On 29 June, a reluctant Jacob had told a friend, 'Things have now reached the point where we are to conclude a pact with the devil himself — in other words the generals — and make a *Putsch* together.'[74]

Leber too had been reluctant to talk to them.[75] There was the constant fear that the Gestapo would have infiltrated the group as they had done so many times before resulting in the arrest and judicial murder of thousands of Communists. At the first meeting there had been three Communists there, including one called Rambow, although only two had been announced. Leber's suspicion was aroused and he refused to attend the next meeting; a few days later all four, with the exception of the Gestapo V-mann, were arrested.

Trott dashed off to Wannsee to warn Stauffenberg. Haeften was clearly stunned by the news. 'Gradually they'll arrest us all, one after the other, that is the way it is going.' Stauffenberg was considerably alarmed; he kept crying out to Trott, 'We need Leber, I'll get him out! I'll get him out!' Two days before the plot, Stauffenberg made the same thing clear to Leber's wife, Annedore. 'We are all conscious of our duty,' he wrote. Leber's reaction to arrest had been characteristic, 'I have only one head,' he said, 'and I can think of no better cause than this to lose it in.'[76] Over the next few weeks both Leber and Reichwein were horribly tortured. At his trial Reichwein could no longer speak.

While Trott was with Stauffenberg, Nostitz remained behind with Haeften. They sat outside on the terrace while Haeften spoke of his wife and youngest child – Nostitz' godchild. Haeften saw the elimination of Hitler as a religious mission – he was, he said, the embodiment of evil.

When Trott returned he was holding in his hand a copy of his memorandum, 'Germany between West and East'. He told the others that he did not want it to be destroyed at any price. Nostitz remarked that the subject would have made his grandfarther, Ambassador von Schweinitz, happy. Together they buried it in the hollow of the garden steps, stacking up the flower pots on top of the steps for added concealment. They went to bed at one, Nostitz lying awake with the full moon shining in through the window. 'Morning came without our being "disturbed"; the two arrests were therefore in the nature of an isolated act.' The next day Nostitz took the train to Potsdam.

Potsdam was as yet undamaged by the war, still very much the city of Frederick the Great with its parks and canal and the Hawel Lakes. 'Only a few months later this wonderful image of the Prussian spirit sank under soot and ashes.' Nostitz was on his way to the house which Count Schwerin shared with Eduard 'Colombo' Brucklmeier. Brucklmeier had joined the Foreign Service in 1927, in the same year as Nostitz and Kessel. He had been in Ribbentrop's private cabinet from 1939–40, but had been a sacked as the result of a denunciation. He now worked for the High Command, although he also undertook tasks for the opposition. He was arrested at the beginning of August and hanged.

The house was a small villa in the Markgrafenstrasse, where guests had been invited for dinner at eight. When Nostitz got there he found 'Uwi' Schwerin, Fritzi Schulenburg, Peter Yorck, Stauffenberg's brother Berthold and Werner Haeften all of whom were revelling in the products of Schwerin's Mecklenberg estate. A little later Adam Trott join them for these unrationed delicacies.

The evening was so delightful that later, Nostitz

felt ashamed to speak about it. There they sat, the men who, a few weeks later would be dragged to the gallows as *Untermenschen* [subhumans]: Ulrich-Wilhelm Graf von Schwerine Schwanenfeld, 'Uwi', and old schoolfriend [from Rossleben], who had since become a fully grown and above all totally scrupulous and liberal nobleman at the height of his powers. For years his political passion had been absorbed by his struggle for his inherited Polish estate and in his deep-seated hatred for the wrecker of everything which he bore in his heart, everything which we loved and cherished; Fritz Graf von der Schulenburg, our fierce, but good-natured, lugubrious-looking robber baron with his reactionary-style monocle fixed in his eye. Always ready to leap to the attack when something monstrous presented itself, he was the man with the gold Party badge and the SA uniform, neither of which he would wear any more, ever since the time, as he put it, through the death of Strasser, national Socialism became National Socialism. The one time Assistant to the Police President of Berlin, the Ministerial Director of the Reichs Ministry of Supply and the just designated Head of Military Administration for Southern France, he used all three posts, won for him by the seniority of his rank in the Party or, like the last, acquired for him by like-minded friends, in order to dig a grave for the regime; the man I had not previously met, Berthold Schenk, Graf von Stauffenberg, the brother of Claus, a judge in the Naval High Command, a refined, serious man with a pensive, donnish head, who, like his brother, had been very close to Stefan George; the big blond youth Werner von Haeften, Claus Stauffenberg's adjutant, despite his thirty-six years still in the full flush of youth and irradiating a splendid good humour; and finally Peter Yorck and Adam Trott.

There they all sat, the criminals of the Führer and people – *Führer und Volk*, 'The Body Snatchers' as Freisler called them. It was a long evening. The culminating point of a friendship which goes no further. The evening made us relaxed, young and glad.

Nostitz remembered that in the course of the evening

[Fritzi] Schulenburg asked me, exactly like Trott the night before, but above all Berthold Stauffenberg, whether it was necessary to think about the plot. I believe that these friends were happy. As Uwi took me to my nearby billet at 3 o'clock that morning and we said goodbye to one another, I had no thought that of this circle, I was to be the only one to survive.[77]

On 7 July Nostitz returned to Geneva. On his way to Berlin he was held up for two hours as a result of an air raid. Once again he saw Trott in his Kurfürstenstrasse office, though this time he was obliged to talk to Six about the latter's ideas on propaganda. At the end of this painful discussion Nostitz could imagine what a 'ticklish existence' it was for his friend, constantly strung between this fanatical Nazi and his Resistance work.

As a result of his conversation with Stauffenberg on the evening of 5 July, Trott was able to break the news of the final go-ahead to his friends the following morning. Furtwängler was one of those he summoned to his office, 'He had two bits of news for me, one sad the other exciting. 'Der Julius' [Leber] had been arrested as a result of his contacts with the Communists. That was the bad news, which really did not greatly surprise me. The good news was that it was going ahead on 15 July.' As is well known, the final attempt was called off 'on technical grounds' once again and fixed for five days later. 'So highly prized was Leber's ability and intelligence in the underground movement that Colonel Stauffenberg was to do anything he could to free him by force before the events of 20 July came to a head.'[78]

The night after Nostitz' departure for the safe haven of Switzerland, there was another discussion at Trott's flat in the Rheinbabenallee. Yorck was there and Haeften, who had brought a friend, a theologian called Herbert Krimm. Once again they went over the now familiar ground of whether it was 'right' to kill Hitler. Peter Yorck expressed reservations about the morality of tyrannicide. As the argument was not going his way, Yorck fell silent and, using the pretext of discovering an eavesdropper, walked out on to the balcony. The discussion reached no conclusion – except that Trott advanced the obvious point that things had now gone too far to conceive of turning back.

It was crucial to act quickly, not only for the sake of Leber and Reichwein and the others who had been arrested in the last few months but also because Himmler and the Gestapo were closing in on the group. Some time in that summer, General Olbricht told Schlabrendorff,

I have bad news for you: in fact we have never had worse news. A short time ago
Admiral Canaris came to see me and told me of an interview with Himmler.
Quite bluntly Himmler said that he knew very well that plans for a rebellion
were being hatched in influential army circles. But, he continued, they would
not succeed because the Gestapo would intervene in time. He was looking on
and waiting only in order to find out who stood behind these plans for high
treason. Now he knew, and he was going to deal effectively with such men as
Beck and Goerdeler.[79]

A warning was issued to Goerdeler as a result and he went into
hiding. Although he was aware that a plot was about to take place, he
was never given any precise details as the plotters did not trust his
discretion. As regards Himmler, he was obviously in two minds about
the action against Hitler, as his own secret dealings with the enemy
make clear. When the conspirators did actually go into action on 20
July Himmler had done nothing to prevent the *coup* from taking place.
When questioned later about precisely this he replied that the plot
was hatched by the army, and that it was the army's job to put it down.

Indiscretion was not just the fault of Goerdeler. Reading the diaries
of Missie Vassiltchikov or Ursula von Kardorff one has the impression
that every girl in Berlin was aware of what was going on. Sometime in
the middle of July, Dulles gives an example of how generally known
the preparations were.

About the same time a naval officer in the Abwehr, who was aware of the plans
for the plot, attended a party given by one of the social leaders of Potsdam, Frau
von Bredow, granddaughter of Bismarck, whose personality was so vigorous
she was called 'the only male descendent of the Iron Chancellor'. There the
naval officer to his astonishment heard a young fellow officer say quite openly
that an attempt on Hitler's life was being planned.[80]

It is perhaps a testament to how little the Nazis had infiltrated the
Berlin 'social set' that nothing of this appears to have leaked out.

Trott was still having regular meetings with Stauffenberg, or so it
appears from the scant indications he gave between the attempt and
his arrest. One night in July, Stauffenberg had spent the night in the
Rheinbabenallee. On another occasion he had taken refuge from an
air raid in the Trotts' cellar. One thing they must have discussed was
the still unconcluded business in Stockholm; the Russians, in the
person of Ambassador Kollontay, had to be prepared for the
emissaries who would be sent out after the bomb went off. For the
East it would be Ambassador von der Schulenburg and Köstring. In the
West negotiations were to be carried out by General Falkenhausen
and Trott himself.

It was probably for this reason that Trott saw the conductor Leo
Borchard on 10 July. Borchard had been born in Russia and spoke the

language perfectly. The story is in the diary of Ruth Andreas-Friedrich. On 11 July she wrote:

> Yesterday Andrik [Borchard] went to see his friend Adam von Trott . . . a man with a good head, a bold heart and one of the most active opponents of the Nazis. When Andrik came back, he paced the room for a long time, cleared his throat, started to speak, stopped, cleared his throat again. 'Can you hold your tongue?' he asked at last.
>
> I looked at him in surprise. 'Do you have to ask that after thirteen years?'
>
> 'That's not it. . . I know. . . But you see it's about. . .'
>
> 'Get on with it,' I urged impatiently.
>
> 'Well, you see, they really are planning something. Rebellion, *coup d'etat,* something of that sort. I have no idea who's in it. It's no business of ours, anyway what matters is that they want to use me.'
>
> 'You? When? For what?'
>
> 'Liaison man, so to speak. I'm to go to Sweden. Do you understand? Get in touch with certain groups there. They'll fix up a conducting tour, and arrange the whole business through official channels.'
>
> 'Suppose they get wise?'
>
> 'The won't get wise, it's all going to be done perfectly legally. And I'm not thinking of telling Mr Hitler about the illegal side of my mission.'
>
> 'When do you think?' I asked breathlessly.
>
> 'Pretty soon, maybe this month. They'll let me know – telegraph, if necessary. I have arranged a code with Trott.'
>
> 'Heavens above, how thrilling! It's coming at last! Really coming! What are they really planning on? Assassination? Army revolt? Are they going to kill Hitler? Do they just want to put him on the shelf?'
>
> But Andrik shrouded himself in silence. 'I haven't the foggiest,' he said. 'Anyway I don't want to know. And I'd advise you not to know anything either. Until. . .well, until it's time.[81]*

That evening Trott dined with Missie Vassiltchikov who had just returned to Berlin from Krummhübel. She was staying in the wrecked Adlon Hotel, which, despite everything, still managed to keep up appearances.

> Adam and I dined there together. We spoke English to the head waiter who was delighted to show how well he still remembers it. Our neighbours began to stare. Adam then took me for a drive during which, without going into

---

* *The failure of the plot removed the necessity for Borchard to play the role intended for him by Trott. The Gestapo never learned of his involvement and he survived the war and the Russian occupation by singing the Russian National Anthem when the Red Guards were on the point of killing him. As a leading musician who had not thrown in his lot with the Nazis he was made the first post-war conductor of the Berlin Philharmonic. Sadly, his new appointment did not last long; like Anton von Webern at the same time in Austria, he was the victim of an over-zealous American sentry who shot him for going through a red light in the car of an English colonel after a concert performance.*

particulars, we discussed the coming events which, he told me, are now imminent. We don't see eye to eye on this because I continue to find that too much time is being lost perfecting the details, whereas to me only one thing is really important now – the physical elimination of the man. What happens to Germany once he is dead can be seen to later. Perhaps because I am not German myself, it may all seem simpler to me, whereas for Adam it is essential that some kind of Germany be given a chance to survive. This evening we had a bitter quarrel about this and both of us got very emotional. So sad, at this of all moments. . .[82]

On 12 July she returned to Krummhübel where the next day she received an apology from Trott.

When Missie Vassiltchikov left Berlin, Trott was still making plans for a further trip to Sweden, but at the last moment he could not get permission to travel. There are no details of his further activities until 16 July, the day after the projected *coup*. On the 15th Stauffenberg had taken the bomb to the meeting of army commanders at the Wolfsschanze in East Prussia, but finding Himmler and Goebbels absent decided not to detonate the fuse. Nonetheless the Walküre orders had been set in motion and were only decommanded in Berlin with the greatest difficulty. There could be no more false alarms.

That evening Ursula von Kardorff returned to her flat in the centre of Berlin to find Fritzi Schulenburg sitting on the sofa. Ursula Kardorff and Leber's wife Annedore worked in the same office, and Schulenburg wanted her to run an errand to the hospital where Frau Leber was at present. She was to 'tell her that his friends had got on to the track of her husband and would resume contact with her.' Later that day she went to the hospital to see Frau Leber who, after checking her credentials, told her of the Gestapo interrogations, the search of the flat, and the stormtroopers' stealing two bottles of Schnaps. Later Schulenburg told Ursula von Kardorff that Frau Leber 'was like a blade of tempered steel, she bends, but she never breaks.'[83]

On Sunday 16 July, Trott was present at an important meeting at the Stauffenberg brothers' home in Wannsee, half-way between Dahlem and Potsdam. Schulenburg was there again, both the Stauffenbergs, Schwerin and Colonel von Hofacker. Caesar von Hofacker was a cousin of Stauffenberg's who was attached to Military Command in Paris. He was there to liaise with the plotters on behalf of General Stülpnagel. Recently Stülpnagel had had some success with other commanders on the Western Front, where it appeared that not only had Field Marshal Günther von Kluge *finally* made up his mind to go along with the plotters, but that also Field Marshall Erwin Rommel had agreed that the time had come to remove Hitler and conclude a peace with the West. The enlisting of Germany's most popular general was a considerable advantage to the group.

Hofacker gave his 'extraordinarily pessimistic' account, as the

Gestapo later called it, of the situation on the Western Front. The main topic of conversation, however, was the post-mortem on the failure of the first attempt at Rastenburg. The Gestapo reports give contradictory reports for the discussions of that day, and it would seem that there were two meetings, Trott being present at both. In the second meeting, Colonel Hansen, Yorck and Colonel Merz von Quirnheim were also there. The latter was one of the closest associates of Stauffenberg on the military side of the conspiracy. He was shot in the courtyard of the Bendlerstrasse on 20 July with Stauffenberg, Olbricht and Werner Haeften. Trott also contributed a pessimistic view: he told the soldiers that he thought the Allies would not drop 'unconditional surrender'.

These meetings finally resolved what was to be done after the *coup* in terms of the Allies. It was decided to despatch two missions, one to the East and another to the West. The idea of pushing for a separate peace had been totally buried. Trott also advanced the view that the Allies would possibly be prepared to negotiate with the Germans provided a change of regime had taken place. Allied lack of assurances towards Germany should not be stressed; it was unthinkable the army would approve continuing a costly war once the Germans had made a genuine call for a truce. In foreign political matters Stauffenberg deferred to Trott.

The next day, 17 July, was the occasion for another meeting, this time at Trott's flat where Berthold Stauffenberg was present. At this meeting there were further discussions on what they would do after the end of the war. That same day Schulenburg had been to see Ursula von Kardorff again, giving her twenty marks to buy roses and a message for Annedore Leber: 'Tell her that I am going to France in three days' time – in three days, on 20 July. And tell her that we are going to do our duty.'

That same day a British plane attacked Rommel's car in Normandy, severely wounding him and putting him out of action till long after 20 July. Two days before, General Falkenhausen had been relieved of his command and sent into retirement in Dresden.

Also on 17 July, Trott met Wilhelm Melchers in the corridor of the Auswärtige Amt.[84] Melchers, who operated the Indian desk in the Foreign Office, had been away on sick leave and only returned that day. Trott told Melchers that the 'day was coming now, that it was well-planned and that Hitler would be killed. Trott was filled with enthusiasm now that the longed-for moment was finally come.' The two diplomats then turned their minds to filling certain positions within the Wilhelmstrasse. As Foreign Minister, Melchers counselled Hassell, Weizsäcker or Nadolny. Then, as they made themselves comfortable in Keppler's office, they turned their minds to the post of State Secretary. For this job, Melchers thought Theo Kordt the best candidate. When it came to the Head of Propaganda, Trott advanced

Councillor von Hentig. 'Do you know him well?' he asked Melchers. 'The soldiers set great store by him.'

Ursula von Kardorff received a further visit from Schulenburg on 18 July. Two men had been asking questions about him at his 'digs'. He seemed nervous, and thought he would go to his wife in Mecklenburg for a few days.

Melchers and Trott continued their discussions in the Auswärtige Amt on the morning of 18 July. Trott expressed the view that in eleven years of Nazism, the Foreign office was still pretty well untainted by Nazism – 'the heart of the office is sound'. During his interrogation a few days later he expressed a similar view; asked to think of any Nazis, he could only mention seven, including Keppler and Six. Melchers was slightly worried that the fact that everyone in the office had had to take out Party membership would count against them in the new regime. Trott comforted him on this subject, telling him that every case would be dealt with on its merits.

That afternoon the talk between Trott and Melchers dealt with broader issues of the plot. After telling him that Hans-Bernd would be in charge of liaison with the army conspirators as a result of his brother's role as Stauffenberg's adjutant, Trott went on to describe how the Walküre orders were arranged to bring about a military takeover in all the major centres of command. There would also be a mobilization of workers' groups and Social Democrats. Here 'he named names'. That same day Trott sent a telegram to Peter Bielenberg in East Prussia: 'I should like to see you soon in Berlin'. Bielenberg did not understand the message and thought matters could wait till the weekend.

On the morning of 19 July, Trott told Melchers that it would be better for him not to be seen talking to him for the next few days. The day before Trott had also sent a telegram to Count Berg, the ordinance officer to Field Marshal Kluge. Berg arrived in Berlin on the 19th in Kluge's plane. Trott told him to wait at his home until he received notification from him to act. It is hard to see now what Berg's role was meant to be. He never received the call.[85] Trott was busy that day calling people to Berlin whom he wanted at his side after the *coup*. Professor von Selle in Königsberg was one of these. Peter Bielenberg was another. He also wrote a letter to Clarita, which she immediately destroyed after memorizing one or two essential parts. 'That I have written so little to you over the past few weeks has nothing to do with my having too little, rather too much, to tell you . . . In the next few weeks you may not hear from me for a long time. . .'

Trott had lunch at the Gersdorffs' house; the summer weather had made the guests indifferent to the fact that the windows had all been blown out in the November raids. Missie Vassiltchikov had left Krummhübel that morning to be on hand for the *putsch*. After lunch she had a long talk with Trott.

He looks very pale and strained, but he seems glad to see me. He is appalled that Loremarie Schönberg should be back in town and is very unhappy about her unceasing efforts to bring together people whom she suspects of being sympathetic to what I call *die Konspiration* [the plot], many of whom are already deeply involved and are having a hard enough time as it is staying above suspicion. Somehow she has found out also about Adam's involvement and now keeps pestering him and his entourage among whom she has acquired the nickname 'Lottchen' [after Marat's assassin Charlotte Corday]. To many she is a real security risk. He told me that she even complained about my being unwilling to take an active part in the preparations.

The truth is there is a fundamental difference in outlook between all of *them* and me: not being German, I have never attached much importance to what happens afterwards. Being patriots, *they* want to save their country from complete destruction by setting up some interim government; whereas *I* am concerned only with the elimination of the Devil. Besides, I have never believed that even such an interim government would be acceptable to the Allies, who refuse to distinguish between 'good' Germans and 'bad'. This is of course a fatal mistake on their part and we will probably all pay a heavy price for it.

We agreed not to meet again till Friday. After he had gone, Maria Gersdorff remarked: 'I find he looks so pale and tired; sometimes I think he is not going to live long.'[86]

Trott went back to the flat in the Rheinbabenallee that evening where he was joined for a last talk by Claus Stauffenberg.[87] Stauffenberg had stopped off to offer up a prayer at the little village church in Dahlem. It was Niemöller's church. After his visit to Trott, Stauffenberg went home to Wannsee, where he spent the evening reading his brother Alexander's latest poems with Berthold.

On 19 July, Trott told Melchers and Werth that Stauffenberg was going to act the next day. That evening the officer had shown the bomb to his brother in Wannsee: two packets of British-made explosive acquired from Colonel von Freytag-Loringhoven of the Abwehr. The fuse, too, was British, as so far the Germans had not yet perfected the development of silent fuses. On the morning of 20 July, accompanied by his adjutant Werner von Haeften, Stauffenberg flew to Rastenburg for the conference.[88]

In the Wilhelmstrasse it was a morning of great excitement, with all those actively involved at their stations ready to go into action once it was clear that Hitler was dead and the Walküre orders had been set in motion.[89] Keppler was fortunately away in Krummhübel and Trott was free to use his office as the centre of operations. Sadly, it was not the nicer of Keppler's two secretaries who was on duty that day, but one whom Werth called 'the denouncer'.

Werth went to see Trott in Keppler's office at around 11 a.m. With Haeften and Melchers they waited, went out to get something to eat and eventually settled down to dictating some office work. It was at two that they received the codeword *panta rei* (Greek for 'all is in flux'), which meant that the plans worked out with Stauffenberg were to be put into action.

At three, Trott telephoned Melchers in his office and asked him to come up to the State Secretary's office.

Trott was conspicuously pale. After I had closed the door to the outer office in which his secretary was working, he came up to me, speaking softly. 'It has been done.' I stared at him, speechless, as he raised his hand and made as if to fire a pistol. I asked him, 'And you have received an absolutely trustworthy report?'

Trott told Melchers that he had received the agreed signal from the officers concerned, and that the whole administrative quarter of Berlin would soon be sealed off by the army. At that point Melchers and Trott opened the window, noting a regular flow of traffic below. Melchers grabbed Trott's hand and said, 'I still find it hard to believe that this *coup* has really been brought off. We will never forget 20 July.' The two men fell silent for a while, then with a gesture towards his desk on which there lay a letter formally signed with the words *Heil Hitler*, Trott exclaimed, 'I won't need to sign letters with this miserable greeting any more.'

Stauffenberg's bomb had indeed gone off as planned in the bunker at Rastenburg, at the last moment Stauffenberg and Haeften had been interrupted in the process of priming the fuse and had had to jettison half the explosive. The wooden bunker had recently been lined with a concrete jacket, but the fact that the windows were open on to the hot summer day and that the long room was able to absorb some of the blast contributed to the limited effect of the explosion which amounted, as Stauffenberg later told General Fromm, to that of a fifteen-centimetre shell. Sadly, it was not sufficient and Hitler had only sustained minor injuries.

Given the timing of Trott's summons to Melchers, Trott must have received a call from Tempelhof Airport when Stauffenberg and Haeften arrived back in Berlin. Both men were convinced that Hitler was dead and that no one could have survived the blast. The Walküre orders, which should have been issued immediately after the explosion, were not given until Stauffenberg returned to Berlin. This resulted in considerable loss of time, further reducing the plot's chances of success.

Melchers advised Trott to act with caution. Trott agreed. 'You're quite right, that's it for now. I must tell some other friends what has happened. We can't do anything for the time being. Please keep quiet and speak to no one until Haeften arrives.' 'I hope he gets back safe and sound before the area is cordoned off.' Melchers countered, 'Now, he will be able to obtain a pass from the soldiers!' Trott smiled. 'Something will be forgotten in all this excitement... In moments like these the oddest things can happen.'

As Melchers left Keppler's office he ran into Legationsrat Dörtenbach. The diplomat told him that he had heard on the radio that there had been an attempt on Hitler's life but that the Chancellor was 'as good as unharmed'. Melchers was inclined to think this was a trick and therefore went to see another official, Legationsrat Ullrich, whom he knew to keep a wireless set beside his desk. Ullrich had not heard the broadcast, but when Melchers told him what Dörtenbach had said, he predicted a 'new scourge'.

Melchers decided that it was worth relaying this to Trott, and called him on the internal line. Trott told him to come back to Keppler's office. When he got there he found Alex Werth sitting on a chair. Trott had already heard about the broadcast from Werth. Trott expressed the hope that this had been 'just a tactical move'.

There was still no further news from the Military High Command in the Bendlerstrasse. Werth called round but could get no information. Finally he decided that if the military plans went ahead, this would prove whether Hitler was actually dead or not. When at four or so, the street showed obvious signs of being cordoned off and steel helmeted soldiers took up their positions along its length, there was a feeling of relief all round. 'Thank Heavens,' cried Trott. 'So the thing has worked!' There was no question about it, he told the others; now they all had to keep their heads like the soldiers, there was no turning back.

Melchers then left the office to try to get more information. On his way he met Bergmann who said, 'Melchers, what's coming isn't going to be fun.' and told Melchers to take great care. In the meantime Haeften had at last gone to Keppler's office. Werth was temporarily absent but returned a few minutes later. He found Trott and Haeften speaking softly to one another. Haeften appeared to know nothing of the broadcast. 'They kept saying that everything had been so well prepared that it was impossible that anything could go wrong.' Haeften was expecting to hear any moment from the soldiers what to do next. In his pocket he possessed full instructions and an authority in writing telling him who was to be arrested immediately.

Haeften went to Councillor Bergmann, the Assistant Chief of Personnel in the Auswärtige Amt. 'Herr Bergmann,' he said. 'Hitler is dead. The counter revolution is now taking place. In an hour at the latest we, that is my friends and I, will be the representatives of the new government in the Foreign Office. We hope that you're with us in this, and I tell you this is so that you do what you think best.' A cautious civil servant, Bergmann told Haeften that he would be better to keep it to himself and not mention it to anyone. Haeften replied that his was impossible, things had already gone too far.

Trott, checking to see that the sentries were still in the street, tried in vain to contact Haeften's brother. When Haeften returned he told him what Bergmann had said, adding that he had pretended not to hear. Trott then asked Melchers whether Bergmann was entirely trust-worthy and Melchers replied that Trott need have no worries on that score.

Haeften once again tried to contact his brother in the Bendler-strasse, only to be told that he could not be reached. Haeften then asked the switchboard to tell him why the Wilhelmstrasse was cordoned off. Receiving no explanation he asked that a message be left telling Werner Haeften to call him as soon as possible. At that point both Werth and Melchers left the room. Trott and Haeften were left alone together trying to decide whether to initiate Herbert Blanken-horn and Councillor Werner-Otto von Hentig into the plot. Werth went down to the press section where predictably, no one had any news to give him.

When Melchers returned he found Haeften in the ante-room trying to get through to his brother. The secretary had disappeared. For the first time Melchers began to doubt whether it was wise to keep ringing up the Bendlerstrasse, '... we all clung to the idea that had the plot not succeeded then their administrative quarter would no longer be cordoned off.' Haeften and Trott were constantly looking out of the window.

Then the ghastly moment came: the street was freed again, men and cars were on the move and people coming and going from the houses across the way. Under Secretary Hencke [who had been having problems getting to an appointment] was seen to leave the building. Once again Haeften sat down at the telephone and tried to get through to his brother.

It was now 7 p.m. and Haeften had gone 'as white as a sheet'.

In the Bendlerstrasse itself, the late issue of the Walküre orders had scuppered the remaining chance of success. Although various regional commands had carried out the orders, notably Paris, General Fromm (who previously had been so keen that the plotters rid him of his arch-enemy Field Marshal Keitel) had refused to act. The man of the hour was Joseph Goebbels who managed to talk round Remer, the officer in charge of the guards battalion, and get Hitler on the telephone to prove to him that he was alive. After that the plot fell apart. Soldiers stormed the Bendlerstrasse building. Beck tried to shoot himself and bungled it, a sergeant having to administer the *coup de grâce*. In the early hours of the following morning Stauffenberg, Olbricht, Werner Haeften and Merz von Quirnheim were shot on Fromm's orders in the courtyard of the Bendlerstrasse building. Fromm did this in order to remove the evidence of his own involvement but it did him no good in the long run. He was shot himself the following March on charges of 'cowardice' during the events of 20 July.

In Rastenburg Hitler, his eardrums burst and with bad cuts and bruises (his trousers had been blown off by the blast), entertained Mussolini to tea. In front of the astonished Italian dictator he began to brood menacingly, while Göring decided to settle an old score with his detested rival Ribbentrop.

Now he blamed him for the bankruptcy of Germany's foreign policy and threatened to hit him with his marshal's baton. Eyewitnesses unanimously reported the following exchange: 'Shut up you champagne salesman!' 'I am still Foreign Minister, and my name is *von* Ribbentrop.' Hitler had listened to all this in brooding silence. When someone mentioned 30 June 1934, he flared up, uttering furious threats that from now on he was going to be ruthless. He would wipe out the lot of them and throw women and children into concentration camps – no mercy was to be shown to anyone![90]*

In the Wilhelmstrasse, Melchers implored Trott and Haeften to stop using the telephone now that the street showed every sign of having returned to normality. He also counselled that they leave the room without delay. Werth supported Melchers and, at eight or so, the two of them left the Foreign Office and went straight to the Foreign Press Club.

In the early afternoon, before Trott had seen Melchers and Werth, he had been working on a radio broadcast on the new government's foreign policy with Dr Fritz Theil,

a radio operator who had been working closely with Hofacker and Schulenburg, as well as Trott. The intention was to give the German public the conclusions of 'Germany Between East and West'. After Theil had left the Foreign Office he had gone to the Foreign Press Club [then in Ribbentrop's house in the Lenzallee in Berlin Schmargendorf], so as not to be stopped at the barriers when the moment came to act. The car due to fetch Theil that afternoon did not arrive. From time to time Trott called him to reassure him. Finally Trott telephoned at nine thirty that evening to tell him to make good his escape at once.[91]

On leaving the AA building Melchers went across the road to the Adlon Hotel, where he was living, telling Trott that he could reach him

---

* *The scene is also admirably painted by Hugh Trevor Roper in* The Last Days of Hitler, *'When a staid German general compared Göring to Elagabalus, he was not exaggerating. In the absolutism, the opulence and the degeneracy of the Middle Roman Empire we can perhaps find the best parallel to the high noonday of the Nazi Reich. There, in the severe pages of Gibbon, we read of characters apparently wielding gigantic authority who, on closer examination, are found to be the pliant creatures of concubines and catamites, of eunuchs and freedmen; and here too we see the élite of the Thousand Year Reich as a set of flatulent clowns, swayed by purely random influences. Even Mussolini was embarrassed, but then Mussolini had, after all, like Goebbels, a Latin mind; he could never be at home among those cavorting Nibelungs. Goebbels incidentialy was not present at this Mad Hatter's tea party; he was in Berlin, giving orders for the suppression of the revolt.'*

there. On his way out of the building he again dropped in on Legationsrat Ullrich. At the Adlon Melchers ate with several colleagues. On his way to bed 'exhausted and disappointed beyond measure' he crossed Ulrich von Hassell in the corridor. In the middle of the night he heard Hitler's broadcast on the wireless and realized there was no longer any hope. Trott himself stayed in Keppler's office until eleven. He had been casting around for an alibi to explain the comings and goings from the office. He thought he would be able to pass them off as the result of his illness and absences from the office over the past four months. Werth in particular he had needed to see on official business. At eleven, he walked over to the Foreign Press Club where he exchanged a greeting with Werth who was still there. He then went home. Despite his quest for an alibi he can have been in little doubt as to the fate which awaited him.

Nobody knows whether Trott heard Hitler's speech on the radio which was broadcast at 1 a.m. on the Friday morning. He must already have been aware that the plot had failed utterly. The talk surprised Klaus Bonhoeffer and the two John brothers, who were celebrating Hitler's death over a bottle of German sparkling wine.[92] Over the next few days Trott saw his cousin Teddy Götz to whom he expressed the feeling of being like 'a tree without branches'.[93]

The next morning he went into work as usual where he ran into Melchers. When Melchers began to rail at the blunders of the military, Trott silenced him. 'Are you indignant?' he asked. 'You should consider the fact that those people will have to give their lives for what they have done.' Haeften in his biblical style murmured that 'Hitler was in league with the Devil.'[94]

Melchers asked him if there were any other group in whom some hope lay. 'No there is no hope,' said Trott, 'and none for the future. It is all finished now and we will have to suffer the consequences. No stone will be left unturned. Hitler will continue this crackpot war – the real nihilist that he is – until everything has been destroyed.' He then expressed some satisfaction that the plot had none the less taken place – that it was a historical fact – that was at least something.

Trott was still occupying Keppler's office. Melchers joked with him that he would now hang up a print over his desk 'of Critias' statue of Harmonias and Aristogeiton, the Athenian tyrannicides; the Nazis wouldn't know what it meant. Trott smiled, adding that it would go very well next to my picture of Galileo, which Trott knew I had once had hanging in my room, a man who had, like all of us, had to swear an oath against his own convictions.'[95]

On 21 July a few of the other plotters were able to meet up and take stock of the situation. Otto John called Trott who came to see him that afternoon. Trott urged John to fly to Madrid.[96] This he did on 24 July, becoming one of the very few conspirators close to the plot to escape the noose. After seeing John, Trott went for a walk in the Grunewald with Blankenhorn, who suggested he destroy all his papers. This Werth and Trott did over the weekend.

Another to escape was Count Berg, who called Trott that day to encourage him to leave in Kluge's plane and hide out in France with him. Trott refused. When Berg returned to Kluge's headquarters, the Field Marshal, who had baulked at joining the conspiracy at the last possible moment, told Berg to get taken prisoner otherwise he would be certainly arrested and executed.[97]

Others suggested possible means of escape to Trott, but he would hear none of them. Furtwängler, who came from a village which bestrode the German-Swiss border, knew of a sure means across the frontier.[98] Waltraud von Götz knew a way to get him into Poland but again he would not listen.[99] To Furtwängler he said, 'I shall take the full blame for everything.' Then he added, 'Have you still got a copy of our paper "Germany Between East and West?" It would be a pity if it were to get lost. You will see that everything will turn out as we predicted — *Leben Sie wohl!*'[100]

On the Eastern Front the news of the plot's failure reached Major General Henning von Tresckow. Calling his friend Fabian von Schlabrendorff to him, he delivered what is possibly the most moving judgement of all on the tragic events. Tresckow was completely calm when he took his leave of Schlabrendoff. He said:

> Now everyone in the world will turn upon us and sully us with abuse. But my conviction remains adamant – we took the right course. Hitler is not only the arch-enemy of Germany, he is the arch-enemy of mankind. In a few hours time I shall stand before God to answer for my actions and omissions. I believe that I will be able with a clear conscience to vouch for everything I have done in the fight against Hitler.
>
> God once promised Abraham that he would spare Sodom if ten just men could be found in the city. He will, I trust, spare Germany because of what we have done and not destroy her. None of us can complain of his lot. Whoever joined our movement donned the shirt of Nessus. The moral worth of a man is certain only if he is prepared to sacrifice his life for his convictions.

Tresckow drove out to no-man's-land in the company of Major Kühn (who later that day deserted to the Russian lines). In a wood, he sent Kühn back to the car for his map. During his absence, Tresckow blew his head from his body with a grenade.[101]

On 22 July, Missie Vassiltchikov finally found an opportunity to talk to Trott. She was a little shocked to find Haeften in the office eating cherries out of a paper bag after his brother had been shot 'like a dog'.

> I went down to Adam's room. I found him with one of his assistants, who soon

left. Adam threw himself down on a sofa and, pointing to his neck, said 'I'm in it up to here.' He looked dreadful. We talked in whispers. The sight of him made me unhappier still. I told him so. He said yes, but to me it was merely as if I had lost the favourite tree in my orchard, whereas for him it's everything he had hoped for that was gone. The intercom rang: our boss Dr Six wanted to see him . . .

When I went over to Maria Gersdorff, I told her how anxious I was about Adam. 'But why?' she asked. 'He knew Stauffenberg only slightly, didn't he? No I am certain he is not deeply involved!'

'No,' I said. 'Not really involved at all.'

Trott joined Missie's group of friends at Princess Aga Fürstenberg's for tea. 'He had been with Dr Six, trying to put him off the scent. He looked like death. I drove back with him to his house and sat on the balcony in the sun while he changed.' When he came back out he told her about Stauffenberg: 'a wonderful man, not only brilliantly intelligent but also with exceptional vitality and drive . . . He had lost in him, Adam said, his closest friend. He seemed completely crushed.'

Trott told Missie Vassiltchikov that he knew he would be arrested, he was far too deeply involved. He had decided to send away his maid Emma 'as she had witnessed many meetings in this house, and, if questioned, might talk. He feared that Helldorf, too, might break down under torture.' Trott wondered aloud whether it might not be possible to have an article published in the London *Times* explaining 'what these men represented.'

In this long talk with Missie, Trott revealed something of the very odd behaviour of Doctor Six.

> He thinks that Dr Six suspects something too, as he keeps pressing Trott to go to Switzerland. I also insisted that he should go – immediately. But no, he will not, because of his wife and children. He [Trott] said that if they arrested him, we would deny everything – in order to get him out again. Six was aware of his activities abroad, and his interest in the results of his negotiations made him value Trott's life.[102]

Curt Bley shot up to Berlin as soon as he heard of the plot. He knew that Trott would have been involved. They spent the day together and that night Bley stayed in the spare bed which had been occupied last by Stauffenberg. Trott explained to Bley the reasons why he refused to flee. He cared too much about the fate of his wife and family and felt that he should stand with the others. Talking of 20 July he expressed the view that the 'sons had rectified the sins of the father'. 'I do not fear death,' he told Bley. 'I fear only the humiliations I shall have to face on the way to the scaffold.'

Bley said goodbye to Trott on the doorstep of his house the following morning, 25 July. An hour later Trott was arrested.[103] Missie had called him later that morning at home when he was still at liberty, 'but later when I droppped by his office, he was not there, only his secretary – a nice girl and a friend – with a scared expression on her face'. After lunch she returned to this office.

> This time Adam's secretary tried to shove me out of his room. I pushed past her and marched in. At his desk a small man in civilian clothes was going through his drawers. Another one lounged in an armchair. The swine! I glanced at them more closely to see whether they had anything in their buttonholes, but then remembered that they wear their Gestapo badge inside. I asked the secretary ostentatiously: 'Wo ist Herr von Trott? Noch immer nicht da?' [Where is Herr von Trott? *Still* not there?] They both looked up. When we had left the room, she looked at me beseechingly and put her finger to her lips.[104]

She learned the full story from Judgie Richter, he told her: 'It's too late. They picked him up at noon. Luckily Alex Werth was with him and drove after them in another car, and hopefully he will soon be back with some indication of why Adam has been arrested.' Richter told her that the Gestapo had arrived while he was in the morning conference and had physically restrained his secretary from warning him that they were lying in wait. Keppler was expecting him for lunch at the Adlon. Meanwhile Dr Six was interested in getting him released and sent his ADC round to find out what the charges were. Ironically, Six and the SS were the strongest card Trott possessed, but it is doubtful that Trott even knew this.[105]

Haeften was arrested the day before Trott and tried hard to protect Trott during his initial interrogations.[106] On 25 July, the Gestapo had a session with Berthold Stauffenberg during which certain details concerning Trott's involvement came to light. Trott was already damned by Claus Stauffenberg's driver's log-books, which recorded the number of times that his employer had stopped off to see Trott in Dahlem.[107] No one can be blamed for Trott's arrest. As he had been the first to say, he was far too deeply involved.

The Gestapo prison was filling up with suspects and after a time some of the detainees were transferred to local prisons and concentration camps – whence they were taken to Berlin for the brutal sessions with Leo Lange and others. They were badly tortured: Gerstenmaier was beaten with a stick studded with nails;[108] Schlabrendorff was tortured on the rack besides more banal forms of beating and humilation.[109] From the unreliable testimony which Trott gave in the course of these interrogations it is clear that he was to some extent playing Scheherazade with the Gestapo, telling them interesting tit-bits in order to prolong his life.[110] This is what he told Missie Vassiltchikov he would do. He was particularly careful only to attribute blame to those he knew to be dead or out of danger. With so many plotters in the prisons, the Gestapo could not prevent a 'bush telegraph' from transmitting the news of executions and suicides to the inmates. To keep his torturers keen he poured a certain amount of scorn on Stauffenberg's wisdom in foreign policy, claiming that he was only an adviser and had only the vaguest notion of what he intended to do.[111] He let them know something of his journeys abroad, stressing his own role in the negotiations with the Allies. If his life hinged upon anything it was on his use to the SS as a negotiator should they wish to push further to conclude a separate peace.[112]

For the time being the SS were holding their options on Trott open. Missie Vassiltchikov learned on 27 July that a list had been found proposing Trott as Under Secretary of State at the Foreign office after a successful *coup*. 'Six seems still half inclined to try and extricate him. Alex Werth is badgering him day and night to do so.'[113] The Under Secretaryship of State was the very least proposed for Trott. After the war, Sebastian Haffner put it out that Trott would have been Foreign Minister. Given his closeness to Stauffenberg and the latter's lack of sympathy for the *Alte Herren*, he may have had a point.[114]

After the war Clarita von Trott was able to glean something of the SS position on Trott at the time of his arrest through an interview with Six's assistant, Dr Horst Mahnke. Mahnke had been examined about Trott and Haeften by the Gestapo man Huppenkothen, who wanted to know who had been responsible for Trott and Haeften's trips abroad. Mahnke had told him the half-truth that it was Six.

Huppenkothen: 'Did Brigadeführer Six have the authoriy to send an official abroad in order to negotiate peace with the enemy?'
Mahnke: 'Under certain circumstances. All possibilities must be looked into.'
Huppenkothen: 'Were reports made of these trips?'
Mahnke: 'Yes.'
Huppenkothen: 'These reports were being used by Stauffenberg?'
Mahnke: 'They were also being used by Schellenberg.'[115]

Mahnke did not save Trott and Haeften's lives but he was responsible for shielding the other members of the office who were implicated.

On 29 July, Missie reported Trott's position as being 'stationary'.[116] Trott was using his continuing interrogations to shield people. Weizsäcker, who was safe in the Vatican, was 'mentioned as the leader of the opposition',[117] while it was suggested by Trott that Stauffenberg had had contacts with a representative of Eisenhower from which he had acquired certain information – information which, in reality, had been brought by Otto John. Trott was not certain that John was one-hundred-per-cent safe from the Gestapo in Spain.[118] Trott also stressed Anglo-American fears of Russia in a bid to lead the SS to negotiate on that basis.

On 31 July, Missie Vassiltchikov learned of Six's violent outburst against Trott and Haeften when he had declared, '*Wir haben zwei Schweinehunde unter uns gehabt.*' ('We had two *Schweinehunde* in our midst.') Yet Trott's nameplate remained on his door for the time being. And Missie thought that Six was treating her with 'unusual consideration'.

In due course, the Gestapo rounded up Trott's wife and children. The children were taken from Imshausen on 13 August when Clarita was in Berlin trying to gain access to her husband. Clarita got as far as the courthouse on the 15th but the officials would not let her into her husband's trial. She was herself arrested on the 27th. Hitler looked as if he was going to pursue the threats he made on 20 July to the letter.

On 3 August, Peter Bielenberg, who had got wind of Adam von Trott's arrest from the factory he managed in Grandenz in East Prussia, dropped in to see Werth at the IA. Werth was not there but he was able to speak to Missie Vassiltchikov.

> We sat on the stairs and I told him all there is to tell. He insisted there must be a way of fighting Adam free. He said that he is imprisoned outside Berlin, but every morning he is brought with a one-man escort from the jail to Gestapo HQ in the Prinz Albrechtstrasse for interrogation. The way to do it would be to ambush the car, after which Adam would be smuggled over to the Warthegau [a partisan-controlled part of Poland] and hidden with Polish partisans with whom Peter (who manages a factory there) is in touch. What a relief to hear someone ready to act and willing to take on even the SS! Actually, when one considers how many key officers were part of the conspiracy, and not all would have been arrested as yet, this *does* seem feasible.*

When Bielenberg got back to the factory on 6 August, with the intention of taking some weapons from the armoury in his bid to free Trott, he found the Gestapo there waiting for him. For a time he thought he had been betrayed by someone in Berlin.[119] In fact, Bielenberg's betrayer was his secretary, who had taken Trott's telegram of the 18th to the Gestapo.

Peter Bielenberg's brave attempt was the last chance to save Trott before his trial before the notorious Volksgerichthof. The frightful Roland Freisler had 'been on excellent form', Lorenzen remarked, at the trials of Generals Hase, Stieff and Hoeppner, and Peter Yorck on 8 August. He had called Stieff (a short man) a 'poisoned dwarf'[120] and insulted the defendents in the way that had made him famous. At Moltke's trial in January a copy of the *Criminal Code* could not be found in the courthouse.

---

* *Peter Bielenberg points out that this account is slightly garbled. For one thing Loremarie Schönberg was present, though she is not mentioned. Trott was imprisoned at Orienburg concentration camp and driven in each day with Gottfried Bismarck. There was a good stretch of country road between the camp and Berlin. (Conversation with Peter Bielenberg, July 1989)*

Trott stood trial with Haeften, Helldorff and three others on 15 August. On 11 August the Foreign Office had received notice from Dr Sonnenhol of the Gestapo that 'von Trott zu Solz will be condemned to death at the next session of the Volksgerichthof, probably Tuesday or Wednesday of next week.'[121] Freisler was in no doubt as to his brief. Trott defended himself well against the charges and against Freisler's impertinence. The 'German Vischinsky' referred to him throughout as 'Count' Trott zu Solz, and mocked his war service and his Oxford education. The prosecution's case was based upon his friendship with Stauffenberg and to this Trott, despite his sang-froid, had no defence.[122] Freisler asked him if he was aware that his participation in the discussions was tantamount to attempted murder. Trott replied coolly, '*Gewiss*' – 'Certainly'.[123]

Trott was not able to bring off the same *coup* as Haeften that morning – namely to perform the virtually impossible by reducing Freisler to silence. Asked what he thought of Hitler, Haeften had replied, 'I have the conviction that Hitler will go down in history as the personification of evil.'[124] A film was taken of the trial from which photographs show Haeften's sad pale eyes. One still photograph shows Trott looking possibly at Haeften with a warm half-smile of encouragement. Another shot shows Trott between two guards with a look of fierce hatred on his haggard face.

Baron Anton Saurma von der Jeltsch was present at the trial. 'Adam had caught sight of him, had made no sign of recognition, had looked at him fixedly for a long time and had then started to sway back and forth from the waist in a rocking kind of movement. He wore no tie,* was clean-shaven and very pale.'

All the defendants were condemned to death. In his summing up Freisler characterized Trott as the sort of spineless intellectual one might find in the Romantisches Café on the Kurfürstendamm. He attributed his lack of moral fibre to two years at Oxford and two years travelling round the world.†[125]

The other convicted 'traitors' were dragged off, stripped naked and led to the gallows where they were hanged with thin cord which slowly strangled them without breaking their necks. Death could take anything up to half an hour during which time the unfortunate victims

---

* *This was theoretically to prevent the men from hanging themselves. Their braces and belts were also removed, adding to Freisler's pleasure as, in forcing them to grab at their trousers to keep them up he was able to humiliate them further.*

† *'It has only now become known that in the daylight attack last weekend, the President of the People's Court, Dr Freisler, and most of his colleagues were killed. Freisler's death has aroused considerable excitement in Berlin and is regarded as an act of just retribution for the revolting manner in which he conducted the case against those accused of the July Plot.' (Studnitz, Diary, entry for 9 February 1945.)*

were sometimes filmed or sometimes mocked by the executioners.[126] Trott, however, was spared for another eleven days. A sinister note had been entered into the Gestapo reports: 'Since Trott has obviously withheld a good deal, the death sentence delivered by the Volksgerichthof has not been carried out, so that [he] may be available for further clarification.'[127] Trott's 'Scheherazade' policy had worked, but at what a price! His agonies were now to continue for another eleven days.

According to Mahnke, he and Schellenberg's assistant, Dr Schmidz, recommended to Himmler that the sentences on Haeften and Trott be commuted to life imprisonment as a result of their usefulness to Germany. Schellenberg sent the recommendation to Himmler who spoke to Hitler himself. Hitler threw a tantrum. There was to be no sparing of Trott or Haeften.[128]

The bush-telegraph of the cells accurately recorded the moment when Trott was deemed to be of no further use to the SS. August 25th was Eugen Gerstenmaier's birthday and the prison guard brought him some plums and rolls as a treat. Biting into a roll he discovered a letter from his wife in which was written, 'Adam von Trott must immediately reckon with death.'[129]

Death came the following day.

On 15 August, only six days after his own – thirty-fifth – birthday he had written to his wife:

You will know . . . that what hurts me most is that I may never again be able to place my experience at the service of this country. I wanted to use those special abilities which I have been able to develop by what was, perhaps, a too-single-minded concentration on foreign affairs and Germany's position in the balance of power. Here I could still have been useful. I should like so much to be able to make some sort of summary of my ideas and proposals which might help other people, but I don't suppose that will be possible now. It was all an attempt, arising out of the love for my country (for which I must thank my father) and from the knowledge of her strength, to protect her immutable rights in the changes and chances of the modern world. I wished to preserve her profound and indispensable contribution to civilization against the encroachment of powers and beliefs foreign to her. That is why I always hurried back eagerly from foreign countries with all their enticements and opportunities to this one which I felt I was called to serve. What I have learned and what I was able to do for Germany abroad would certainly have helped a good deal now, because there are so few people who have enjoyed such diverse opportunities in the last years [as me]. So I must hope that even without me, understanding and assistance will be forthcoming from many of these connections, should it ever be wanted or necessary. But the sower would rather not leave his seed for others to care for, between the sowing and the harvest there are so many storms.[131]

After the war the British estimated that 4,980 people were judicially murdered as a result of the July Plot. Some of those killed were known opponents who were rounded up in the weeks following the *coup* and who had no connection with the plot itself.[132] Not only did the blood bath turn out to be the long-awaited attack on the German nobility, many of whom were among the victims, it also substantially destroyed the cadre most likely to administer a non-Nazi Germany.

In the concentration camps the failure of the plot provided the cue for the murder of a large number of Communists who had been in detention since 1933 or 1934, including their leader Ernst Thälmann. The number of Communists killed during the Third Reich is estimated to have been as high as 30,000.[133] The brutalities continued right up to the moment that the Allied armies reached the camps. The last executions of Resisters in Berlin took place after the Russians had actually entered the city. Amomg the victims were Albrecht von Bernstorff and Herbert von Mumm.

The failure of the July plot was the fault of the Resisters themselves. They would have been the first to say – had they lived – that it was a *German* affair and that the Germans should take the credit or the blame for success or failure. That it failed in no manner detracts from the nobility of the plotters' actions and from the heart-rending tragedy of its *dénouement*. In the deaths of these men and women must lie a small degree of atonement for the barbarities commited by branches of the German administration before and during the Second World War.

But if, like Trott, the Germans rightly chose to bear the major share of the blame for the failure to remove Hitler from power, the Allies too must take some responsibility. Why was not a shred of encouragement offered to Hitler's opponents? After 20 July, Trott told Teddy Götz that the English must also bear a measure of guilt for the disaster.[134] The scales had begun to fall from his eyes. Trott loved Germany, but he also reserved a place in his heart for Britain and America. The one had given him Oxford, the other the legacy of John Jay which he derived from his mother. Even more than forty years later one asks what would it have cost to make some statement of support to the German opposition? How much were the Allies kidding one another with those sterile formulae of 'absolute silence' and 'unconditional surrender', the broken gramophone records by which they thought they held together their flimsy Alliance. How much could we, clinging to these phrases, expect to win the war *and* peace? How much did we deserve to?

306

Sources

The manuscript sources for Adam von Trott's life are for the main part in the possession of his widow in Berlin. From his letters and papers she made a compilation in 1957, which was distributed to his friends; this is referred to below as '*Materialsammlung*'. Trott's letters to Diana Hubback are in the possession of Balliol College, Oxford. Most of his letters to Sheila Grant Duff were included in Klemens von Klemperer, (ed.) *A Noble Combat* (Oxford 1988). Rhodes House in Oxford also possesses a number of useful documents.

The first biographical sketches of Trott were the *Berichte* written by his friends after his death and now kept in Berlin. Christopher Sykes' biography, *Troubled Loyalty* (London 1969), was in response to a commission from a Trott Committee, set up by Trott's friends in the late 1950s. Sykes produced very much his own book, which was a disappointment to many people who had known its subject. Henry Malone's doctoral thesis, 'Adam von Trott zu Solz' (Austin, Texas, 1980) was an impressive attempt to refute Sykes, but sadly only goes as far as 1938. Malone's thesis has been published in German as *Adam von Trott zu Solz, Werdegang eines Verschwörers, 1909*-1938 (Berlin 1986).

Other bibliographical references will be found in the notes.

Translations from the German are my own unless the title of the book is given in English. My thanks to Lisa Barnard and André Dominé for their help.

Photographs are reproduced by permission of Clarita von Trott, the National Portrait Gallery, the World Council of Churches, the *Washington Post, Svenska Dagbladet,* the Imperial War Museum and the Bundesarchiv.

Notes

Introduction

1. Rhodes House. Trott's Personal File.
2. Rhodes House. See Allen's attitude to Trott's postponed third year.
3. Rhodes House. Personal File.
4. Ibid.
5. Rhodes House. Personal File.
6. Copy in Rhodes House. Personal File.
7. Henry Malone, 'Adam von Trott zu Solz', unpublished Ph.D. thesis, University of Texas at Austin, 1980.
8. Rhodes House. Personal File.
9. Ibid.
10. Compare attitudes to Moltke in particular. See A.L. Rowse, *All Souls and Appeasement*, London 1961, and Balfour and Frisby, *Helmuth von Moltke: A Leader against Hitler*, London 1972.
11. See A.L. Rowse, *All Souls and Appeasement*; Diana Hopkinson, *The Incense Tree*, London 1969; Shiela Grant Duff, *The Parting of the Ways*, London 1982; and Christopher Sykes, *Troubled Loyalty*, London 1968. An exception is Malone, op. cit.
12. Richard Lamb, *The Ghosts of Peace*, 1987.
13. Foreign Office, C 3339/103/18. Copy in Trott Archive.
14. *Observer*, 24 November 1968
15. Malone, op. cit.
16. Quoted in F.W. Furtwängler, *Männer die ich sah und kannte*, Hamburg 1951.
17. Christabel Bielenberg, *The Past is Myself*, London 1968.
18. See *Poems of Deliverance*, London 1946. The relevant poems are entitled 'In Memory A v T' and 'Dream Sonnet (1)'. The latter is particularly lurid.
19. Letter to Diana Hubback in August 1934. Quoted in *The Incense Tree*.
20. In a conversation with Hugh Trevor Roper after the war (Malone, op. cit). In his autobiography, *Memories*, London 1966, Bowra wrote 'my rejection of him remains one of my bitterest regrets'.

21. Shiela Grant Duff, *A Noble Combat*, Oxford 1988.
22. Conversation with David Astor, February 1988.
23. Shiela Grant Duff, *The Parting of the Ways*, London 1982.
24. Quoted in Margret Boveri, *Treason in the Twentieth Century*, translated by Jonathan Steinberg, London 1961. See also *Wir Lügen Alle*, Freiburg im Breskau, 1965.
25. Conversation with Clarita von Trott, October 1988 and notes, 1989.

1

1. *Genealogisches Handbuch des Adels*, Vol. XIV (Adelige Häuser A), 1977. I am grateful to Dr J. G. Coates of Montgomery, Powys, for sending me the extract relating to the Trott family.
2. Malone, op. cit.
3. See Gregory Pedlow, *The Survival of the Hessian Nobility 1770–1870*, Princeton 1988. I am particularly indebted to this book for the history of the Trott family over the period.
4. Quoted in Pedlow, op. cit.
5. Quoted in Malone, op. cit.
6. Pedlow, op. cit.
7. Edward Crankshaw, *Bismarck*, London 1981.
8. Malone, op. cit.
9. Crankshaw, op. cit.
10. Clarita von Trott, '*Eine erste Materialsammlung Sichtung und Zusammenstellung, Den Freunden vorgelegt*', typescript, 1957. Hereafter, '*Materialsammlung*'.
11. A.L. Rowse, *A Cornishman Abroad*, London 1965.
12. '*Materialsammlung*'.
13. Conversation with Clarita von Trott. Also 'Materialsammlung'.
14. '*Materialsammlung*'.

2

1. See Pedlow, op. cit. Forest represented some sixty-one per cent of land in Hesse-Kassel and was the chief source of wealth among the nobility. Moreover, incomes from land had risen steadily from the middle of the century.
2. Golo Mann, *The History of Germany since 1789*, Penguin 1974.
3. Malone, op. cit. Rowse (*A Cornishman Abroad*) was given one of these visiting cards when he first met Trott.
4. Malone, op. cit; the same story is recounted in Sykes, op. cit.

5. See R.G.S. Weber, *The German Student Corps in the Third Reich*, London 1986.
6. See Ernst-Friedemann Freiherr von Münchhausen in *Corps-Zeitung der Göttinger Sachsen*, autumn 1959.
7. Malone, op. cit.
8. W.A. Visser't Hooft, *Memories*, Amsterdam 1971. I was unable to trace the English-language edition of Visser't Hooft's book and am immensely grateful to Marielle Ruskauff for translating large passages of it for me.
9. Malone, op. cit.
10. Conversation with Diana (née Hubback) and David Hopkinson, 9 August 1988.
11. Letter from Trott to Diana Hubback, 19 October 1932.
12. Malone, op. cit. Sykes, op. cit., gives the name of Trott's intermediary with Selbie as Miss Denham.
13. Humayun Kabir to Clarita von Trott.
14. Ibid.
15. A.L. Rowse, *A Cornishman at Oxford*, London 1965.
16. Ibid.
17. Ibid.
18. Malone, op. cit.
19. *A Cornishman Abroad.*
20. Ibid.
21. Conversation with David Astor, February 1988.
22. *A Cornishman Abroad.*
23. Ibid.
24. Conversation with Clarita von Trott, October 1988. Frau von Trott showed the author a photograph of the lady in question.
25. Malone, op. cit.
26. Copy in Trott Archive, Berlin.
27. *All Souls and Appeasement.*
28. Albrecht von Kessel to Clarita von Trott.
29. Malone, op. cit.
30. Ibid.
31. Malone, op. cit. The influence of Hegel on Trott's mind was 'vastly overrated' (Richard Crossman in the *Observer*, op. cit.). It is also a theme very dear to Dr Rowse (cf. *A Cornishman Abroad, All Souls and Appeasement* and his subsequent writings on the subject).
32. Alexander Werth to Clarita von Trott, 1957.
33. Conversation with Clarita von Trott, October 1988.
34. Trott later introduced Diana Hubback to Golfing. See *The Incense Tree.*
35. Malone, op. cit. Sykes translates *voll befriedigend* as a 'good second', ignoring the *summa cum laude* which Trott achieved in his dissertation.
36. Malone, op. cit.

37. For the history of the scholarships see *The First Fifty Years of the Rhodes Trust and the Rhodes Scholarships*, 1903–1953, Oxford 1955.
38. *Rhodes Scholarships, Records of Past Scholars, 1903–1916.*
39. Rowse makes this contention in *All Souls and Appeasement.*
40. See Rowse, *A Cornishman Abroad.*
41. Trott was particularly aggrieved by Mierendorff's death. According to his widow, he exclaimed, 'And he had only just begun to call me Adam!' Conversation with Clarita von Trott, October 1988.
42. Eberhard Zeller, *The Flame of Freedom*, London 1967.

3

1. Malone, op. cit.
2. Harold Nicolson, *Peacemaking*. A special Balliol dinner was held in Paris at the Majestic Hotel.
3. Sykes, op. cit.
4. *A Cornishman Abroad.*
5. '*Bericht über das erste Studienjahr in Oxford*', Trott Archive. This report was presumably written for the sake of the German Rhodes Selection Committee.
6. Malone, op. cit. The lecture was later printed in book form.
7. '*Materialsammlung*'; also Malone, op. cit.
8. Patricia Russell to Clarita von Trott.
9. Conversation with Christabel Bielenberg, April 1988.
10. Diana Hopkinson, *The Incense Tree*, London 1968.
11. Letter to Diana Hubback, December 1931.
12. *The Incense Tree.*
13. Ibid.
14. Ibid.
15. Ibid. In Shiela Grant Duff's book *The Parting of the Ways* it is Diana Hubback who is dancing with Trott. Diana Hopkinson (conversation, August 1988) insists that it is Shiela Grant Duff who is mistaken. After the dance Trott wrote to Diana Hubback asking her to remember him to Sheila [*sic*]. Letter, December 1931.
16. *The Incense Tree.*
17. Ibid.
18. Letter from Trott to Diana Hubback, May 1932.
19. Friedrich Hölderlin, *Gesammelte Werke*, Tausend 1955.
20. C.E. Collins to Diana Hopkinson, 1946.
21. Ibid.
22. Conversation with Diana and David Hopkinson, August 1988.
23. C.E. Collins to Clarita von Trott.
24. Letter to Diana Hubback, 1 July 1932.
25. *The Incense Tree.*

26. Malone, op. cit.
27. Ibid.
28. Ibid.
29. Letter to Diana Hubback, Imshausen, 28 August 1932.
30. *The Incense Tree.*
31. Patricia Russell to Clarita von Trott.
32. Sykes, op. cit.
33. Letter to Diana Hubback, July 1932. He possibly went on to stay with Rowse, who lived in Cornwall. Rowse tells that Trott stayed with him there, see '*In Memoriam* A *v* T' in *Poems of Deliverance.*
34. Letter to Diana Hubback, 19 July 1932. In his letter Trott expresses Mrs Dyer-Bennett's desire to become 'good friends' with Diana Hubback.
35. Letter to Diana Hubback, 1 July 1932.
36. Collins, *Balliol Record*, 1987.
37. Letter to Diana Hubback, August 1932. Trott's attitude was certainly influenced by the need to comfort Diana Hubback on her decision to abandon her studies.
38. On one of her visits they had tea in Corpus Christi College with Charles Henderson, the don with whom Trott had stayed in Cornwall the previous summer. After tea, Henderson let them out into the by-now-closed Christ Church meadows behind the college. Later he wrote to Diana Hubback, 'I enjoyed letting you and Adam into the Meadows; it seemed like undoing the bad day's work of the God of Genesis when he thrust Adam and co. out of paradise.' *The Incense Tree.*
39. Isaiah Berlin, *Balliol Record*, 1986.
40. Malone, op. cit.
41. Letter to Diana Hubback, November 1932.
42. Letter to Diana Hubback, November 1932.
43. Balogh had been introduced to Trott by Diana Hubback's mother. Conversation with David and Diana Hopkinson, August 1988.
44. *The Incense Tree.*
45. Letter to Diana Hubback, December 1932.
46. Malone, op. cit. Also Sykes, op. cit.
47. Ibid.
48. 'Adam von Trott, a Personal View' in *The Challenge of the Third Reich*, edited by Hedley Bull, Oxford 1986. Adam von Trott Memorial Lectures delivered in Balliol Hall in Hilary term 1983, Oxford 1986. Trott described Astor to Diana Hubback as 'a good old Teuton' in a letter dated 26 January 1934.
49. Letter to Diana Hubback, February 1933. Rees was then working as a journalist and translator in Berlin.
50. Later Sir John Cripps (assistant-editor of the *Countryman*, 1947–71).
51. Letter to Diana Hubback, April 1933.

52. Letter to Shiela Grant Duff in *A Noble Conflict.* ed. Klemens von Klemperer, March 1933.
53. *The Incense Tree.*
54. This is now the accepted version among historians (see Martin Broszat, *The Hitler State*, London 1981). Broszat cites the findings of Fritz Tobias in *Der Reichstagbrand: Legende und Wirklichkeit*, Rastatt 1962. The Communist historian Allan Merson (*Communist Resistance to Hitler*, London 1983) refuses to accept the version of the events and describes van der Lubbe as 'an anarchist'.
55. See Krausnick and Broszat, *Anatomy of the SS State*, London 1968.
56. Günther Weissenborn, *Der Lautlose Aufstand*, Hamburg 1954.
57. Ibid. For the activities of the Gestapo at the time, see Hans Bernd Gisevius, *To the Bitter End*, London 1958, and Rudolf Diels, *Lucifer ante Portas*, Stuttgart 1950.
58. Letter to Shiela Grant Duff, March 1933.
59. Letter to Diana Hubback, April 1933.
60. Isaiah Berlin, *Balliol Record*, 1986.
61. Malone, op. cit. '[they had probably met with Cripps in the House of Commons] ... I was very glad to see you and talk to you. Long years ago all the kind of difficulties which face you, faced my generation. This has been the case throughout the ages. We must all choose according to our right and conscience which side we will be on. Sometimes as in yours the path of right and duty is chock full of difficulties. But that which we think as of "God" does give us light and guidance if we strive to overcome ambition and self ...' etc.
62. Professor Brock to Clarita von Trott, 1948.
63. Letter to Diana Hubback, May 1933.
64. Letter to Diana Hubback, May or June 1933.
65. Jo Grimond, *Memoirs*, London 1979.
66. Letter from Tarbert Lodge, Jura, July 1933.
67. Letter to Shiela Grant Duff, July 1933.
68. Ibid.
69. '*Materialsammlung*'.
70. *The Incense Tree.*
71. Malone, op. cit. Sykes (op. cit.) poured scorn on the idea of Trott succeeding in the fellowship exam.
72. Malone, op. cit.
73. Ibid.
74. Ibid.

4

1. Countess Spinelli (née Ingrid Warburg) to Clarita von Trott, 1979. Countess Spinelli asserts that Trott looked like Valéry Giscard d'Estaing.

2. Curt Bley to Clarita von Trott.
3. *The Incense Tree.*
4. Letter to Shiela Grant Duff, 28 August 1933.
5. *The Incense Tree.*
6. Letter to Diana Hubback, 10 September 1933.
7. Ibid.
8. Balfour and Frisby, op. cit.
9. Margret Boveri to Christopher Sykes, May 1968. Copy in the Trott Archive, Berlin.
10. Letter to Shiela Grant Duff, November 1933.
11. Letter to Diana Hubback, November 1933.
12. Ibid.
13. Letter, 14 November 1933.
14. Rhodes House Archive, letter dated 12 December.
15. Balfour and Frisby, op. cit.
16. Malone, op. cit.
17. Letter to Diana Hubback, 8 December 1933.
18. Ibid., December 1933.
19. See Krausnick and Broszat, op. cit.
20. Allan Merson, *The Communist Resistance to Hitler'*, London 1983.
21. Ibid.
22. Ibid.
23. Ibid.
24. *The Incense Tree.*
25. Ibid.
26. Letter to the author from C.E. Collins, 19 April 1988.
27. Letter to Diana Hubback, 22 January 1934.
28. Ibid.
29. Letter to Diana Hubback, 4 February 1934.
30. Ibid.
31. Letter to Diana Hubback, (late) February 1934.
32. Malone, op. cit.
33. Conversation with Countess Spinelli, June 1989.
34. Malone, op. cit.; this is what inspired Con O'Neill's reaction, see above p.3.
35. Quoted in Malone, op. cit.
36. Letter to Diana Hubback, February 1934.
37. Malone, op. cit.
38. Ibid.
39. *A Noble Combat.*
40. *The Incense Tree.*
41. *The Parting of the Ways.*
42. Ibid.
43. '*Materialsammlung*', quoting an extract from Shiela Grant Duff's diary.
44. *The Parting of the Ways.*

45. Ibid.
46. Letter to Shiela Grant Duff, 3 October 1934.
47. Letter to Diana Hubback, 6 November 1934.
48. Malone, though he is wrong about Leverkühn's having been a Rhodes Scholar.
49. See Goronwy Rees, op. cit. I a grateful to Robin Chapman for talking to me about Rees and for giving me a copy of his play, *One of Us* (London 1986) in which the two main protagonists are Rees and Guy Burgess.
50. Letter to Diana Hubback, 17 December 1934.
51. Leverkühn was the German defending counsel in the trial of Field Marshal Manstein in 1949. His British counterpart was Sir Reginald Paget. See the latter's book, *Manstein, His Campaigns and his Trial,* London 1951. He was also involved in the case to prove 'Anastasia' was the true daughter to Tsar Nicolas II.
52. '*Materialsammlung*'.
53. Letter to Shiela Grant Duff, 29 December 1934.
54. Fabian von Schlabrendorff, *Offiziere gegen Hitler* 1946; most recent English edition, *Officers against Hitler*, London 1966.
55. Malone, op. cit.
56. '*Materialsammlung*'.
57. Letter to Diana Hubback, 17 January 1935.
58. *The Incense Tree.*
59. Ibid.
60. R.G.S. Weber, op. cit.
61. Ibid.
62. Conversation with Clarita von Trott, October 1988.
63. '*Materialsammlung*'.
64. Weber, op. cit. See also A.A. Löwenthal, *Gesammelte Werke*, Tübingen 1958.
65. Merson, op. cit.
66. Conversation with David and Diana Hopkinson, August 1988.
67. Merson, op. cit.
68. Weisenborn, op. cit.
69. *The Incense Tree.*
70. Naomi Shepherd, *Wilfrid Israel,* London 1984.
71. Ibid.
72. Ibid.
73. Julie Braun-Vogelstein, *Was Niemals Stirbt,* Stuttgart 1966
74. Trott was frequently troubled by painful boils.
75. Ibid.
76. Ibid.
77. Martin von Katte, 'Adam von Trott zu Solz' in *Wandlung und Wiederkehr: Ernst Jünger zum 70 Gebürtstag.*
78. Bruce Chatwin's article, which coincided with the publication of Jünger's *Diaries* in Germany, wrongly insisted it was Adam von

Trott who inspired the book. George Steiner in the Penguin edition of *On the Marble Cliffs* further complicates the story by implying that the meeting described in the book was a sort of premonition. The novel was published in 1939.

5

1. Butler, *Lord Lothian*, London 1960.
2. Bernstorff to Lothian, Rhodes House.
3. Letters to Diana Hubback, 19 April 1935 and May 1935.
4. Shiela Grant Duff to Trott, Paris, 11 June 1935.
5. Letter to Shiela Grant Duff, 26 June 1935.
6. Letter to Diana Hubback, 8 June 1935.
7. Quoted in Malone, op. cit.
8. Joachim Maas, *Kleist*, New York 1983.
9. Malone, op. cit.
10. Letter to Diana Hubback, 26 June 1935.
11. Malone, op. cit.
12. Letter to Shiela Grant Duff, 30 June 1935.
13. Malone, op. cit.
14. Letter to Diana Hubback, 20 July 1935.
15. *The Incense Tree.*
16. Letter to Diana Hubback, August 1935.
17. Martin von Katte, op. cit.
18. Quoted in Malone, op. cit.
19. Letter to Diana Hubback, 20 September 1935.
20. This is Malone's theory. Leverkühn's help later on with Donovan and perhaps in his (Trott's) attempted transfer to Ankara during the war might have come in very useful.
21. Letter to Diana Hubback, 20 September 1935.
22. *The Past is Myself.*
23. *The Parting of the Ways.*
24. Malone, op. cit., who quotes the letter to this father.
25. *The Parting of the Ways.*
26. 'Materialsammlung'.
27. Mommsen, in Bull (ed.), *The Challenge of the Third Reich*, op. cit.
28. Rhodes House Archive.
29. Letter to Diana Hubback, Christmas Day 1935.
30. Malone, op. cit.
31. Letter to Shiela Grant Duff, in *A Noble Combat.*
32. Letter to Shiela Grant Duff, 10 January 1936.
33. Ibid.
34. Letter, Shiela Grant Duff to Trott, 28 January 1936.
35. Letter to Shiela Grant Duff, 9 February 1936.
36. Countess Russell to Clarita von Trott.

37. Quoted in Malone, op. cit.
38. Letter to Shiela Grant Duff, 16 March 1936.
39. Letter to Diana Hubback, 15 June 1936.
40. *The Parting of the Ways.*
41. Malone, op. cit.
42. Letter to Diana Hubback, 23 October 1936.
43. Hildebrandt, *The Foreign Policy of the Third Reich* (trans. Anthony Fothergill), London 1973.
44. Letter to Shiela Grant Duff, 3 November 1936.
45. Letter to Diana Hubback, November 1936.
46. Woodward to Allen, 27 November 1936, Rhodes House.
47. Woodward to Lothian, 23 November 1936. Rhodes House.
48. Lothian, 27 November 1936, Rhodes House.
49. Lothian to Ned Carter, 10 December 1936.
50. Letter to Shiela Grant Duff, 27 November 1936.

6

1. Letter to Shiela Grant Duff, 7 January 1937; also letter to Diana Hubback, 4 January 1937, in which he says he will be staying with the former ambassador to China. For some reason, Trott maintains discretion with Shiela Grant Duff.
2. Letter to Diana Hubback, 24 January 1937.
3. Letter to Diana Hubback, from Paris, February 1937.
4. Werth to Clarita von Trott.
5. Letter to Shiela Grant Duff, March 1937.
6. *All Souls and Appeasement.*
7. For Moltke see Ger van Roon, *Neuordnung im Widerstand,* Munich 1967, and Balfour and Frisby, op. cit.
8. To Christopher Sykes, May 1968.
9. Balfour and Frisby, op. cit.
10. *All Souls and Appeasement.*
11. Balfour and Frisby, op. cit.
12. Ibid.
13. *All Souls and Appeasement.*
14. Letter to Shiela Grant Duff, March 1937. Malone mentions a hat and a suit as other parts of Nancy Astor's largesse.
15. Letter to Shiela Grant Duff, March 1937.
16. '*Materialsammlung*'.
17. Letter to Shiela Grant Duff, beginning of March 1937.
18. Anthony Cave Brown, *The Last Hero, Wild Bill Donovan,* London 1982.
19. Corey Ford, *Donovan of the OSS,* London 1971.
20. '*Amerikanische Eindrücke*'.
21. Letter to Shiela Grant Duff, about 26 March 1937.

22. '*Amerikanische Eindrücke*'.
23. Letter to Shiela Grant Duff, about 26 March 1937.
24. Letter to Shiela Grant Duff, 28 March 1937.
25. Diary extracts in the possession of Clarita von Trott, Trott Archive.
26. Malone, op. cit. The letter is in the Trott Archive.
27. Letter to Shiela Grant Duff, 14 April 1937.
28. Letter to Shiela Grant Duff, 28 March 1937.
29. Letter to Shiela Grant Duff, 28 March 1937.
30. Ibid, 18 April 1937.
31. Letter to Diana Hubback, 4 April 1937.
32. Letter to Shiela Grant Duff, 18 April 1937.
33. Letter to Diana Hubback, 20 April 1937.
34. Ibid.
35. Letter to Diana Hubback, April 1937.
36. Ibid.
37. Letter to Diana Hubback, 18 April 1937.
38. '*Materialsammlung*'.
39. Sykes, op. cit.
40. '*Amerikanische Eindrücke*'.
41. Lord Tweedsmuir to Rt Hon. W.L. Mackenzie King, 5 May 1937.
42. Peter Ludlow, in *Das andere Deutschland im Zweitem Weltkrieg*, Herausgegeben von Lothar Kettenacker, Veröffentlichungen des deutschen Historischen Instituts, London 1977.
43. Letter to Shiela Grant Duff, May 1937.
44. Ibid, about 10 May 1937.
45. '*Amerikanische Eindrücke*'.
46. *Was Niemals Stirbt*.
47. Letter to Diana Hubback, April 1937.
48. *Was Niemals Stirbt*.
49. Letter to Eleonore von Trott, '*Materialsammlung*'.
50. Hasso von Seebach, in '*Materialsammlung*'.
51. Letter to Diana Hubback, 15 June 1937.
52. Ibid. 15 June 1937.
53. Malone, quoting letter from Diana Hubback.
54. Letter to Diana Hubback, 15 July 1937.
55. Letter to Diana Hubback, 12 August 1937.
56. Letter to Diana Hubback, on the China Sea, 12 August 1937.
57. Letter to Shiela Grant Duff, 3 June 1937.
58. Letter to Diana Hubback, 12 August 1937.
59. Letter to Shiela Grant Duff, undated.
60. Letter to Shiela Grant Duff, 20 August 1937.
61. Falkenhausen's memoirs have been edited as *Memoires d'outre guerre*, Brussels 1974. Sadly, however, the publishers included nothing on his meeting with Trott in China. For Falkenhausen and the Chinese, see Hsi-Huey Liang, *The Sino-German Connection: Alexander von Falkenhausen between China and Germany,*

1900–1941, Amsterdam 1978. This book contains a great deal of inaccurate information about Trott.

62. Letter to Shiela Grant Duff, 20 August 1937.
63. Letter to Shiela Grant Duff, 31 August 1937.
64. Ibid.
65. Letter to Shiela Grant Duff, September 21 1937.
66. Ibid.
67. Letter to August von Trott, quoted in Malone, op. cit.
68. Malone, op. cit.
69. Letter to Diana Hubback, 30 September 1937.
70. Malone, op. cit.
71. Letter to Shiela Grant Duff, 20 October 1937.
72. Ibid, written the next morning.
73. Quoted in Malone, op. cit.
74. Malone, op. cit.
75. Letter to the author from Sir Harold Acton, March 1989.
76. Harold Acton, *More Memoirs of an Aesthete*, London 1970.
77. Letter to Diana Hubback, 24 October 1937.
78. Ecke in '*Materialsammlung*'.
79. Letter to Shiela Grant Duff, 6 November 1937.
80. '*Materialsammlung*'.
81. Letter to Shiela Grant Duff, 21 October 1937.
82. Martin von Katte, op. cit.
83. Letter to Millar, 8 February 1938.
84. For the political thinking of the Kreisau Circle, see Ger van Roon, op. cit. For Goerdeler and Beck's political thought, see Beck und Goerdeler, *Gemeinschaftsdokumente für den Frieden, 1941–1944*, Herausgegeben von Wilhelm Ritter von Schramm, Munich 1965. A discussion of Popitz' thinking is found in Peter Hoffmann, *Widerstand, Staatsstreich Attentat: der Kampf der Opposition gegen Hitler*, 3rd ed., Munich 1979, (English edition: *The History of the German Resistance*, London 1977).
85. Malone, op. cit.
86. Ibid.
87. Trott to Lothian, 1 July 1938.
88. Millar to Leo Amery, 8 February 1938.
89. Lothian to Halifax, 2 August 1938.
90. Malone, op. cit.
91. Letter to Shiela Grant Duff, 15 March 1938.
92. Ibid.
93. Letter to Shiela Grant Duff, 1 April 1938.
94. '*Materialsammlung*'.
95. Letter to Shiela Grant Duff, 31 August 1937.
96. *Europe and the Czechs.*
97. Ibid.
98. Letter to Shiela Grant Duff, 20 July 1938.
99. Letter to Shiela Grant Duff, 3 July 1938.

100. Letter to Shiela Grant Duff, 20 July 1938.
101. Ibid., 10 August 1937.
102. Shiela Grant Duff to Trott, 1 September 1938.
103. '*Materialsammlung*'.
104. Letter to Lord Lothian, 11 October 1938.
105. Ibid.
106. Letter to Shiela Grant Duff, 1 October 1938.
107. Ibid, 28 September 1938.
108. Ibid, 1 October 1938.
109. Ibid. 6 October 1938.
110. Letter to Shiela Grant Duff, 10 November 1938.
111. Information from David Astor and Christabel Bielenberg, April 1988.
112. Martin von Katte, op. cit.
113. Rhodes House, 14 November 1938.

7

1. *The Parting of the Ways.*
2. Letter to Diana Hubback, 30 December 1938.
3. Letter to Diana Hubback, 30 December 1938.
4. After his brother's death Werner von Trott remained aggressive towards those people who praised his brother's actions during the war. After the cross was set up on his land at Imshausen he reportedly made life difficult for those people who wished to pay their respects.
5. Letter to Shiela Grant Duff, 6 December 1938.
6. Helmut Conrad to Clarita von Trott.
7. Letter to Shiela Grant Duff, 6 December 1938.
8. Krausnick and Broszat, op. cit.
9. Ulrich von Hassell, *The von Hassell Diaries, 1939–1944*, Introduced by Allen Welsh Dulles, London 1948.
10. Letter to Shiela Grant Duff, 30 December 1938.
11. *The Parting of the Ways.*
12. Peter Bielenberg before the Nuremberg Tribunal, included in Hjalmar Schacht, *Account Settled*, London 1949.
13. Friedemann Freiherr von Münchhausen in the *Corps Zeitung der Göttinger Sachsen*, 1959.
14. Albrecht von Kessel, *Bericht*, 1945.
15. *The Past is Myself.*
16. Ibid.
17. Letter to Eleonore von Trott, 24 February 1939.
18. Monsignor Hugh Montgomery to Christopher Sykes, 1964.
19. Letter to Shiela Grant Duff, March or possibly April 1939.
20. Sykes (op. cit.) who interviewed Sir Geoffrey Wilson.

21. Conversation with Peter and Christabel Bielenberg, July 1989.
22. Peter Bielenberg, notes for Christopher Sykes, 1968.
23. Letter to Eleonore von Trott, 29 April 1939.
24. For Weizsäcker, see the latter's *Memoirs* (English ed.), London 1951.
25. Ibid.
26. Margret Boveri, *Der Diplomat vor Gericht*, Berlin-Hannover 1948.
27. See Ritter, *The German Resistance, Carl Goerdeler's Struggle Against Tyranny*, London 1958. The English version is slightly shortened from the earlier German edition.
28. Schlabrendorff, op. cit.
29. Peter Bielenberg, notes to Christopher Sykes.
30. Letter to Diana Hubback, May 1939.
31. See Hon. David Astor in the *Manchester Guardian*, 7 June 1956.
32. William Douglas Home, *Half Term Report*, London 1956.
33. Malone, op. cit.
34. David Astor in the *Manchester Guardian*, 1956.
35. David Astor, 'Why the Revolt Against Hitler Failed', *Encounter*, 1969.
36. David Astor, notes written for the author, 1989.
37. David Astor in *Encounter*, 1969, and in Bull, *The Challenge of the Third Reich*, Oxford 1986.
38. Peter Bielenberg, notes to Christopher Sykes.
39. Astor in the *Manchester Guardian* and Hoffman, *History of the German Resistance*.
40. Butler, *Lothian*.
41. Hildebrandt, *Foreign Policy of the Third Reich*, London 1970. See also Andreas Hillgruber, *Germany and the Two World Wars*, 1981. The historian does not allude to the Foreign Office Resisters in his account of policy at the time.
42. Letter to Eleonore von Trott, June 1939.
43. *All Souls and Appeasement*.
44. Stephen Spender, *Horizon*, 1940.
45. Bowra, op. cit. Sykes interviewed Bowra and got a rather fuller description of that last meeting than is printed in Bowra's book.
46. Bowra, op. cit.
47. Ibid.
48. Letter to Eleonore von Trott, 15 June 1939.
49. Conversation with David Astor, February 1988.
50. Letter to Shiela Grant Duff, 19 June 1939.
51. Letter to Diana Hubback, June 1939.
52. Sykes, who interviewed Crossman. Sykes was not aware of the existence of Crossman's Foreign Office memo and gave out that Crossman remained loyal to Trott to the end.
53. Barbara Bosanquet, *Bericht*.
54. Quoted in Sykes, op. cit.

55. For a discussion of this issue, see Sebastian Haffner, *The Meaning of Hitler*, London 1979.
56. See Paul Schmidt, *Hitler's Interpreter. The Secret History of German Diplomacy 1935–1945*, London 1951.
57. Sykes, op. cit.
58. Astor in Bull, op. cit., and in conversation with the author, February 1988.
59. Conversations with David Astor, June 1989, and Peter and Christabel Bielenberg, July 1989.
60. Sykes, op. cit.
61. Letter to Diana Hopkinson, August 1939.
62. *The Past is Myself.*
63. Sykes, op. cit.
64. Wilhelm Ritter von Schramm, op. cit.
65. Letter to Shiela Grant Duff.

8

1. Hassell, op. cit.
2. Ibid.
3. Hoffman, op. cit.
4. Ibid.
5. Falkenhausen, op. cit.
6. Rhodes House.
7. Telegram from Carter, 15 August 1939. Rhodes House.
8. Hoffman, op. cit. Also Harold S. Deutsch, *The Conspiracy against Hitler in the Twilight War*, Minneapolis 1968.
9. In letters to his mother, etc. Also a letter to Clarita Tiefenbacher, 24 July 1939.
10. Sykes, op. cit.
11. Ibid.
12. Rhodes House.
13. FBI case number 862 20211.
14. Letter from Ingrid Countess Spinelli to Clarita von Trott.
15. Ibid.
16. See Richard Löwenthal in Kettenacker, op. cit.
17. Ingrid Countess Spinelli, *Bericht.* Also conversation with the author, 1989..
18. Schlabrendorff, op. cit.
19. Alexander Böker to Clarita von Trott: '*Wheeler-Bennett ist überhaupt eine schlechte Quelle in alle deutschen Dingen . . .*' In the winter of 1940-1, '*seine Haltung abrupt geändert, und seiner deutsche Freunde – darunter auch Brüning – mehrer oder weniger fallen gelassen*'. . . '*Die Behauptung Wheeler-Bennett's, Adam sei von fast alle Emigranten mit Misstraut betrachtet worden, ist völlig unzutreffend.*'

20. FBI file.
21. For Scheffer, see Boveri, *Wir Lügen Alle* and *Treason in the Twentieth Century.*
22. See Hoffmann, op. cit.
23. Hans Rothfels, *The German Opposition to Hitler*, London 1961.
24. Butler, *Lothian*, London 1960.
25. Hoffman, op. cit.
26. Ibid.
27. The extracts from Felix Morley's diaries were sent to Clarita von Trott after the war. The piece quoted is printed in Mother Mary Gallin, *German Resistance to Hitler: Ethical and Religious Factors*, Washington DC 1962.
28. Quoted in Gallin, op. cit.
29. Hoffmann, op. cit.
30. Quoted in Sykes, op. cit; also Hoffmann, op. cit.
31. FBI file.
32. Countess Moltke to Clarita von Trott, 28 October 1949.
33. Letter to Diana Hopkinson, 11 October 1939.
34. Ibid, 12 November 1939.
35. For the Burgerbräu Keller incident, see Zeller, op. cit. and Hoffmann, op. cit.
36. See Schellenberg, *Memoirs*, 1956. Schellenberg's posthumous memoirs contain much which is fantastical in the extreme. The English edition provides a lively introduction by Alan Bullock.
37. For a discussion of British policy at the time, see Peter Ludlow in Kettenacker, op. cit.
38. The letter is among those left with Mrs Braun-Vogelstein in New York and returned to Clarita von Trott after the war. It is reproduced in Shepherd, op. cit.
39. *Treason in the Twentieth Century.*
40. Letter to David Astor, end of 1939 (undated), Trott Archive.
41. Letter to Diana Hubback, 15 January 1939.
42. *Spiegelbild einer Verschwörung, die Kaltenbrunner-Berichte an Bormann und Hitler über das Attentat vom 20 Juli 1944,* Geheime Dokumente aus dem ehemaligen Reichssicherheitshauptamt, Stuttgart 1961. A further volume was edited by Hans-Adolf Jacobsen and published in 1983. See also Mother Gallin, op. cit. For the history of the Churches under Nazism, see Annedore Leber (ed.), *Conscience in Revolt*, translated by Rosemary O'Neill and with an Introduction by Robert Birley, London 1957. Also Terence Prittie, *Germans Against Hitler*, and with an introduction by Hugh Trevor Roper, London 1964.
43. *Was Niemals Stirbt.*
44. Ibid.
45. There is no evidence that he saw Madame Gorky; Trott was ill at the time of his visit to Moscow.

46. The packet is now in the possession of Clarita von Trott in Berlin.
47. Letter to Diana Hopkinson, 18 January 1940. By this time Mrs Hopkinson's husband was in the British army. She no longer thought it prudent for his sake to reply to Trott's last letters.
48. Klaus Mehnert to Clarita von Trott, undated. Russian Germans like Hilger played an considerable role in the making of National Socialism, with a high percentage of early Nazis coming from Russia and the Baltic States. For an analysis of their role see Walter Laqueur, *Russia and Germany, A Century of Conflict*, London 1965.
49. See Ingeborg Fleischhauer, *Die Chance des Sonderfriedes, Deutsch-sowjetische Geheimgespräche 1941–1945*, Berlin 1986 and Paul Schmidt, op. cit.
50. Ibid.
51. & 52. These notes are to be found in the Trott FBI file; both are quoted in Sykes, op. cit.
53. FBI file.
54. Ibid.
55. Ibid.
56. Ibid.
57. Ibid.

9

1. '*Materialsammlung*'.
2. 'Adam von Trott, A Memoir', typescript by Diana Hopkinson.
3. Otto John, *Falsch und zu spät*, 1984.
4. Letter from Achim von Arnim to the Control Commission, 1946.
5. '*Materialsammlung*'.
6. Ibid.
7. See *Politisches Archiv Auswärtiges Amt Bonn, Personalakte Trott.*
8. *The Past is Myself.*
9. Annedore Leber, op. cit.
10. Schacht, *Account Settled.*
11. Hsi-Huey Liang, op. cit. There are three letters from the General to Trott, dated 5 April 1939, 5 April 1940 and 16 April 1940.
12. See Otto John, *Twice through the Lines*, London 1969 and *Falsch und zu spät*, 1984.
13. Conversation with Clarita van Trott, July 1989.
14. See Balfour and Frisby, op. cit; also in *A German of the Resistance. The Last Letters of Helmuth James von Moltke*, OUP, 1946. The article, which is unsigned, is presumably the work of Moltke's friend Lionel Curtis.
15. See Hans-Georg von Studnitz, *While Berlin Burns. Diaries 1943–*

1945, London 1963. Studnitz was the press attaché to the Auswärtige Amt.

16. As it slowly dawned on Joseph Goebbels that the war was lost he began increasingly to blame defeat on the fact that the Nazis had failed to 'revolutionize' the army after the Night of the Long Knives. Tagebücher, 1945.
17. Quoted in Balfour and Frisby, op. cit.
18. Schlabrendorff, op. cit.
19. Roger Manvell and Heinrich Fraenkel, *The Canaris Conspiracy*, London 1969.
20. Balfour and Frisby, op. cit.
21. Ibid.
22. Hoffmann, op. cit.
23. For Schulenburg, see Albert Krebs, *Fritz-Dietlof, Graf von der Schulenburg, zwischen Staatsraison und Hochverrat*, Hamburg 1964.
24. Balfour and Frisby, op. cit.
25. Ibid.
26. '*Materialsammlung*'.
27. Tatiana, Princess Metternich, *Five Passports in a Shifting Europe*, London 1976 (new edition 1988).
28. Ibid. Tatiana Vassiltchikov was shortly to marry Paul Metternich, at which point she gave up working. Her sister Marie ('Missie') carried on working at the IA till after the July Plot, when she moved to Vienna to become a nurse.
29. Werth to Clarita von Trott, 1957. Typescript. Also Clarita von Trott, notes to the author, 1989.
30. See Franz-Josef Furtwängler's series of pen-portraits, *Männer die ich sah und kannte*.
31. Werth, *Bericht*.
32. Ibid.
33. An interesting early work which attempts to laugh back at Lord Haw-Haw is *Lord Haw-Haw of Zeesen* by Jonah Barrington with illustrations by Fenwick, London (nd). Barrington was the creator of the name Lord Haw-Haw, which came into being in the columns of the *Daily Express* on 18 September 1939, 'three days after the birth of Winnie the Whopper of Warsaw'.
34. For the business of looking after Amery, see Hans-Georg von Studnitz, op. cit.
35. Werth, *Bericht*.
36. Ibid.
37. Letter to Eleonore von Trott, 26 April 1940.
38. Quoted in '*Materialsammlung*'.
39. '*Materialsammlung*'.
40. For Bonhoeffer, see Eberhard Bethge, *Dietrich Bonhoeffer: Theologe, Christ, Zeitgenosse*, Munich 1967.

41. For Niemöller, see James Bentley, *Martin Niemöller*, Oxford 1984.
42. Ger van Roon, *Neuordnung in Widerstand.*
43. Eugen Gerstenmaier, *Streit und Friede hat seine Zeit, Ein Lebensbericht*, Frankfurt, Berlin, Vienna, 1981.
44. See Ronald Jasper, *George Bell, Bishop of Chichester*, London 1967.
45. Gerstenmaier, *Streit und Friede.*
46. Eugen Gerstenmaier, 'The Church Conspiratorial', in *We Survived: Fourteen Histories of the Hidden and Hunted in Nazi Germany*, Erich Boehm, Santa Barbara 1966.
47. Gerstenmaier, *Streit und Friede.*
48. Ibid.
49. Quoted in Ger van Roon, *Neuordnung un Widerstand.* For Leber, see also *Ein Mann geht seinem Weg*, Berlin, Frankfurt am Main 1952, which is a collection of his speeches and diaries. More recently there have been two books by Dorothea Beck, *Julius Leber, Schriften, Reden, Briefe. 1920–1945*, Herausgegeben von Dorothea Beck und Wilfried Schoeller, Munich 1976; and *Julius Leber, Sozialdemocrat zwischen Reform und Widerstand*, Einleitung von Willy Brandt, Vorwort von Hans Mommsen, Berlin 1983. See also Michael Balfour, *Withstanding Hitler 1933–45*, 1988.
50. Ger van Roon, op. cit.
51. Furtwängler, *Männer die ich sah und kannte.*
52. Ibid.
53. Ibid.
54. Ibid.
55. Ibid.
56. Furtwängler to Clarita von Trott 1946.
57. *Männer die ich sah und kannte.*
58. Discussion with David Astor and Christabel Bielenberg, April 1988.
59. *The Past is Myself.*
60. *Männer die ich sah und kannte.*
61. Balfour and Frisby, op. cit.
62. Ibid.
63. Peter Bielenberg notes for Christopher Sykes, undated.
64. David Astor to Clarita von Trott.
65. Visser't Hooft, *Memoirs.*
66. Merson, op. cit.
67. See Hoffmann, op. cit. See also Schlabrendorrf, op. cit., who was a friend of Halem's.
68. *Das Gewissen Entscheidet*, Herausgegeben von Annedore Leber, Frankfurt 1957.
69. Hoffmann, op. cit.
70. Hoffmann, op. cit., whence the quotation. The rest from Schlabrendorff, op. cit.

71. Marie 'Missie' Vassiltchikov, *Berlin Diaries 1940–1945*, ed.
George Vassiltchikov, London 1985. Peter Bielenberg and Trott
were not at university together – except that is, in the imagination
of Denis Potter.

72. *Berlin Diaries*, 8 August 1940.

73. Ibid, 10 November 1940.

74. Ibid, 18 December 1940.

75. Ibid, 23 December 1940.

10

1. See the autobiographies *The Incense Tree* (Diana Hopkinson) and
The Parting of the Ways (Shiela Grant Duff).

2. Letter from Humayun Kabir to Clarita von Trott.

3. *India, What Next? Why the Talks Failed. The Congress Reply*,
Jawaharlal Nehru and Abdul Kalam Azad answer Sir Stafford
Cripps, April 1942; also *A Summary of the Proposals*.

4. *The Lost Hero: A Biography of Subhas Bose*, Mihir Bose, London
1982. The account of Bose's life before his arrival as Orlando
Mazzotta in Berlin is taken from this book except where otherwise
stated.

5. Alexander Werth, *Der Tiger Indiens, Subhas Chandra Bose, Ein
Leben für die Freiheit des Subkontinents*, Munich and Esslingen
1971. In reality this book by Trott's former friend and collaborator
in the Sonderreferat is the work of several hands. Werth was an
enthusiastic supporter of Bose's cause and continued to work for
Bose's memory till the end of his life.

6. *Mein Kampf*, London 1940. The passage comes from p.559 of the
Methuen edition. Quotations of this passage vary.

7. *Life and Times of Subhas Chandra Bose as Told in His Own
Words*, compiled and edited by Madan Gopal, Delhi 1978. The
phrase was later used in an Azad Hind broadcast on 25 March 1942
from Berlin.

8. Milan Hauner, 'The Place of India in the Strategic and Political
Considerations of the Axis Powers, 1939–1942', unpublished Ph.D.
thesis, Cambridge 1972.

9. *The Past is Myself*.

10. Conversation with Clarita von Trott, October 1988.

11. Alexander Werth and Walter Harbich, *Netaji in Germany*, Calcutta
1970. Werth's contribution was a reworking of his Netaji oration of
23 January 1969 – i.e. the day fixed as Indian Independence Day by
Bose and his German friends in 1943.

12. Ibid.

13. *A Beacon across Asia. A Biography of Subhas Chandra Bose*, eds
Sisir K. Bose, Alexander Werth and S.A. Ayer, New Delhi 1973.

The parts relating to Bose's German existence were written by Werth.

14. *Tiger und Schakal, Deutsche-Indien Politik, 1941–1943 Dokumentarbericht*, Reimund Schnabel, Vienna 1968. This work is chiefly a collection of documents relating to events concerning Bose, many of which are signed by or addressed to Trott.

15. Hugh Trevor Roper, *Last Days of Hitler*.

16. Schnabel, op. cit.

17. *Netaji in Germany*.

18. Furtwängler, op. cit.

19. Mihir Bose, op. cit.

20. *Netaji in Germany*.

21. Schnabel, op. cit.

22. Mihir Bose, op. cit.

23. For the daughter: Mihir Bose. For their living together in Berlin, Werth's *Bericht* to Clarita von Trott. This lengthy document is much more open on Bose's German existence than any of his other three works on the subject. It is also an invaluable account of Trott's relations with Bose.

24. Werth, *Bericht*.

25. Ibid.

26. Furtwängler, op. cit.

27. Mihir Bose, op. cit.

28. Furtwängler, op. cit.

29. Mihir Bose, op. cit.

30. Furtwängler, op. cit.

31. Ibid.

32. '*Materialsammlung*'.

33. Werth, *Bericht*.

34. '*Materialsammlung*'.

35. Ibid.

36. Figures from Schnabel and Werth.

37. Schnabel, op. cit.

38. Schnabel prints Furtwängler's letters from Bangkok.

39. Studnitz, op. cit.

40. '*Materialsammlung*'.

41. Furtwängler, op. cit.

42. Trott's brother Heinrich was a case in point, though, as Sykes points out, it landed him in a difficult position when he was captured with the Indian troops at the end of the war, the French Resistance murdering the Indians to a man and Trott's own life only being preserved by a whisker. Another whom Trott tried to get into the Indian Legion after his name had been connected with the Rote Kapelle group had been Curt Bley.

43. Werth, *Bericht*.

44. See Colin Cook, *Life of Sir Stafford Cripps*, London 1957; also

'India 1939–1942. A Summary of Events up to and Including the Cripps Mission', prepared by Agatha Harris and Gerald Bailey, Peace Aims Pamphlet no. 14.

45. Schnabel, op. cit.
46. Werth, *Bericht.*
47. Mihir Bose, op. cit.
48. '*Materialsammlung*'.
49. Ibid, quoting Furtwängler to Ricarda Huth.
50. Letter printed in Schnabel, op. cit.
51. Hassell, op. cit.
52. '*Materialsammlung*'.
53. *Männer die ich sah und kannte.*
54. *Netaji in Germany.*
55. A description of Trott's role in the *Führerbetreff* is given in each of the three published works by Werth. It is not, however, in the *Bericht* on which Frau von Trott's 'Materialsammlung' account is based. I can only suppose this is why the meeting is such a glaring omission from Syke's account in *Troubled Loyalty.* Sykes mentions Trott meeting Hitler once, but only to say that Trott was disturbed by the Führer's piercing stare.
56. Hildebrandt, op. cit.
57. Mihir Bose, op. cit.
58. Keppler (letter) printed in Schnabel, op. cit. Other sources give a much earlier date for the foundation of the Sonderreferat. Keppler's letter is more than conclusive proof.
59. *Personalakte*, Foreign Office, Bonn.
60. Ibid.
61. Gottfried von Nostitz to Clarita von Trott.
62. *Tiger und Schakal.*
63. Schellenberg, op. cit.
64. Falkenhausen, op. cit.
65. *Tiger und Schakal.*
66. *Netaji in Germany.*
67. Studnitz, op. cit.

11

1. See Ruth Andreas-Friedrich, *Berlin Underground*, New York, 1947.
2. For Düsseldorf, see Bernt Engelmann, *In Hitler's Germany*, London 1988.
3. For the Weisse Rose group, see Inge Scholl, *Die Weisse Rose*, Frankfurt-am-Main 1988 (new edn); English translation: *Six Against Tyranny*, London 1955.
4. Hassell, op. cit. For Trott's reaction: conversation with Christabel Bielenberg, April 1988.

5. *Die Weisse Rose.*
6. Schlabrendorff, op. cit.; Zeller, op. cit.
7. See *Spiegelbild einer Verschwörung.*
8. Schwerin's attempts appear in the edited films of the trial.
9. Hassell, op. cit. Moltke's job meant that he was privy to more information than others in the High Command when it came to German atrocities.
10. Zeller, op. cit., quoting letters published in the *Zeitschrift für Zeitgeschichte.*
11. Ibid.
12. For Tresckow, see Schlabrendorff, op. cit., and Zeller, op. cit. There is a biography by Bodo Scheurig, Oldenburg 1973.
13. See Allen Dulles, *Germany's Underground,* New York 1948.
14. For Goerdeler, see Ritter, op. cit.
15. Clarita von Trott, notes written for the author. She quotes from the Hammerstein family papers.
16. Schlabrendorff, op. cit.
17. Quoted in Zeller, op. cit., and elsewhere.
18. Schlabrendorff, op. cit.
19. Ibid.
20. From *Das Ziel,* quoted in Schramm, op. cit. Schramm sets out to prove how much Beck was jointly responsible for the memoranda which had been previously attributed to Goerdeler alone.
21. Schramm, op. cit.
22. Zeller, op. cit., quoting Pechel, *Deutsche Widerstand,* Zurich 1947. The note is appended to a letter from the time of Munich. The precise date of the note is not known.
23. In '*Materialsammlung*' Clarita von Trott refers to Yorck's house as the '*Hauptquartier*'. Christabel Bielenberg told the author that their home in Dahlem was a 'Berlin branch' of the Kreisau Circle.
24. *Spiegelbild einer Verschwörung,* Vol. 2, ed. Hans-Adolf Jacobsen, 1984.
25. The decision to write papers seems to have been informally taken. The 'Comments on the Peace Plans of the American Churches' has been seen (van Roon, op. cit.) as a collective effort. As has been seen, the peace moves through Visser't Hooft and Schönfeld were jointly composed by Trott, Gerstenmaier and Haeften, and amended by Kessel and Nostitz.
26. Conversation with Peter Bielenberg, July 1989.
27. *A German of the Resistance. The Last Letters of Helmuth James von Moltke,* OUP 1946.
28. Gerstenmaier, *The Church Conspiratorial,* Boehm ed., op. cit.
29. See Ger van Roon, op. cit.
30. van Roon, op. cit. See also '*Amerikanische Eindrücke*'. These were the views Trott held both times he had visited America.

31. Moltke to Freya in *Briefe an Freya 1939–45*, ed. C.H. Beck, 1988.
32. Furtwängler, op. cit.
33. *Briefe an Freya.*
34. Balfour and Frisby.
35. Helmut Conrad to Clarita von Trott, 1957.
36. For John's contacts with Louis Ferdinand, see *Twice through the Lines* and *Falsch und zu spät.*
37. Schramm, op. cit.
38. Hassell, op. cit.
39. Ibid.
40. Ibid.
41. Ibid.
42. Ibid.
43. See Ritter, op. cit., and Zeller, op. cit.
44. Trott to Diana Hopkinson. The letter was clearly intended for general distribution.
45. See *Treason in the Twentieth Century.*
46. Hassell, op. cit. Goerdeler had reacted to German defeat by promoting civil disobedience in East Prussia; see also Ritter, op. cit.
47. *Treason in the Twentieth Century.*
48. Ibid.
49. Professor Patijn, in *Wending*, July/August 1964. A translation into German is to be found in the Trott Archive in Berlin.
50. *Personalakte*, Foreign Office, Bonn.
51. Patijn, op. cit.
52. *Personalakte*, Foreign Office, Bonn.
53. Ibid. The idea of Bose urging moderation seems unlikely.
54. Hassell, op. cit.
55. Ibid.
56. Balfour and Frisby, op. cit.
57. *Streit und Friede.*
58. Ibid.
59. Kettenacker, op. cit. The summary of approaches to the Foreign Office is included in the documents printed at the end of the book.
60. See Rhodes House and Visser't Hooft, 'How the Revolt against Hitler Looked from Geneva' in *Encounter*, 1969.
61. Kettenacker, op. cit., and Lamb, op. cit.
62. Lamb, op. cit.
63. Ibid.
64. Ibid.
65. Ibid.
66. Jasper, *Bell.*
67. Ibid.
68. Ibid.

69. From Bishop Bell's article in *Das Parlament – Sonderausgabe von 20 Juli 1952*. I have been unable to find an English version of this text and offer readers a translation from the German.
70. See Bethge, op. cit.
71. Jasper, *Bell*.
72. Kettenacker, op. cit.
73. Visser't Hooft, *Memoirs*.
74. Lamb, op. cit., and *Streit und Friede*.
75. Printed in Lamb. The text is also in the Trott Archive in Berlin where Mr Lamb has deposited copies of the Foreign Office papers relative to Trott.
76. Lamb, op. cit.
77. Ibid.
78. Ibid.
79. Ibid.
80. Ibid.
81. Information supplied by the FBI to Mr Brian Harte.
82. Lamb, op. cit.
83. See Bernd Martin, '*Deutsche Opposition und Widerstandskreise und die Frage eines separaten Friedensschlusses im zweiten Weltkrieg*' in K-J. Müller (ed.), *Deutschen Widerstand 1933—1945*, Paderborn 1986.
84. Ibid.
85. Jasper, *Bell*.
86. Visser't Hooft, *Encounter* 1969.
87. Balfour and Frisby, op. cit.
88. Hsi Huey Liang, op. cit.
89. '*Materialsammlung*'.
90. Balfour and Frisby, op. cit.
91. Curt Bley to Clarita von Trott; also a letter to Heinrich von Trott and John, op. cit. John had become a friend of Bley through Trott.
92. See *Twice through the Lines*.
93. Hoffman, op. cit. Ingeborg Fleischhauer gives the dates as 18–21 September but it is improbable that Trott would have sent the letter to Harry Johansson from Germany.
94. *Spiegelbild einer Verschwörung*.
95. Hoffman, op. cit.
96. Ibid.
97. Missie Vassiltchikov, op. cit.
98. '*Materialsammlung*' and a conversation with Clarita von Trott, Berlin, October 1988.
99. Furtwängler, op. cit.; also '*Materialsammlung*'.
100. *Twice through the Lines*.
101. *Widerstand, Kirche, Staat, Eugen Gerstenmaier zum 70 Geburstag*. Herausgegeben von Bruno Heck, Frankfurt and Vienna

1976. Gerhard Leibholz, *Die Deutschlandpolitik Englands im Zweiten Weltkreig und der Widerstand.*

102. Quoted in Bull, op. cit.
103. *Treason in the Twentieth Century.*
104. Ibid.
105. Visser't Hooft, *Memoirs.*
106. Dulles, *Germany's Underground,* New York 1947.
107. Ibid.
108. Gisevius, *To the Bitter End.*
109. Dulles, op. cit.
110. Ibid.
111. Bernd Martin, op. cit.
112. See Heinz Höhne, *Canaris,* London 1979.
113. Ibid.
114. Ibid.
115. Ibid.
116. *Briefe an Freya.*
117. Hassell, op. cit.
118. Balfour and Frisby, op. cit.
119. *Streit und Friede.*
120. Balfour and Frisby, op. cit.
121. Bishop Bell, *Germany and the Hitlerite State,* London 1944.
122. Ibid.
123. Ibid.
124. Balfour and Frisby, op. cit.
125. Gisevius, op. cit.
126. Hoffmann, op. cit.
127. Dossier Kreisauer Kreis: *Dokumente aus dem Widerstand gegen den Nationalsozialismus, Herausgegeben von Roman Bleisten,* Frankfurt 1987.
128. Bernd Martin, op. cit.
129. Ibid.
130. Letter from Erich Vermehren to the author April 1989, also telephone conversation with Nicolas Elliott the same day.
131. Hassell, op. cit.
132. Ibid.
133. *Briefe an Freya.*
134. Falkenhausen, op. cit.
135. Rhodes House. At the time of the plot Snowden was imprisoned only ten kilometres from Imshausen. He was told by the guards that the rest of the family had been disposed of in the same way as Trott and that the house was shut up.
136. Hildebrandt, op. cit.
137. Ibid.
138. Ritter, *Goerdeler.*
139. Missie Vassiltchnikov, op. cit. Trott seemed suspicious of Helldorf

at first as did everyone in the Resistance who had got to know him only recently. Despite his Nazi record, he had been working closely with Gisevius since 1938.

140. Ivar Andersson (diaries and notes in the possession of Clarita von Trott).
141. Ibid.
142. Inga Kempe (notes in the possession of Frau von Trott).
143. Ibid.
144. Lamb, op. cit.; also Kettenacker, op. cit.
145. Peter Kleist, *A European Tragedy*, Isle of Man 1965. Peter Kleist remained a strong nationalist after the war, writing a pamphlet entitled '*Wer ist Willy Brandt*' in 1973 in which he cast doubt on Brandt's right to govern as one who had emigrated during the war.
146. '*Materialsammlung*'; also conversation with Frau von Trott, October 1988.
147. Hoffmann, op. cit.; the text of the memorandum is reproduced in van Roon, op. cit.
148. Ibid.
149. Lamb. Lamb does not, however, share the author's view that the Allies can only have been confused by the fact that both the Resistance and the SS were both seeking a similar 'Western Solution'.
150. Missie Vassiltchikov, op. cit.
151. Studnitz, op. cit.
152. Ursula von Kardorff, *Diary of a Nightmare*, London 1965
153. Studnitz, op. cit.
154. Missie Vassiltchikov, op. cit.
155. Ibid.
156. Balfour and Frisby, op. cit.
157. Hassell, op. cit.
158. Conversation with Clarita von Trott, October 1988.
159. Balfour and Frisby, op. cit.
160. Ibid.
161. Hassell, op. cit.
162. Ibid.
163. Ibid.
164. Weissenborn, op. cit.

12

1. Yorck had qualms on 7 July and Trott had to tell him that things had gone too far to turn back.
2. Julius Leber, *Ein Mann geht seinen Weg.*
3. See Dorothea Beck, *Julius Leber.*

4. See *Ein Mann geht seinen Weg.*
5. '*Materialsammlung*'.
6. Conversation with Christabel Bielenberg and David Astor, April 1988.
7. For Stauffenberg, the classic biography is Joachim Kramarz, *Stauffenberg. The Life and Death of an Officer*, with an introduction by H.R. Trevor Roper, London 1967. For an East German view, see Finker, *Stauffenberg, und der 20 Juli 1944* (2nd edn), Berlin 1971.
8. Rothfels, op. cit.
9. Krebs, op. cit.
10. Kardorff, op. cit.
11. Zeller, op. cit., quoting a manuscript by Thiersch.
12. See *Männer die ich sah und kannte*; also Klaus-Jürgen Müller in Müller (ed.), op. cit.
13. *Männer die ich sah und kannte.*
14. Studnitz. For Bismarck, see Missie Vassiltchikov, op. cit. Missie lived with Bismarck in Potsdam where he was Regierungspräsident.
15. Letter to Barbara von Haeften, 5 January 1944. This is a reference to Emma, and not to Trott's daughter, Clarita junior, born in November.
16. Studnitz, op. cit.
17. Hassell, op. cit.
18. *Personalakte*, Foreign Office, Bonn. Trott hid his copy in the garden, under the balcony; another was lodged in the Bielenberg's garage; Franz Josef Furtwängler hid another in a metal box in the garden of a friend; another was mislaid by Theordor Stelzer in Scandinavia. The memo suffered from very poor luck all in all. Recently Trott's younger daughter told the author she had made a new attempt to locate the paper in the former Bielenberg residence, but had found nothing.
19. Otto John, *Falsch und zu spät.*
20. Missie Vassiltchikov, op. cit.
21. For the *Gastarbeiter*, see Detlev Peukert, *Inside Nazi Germany*, translated by Richard Deveson, London 1987.
22. Letter to Clarita von Trott, 29 January 1944.
23. Letter to Eleonore von Trott, 10 February 1944.
24. Missie Vassiltchikov, op. cit.
25. *Männer die ich sah und kannte.*
26. Inga Kempe to Clarita von Trott.
27. Ibid.
28. The specialist's report is in the Trott Archive.
29. Andersson, *Diary.*
30. Letter to Clarita von Trott.
31. Information from Erich Vermehren.

32. Letter to Clarita von Trott, 14 March 1944.
33. *Männer die ich sah und kannte.*
34. Letter to Clarita von Trott, 26 March 1944.
35. Ibid.
36. Lalli Horstmann, *Nothing for Tears*, London 1953.
37. Lamb, op. cit.
38. Dulles, op. cit.
39. Dulles, op. cit.
40. Lamb, op. cit.
41. Missie Vassiltchikov, op. cit.
42. Letter to Clarita von Trott, 1 April 1944.
43. Ibid.
44. Elizabeth Wiskemann, *The Europe I Saw*, London 1968.
45. *The Past is Myself.* Their talk took place in March.
46. Letter to Clarita von Trott quoted in '*Materialsammlung*'.
47. Missie Vassiltchikov, op. cit.
48. Ibid.
49. Ibid.
50. *Treason in the Twentieth Century.*
51. '*Materialsammlung*'.
52. Kessel's account comes from his privately printed diary written in the Vatican, 1944–5.
53. *Allocution prononcée à Caux par M Philippe Mottu*, 20 July 1986. Caux has been established as a European centre for moral rearmament. The text was rendered into English for the Balliol Record, 1987.
54. Schlabrendorff, op. cit. In many ways, considering the better physical shape of Tresckow in relation to Stauffenberg, it was a considerable pity that he was not in Berlin to undertake the work of planting the bomb.
55. *Chief of Intelligence*, London 1951.
56. *Spiegelbild einer Verschwörung.*
57. Letter to Clarita von Trott, 18 June 1944. Quoted in '*Material-sammlung*'.
58. *Ein Mann geht seinen Weg.*
59. See Willy Brandt, *Links und Frei*, Hamburg 1982.
60. See Finker, *Stauffenberg.*
61. *Spiegelbild einer Verschwörung.* Clarita von Trott points out in her notes that her husband's letter of the 18th, which he wrote between the two meetings, points to only one guest. However, she concludes that this might have been for the sake of the censor. (Notes for the author, 1989).
62. Kleist, op. cit., and Fleischhauer, op. cit.
63. Fleischhauer, op. cit., and Ruth Andreas-Friedrich, op. cit.
64. Inga Kempe.
65. Harrison's memo is reprinted in Kettenacker, op. cit.

66. Scott's report as drawn up by Consul Johnson is in Kettenacker, op. cit.
67. Inga Kempe.
68. Missie Vassiltchikov, op. cit. Ingeborg Fleischauer and 'Material-sammlung' suggest he did not return till 3 July, which is clearly impossible unless Missie is mistaken.
69. Ibid.
70. Patijn, op. cit.
71. Horstmann, op. cit. Clarita von Trott distrusts this story.
72. Gottfried von Nostitz' diary of those days is in the possession of Clarita von Trott.
73. Missie Vassiltchikov, op. cit.
74. Merson, op. cit., and Weisenborn, op. cit.
75. See *Ein Mann geht seinen Weg.*
76. Ibid.
77. Nostitz' diary.
78. *Männer die ich sah und kannte.*
79. Schlabrendorff, op. cit.
80. Dulles, op. cit.
81. Ruth Andreas-Freidrich, op. cit.
82. Missie Vassiltchikov, op. cit.
83. Kardorff, op. cit.
84. Wilhelm Melchers' testimony, or *Bericht,* is in the possession of Clarita von Trott.
85. Count Berg to Clarita von Trott.
86. Missie Vassiltchikov, op. cit.
87. Waltraud von Götz to Clarita von Trott.
88. See Hoffmann, op. cit., Zeller, op. cit.
89. The following account of 20 July in the Auswärtige Amt is based on the papers of Alexander Werth and Wilhelm Melchers in the possession of Clarita von Trott.
90. Zeller, op. cit.
91. Hoffmann. Hoffmann gives the location of the Foreign Club as the Leipziger Platz. Werth is adamant that it was now in the private residence of Ribbentrop in Berlin Schargendorf.
92. *Spiegelbild einer Verschwörung.*
93. Götz, op. cit.
94. Melchers, op. cit.
95. Ibid.
96. John, *Twice through the Lines.*
97. Berg to Clarita von Trott.
98. Furtwängler op. cit.
99. Götz, op. cit.
100. Furtwängler, op. cit.
101. Zeller, op. cit., and Schlabrendorff, op. cit.
102. Missie Vassiltchikov, op. cit.

103. Letters from Curt Bley to Heinrich von Trott, 1945, and Clarita von Trott.
104. Missie Vassiltchikov, op. cit.
105. Ibid.
106. *Spiegelbild einer Verschwörung.*
107. Werth, *Bericht.*
108. *Streit und Friede.*
109. Schlabrendorff, op. cit.
110. *Spiegelbild einer Verschwörung.*
111. Ibid.
112. Ibid.
113. Missie Vassiltchikov, op. cit.
114. Quoted in Finker and elsewhere.
115. Clarita von Trott's interview with Horst Mahnke, 1958.
116. Missie Vassiltchikov, op. cit.
117. Wiezsäcker, *Memoirs.*
118. *Falsch und zu spät.*
119. Missie Vassiltchikov, op. cit.
120. *The Past is Myself* and conversation with Peter and Christabel Bielenberg.
121. *Spiegelbild einer Verschwörung.*
122. In the possession of Frau von Trott, Berlin.
123. Mahnke, op. cit.
124. This was pointed out to the author by Christabel Bielenberg. In the film of the trial Trott remains upright and calm, despite Freisler's badgering (copy in the Imperial War Museum, London.)
125. Hoffmann, op. cit.
126. Todesurteil.
127. Zeller, op. cit., Hoffmann, op. cit.
128. *Spiegelbild einer Verschwörung.*
129. Mahnke, op. cit.
130. *Streit und Friede.*
131. Malone, op. cit. I have slightly adapted the English.
132. Hoffmann, op. cit.
133. Merson, op. cit.
134. Götz, op. cit.

Index

353